P9-CAN-298

THE WORLD ALMANAC® OF THE
SOVIET UNION

THE WORLD ALMANAC® OF THE
SOVIET UNION
FROM 1905 TO THE PRESENT

Warren Shaw

David Pryce

First published in 1990.

Library of Congress Cataloging-in-Publication Data
Shaw, Warren.
    The world almanac of the Soviet Union : from 1905 to the present /
Warren Shaw and David Pryce.
        p.   cm.
    Includes bibliographical references and index.
    ISBN 0-88687-565-X : $24.95
    1. Soviet Union—History—20th century—Biography.   2. Soviet
Union—History—20th century—Chronology.   3. Soviet Union—
Miscellanea.   I. Pryce, David.   II. Title.
DK246.S5   1990
947.084—dc20   90-46041
                                                              CIP

Printed in the United States of America

Cover design: Suzanne Reisel
Interior design: Bea Jackson

World Almanac
An Imprint of Pharos Books
A Scripps Howard Company
New York, NY 10166

10 9 8 7 6 5 4 3 2 1

CONTENTS

To the Reader

Our intention in writing this book was to give the student or interested reader detailed background on the Soviet Union from the 1905 revolution to the present. We were mainly concerned with plotting the political and economic developments in the USSR and describing its external relationships. We did not pretend nor aspire to a total account of all aspects of Soviet life—such a vast enterprise is beyond the scope of a single volume.

The book is divided into three sections: topics, biographies, and chronology. There is some cross-referencing when the need is apparent, and the biographies and topics are in alphabetical order. The choice of spelling may appear abitrary. Neither the style of the U.S. Library of Congress nor the British National Standard has been followed—we have preferred to use the spelling most frequently seen in current periodicals and newspapers. This inconsistency will irritate some scholars, but ease the understanding of most readers.

PREFACE

On January 18, 1918, the Bolsheviks under the leadership of Lenin dissolved the Constituent Assembly and instituted one-party rule in Russia. On February 7, 1990, the Central Committee of the Communist party under its chairman Mikhail Gorbachev repealed Article 6 of the constitution and abandoned the party's claims to the monopoly of power, thus opening the way for multi-party democracy.

Between those two dates, the Biblical span of a man's life, is contained the most extraordinary story of the twentieth century and one which has profoundly affected the lives of everyone now living. The story begins with the abortive 1905 revolution, followed shortly by the successful revolutions of 1917, the fall of the czar, the establishment of communist rule under Lenin, and, after his death, the transformation, under the brutal dictatorship of Stalin, of the backward peasant economy into a major industrial power, dividing the world into power blocs dominated by a terrifying nuclear arsenal.

In 1956 came Khrushchev's revelations of Stalin's crimes and the extent of his tyranny, along with a freeing of a vast number of political prisoners. But under Brezhnev the initial impulse toward greater freedom was once again supressed, and it was not until Gorbachev was declared general secretary in 1985 that the startling changes now taking place in the Soviet Union and whole eastern bloc began.

Gorbachev introduced the twin concepts of *perestroika* and *glasnost*. *Perestroika* has a political and economic wing. Politically, it has led to the formation of the Congress of People's Deputies, and the emergence of dozens of new political parties whose candidates include many who, twenty years ago, would have been confined to labor camps. In economic terms, Gorbachev has aimed to introduce elements of the market economy through the formation of cooperatives, joint ventures with the West, and even plans to create a Moscow stock exchange.

Externally, Gorbachev has created an immensely favorable impression on the world scene. His unilateral announcement of cuts in conventional arms and his wide-ranging agreements with the United States on nuclear forces lowered international tensions. At the same time, he presided over the collapse of Communist regimes in Eastern Europe, starting with Hungary and Poland and extending to the dramatic collapse of Ceaucescu in Romania in December 1989. And the Warsaw Treaty organization has recently declared itself in favor of becoming a political rather than a military body.

In some ways it is possible to compare Gorbachev's situation with that of Stolypin, the reform-minded prime minister under czarist Russia at the beginning of the century.

Both men inherited a rigid bureaucratic system with an oppressed peasantry and an inefficient industrial structure. Both attempted to introduce elements of a market economy and democracy. Stolypin was assassinated, probably with police collusion. Gorbachev's popularity and prestige in the Soviet Union are threatened by the very liberation of the twin forces of nationalism and democracy in the country.

Gorbachev has problems that Stolypin does not face. For the first time in their history, the republics that make up the Soviet Empire are using the rights granted to them under the constitution to declare their independence. At the same time, bitter ethnic struggles have broken out in the Caucusus and in Central Asia.

A command economy responds only sluggishly to attempts at reform and the queues for food and consumer goods grow longer, while Gorbachev's rivals, both radical and conservative, become more vocal. Boris Yeltsin, his leading opponent and president of the Russian Soviet Federated Socialist Republic (RSFSR), the largest of the republics, has accused him of being both too radical and not radical enough.

The situation is threatening and unpredictable. To what extent it is possible for the Soviet Union to change its nature both constitutionally and economically without disintegrating into chaos is hard to say; there are no real historical parallels. The possibility of extreme reaction, even of a return to a hard-line regime backed by the army must exist, though the Red Army has no tradition of taking hand in politics. It may be that some form of federation will emerge. Whatever happens we should not forget the astonishing changes that have taken place in the Soviet Union and Eastern Europe, changes that have brought about the possibility of an infinitely better life for so many millions after years of dark and terrible repression.

Our particular thanks for help in this project go to Leonora Collins for her assistance in Russian studies, the research facilities extended by the London Library and the Library Services of the Royal Borough of Kensington and Chelsea and the Novosti Press Agency.

In conclusion, we would like to thank the publisher not only for encouragement but also for being so flexible with their production scheduling, allowing us to record events in the chronology within three months of publication.

Warren Shaw and David Pryce
London, 1990

PART ONE

TOPICS

AEROFLOT

The Soviet airline was set up in 1928, as part of the 1923 five-year plan, under the name of Dobroflot, but it was restructured in 1932 under its present title. By 1935, services spanned the whole of the USSR. At the end of World War II, after a relatively slow beginning, Aeroflot expanded its services with the Lisunov LI-2, aircraft based on the Douglas DC-3. It is now the world's largest airline, carrying an estimated 15 percent of all passenger traffic.

In the 1950s the airline had a generation of turboprop and turbojet aircraft of which the TU-104, with a hundred passengers with a range of 1,900 miles, was the main carrier. The next most effective long-range aircraft was the TU-114, with a range of 5,600 miles. In 1973 the TU-144, a supersonic plane resembling the British-French Concorde was exhibited at the Paris Air Show, where it crashed. A later version went into service on internal flights in the USSR, but was withdrawn in 1977.

By 1980 Aeroflot was serving all the major cities of Europe, Africa, the Middle East, and South and Southeast Asia, including a direct flight to Havana from Moscow. The most common Aeroflot plane now is the IL-62, carrying up to 180 passengers, and the IL-86, in service since 1977, capable of carrying 350 passengers.

AFSR. See WHITE ARMIES.

AFGHANISTAN

Area: 251,773 square miles
Population: 16,592,000
Capital: Kabul; population, 1,200,000

Soviet Aid and Diplomacy under Khrushchev—In the 19th century Afghanistan was the buffer state between the expanding Russian Empire in Asia and the British Empire in India with its interests in Persia. Afghanistan's frontier with British India (the Northwest Frontier), which ran along the mountains south of the Hindu Kush, ignoring the tribal and clan boundaries, became the Pakistan frontier in 1947 when that nation was born. The Russian frontier lay mainly along the Oxus (Amu Darya) River to the Pamirs; it was established at the end of the 19th century and was confirmed when the Soviets took over the kingdom of Bokhara, Afghanistan's last independent northern neighbor, in 1920.

After the death of Stalin, the Soviet Union took a fresh look at the world outside and, in particular, its neighbor Afghanistan. The Bandung Conference had shown the great powers that the smaller nations of the Third World could, united, have more muscle than had been appreciated. Afghanistan was of obvious interest: a long-standing quarrel with Pakistan arising from the Afghan claim to the whole tribal area had resulted in the closure of that frontier to Afghan trade. The Soviet Union offered and encouraged an alternative route and sent a large trade mission to Kabul. At this time the United States was also offering aid to Afghanistan through agricultural development (the vast and ambitious Helmand Valley Authority). The Soviets, in direct competition, built grain silos that housed the U.S.-donated grain and also constructed new roads in and out of the capital, Kabul.

In 1955 to show their sincere friendship Nikolai Bulganin and Nikita Khrushchev paid a state visit to Afghanistan (countered shortly afterwards by a visit from U.S. vice-president Richard Nixon). The Soviet Union then stepped up its involvement, and new projects included the huge engineering project of the Salang (Phuket) Tunnel, through the Hindu Kush, which allowed trade to move north and south year round. This was followed by a military aid program by which the Afghan defense forces were re-equipped and given jet fighters.

The Soviets made little move to exercise direct political influence at this stage and were content to deal with the dictatorial Daoud Shah, uncle of the king and prime minister from 1953 to 1963. But the political climate among the educated Afghans moved steadily away from traditional conservative Muslim and tribal ways to more democratic liberal and international ideas. Women were encouraged to appear in public without the veil and religious leaders who protested against this were jailed. As part of his strengthening of the Afghan central government, Daoud Shah used troops to collect taxes and enforce his rule.

From the Soviet point of view this development of a strong and friendly government in its neighbor was most satisfactory. U.S. influence was weakened by the massive Soviet programs and the Khrushchev policy of trade and aid with little attempt at political infiltration seemed to have paid off.

1963–1979—By the mid-1960s Afghanistan had changed enormously. Tourists from all the world visited Kabul, and the social contrasts between the city and the mountain villages increased. The small pro-Soviet Marxist parties began to divide into urban and rural factions, but were both remote from day-to-day life. In July 1973, the Parcham urban faction, with Daoud Shah, carried out a coup expelling the king. But when Daoud seemed to turn against the Parcham in April 1978, they liquidated him with their Soviet-acquired military power. A Democratic Republic of Afghanistan was proclaimed. But the Parcham was not in touch with the country and local uprisings broke out. The rural Khalq faction disputed power, and the Soviets found their ally in danger of civil war.

1979–1988—In late December 1979 Soviet armed forces moved into Afghanistan. They killed the Parcham leader and put the Khalq in power because they believed the latter to be the faction most likely to gain wide popular support. But rather than settling matters, the invasion roused the whole country. Resistance forces, labeled generally Mujahideen, appeared and were supplied with arms from U.S. and Arab sources through Pakistan and Iran—sometimes for anti-Soviet motives, sometimes for patriotic Afghan motives, and sometimes in support of Islam. Their increasingly sophisticated weapons denied the Soviets any chance of success.

In 1986 a more moderate leader was found in the Parcham, Dr. Sayid Mohammed Najibullah, and the Soviet Union under Mikhail Gorbachev began to find a way out. Not only was the war unwinnable, but it was having a negative effect in the USSR. In eight years, over 13,000 Soviet soldiers had been killed. Soviet conscripts from Central Asia (usually in the ranks without technical skills) were not sent to Afghanistan, since they were regarded as unreliable against fellow Muslims, which increased the proportion of ethnically Russian casualties and exacerbated dislike of the war within the USSR. Returning soldiers reported against the war's aims and its conditions. There was also evidence of drug abuse among returning soldiers.

On February 8, 1988, Gorbachev announced that Soviet troops would begin to withdraw on May 15. In April, at Geneva, Afghanistan and Pakistan signed agreements to cease interference in each other's lands, to help refugees, and to cooperate with the withdrawal of Soviet troops. This was followed by guarantees by the USSR and the United States to respect these commitments. The Soviet troops withdrew according to the planned timetable and Afghanistan has, since then, settled into its own civil war.

AGRICULTURE

Background—During the 1905 Revolution there were uprisings among the peasantry, and after the revolution was suppressed, reforms that enabled peasants to buy and sell land removed more than 2 million households from the landless communes that hired out peasant labor. This was particularly marked in the rich black earth country of western Russia, the Ukraine, and the North Caucasus. Peter Stolypin said that the government was placing its wager "not on the needy and the drunken but on the sturdy and strong." While these reforms did create a class of strong peasants (kulaks), they also led to increasing bitterness among the remaining people. This was fertile ground for the revolutionary doctrines of the various socialist parties contending for future power in Russia at the time.

The Socialist Revolutionaries were in direct succession to the 19th century radical Narodniks and, above all, were the champions of the peasants. They believed that socialism would develop

naturally in the countryside through the activities of the peasant communes. Followers of Marx, such as Georgy Plekhanov and, even more so, Lenin, were totally opposed to such a notion, realizing that it would be necessary to create large-scale agricultural units to supply a socialist economy. There was also a powerful bias against the peasantry in the Bolshevik party, which believed them to be a naturally reactionary force and a breeding ground for capitalism. But no party could afford to ignore the peasants. They represented 80 percent of the population and contributed 50 percent of the national income.

During World War I the agricultural sector was affected more drastically than the industrial. The best manpower went to the front and replacements for worn-out agricultural machinery and implements were unobtainable. Food production slumped, and the combination of hunger in the cities and the conduct of the war revived all the forces that had erupted in 1905. When the revolution took place there were sporadic seizures of landlords' lands by peasants in various parts of the country, despite exhortations by the Provisional Government to await the decision of the Constituent Assembly.

The first All-Russian Congress of Soviets in June 1917 had a Socialist Revolutionary majority and, although their agrarian policy was very similar to the Bolsheviks (in fact, Lenin later adopted it for the Bolsheviks), there was a significant difference: the Socialist Revolutionaries backed the Provisional Government in telling the peasants to wait for the Constituent Assembly before expropriating land, while Lenin backed their seizures of land and further added that large estates should be transformed into model farms run by local soviets. But this argument was interrupted by the success of the October Revolution and all that this brought in its wake.

1917 October Revolution—Lenin realized that the vital issues to the peasants—the vast mass of the population—were the war and the land. At the first All-Russian Congress of Soviets on October 26 the Decree on Land was submitted and passed unanimously; this declared all private property in the land abolished and called for all land—private, state, and church—to be handed over to rural district land committees. The small holdings of working peasants and Cossacks were exempted.

This was certainly one of Lenin's most ingenious political moves. It had the effect of making the Bolsheviks popular while preparing the ground for the division of the Socialist Revolutionaries.

The split was widened when Andrei Kolegaev, a prominent Left Socialist Revolutionary, was appointed people's commissar for agriculture. On January 18 the third All-Russian Congress of Soviets approved a draft law on the socialization of land. Appropriately, this was the 57th anniversary of Czar Alexander's decree emancipating the serfs. One of its clauses stressed the objective of a socialist agricultural program to be as follows: "To develop the collective system of agriculture, as being more economical in respect both to labor and of production, at the expense of individual holdings, in order to bring about the transition to a socialist economy."

During the next four or five months a massive redistribution of land took place throughout most of European Russia. But, except in areas where the power of the soviets was firmly established, the distribution of land was often haphazard—in some places peaceful, in others leading to violence and destruction of property and equipment. It has been calculated that of the seized land 86 percent went to the peasants, 11 percent to the state, and 3 percent to collectives. Owing to the strength of the Socialist Revolutionaries in the local land committees, the well-off peasants probably did better from the transfer than did the poor peasants.

The harvest of 1917 was a poor one largely because of the war, and by January 1918 the food shortages in the cities were becoming acute. At a meeting of the Petrograd Soviet, Lenin proposed searching all storage areas where grain might be being hidden and immediately shooting any speculators.

War Communism, 1918–1920—The people's commissar for supply organized armed bands of men to go into the villages to offer goods to the peasants in exchange for grain or, where that proved unproductive, to take grain by force. Neither means proved effective. The peasants would not give up grain without goods and the goods offered were of little interest to them. This attitude and the menacing approach of a civil war led to the decree of June 18 setting up the Committees of Poor Peasants. Membership in these was open to anyone in the rural community. Their purpose was to extract grain from the kulaks and the rich. Lenin regarded this as a vital step in the progress of the revolution. It meant the beginning of the true socialist revolution in the countryside in which the poor peasants, led by the industrial proletariat, took decisive action against the bourgeoisie, in the guise of the kulaks. It also signaled the first step in what was to become known as War Communism.

The result of all these measures was that peasants hid their grain and refused to sow more than would feed their families. With the end of the civil war by the autumn of 1920, it was apparent that there had been an appalling decline in agricultural production. The redistribution of land had led to the virtual elimination of the large estates, but the natural unit for agriculture had now become the peasant small holding: a plot of up to 10 acres cultivated by the labor of a peasant family owning a horse. This unit represented 86 percent of all holdings, while the collective—the desired socialist solution—had everywhere met with almost total failure.

The area of sown land in Russia had declined from 105 million hectares in 1913 to 75 million in 1920, and the grain harvest of 80 million tons in 1913 had dropped to less than 50 million in 1920. What was worse, the small peasant holdings not only produced less but they consumed more, and even if they produced a surplus it was more difficult and expensive to collect. The Eighth Congress of Soviets recognized that the real problem for Soviet agricultural policy was not to find the means of collecting crops but to discover an effective way of increasing production. This led directly to the New Economic Policy (NEP).

NEP, 1921–1927—At the 10th Party Congress in March 1921, Lenin announced a series of measures aimed at encouraging the production of surpluses. These consisted of a tax in kind based on a percentage of crops harvested, calculated to favor the middle and poor peasants, and freedom to trade surpluses in the marketplace. A fund was promised to provide agricultural equipment and

consumer goods. Almost immediately the area of sown land in some provinces increased by up to 15 percent, though it was offset by decreases elsewhere. Much more seriously, a severe drought affected the harvests of 1920 and 1921. The state had to supply large quantities of relief supplies to which were added considerable quantities from abroad. Herbert Hoover's American Relief Administration was a major force in famine relief.

In 1922 there was a massive agricultural campaign, including an agricultural exhibition held in Moscow, that was rewarded by an excellent harvest. The effects of the NEP were considerable and lasted for almost the next 10 years. The peasant, and in particular the well-off and energetic peasant, was given the chance of treating his holding as his own, of employing hired labor on it if he so wished, and of selling its produce where he wished. Essentially his obligation to the state was that of a taxpayer. Lenin continued to say that the ideal socialist development was large-scale agriculture but he did little in practical terms to bring it about. So little indeed that by 1927, 98.3 percent of all land was in the hands of individuals and only 1.7 percent was in the hands of collectives or state farms.

The agricultural policies of the NEP were criticized as were the rest of its policies—first on ideological grounds, particularly by the left, including Trotsky and Kamenev, and second by industrial workers who felt that they were being discriminated against. Much debate went on about these issues but that was normal during the 1920s in the country, and by 1925 the sown area had increased to 104 million hectares and the grain harvest had climbed from 50 million tons to 72 million. The NEP could be seen to be working.

Collectivization, 1927–1936—By 1927 Stalin believed that "The Soviet regime was walking on two unequal legs, the socialist sector in towns and the private sector in villages and that this could no longer go indefinitely." The idea of collectivization was not a new one and, in fact, Stalin was taking the left-wing policies of Trotsky and Zinoviev to their logical conclusions. The five-year plan was not officially promulgated until April 1929, but many of the measures contained in it were already being put into effect.

Soviet agricultural policy now had as its main thrust the herding of peasants into collectives. They either went to voluntary collectives, such as the kolkhoz, working on a cooperative basis and sharing the profits from the produce which now had to be sold to the government, or joined a sovkhoz, which as a state farm paid a wage. The inhabitants of the kolkhoz were permitted an acre or less of land on which they were allowed to keep a cow, a pig, four sheep, rabbits, and poultry.

Since not more than 2 percent of the land was collectivized by 1927, it was plain drastic measures would have to be taken in order to meet the targets set out by the party. The collectivization policy was aimed at the whole peasant population, but it was now being proposed that the land belonging to the kulaks should be expropriated and the owners expelled from the community. Kulaks were defined by the Sovnarkom as peasants who: (1) hired permanent workers, (2) owned an industrial enterprise—a flour mill for example, (3) hired out agricultural machinery, and (4) had any member of their family involved in usury. Stalin claimed that the kulaks represented 5 percent of the population, though 3 percent is a more generally accepted estimate.

Pravda published an article entitled "Neither Terror Nor Dekulakization, but A Socialist Offensive On NEP Lines." This was in June 1929. By December Stalin had ceased to pretend. "Now we are able to carry on a determined offensive against the kulaks, eliminate them as a class. It is an integral part of the formation and development of collective farms. Consequently it is ridiculous and foolish to discourse at length on dekulakization. When the head is off, one does not mourn for the hair." Action against the kulaks started almost immediately, though official instructions were only issued in February of next year. There are no official figures as to the number of households "dekulakized," but about 1 million seem to have been affected, a total of at least 4.5 million people. Their fate depended upon what category they came under. The "actively hostile" were handed over to the OGPU (State Political Administration) and sent to camps while their families were deported to distant regions such as Siberia or the Far East. The second category, the "most economically potent," were deported outside the region of their residence. The final group, those with little land and a minimum of capital, were allowed to remain in the region but were given the worst land.

It is of course true that in the Caucasus and the Ukraine richer peasants did own a disproportionate percentage of the land compared to other parts of the country, and that more of them had joined the White Armies in the civil war than their poorer neighbors. However, the basic reason for the assault on the kulaks was the belief, not confined to Stalin, that they were "a petit bourgeois class of aspiring capitalists who were hostile to the socialist revolution." As a class they paid for their beliefs and attitudes under Stalin.

Deprivation was not confined to the kulaks. In the winter of 1930–31 collectivization and confiscation were being employed against the whole spectrum of peasants in the Ukraine and, by 1933, also in Siberia. Livestock was compulsorily purchased, though frequently the peasants slaughtered their beasts before this could happen. In Kazakhstan there was a disastrous decline in the sheep population leading quite directly to a decline of Kazakhs themselves, with as many as 20 percent dying of famine. Another method used to persuade peasants to join collectives was the imposition of arbitrary demands for grain. Failure to meet these demands was punished by fines, confiscation of property, and even imprisonment. The human cost of collectivization was high: the estimated death toll is, between 1930 and 1937, 11 million, added to which another 3.5 million who died later in camps. Of these deaths, 5 million were in the Ukraine, 1 million in the north Caucasus, and another million in the Kazakhstan disaster.

Agriculture, 1936–1941—Collectivization was more or less complete by 1936, and the pattern of collective institutions remained primarily the same from the time of the kolkhoz congress until after the death of Stalin. In 1937 there were nearly a quarter of a million kolkhozes and 4,000 sovkhozes. In the kolkhoz the peasants grew grain and industrial crops, cotton, and so on, but the supply of meat and vegetables came almost entirely from their private holdings, and the same applied to fruit, eggs, and poultry.

Collectives 1928–1937			
	1928	1932	1937
Households collectivized (%)	1.7	61.5	93.0
Sown area collectivized (%)	2.3	77.7	99.1
No. of kolkhozes (thousands)	33.3	210.6	242.5
No. of sovkhozes (thousands)	1.4	4.3	4.0
No. of MTS (thousands)	—	2.4	5.8

Source: Adapted from Munting, *The Economic Development of the USSR*, 1982

Payment for collective work was not good, and the kolkhoz had to pay for the services provided by the MTS (Motor Tractor Stations), which provided agricultural machinery and also exercised political control over the collectives. The constant problem therefore was to exert pressure on the peasants to work for the collective when it was in their interests to work for themselves. In 1939 an edict defined the number of hours to be worked for the kolkhoz but enforcing it was not easy, particularly when industrial prices rose more sharply than agricultural incomes, the "scissors crisis."

The sovkhoz, although they had more access to capital goods than the kolkhoz and had a fully paid staff of workers, did very little better in production terms. But the harvest of 1937 at 87 million tons was the best since the revolution.

The harvests declined sharply for the next two years. But in 1939 at the outbreak of World War II there was a record harvest of 95 million tons, of which procurements for the state amounted to 36 million tons. It might be said that Stalin had won his battle against the peasants, a contest which, according to Franklin D. Roosevelt, he compared to the terrible experience of war against the Germans.

It has been said that the survival of the peasantry from 1930 onward was due to the toleration by the government of private food growing. Comprising 3.5

percent of the sown area, this produced 45 percent of all agricultural output including 71 percent of milk, 70 percent of meat, and 43 percent of wool. Noncollectivized agriculture has been called, appropriately, the "giant dwarf."

The introduction of compulsory work units on the kolkhoz further increased peasant grievances and led to a further decline in their standard of living. Vast and ill-conceived plans like Stalin's dream of growing cotton in the Ukraine, and huge plantings of a supposed rubber-bearing plant, the *kok-sagyz*, did little to increase agricultural production at a critical time for the USSR.

World War II, 1941–1945—Soviet agriculture was hit almost immediately by the rapid advances made by the German army in the summer of 1941. Much of the best agricultural land in the Ukraine and northern Caucasus was lost to the government, and it has been estimated that by the end of November 1941, 38 percent of grain production, 84 percent of sugar, and 60 percent of pig production was held by the invading Germans. Unlike the industrial capacity, much of which was removed to the east, good agricultural land could only be made up for by increased production off worse land. By herculean efforts this was achieved, though by the end of 1942 the Nazi occupation of the northern Caucasus and the Don area had deprived the country of almost all its first-rate grain-growing areas. The grain harvest in 1942 was reduced to 30 million tons.

The invading Nazis used the kolkhoz to supply their forces and, particularly in the Ukraine, they were at first welcomed by the peasants who had every reason to dislike their own regime. But the brutality of many of the occupying units soon turned the peasants against them and drove the more adventurous members into joining the partisan units.

Total food rationing was introduced in July 1941, and as the war went on the share of the free market in supplying foodstuffs and other products increased, until in 1945 it was more than 45 percent.

1946–1953—Announcing the Fourth Five-Year Plan in 1946, the Central Committee spelled out the situation in the Soviet Union. There were 25 million people homeless, 1,700 towns and 70,000 villages destroyed, and, because of terrible casualties estimated at 20 million, an acute shortage of agricultural labor. Despite this the plan called for a huge increase in agricultural production. Stalin was determined to regain complete control over the kolkhozes and to tax them as onerously as in the 1930s to make them pay for the reconstruction of the country's economy. Like the First Five-Year Plan, if one can ignore the ruthlessness of its execution, it was a brilliant success.

A council of kolkhoz affairs was established to ensure strict observance of the kolkhoz statute. Procurement prices of crops were not increased but taxes were. In 1948 there was drought and, partly as a result of this, Stalin announced plans for the "great transformation of nature." To deal with future shortages of water, vast belts of forest shelter trees were to be planted, canals were planned, and irrigation schemes announced. The trees refused to grow but the cost was taken from the kolkhoz's income. A new system of crop rotation was introduced by direct command of the commissariat for agriculture, without regard for local conditions.

The kolkhoz growing cotton or other

industrial crops or those near large towns with a ready market for their privately grown produce did quite well, notwithstanding. But the more remote collectives did very badly. For some products such as potatoes the payments were less than the cost of production. At the same time many kolkhoz were amalgamated to form larger units. In 1950 there were 250,000; by 1952 this had been reduced to 97,000.

In 1952 the Sixth Five-Year Plan was announced, which called for increases of 40 percent in grain production, 80 percent in meat, and 50 percent in milk. However, the death of Stalin early in 1953 and the subsequent struggle for power among his successors meant that it was never put into effect.

Khrushchev Revolution, 1953–1954—In the power struggle after the death of Stalin, Khrushchev had emerged as a powerful figure, and in 1954 he was put in charge of agriculture. Khrushchev's first moves were directed at improving the lot of the kolkhoz. He had been deeply involved in the agricultural field under Stalin and, coming from a peasant background himself, was totally committed to improving their lot. The following measures were introduced immediately:

1. The state was to pay transport costs of procured produce.
2. Debts of the kolkhoz were to be written off.
3. MTS charges were to be fixed and not based on a percentage of the harvest.
4. Work minimums for members were to be decided by the kolkhoz itself.
5. Peasants could consume more of their own produce produced on

private plots or, if they wished, sell it in the marketplace.
6. Compulsory procurement prices were to be increased and there was to be an increase in state investment.

Virgin Lands Program, 1954–1958—In addition to the above reforms, in January 1954 Khrushchev first proposed the Virgin Lands program, an attempt to solve at a stroke the perennial problem of the Soviet Union: feeding itself. There seemed to be an absolute limit to increasing yield by more intensive cultivation of the existing sown area, so logic demanded an increase in the absolute amount of land under cultivation, by plowing virgin land, hitherto used only for grazing.

Khrushchev also wished to shift the production of grain into the Virgin Lands so as to allow the cultivation of fodder, in the shape of corn, in the more naturally fertile areas of the Ukraine and the Caucasus. The areas chosen were in northern Kazakhstan, the southern part of Siberia, and in the southeast of European Russia. Between 1953 and 1956, cultivated land was increased by 35 million hectares. In 1954 the harvest was excellent but in 1955 there was a drought. In 1956 there was another good harvest. Meanwhile, in January 1955, Khrushchev had got the Central Committee to agree to a concentration on corn, increasing it from 3.5 to 28 million hectares.

He also continued the policy of amalgamating the kolkhoz or turning them into state farms. By the end of his period in office in 1965 they had been reduced to 36,000 from 125,000 in 1950. There were also reforms of the pricing structures, and in February 1958 the MTSs were abolished and their equipment sold to the kolkhoz. There were also moves to restrict the amount of private land available to the kolkhoz and the food they could sell in the market. This was in the year following Khrushchev's success in fighting off the attempt of the old guard—Molotov, Kaganovich, and so on—to unseat him.

1958–1964—Khrushchev's agricultural reforms suffered from major faults. Shutting down the MTSs and selling their equipment to the kolkhoz, and forcing them to rely more on their collective income and less on the earnings from their private plots, was neither successful or popular. The kolkhoz had to pay for the equipment, which meant they had less to invest.

The new Territorial Production Administrations he set up were inefficient and the price structure had become chaotic. His intensive corn production was not a success and led to the extensive slaughtering of cattle because of both grain shortages and a desire to increase short-term meat production.

Finally the great Virgin Lands campaign was a disappointment, the hoped for huge increases in grain production were short-lived, owing to the nature of the soil and the climate in the chosen areas, and also to the quality of labor and management available. In 1963, the year of the 21st Party Congress, Khrushchev had come to the conclusion that increasing agricultural production by the extensive method—that is, plowing more land—had to be succeeded by the intensive method—that is, the use of fertilizers. He therefore called for the expansion of agro-chemical production, at one time suggesting a requirement of 100 million tons by 1970. His efforts to fight off his critics were in no

way assisted by the fact that large quantities of grain had to be imported from the West. In October 1964 Khrushchev was dismissed from office.

AGRICULTURAL OUTPUT, 1958–1965
(1958 = 100)

	Total	Crops	Livestock
1958	100.0	100.0	100
1959	110.4	95.0	108
1960	103.0	99.4	107
1961	106.0	101.0	112
1962	107.0	101.0	115
1963	99.0	92.0	108
1964	113.0	119.0	106
1965	114.0	107.0	123

Brezhnev and his Successors, 1965–1985—When Brezhnev and Kosygin succeeded Khrushchev, they set about reversing many of his agricultural reforms. Restrictions he had placed on the private plots were relaxed and procurement prices were raised. Kolkhoz prices for agricultural machinery were reduced and Vladimir Motshevich, who had been fired by Khrushchev, was brought back as minister of agriculture, while the Territorial Production Administrations were reduced to purely local functions. Under the dual leadership, soon to be reduced to Brezhnev on his own, agricultural production once more increased. Indeed, Brezhnev in his speech introducing the Food Program in May 1982, was able to claim an increase in gross agricultural production of 50 percent. What he did not say was that these achievements had been affected by considerable and growing increases in food subsidies—necessary in order to keep consumer prices at an artificially low level—and by a continual increase in the percentage of investment going into agriculture. While the share of national income from agriculture was in continual decline, there was the rising cost and embarrassment of grain imports from the West, more specifically from the United States.

This situation, though not alluded to in the speech, was prominent in the minds of the Politburo and was brought sharply into focus by the U.S. grain embargo in January 1980. The fact that, under pressure from U.S. farmers, President Ronald Reagan dropped the embargo in April 1981 did not lessen its effect on the USSR.

The Food Program was launched in May 1982 with the avowed intention of making the Soviet Union self-sufficient in its food and fodder requirements. It indicated a considerable body of support for agricultural reform in the Politburo already.

GRAIN PRODUCTION AND NET IMPORTS
(million tons)

	Production	Net imports	All grain	Imports from USA	Net imports as % of domestic production
1970	186.8	−7.2	180	0	0
1971	181.2	1.4	182	2.9	0.8
1972	168.2	21.0	189	13.7	12.5
1973	222.5	5.2	227	7.9	2.3
1974	195.7	0.4	196	2.3	0.2
1975	140.1	25.4	165	13.9	18.1
1976	223.8	7.7	230	7.4	3.4
1977	195.7	16.8	213	12.5	8.6
1978	237.4	12.8	250	11.2	5.4
1979	179.2	30.2	209	15.2	16.9
1980	189.2	34.3	224	8.0	18.1
1981	160.0	45.5	206	15.4	28.4
1982	180.0	40.3	220	6.2*	22.4
1983	190.0	33.9	224	14.1*	17.8
1984	170.0	45.0	215	18.3*	26.5
1985	178.0	30.0	-	-	16.85
1986	210.0	26.0	-	-	12.38
1987	211.3	30.0	-	-	14.20
1988	195.0	41.0	-	-	21.03
1989	209.0	41.0	-	-	19.62

*Wheat and corn only

The Food Program, when it finally appeared, contained more rhetoric than novelty. In many ways it appeared to be a continuation of the policies adopted in the 1970s. These included increased procurement prices and additional subsidies for unprofitable farms. However, behind the scenes there were other forces at work, indicated by the fact that from 1980 onward there had been a slight but continuing decline in the percentage of investment in agriculture. But Brezhnev was not the man to make decisive strategic moves, and in March 1985 his policies were overturned by Mikhail Gorbachev.

Gorbachev, 1985– —Mikhail Gorbachev's background fits him almost uniquely to deal with the agricultural problems of the USSR. He is a qualified agro-economist, and after 20 years' work in party organizations in Stavropol, he took charge of the Agricultural Department of the Central Committee in 1978 and obtained a full seat on the Politburo only two years later. He has made several statements concerning agriculture. In September 1985 at Tselinograd (the town named after the Virgin Lands program) he said, "The problem of providing the population with foodstuffs has not been completely solved. The demand exceeds the supply." For this he blamed the growth of cash incomes compared to food production. He said: "Meat is sold in our stores at prices that are only one-third to one-half the cost of production. At present this disparity is covered by state subsidies amounting to 20 billion rubles a year."

At the 27th Party Congress, Nikolai Ryzhkov, chairman of the Council of Ministers, suggested that capital investment in the agro-industrial complex would grow at a mere 22 percent compared to the overall growth of the economy at 36 percent. This was a further move in the direction of shifting investment away from this sector. Gorbachev himself continually emphasized that "We must face up to real problems." Some hint of how this might be done came in a speech he made to the Supreme Soviet concerning the 1986 plan for agriculture, in which he noted the introduction of methods such as cost-accounting, self-financing, and self-recoupment for all collective and state farms. The farms will be given more autonomy, he added, but concluded, "As in previous years, the state will subsidize the output of staple products."

The removal or drastic reduction of subsides, which would mean substantial rises in the price of food to the consumer, is a nettle that he has not as yet quite dared to grasp—a problem that is not unique to the USSR.

AIDS

Until 1989 the disease AIDS was dismissed as a phenomenon of the capitalist world and non-Soviet citizens were accused of being its carriers. In October 1985 the *Literary Gazette* claimed that AIDS had been created by Western scientists working on germ warfare, but AIDS had already been detected in the USSR in 1978. However, by September 1987, AIDS was no longer presented as a Western problem: millions of copies of an informative booklet were issued and a program to train 2,000 specialist physicians was announced. In February 1989 *Pravda* and *Trud* reported an emergency meeting of the Ministry of Health, stating that there were 150 people known to be infected in the USSR and that by the year 2000 there

could be 15 million carriers and hundreds of thousands dying or dead. In fact, by the end of 1988, there were already over 700 H.I.V.-positive cases. In one Caucasus town 27 infants had been found infected from unsterilized syringes. With homosexuality illegal, and therefore kept hidden, and with 40,000 intravenous drug users in Moscow alone, the task of containing the infection is clearly formidable.

AIR FORCE

In 1917 there were over 2,000 aircraft in Russian military service. By the collapse of the czarist government in 1917 and the Brest-Litovsk Treaty in 1918, much of this strength had been destroyed. Furthermore, the Bolshevik leaders had no experience in air warfare and regarded the machine as some sort of middle-class luxury, despite the substantial air force they had inherited from the czarist army. The German advances of 1918 and the civil war reduced the surviving planes to just over 300 by the end of that year.

The Red Air Fleet, set up in May 1918—short of fuel, lubricants, and spare parts—played a limited role in the fighting against Anton Denikin and Baron Peter Wrangel. The air fleet and its supporting industry, for the reasons given, were in decline, despite the existence of design teams of high quality, such as that started by Nikolai Zhukovski and carried on by Andrei Tupolev. In the 1920s machines were bought from abroad, but the Soviet-German trade agreement of 1921 was used as a cover for the manufacture of German planes in the Soviet Union and, after the 1922 Treaty of Rapallo, the secret training of German air crews at the Lipetsk Air School. New engineers and designers were produced from the Zhukovski Academy, the most distinguished being Sergei Ilyushin in 1926, Alexander Yakolev in 1931 and Anastasy Mikoyan in 1936. Between 1923 and 1940 over 6,000 pilots were trained by the Air Fleet Academy at Kacha in the Crimea, where there was good flying weather year-round and also a center for glider training.

In 1924, as Trotsky's control of the armed forces was removed, the command of the Red Air Fleet was given to Petr Baranov with the German-speaking Latvian Alksnis as his deputy. Stalin became dissatisfied with the results of Soviet aircraft design and designers were subjected to continual surveillance by the NKVD—some teams having to continue their work while interned. By 1938 the air fleet's frontline strength was assessed by the Germans at over 6,000 aircraft (Soviet figures were deliberately obfuscated).

In 1933 Baranov died in an air crash and was succeeded by Alksnis, who, because of his sympathy with the military ideas of Mikhail Tukhachevsky, was arrested on November 23, 1937, and shot on October 28, 1938. This was part of Stalin's purge of the military, and all the senior Red Air Force command also went to their deaths.

The Spanish Civil War gave the Red Air force an opportunity for combat experience, and the first 18 I-15 fighters were shipped to Cartagena on October 13, 1936. Probably up to 1,500 planes were sent to Spain and up to 770 aircrew served for some time from 1936 to 1938. The Soviet aircraft outmatched the first German aircraft they met, giving the Republicans air superiority until the Messerschmitt BF-109 altered the balance in mid-1937.

Vasili Blyukher's defense of the east-ern frontiers against Japanese incursions from 1931 on provided another opportunity to exercise the Red Air Force. Some 400 aircraft and 40 instructors went to China in 1937. On May 20, 1939, a series of air battles against the Japanese air force started in northern Manchuria, continuing until September 16. Accurate figures are unavailable from either side, but Soviet losses of 202 and Japanese of 162 planes are likely. General Zhukov's ground offensive was accompanied by the then-massive air support of 200 bombers covered by 300 fighters.

The Red Air Force was a world pioneer in the use of parachute troops; the first demonstration was in August 1931 when 19 men were dropped to seize a landing area for troop-carrying planes and by 1935 there was an entire airborne brigade. Although by the time of the German invasion in 1941 there were at least three fully equipped and trained brigades, and the framework of three airborne corps, paratroops were not used until early in 1942 as part of the Soviet counteroffensive, but the results were disappointing and Stalin ordered their employment as infantry.

The next wartime use of the air force after the Manchurian campaign was against Finland in 1939, where 900 aircraft were opposed by less than 100 Finnish machines. In three and a half months Soviet losses were heavy, over 800 to the Finns' loss of 70.

World War II—In 1941 the Red Air Force was large but obsolete, and its poor showing in Finland led the Germans to rate it very poorly. When they attacked, the slow and heavy Russian bombers were shot down in large numbers by the BF-109 fighters and the powerful German anti-aircraft artillery. The purges of air force commanders and the extraordinary detention of Tupolev on the charge that he had given the Germans the design of the BF-109 further led the Germans to underestimate the Red Air Force and its aircraft industry.

On the first day of the German attack 1,800 Soviet aircraft were destroyed, mostly sitting on the airfields. The Red Air Force was no longer in a state to attack or defend, but the loss was not so much of air crew as of obsolete aircraft. When the rapid German advance began to leave its base airfields far behind, their aircraft began to encounter new and improved aircraft, including British Hurricane and American P-40 fighters, but especially the new YAK-1 fighter and the ground-attack IL-2 Stormovik. Equipping aircraft with cannon and rockets improved their firepower, but heavy or long-range bombers were lacking. Nor did the Red Air Force at this time have more than the rudimentary use of radar. Between January and May 1942 an encircled German army had to be supplied by air, and the Red Air Force took the opportunity to revenge itself, destroying 262 Junkers transport planes and their air crews and showing that the BF-109 did not necessarily control the skies.

The battle of Stalingrad repeated the Red Air Force's experience of dealing with a surrounded German army, and in 10 weeks the Germans lost 488 planes in attempts to drop supplies.

The Soviets developed three women's air regiments in 1941, two of bombers and one of fighters, as well as employing women pilots individually in other units, both combat and transport. Lidya Litvyak was a fighter ace with 12 victories before she was shot down at the age of 22.

In 1943 aircraft production was re-established and the Red Air Force increased its size to 8,300, twice that of the Germans. Part of this was the supply of aircraft from the United States and Britain (some 20,000 during the whole war). At the Battle of Kursk, the German Luftwaffe was to have swept the sky clear for the army's advance, but the Red Air Force withstood this and attacked the German air bases while harassing the assembling troops. On the day of the German attack, July 5, the Soviets sent in a wave of ground attack planes but these were countered by a prepared massive force of Messerschmitt and Focke-Wulf fighters, shooting the Red Air Force down in hundreds, claiming over 600 in two days. But the Germans found the pace difficult to maintain and the Soviets continued to attack the German Panzers with Stormoviks en masse. When the counterattack began on July 12, huge air reserves had been brought in and the Soviet armor rolled forward. The Luftwaffe's command of the sky had been only local and temporary.

Postwar—By the end of the war the Red Air Force had expanded hugely, the aircraft factories turning out over 40,000 machines in 1944, giving an active frontline strength of 18,000. But the postwar period saw most of these planes become obsolete; the jet plane had appeared and the early German types were captured at the end of the war in 1945 and tested in the USSR. On May Day 1947, two groups of 50 YAK-15 and MIG-9 jet fighters flew over Moscow. The first jet bomber, the IL-28, was shown in 1950. In the Korean War the Soviet-built MIG-15, flown by Chinese pilots, met and showed its superiority to the American F-51, but was mastered by the F-86 Saber. The superior MIG-17 appeared at the end of the war. From now on, Western military analysts would look anxiously at new Soviet aircraft developments.

Khrushchev appreciated that Soviet air power required advanced weapons research and development, particularly in rocket development and in space. He successfully conducted an aspect of the cold war by demonstrating each May Day progressively greater rocketry, giving weight to the USSR's world position. Khrushchev seemed to indicate that the Soviet Union would move away from long-range bombers to rocketry. However in 1954 a Moscow air display showed new big bombers, and in 1955 the turboprop TU-20 (called Bear by NATO) was seen. Clearly, it could deliver an attack on North America, flying over the Pole and back. In the 1970s and '80s Bear was followed by Bison, Backfire, Blinder, and Badger bombers. The MIG-25 (Foxbat) outclassed all other combat aircraft on its appearance in 1970; it has been developed as a high-altitude, all-weather interceptor and reconnaissance plane.

Experience in Afghanistan showed the development of frontal air attack units, with helicopters and ground attack, rocket-firing aircraft. While the Strategic Rocket Forces launch the space vehicles, the cosmonauts are generally air force men, and this is seen as part of their professional future.

ALBANIA
Area: 11,000 square miles
Population: 3,201,000
Capital: Tirana; population, 272,000

The People's Socialist Republic, with a party membership of 122,600, is the least developed country in the Balkans. Its economy is largely agricultural with some mining. Seventy percent of the population are Muslim, though all places of worship were closed in 1976.

Before World War II, Albania was ruled by the self-crowned King Zog, and from 1939 to 1944 was occupied by Italy. Local Communists, aided by the Yugoslav partisans, formed the National Liberation Front, which established a government without opposing parties in November 1944 under the leadership of Enver Hoxha.

In 1948, Hoxha broke off relations with Yugoslav leader Tito and moved closer to the USSR. This came to an abrupt end after Khrushchev's denunciation of Stalin at the 20th Party Congress in 1961. Hoxha turned to the Chinese and Mao Tse-tung, deeply at odds with the USSR, was pleased to find a sympathetic communist ally in Europe. China supplied more than 700 million dollars' worth of aid including economic and military advisers. By the late 1970s, China was set on improving relations with the West, and in 1978, it withdrew its aid to Albania and its civilian and military mission, leaving Albania even more isolated. Hoxha died in 1982 and was replaced by Ramiz Alia but the party still strongly resisted any of the ideological changes that were beginning to make themselves felt in other Communist states. However the dramatic events of the last months of 1989 have had some effects. There is no sign of a change in the one party system, but there have been reports of internal protest meetings. On the economic front, a system of wages based on results produced has been introduced in some areas, while in diplomatic circles there is talk of the possibility of reopening relations with both Moscow and Washington.

ANARCHO-COMMUNISTS

A small group in 1917 deriving from the 19th-century Anarchists, particularly from Mikhail Bakunin. They were openly against any parliamentary system. Although they were briefly allied with the Bolsheviks in order to achieve a revolution, and played an important role in the fighting both in the October Revolution and in the anti-Denikin warfare in the Ukraine in 1919, they underestimated the Bolsheviks and were eliminated as enemies.

Leading personalities among them were Bleikhman and Boris Volin. Probably the best known was the veteran Peter Kropotkin, who returned from exile in 1917 but his association with the Provisional Government isolated him from his fellow anarchists.

APPARAT

The party machine, the organization of professional party workers and office holders, controlling all levels of Soviet life.

APPARATCHIK

Colloquial (and often derogatory) term for a party or government official.

AMERICAN RELIEF ADMINISTRATION (ARA)

An agency, directly by Herbert Hoover, which provided help for famine victims after World War I, particularly in the USSR.

ARCHITECTURE

The most significant architectural movement of prerevolutionary Russia was art nouveau, of which the most noted practitioner was F.O. Shekhtel, one of whose villa designs is now the Gorky Museum.

In the immediate aftermath of the revolution there was little possibility of major architectural work. Commemorative buildings such as the Lenin Mausoleum and the *Monument to the Victims of the Revolution* in Petrograd were designed by architects established before the revolution, such as Alexei Shchusev and Lev Rudnyov. With the increased prosperity of the New Economic Policy, and under the sympathetic eye of Anatoly Lunacharsky, the more avant-garde architects such as Grigory Barkhin and Konstantin Melnikov were given a chance and the style they chose was constructivism, based on the theories of painters such as Alexander Rodchenko. By the late twenties constructivism was beginning to be looked on with suspicion because of its formal elements, and the huge industrial and administrative projects being built in the 1930s were all of the neoclassical kind favored by Stalin and the party. There were such vast projects as the Mosvka (Moscow hotel) and the unbuilt Palace of the Soviets, which was to have been over 1,200 feet high surmounted by a 325-foot statue of Lenin (cancelled for fear that the figure of Lenin might be covered by a low cloud in inauspicious weather). One great success for Soviet architecture is the Moscow metro, magnificent by comparison to the London underground or New York subway.

After World War II the main task was reconstruction, carried out with exemplary concentration while the construction of huge wedding cakes such as the Hotel Ukrainia in Moscow went on. There is little indication that the loosening of censorship under Khrushchev and more recently under Gorbachev has made a great difference in architecture in the USSR. Buildings take a long time to plan and construct.

ARMED FORCES

Not all armed forces of the Soviet Union come under the Ministry of Defense. There are also the Border Guards of the KGB and the Internal Security Troops of the MVD, both fully armed for action.

The Border Guards, with ships, tanks, helicopters, and light aircraft, cover the whole frontier of the USSR and are the soldiers with green lapel tabs tourists see at airports.

Other KGB troops are the Kremlin guards, marked by royal blue tabs; they also man other sensitive sites throughout the Soviet Union, such as nuclear weapon stores or communications centers.

The Internal Security Troops of the MVD (with dull brick-red lapels) are the descendants of the Cheka's armed force and have the duty of guarding labor camps, maintaining civil order in the country, or during war, policing the rear of the fighting lines and holding prisoners of war.

The armed forces under the Ministry of Defense are the Army (formerly the Red Army), the Air Force, and the Navy (see entries on each of these). There is also a special feature of the Soviet Union: the Strategic Rocket Forces, which were formed soon after the end of the war when captured German technicians were set to developing rocketry. With the emergence of nuclear warheads, these forces became a high priority in Soviet budgeting. The setback of 1960, when many of its senior staff were killed by an experimental rocket, was overcome and the service has been responsible for launching many Soviet space vehicles.

ARMENI

The Armenians, a people living in both Turkey and the USSR. In the 1880s a group of Armenians in Russia organized the anti-Russian revolutionary federation party Dashnak, which was the leading political force there in 1905.

ARMENIAN SOVIET SOCIALIST REPUBLIC (HAYASTAN)

Population: 3,459,000; 90 percent Armenian

Area: 11,306 square miles

Capital: Erevan; population, 1,186,000

After years of persecution of Christian Armenians by the Ottoman Empire, after the killing of many of their leaders and intellectuals, and their enforced removal from the Turkish border areas in April 1915 during the war with Russia, Armenians wanted safety within the Soviet Union. The dominant political group were the Dashnaks (Dashnaktsutiun, or the Armenian Federation).

In 1918, with the collapse of the Russian Empire, an Armenian republic emerged that was strongly influenced by the power of the Turkish army nearby. Under the terms of the Brest-Litovsk Treaty, Turkey took the province of Kars from Russian Armenia and was awarded control of Batum.

Turkish troops of the Ottoman Empire occupied much of Armenia and Georgia, and in mid-1918 German troops also advanced into Georgia. In December 1917 the Soviets in Petrograd acknowledged the right of Armenians to self-determination in a Decree on Turkish Armenia, which would have made a state including much of the territory taken in Turkey by the czarist armies. Turkey forced the Transcaucasus to declare independence as the Transcaucasian Federation on April 22, 1918. Turkish troops and Azerbaijani Musavats took over Baku in September 1918, which resulted in the massacre of some 30,000 Armenians. As World War I ended, British troops arrived in Baku and Batum. In Baku the British declared the area their "government general" and forced, first, the Azerbaijani and, then, the White troops out.

The Turks, by a treaty of May 11, 1920, recognized a Soviet republic of Armenia under Dashnak control, and the Allied powers also recognized it. In 1920 the Western Allies signed the Treaty of Sèvres with the Turkish Ottoman Empire, ending its rule outside Asia Minor and giving the new Armenian republic parts of Turkey. However, the new ruler of Turkey, Kemal Ataturk, refused to accept the treaty and in September he attacked the Armenians. In a two-month campaign 200,000 Armenians were killed. Following the peace treaty of Alexandropol between Turkey and the Dashnak government of Armenia, land, including Erevan, was yielded to Turkey and Armenia would actually have become a protectorate of Turkey. However the Red Army preempted this, moving into the territory and, on November 29, 1920, declaring a Soviet republic.

Armenia was made part of the Transcaucasian Federal Republic of the USSR in 1922. When this was abolished in 1926, Armenia became one of the USSR's constituent republics.

In November 1920 the Armenian Christian Church (the oldest established state church in Christendom, established A.D. 300) found itself at once freed from the tyranny of the Russian Orthodox Church and faced with the declared atheism of the state, nationalizing its schools and libraries. The Armenians were inured to persecution and survived even the general purges of 1936. During World War II, the Armenian Church made sure that its patriotism was evident. The influence of the church in the Middle East and in the United States has undoubtedly modified the Soviet state's attitude and ensured a policy of coexistence.

In 1988 Nagorno-Karabakh, the Christian Armenian enclave in Muslim Azerbaijan, was the cause of ethnic riots in both republics. As a result the party heads of both Armenia and Azerbaijan were dismissed; 80,000 Azeri refugees left Armenia, and 14,000 Armenians left Azerbaijan. There were strikes, riots, and, as a result, curfews imposed. The leader of the Krunk, the group urging the return of Nagorno-Karabakh to Armenia, Musa Manucharov was arrested (for bribery and embezzlement as head of a building firm).

On December 7, 1988, an earthquake shattered Erevan and Leninakan. As a result, the 1989 election issues in Armenia were dominated by Nagorno-Karabakh and the effects of the earthquake (linked with demands to close a nuclear power station). In protest against Armenian claims on Nagorno-Karabakh, Azerbaijan blocked Armenia in 1989, preventing the railways from carrying goods to Armenia.

Because of the violence in the republic, in reaction to the earthquake and the threat of Azerbaijani attacks, the

1990 elections to the republic's new parliament were postponed.

ART, PLASTIC AND GRAPHIC

Twentieth-century art came to Russia with the movement known as the World of Art; the title came from the movement's magazine published in 1898. The movement, whose credo was essentially "art for art's sake," had a number of important painters, most notably Leon Bakst and Alexander Benois. They became best known for their theatrical and costume design for the ballets of Sergei Diaghilev, who had been a cofounder of the movement. The real significance of the movement lies in the degree to which the rest of Europe was made aware of Russian art. Most of the World of Art group left to live in Western Europe and the United States, but in Russia itself before the October Revolution the neo-primitivist movement led by Mikhail Larionov and Natalia Goncharova was becoming important. In 1910 this group, known as the Knave of Diamonds group, held an exhibition of its work in Moscow and included paintings by Casimir Malevich and Wassily Kandinsky. The movement split and Larionov's group held two major exhibitions, the Donkey's Tale in 1912 and Target in 1913. The other splinter, led by Petr Konchalovsky, promoted such important artists as Nathan Altman and Marc Chagall. Larionov went on to develop a version of cubism called rayonism, while Malevich showed at the Last Futurist Exhibition of Pictures several paintings done in accordance with his theory of suprematism.

After the October Revolution Narkompros (People's Commissariat for Enlightenment) headed by Anatoly Lunacharsky set up a new range of art schools such as Svomas (Free State Art Studios). For the first time avant-garde artists felt that they no longer needed to shock. For the new Commissariat for Popular Culture, Kandinsky ran museums and art galleries in Moscow, Vladimir Tatlin in Petrograd, and Malevich in Vitebsk. At the same time there were other movements such as constructivism afoot. Led by Alexander Rodchenko, this movement declared that easel painting was a useless activity and proposed that artists should now be concerned only with industrial design. In 1922 there was a significant exhibition by the Association of Artists of Revolutionary Russia, which called for a style of heroic realism.

After the dissolution of Narkompros and the decree by the Central Committee in 1932 on the Reconstruction of Literary and Art Organizations, social realism took over from heroic realism as the officially approved style. Abstract art virtually disappeared. Kandinsky left the USSR with Naum Gabo, and of the others some, like Malevich, had died and others had ceased exhibiting. But there was not the same savage persecution of artists as was meted out to writers. Rodchenko went on painting abstracts in his studio in the 1940s. Officially approved painters like Mikhail Avilov and Isaac Brodsky continued to paint portraits, events of the civil war, and scenes on the collective farm. The same thing happened during World War II, with Alexander Gerasimov painting subjects as in *Mother of a Partisan*. After the Khrushchev revolution there was a loosening of constraints, though Khrushchev himself had harsh things to say to painters interested in abstraction in his well-known visit to an exhibition in

1962. Since then there has been a considerable degree of freedom for all types of experimentation, and exhibitions are beginning, in the age of *glasnost*, to be held in the West.

Some of the better-known artists exhibiting in the USSR and the West are two graduates of the Repin Institute of Leningrad, Valerie Lukka and Vyacheslav Mikhailov, both born in 1945 and both working in mixed media with an emphasis on acrylic. Gleb Bogomolov, born in 1933, one of the leaders of the nonconformist art movement has never studied art formally, but is highly thought of by the establishment. His work has been bought for the State Russian Museum in Leningrad. Dmitri Plavinski, born in 1937, is probably the most cosmopolitan artist in the Soviet Union. He studied at the Regional College of Art in Moscow and has had several exhibitions in the United States, Western Europe, and the USSR.

ARTEL

The prototype of the collective farm organization, in which only the land and other means of production were socialized, unlike the earlier type of commune in which everything was held in common and surplus products were delivered to the local soviets in exchange for goods needed by the commune. Distribution of the cultivated produce was allotted in proportion to the work performed by the members. By 1920 there were more than 8,000 artels holding more than 2 million acres.

ATAMAN

A Cossack military leader, sometimes called Hetman.

AZERBAIJAN SOVIET SOCIALIST REPUBLIC

Population: 6,921,000; 78 percent Azerbaijani, 8 percent Russian, and 8 percent Armenian
Area: 33,400 square miles
Capital: Baku; population, 1,757,000
Nakhitchevan Autonomous Soviet Socialist Republic: capital Nakhitchevan; population 278,000.
Nagorno-Karabakh Autonomous Region: capital Stepanakert; population 177,000. An Armenian enclave whose history still causes dispute.

Until 1813, when part of it was ceded to the czar, Azerbaijan (meaning the land of the Azeri people) was all in Persia. In 1917 all the Transcaucasus came under the influence of nationalist revolutionaries, Georgian Mensheviks, Armenian Dashnaks, and Azerbaijani Musavats, the latter being the Muslim Democratic party, a group not unlike its contemporaries, the Young Turks, who were taking over the Ottoman Empire. Baku, an industrial oil town with a large Russian population, was in the hands of a revolutionary government from October with a Musavat majority. The Musavats, moving politically away from the left, withdrew from this government, leaving it in Bolshevik hands in November 1917 and establishing their Transcaucasian Commissariat.

In March 1918 Baku was the scene of ethnic riots, Azeris killing Armenians. At that time, as the Russians came to terms with the Central Powers at Brest-Litovsk, Turkish power grew in Azerbaijan, encouraging the formation of a separate Transcaucasian alliance. There was a proclamation of Azerbaijan independence in May and Turkish troops advanced toward Baku. In August 1918 British forces landed at Baku, ostensibly to defend the area against the Turks, but also to protect the oil fields. They left in September, with a local anti-Bolshevik administration in charge. The Musavat party in Baku made an alliance with the Turks, seen by them as allies but regarded as enemies by the Armenians and Georgians: this resulted in a massacre of some 30,000 Armenians and 26 Bolshevik commissars, the leaders of the earlier attempt at control of the area, who were taken from Baku and shot. Anastasy Mikoyan was a survivor of these events in which British complicity was assumed.

Another British contingent arrived at Baku in November 1918 as World War I ended, being met by an Azerbaijan Musavat government they could not recognize unless it admitted to being a part of Russia. In December a coalition government for Azerbaijan in Baku was accepted by the British who also had outposts at Batum and Tiflis.

On April 28, 1920, Soviet troops entered Baku and with little opposition took control of Armenia. There was an Armenian army of 40,000, equipped by the British and Americans, deployed in Nagorno-Karabakh, the Armenian enclave in Azerbaijan, around which the bulk of the Azeri Musavatists army of 20,000 with Turkish and German arms was stationed. In mediating with Turkey that year the Soviet government accepted the compromise of a previous agreement on a separate status for Nagorno-Karabakh with a largely Armenian people, recognizing the ethnic difference but also the economic reality of its situation.

Azerbaijan entered the USSR as the Autonomous Soviet Socialist Republic on December 31, 1922. It in-cludes the autonomous territories of Nakhitchevan, which is surrounded by Armenian territory, and Nagorno-Karabakh. Today, a further 5 million Azeris, using the common Turkic Azeri language and also following the Muslim Shia faith, live across the frontier in Iran. In 1945 the Soviets, who had occupied northern Iran during the war, attempted to integrate all the Azeri area into the Soviet Union by supporting a puppet Communist government, but were forced out under British-U.S. pressure that contributed to the beginnings of the cold war. Many Azeris are leading figures in modern Iran, and there is a growing interest in Islamic fundamentalism in Azerbaijan. In July 1989 the speaker of the Iranian Parliament, Ali Hashemi Rafsanjani, visited Baku and, speaking at a mosque, promised help in promoting the religion. In January 1990 numbers of Azeri Muslims demonstrated on the frontier with Iran, some swimming over the dividing river, demanding that the border be opened between them and their cousins. This had the effect of giving anxiety to both the Soviet Union and to Iran, neither welcoming the prospect of a larger nationalist Azerbaijan republic.

Nagorno-Karabakh—This enclave, with 75 percent Christian Armenians in Muslim Azerbaijan, has been the cause of riots in both republics. On February 28, 1988, there was a massacre in Sumgait where 26 Armenians and 6 Azerbaijanis died. The party lost control in Nagorno-Karabakh, and as a result the party heads of both Armenia and Azerbaijan were dismissed. When in November 1988 a young Azeri was sentenced to death by a Moscow court for his part in the Sumgait murders, and thousands of Azeris protested, a curfew was imposed in Baku (with 200,000 Armenian inhabitants). In Kirovabad and other towns there was a pogrom of Armenians; 2,000 Armenia women and children were taken out of Nakhitchevan and Kirovabad by truck and helicopter. That month 80,000 Azeris had left Armenia while 14,000 Armenians had left Azerbaijan. In Baku the army cleared the main square where demonstrators had carried red Turkish and green Islamic flags and were said to have burned Christian Armenian crosses.

In January 1989, the parliament of Nagorno-Karabakh was suspended, bringing it under direct Moscow control with the intention of its remaining part of Azerbaijan. In August 150,000 Azeri workers demonstrated in Baku demanding that Nagorno-Karabakh be kept in Azerbaijan, hoisting the flag of the 1918–1920 Azerbaijan Republic. At the same time workers in Nagorno-Karabakh added to the chaos with strikes against Azeri rule.

In January 1990 there were further riots in Baku, attacking Armenians and demanding the return of Nagorno-Karabakh to Azerbaijan's administration. On January 19, after 60 Armenians had been killed, the Soviet military intervened toughly and, from official figures, 147 people were killed. As a result the elections to the republic's parliament were postponed.

AZERI

The people of Azerbaijan. The socialist-nationalist Musavat ("Equality") party was founded among the Azeri in 1911.

BABI-YAR

In Kiev from 1941 to 1943, Nazi execution squads slaughtered over 150,000 men, women, and children and threw them into a ravine, Babi-Yar, near the city. Most of the victims were Jews. Yevgeny Yevtushenko's poem of that name (1961) was central to action against anti-Semitism in the Soviet Union.

BAIKAL-AMUR MAGISTRAL RAILROAD

The direct, northerly route to the Pacific ports avoiding the Trans-Siberian Railroad's detour around Lake Baikal, was completed in 1979 to Komsomolsk-na-Amure.

BALLET

After the departure of Sergei Diaghilev to the West, the great classical tradition in Russian ballet continued. There were contemporary pieces with themes arising out of the revolution, such as Reinhold Glière's *The Red Poppy* in 1927 and the *The Age of Gold* in 1930 with music by Igor Stravinsky. After World War II the great ballerina Galina Ulanova created a sensation with Sergei Prokoviev's *Cinderella*. Then in 1956 there was *Spartacus* by Aram Khachaturian. Both the Bolshoi and the Kirov ballets toured the West and a new crop of great artists including Rudolf Nureyev, Natalia Makarova, and Mikhail Baryshnikov left their companies and found fame in the international ballet world.

BALTIC STATES—ESTONIA, LATVIA, AND LITHUANIA, 1917–1980

Czarist Russia obtained control of the peoples and lands of the Baltic coast, formerly subject to the Swedes and once the estates of German barons, by the end of the 18th century. These countries differed from the rest of the empire in their religious, linguistic, and economic development. The Lutheran and Roman Catholic churches dominated, the languages were distinct from the Slavic Russian, and their traditions of craft, industry, and trade with the rest of Europe had developed a bourgeoisie unlike in any other part of the Russian Empire. Railways and industry were developed earlier than other parts and illiteracy was rare by the beginning of the 20th century.

The 1905 Revolution saw as much unrest in Baltic cities as in any other part of the empire and, although many of the leaders were exiled, a new generation of political leaders was generated by the new Duma.

The collapse of the Russian Empire in March 1917 left Lithuania and half of Latvia under German military occupation. In February 1918 Lithuania and Estonia declared independence. Latvia, with a strong working-class movement having sympathies with the Bolsheviks on the one hand and Baltic German nationalists supported by *Freikorps* (bands of German soldiers fighting for the old landowners) on the other, did not declare independence until November 1918. The three republics signed treaties with the Soviet Union in 1920. Poland, however, as a result of its war with the Soviets, took and kept the ancient cathedral city of Vilnius (Wilno to the Poles) and left the new republic of Lithuania to make do with Kaunas as capital. For their part, the Lithuanians held the largely German city of Memel (Klaipeda) in 1923, which gave Hitler an excuse for expanding his Greater Germany in 1939. Latvian soldiers (the Latvian Rifles) provided the Bolsheviks with their best unit of professional sol-

diers in 1917–18, but Latvia preferred independence, and an attempt at a Communist coup in 1924 failed, resulting in the Communist party there being made illegal.

During the next 20 years each republic, under economic pressure from within and under the shadows of their neighbors—Hitler's Germany and Stalin's Russia—became politically authoritarian and failed to gain other allies. Hitler demanded and took Memel from Lithuania in March 1939 and met no effective protest from the rest of the world. When the Molotov-Ribbentrop pact was signed on August 23, 1939, a secret protocol assigned Latvia and Estonia to the Soviet sphere of influence and part of Lithuania to Germany's. On October 2, 1939, a mutual assistance pact was signed, allowing Red Army bases in Estonia. In June 1940, when Hitler's troops moved into France in the West, Soviet troops occupied the Baltic States completely. Senior Soviet officials were sent to ensure control, Andrei Zhdanov to Estonia and Andrei Vyshinsky to Latvia. Demonstrations called for "people's assemblies" and in July elections were held with massive turnouts and huge majorities of 95 percent and more being claimed. The new governments adopted new Soviet Socialist constitutions and applied to join the Soviet Union. These requests were, not surprisingly, granted in August 1940. Integration into the Soviet system was rapid and determined; by mid-1941 it is estimated that 10 percent of the Latvian population had been deported.

The German invasion of the Soviet Union on June 22, 1941, saw the rapid occupation of Lithuania, with Nazi forces having penetrated into most of Latvia by August and Estonia taken by October.

At first some inhabitants greeted the Germans as liberators and a few set out to reestablish independent republics. A provisional government in Lithuania welcomed the Germans, but it was soon disbanded; the Nazi intention was to make the Baltic States into part of Greater Germany, deporting the Balts and replacing them with German settlers. The area was then called Ostland and given an administration headed by compliant and racially acceptable local people. Workers were drafted to fill vacancies in German industry and ex-soldiers and new conscripts were formed into defense battalions: as support, rather than combat units, they were therefore given the secondary and unpleasant duties of controlling the civilian populations behind the German lines. The SS formed divisions from the Baltic States. In 1944, when the tide of war had turned against the Nazis, many of these recruits began to desert and hide in the woods.

The Jewish communities suffered terribly. Of an estimated 250,000 only 10,000 survived the German extermination camps. Nazi brutality led to the formation of resistance groups. In 1944 Estonian groups had contacts via Finland and Sweden with London, but in general armed resistance was on a small scale. Partisans were more likely to be escaped Jews or Communists helped by others infiltrated or parachuted from Soviet Russia.

In January 1944 the Red Army began to retake the territory, finally bottling up German forces in Kurland from October 1944 until the final surrender in 1945. The Baltic Soviet republics were reestablished but controlled from Moscow with a degree of mistrust. Some who had hidden in the woods were joined by others who hated or were hated by the new regimes. There were Russian and German deserters among them and for eight years—until 1952—there were groups, some as large as 800, hiding, raiding, and robbing. Although any one person may have stayed or survived in the forests up to only two years, probably 100,000 in Lithuania, 40,000 in Latvia, and 30,000 in Estonia took to guerrilla activity at some time or other. A central organization was attempted: in 1947 there was a 17-day officer training course and news sheets were distributed until 1951. The Soviets tried to counter these groups in some instances by offering amnesties and at other times by sending in MVD (International Affairs) special task divisions. There was little tangible help from Western intelligence agencies, although a few parachute drops of men and materials were made. Guerrilla casualties in Lithuania are estimated at between 20,000 and 50,000.

In 1948 the MVD and MGB (State Security) had over 70,000 men with eight regular army divisions engaged against guerrilla activity in Lithuania. There were few pitched battles, for the guerrillas' aim was to disrupt Soviet administration and to unnerve the MVD units by small surprise raids.

Soviet rule reestablished the republics' supreme soviets and ensured a secretariat loyal to the Soviet Union in each; often they were either Russians or local citizens who had spent the war in Russia; in this way, Mikhail Suslov arrived in 1944 to run a special Soviet Union Communist Party Bureau. Collectivization of farming was enforced again and deportation to the interior of the Soviet Union was carried out against tens of thousands of suspected kulaks in 1949. In Estonia, the native party was purged and replaced by what were called Yestonians.

Lithuania was mainly Roman Catholic and the church was associated with opposition to the Soviets. In Estonia and Latvia the prevalent Lutheran Church had not the same grip on the people and did not represent an equal threat. The minor Protestant churches were ordered to join the USSR's Baptist league. The remnants of the Jewish communities never reformed.

With the "thaw" and after Stalin's death there was a reemergence of national identities throughout the Soviet Union and particularly in the Baltic republics with their comparatively advanced economies. Roman Catholic Bishops were consecrated in Latvia and Lithuania in the 1960s. A Union of Fighters for Political Freedom led by naval officers was crushed in Estonia in 1969.

However, Russification continued, partly through the immigration of Russian officials and skilled workers, often moving there with priority in housing over local workers. In 1978 a directive throughout the USSR affected the Baltic States: the use of the Russian language was extended from nursery school to the university. Just as a similar drive to promote the Russian language in the 1890s under the czar had resulted in an increase in nationalist consciousness, so did this directive. (See also ESTONIAN, LATVIAN, and LITHUANIAN SOVIET SOCIALIST REPUBLICS for post-1980.)

BANKING

The Soviet Union's central bank, Gosbank, is part of the new banking system, which in 1990 is still not really functioning. There are specialized banks dealing with housing, agriculture, and industry and now there are 60 commercial banks (28 set up by cooperatives and 32 by state organizations). The banking law of April 1, 1989, makes the state pay interest on its loans to cover the budget deficit. The public's savings accounts are reckoned to be 300 billion rubles; from this the government appropriates what it needs: 63 billion in 1988 to cover its expenditure. When this figure is added to the published deficit, the true annual deficit is about 100 billion rubles, or 11 percent of the gross national product.

Internationally, the Soviet Union has been hampered economically by the 1918 Soviet refusal to recognize debts incurred by any previous government. There are, for example, the $192.6 million lent by the United States to the 1917 pre-Bolshevik Provisional Government and another $75 million worth of czarist Russian bonds held by U.S. citizens. There have been discussions for years on how to clear these debts before the Soviet Union can enter the international markets and raise money through bonds.

BASMACHIS

"Bandits" or "robbers" in the Uzbeki language. Anti-Bolshevik partisans in Central Asia who were not finally suppressed until 1926.

BELORUSSIAN SOVIET SOCIALIST REPUBLIC

Population: 10,141,000
Area: 80,200 square miles
Capital: Minsk; population, 1,543,000

1917–1945—Also known as White Russia, a land taken into the Russian Empire in the 18th century and, like the

Ukraine, speaking a variation of the Russian language and under Polish and Roman Catholic influence. In World War I the Germans advanced into Belorussia, which became a battleground and a place of famine. The czarist military headquarters, the Stavka, was in Mogilev and hundreds of thousands of soldiers were stationed in the territory. The February 1917 Revolution was greeted there with relief, and with hope for peace.

In March 1917 Belorussian nationalists, socialists, and other politicians gathered in Minsk, and by August 5 had formed a rada with a largely Socialist Revolutionary policy, hoping to become something like an autonomous republic under the Petrograd Provisional Government. After the Bolshevik Revolution in October, however, a trainload of troops was sent to Minsk and a Bolshevik coup d'etat took place. The rada acquiesced and Bolshevik rule was established on November 15.

But the war with Germany continued and by the time of the Brest-Litovsk Treaty in March 1918, a large part of the land, including Minsk, was in German hands. The nationalists in the rada saw the opportunity for independence and met on March 25 to declare a national republic. But when the Germans left, the Bolsheviks reoccupied Minsk and their Central Committee decided on December 23 to establish a Belorussian Soviet Socialist Republic.

In March 1919 Polish armies under Josef Pilsudski advanced into Lithuania, the Ukraine, and Belorussia. They proclaimed Belorussia part of Poland and both the nationalists of the rada and the Bolsheviks were forced to flee. It was not until July 11, 1920, that the Red Army retook Minsk from the Poles. On July 19, by a treaty, parts of Belorussia were handed over to Lithuania and finally, under the Treaty of Riga, signed on March 18, 1921, a large area was given to Poland.

The reduced Belorussian Soviet Socialist Republic (areas around Mogilev, Vitebsk, and to the south were added to it in 1924 and 1926) was in economic chaos and peasant uprisings were ferociously put down by the Cheka. The New Economic Policy was enthusiastically accepted and for a time Belorussia flourished. In 1929 Stalin began the program of collectivization. By January 1, 1930, one in five of the 165,000 Belorussian farms had been collectivized and the pace was increased. In common with the rest of the USSR, there were riots in reaction to the demands and repression by the GPU (State Political Administration) with numbers of peasants or kulaks sent to labor camps. In particular the Belorussian nationalists were a primary target together with the organizers of Belorussian schools and education. In the summer of 1933 the party announced the discovery of a Belorussian National Center controlled from Poland, implicating as traitors nationalists freed from Poland.

On September 17, 1939, the Red Army marched into Poland, countering the German invasion from the west. The Belorussian Soviet Socialist Republic was enlarged with territory taken from Poland and, in October, from Lithuania. The NKVD came with the army and arrested all who had been Polish officials. The purges of suspects continued up to June 1941, when the Germans invaded.

Belorussia was overrun in three weeks. The Nazis had plans for Eastern Europe, and some Belorussian land was given to

East Prussia and some to the Ukraine. The remaining territory was earmarked for future German settlement: 75 percent of the present inhabitants were to be expelled or killed and the remainder to be assimilated as Germans. A general commissar, Wilhelm Kube, was appointed in July. The large Jewish population, three-quarters of a million people, was rounded up for extermination. Young people were shipped to Germany as forced labor. A puppet government was set up under a former officer of Baron Peter Wrangel's army, Ivan Ermachenko, but it had no popular support.

The Soviet response was partisan warfare, infiltrating thousands into the forest areas behind the German lines. Sabotage of the Germans resulted in savage reprisals, which in turn added to the hatred of the Germans. Kube was killed by a bomb in his bed, put there by the Belorussian girl he used as servant and bedmate. Terror was again answered by resistance and Soviet partisans by Belorussian nationalists recruited by the Germans. In mid-1942 the capital Minsk was controlled by partisans, and by the end of 1943 over half of Belorussia was in the hands of 300,000 partisans.

By the war's end in 1945 Belorussia was wrecked. Almost 1.3 million people had been killed and still the NKVD sought traitors or suspected collaborators among the survivors. From 1946 to 1948 all managers and party officials were examined, and any hint of "cosmopolitanism" or Western ideas led to dismissal or the labor camp. New senior officials in the Belorussian party were all Russian. Stalin's concept of linguistics was that languages other than Russian were marginal and would die out.

By agreement with the Allies at the 1945 Yalta Conference, the borders of Belorussia were extended to include the land that Poland had taken in the 1920s. To demonstrate the constitutional freedom and eligibility for entry to the United Nations of Soviet republics, Belorussia and the Ukraine were proposed for independent entry as nations. They took their seats on April 30, 1945.

BLACK HUNDREDS

The general name for the groups who roused popular feelings by demonstrations of loyalty to the czar and the Russian Orthodox Church, and hatred of Jews, socialists, and intellectuals. They were small shopkeepers, tradesmen, priests, and minor officials drawn to extremism by the turmoil and class fears of 1905. In the Duma, the Union of the Russian People led by Vladimir Purishkevich represented these extremists. They organized riots and pogroms against their enemies and were unofficially encouraged by the police and openly thanked by the czar. They were an object of hatred, though they ceased to play any role in 1917.

BOLSHEVIK

The "majority." The faction led by Lenin at the Russian Social Democrat Congress in 1903, which obtained a narrow majority over Yuli Martov and those in favor of a broad-based movement. Lenin wanted an elite centralized party of professional revolutionaries and so arranged that the Congress vote out affiliated groups such as the Jewish Bund. The Bolsheviks termed their opponents Menshevik (the "minority") and the name remained with them. The split had become irreversible by the February 1917 Revolution.

The leading figures in 1917 were Vladimir Lenin, Lev Kamenev, Anatoly Lunacharsky, Grigory Zinoviev, and Leon Trotsky (who had sided with neither Bolshevik nor Menshevik until his return to Russia in May 1917).

BOLSHOI THEATRE

The State Academic Bolshoi Theatre of the USSR. The Bolshoi was built in Moscow in 1824 to replace the Petrovsky Theatre for the performance of opera and ballet. The period beginning in 1870 represents the great flowering of ballet and opera in Russia, and the Bolshoi saw productions of Peter Ilych Tchaikovsky's *Swan Lake*, *Eugen Onegin*, and *The Queen of Spades*. Operas by Modest Mussorgsky and Nikolai Rimsky-Korsakov were also performed there, as well as works by Western composers. During the upheavals of the revolution and the civil war, Lenin made special arrangements to keep the theatre open. After the revolution works of a specifically ideological nature were performed, such as Vasilii Zolotaev's *The Decembrists* in 1925 and Sergei Prokoviev's *Love for Three Oranges* in 1927, while at the same time the company continued to perform the classical repertoire both in opera and ballet. Since World War II the same policy has been followed. Some of the better-known postwar works are Prokoviev's *War and Peace* and Aram Khachaturian's *Spartacus*. The company has followed a consistent policy of touring all over the world.

BOROTBISTS

The name of the Ukrainian Socialist Revolutionary nationalists in 1918–1920.

BREST-LITOVSK TREATY

The peace agreement signed in March 1918 between the Bolshevik government and the Central Powers—the German and the Austro-Hungarian empires. Determined to end a futile war (in their eyes), the Bolsheviks tried to negotiate but were forced to accept the Central Powers' terms. Trotsky's revolutionary attitude of "Neither peace, nor war" did not strengthen Russia's bargaining position, and Germany forced upon Russia acceptance of Polish, Georgian, Lithuanian, Latvian, Estonian, and Ukrainian independence. It was signed by Grigory Sokolnikov, because major Bolshevik figures would not risk putting their name to it. There were supplements to the treaty signed with Bulgaria, Rumania, and Turkey. Russia surrendered Kars, Ardahan, and Batum to Turkey. The Left Socialist Revolutionaries voted against the treaty and resigned from Sovnarkom. The treaty was invalidated after the 1918 Allied victory, when different territorial terms were imposed on the Central Powers.

BREZHNEV DOCTRINE

The policy outlined in *Pravda* in September 1968. It declared Moscow's right to intervene with force in its satellite states when they deviate from the Soviet version of socialism. The prime examples were the invasion of Hungary in 1956 and the overturn, the month before the article, of the Czechoslovak government.

The doctrine was abandoned when Mikhail Gorbachev stated in March 1989 on the occasion of the Hungarian premier's visit that "Each ruling Communist party solves tasks in accordance with its historical conditions and national values, and works out its policies in a sovereign fashion." In 1989 a Soviet spokesman referred to the new policy toward satellites as the "Sinatra" policy: "They do it their way."

BULGARIA

Area: 44,365
Population: 9,037,000
Capital: Sofia; population, 1,119,000

The People's Republic claims a party membership of 825,876.

In 1941 Bulgaria, a largely agricultural country with a constitutional monarchy under King Boris III found itself allied with Nazi Germany. In 1944, as German resistance crumbled, Soviet forces occupied the country, and the Fatherland Front, which included Communists, Social Democrats, Agrarians, and others, formed a government. In November 1945 the Fatherland Front, of which 277 out of 364 were Communists, won the election under their leader Georgy Dimitrov (the hero of the 1933 Reichstag Fire trial in Nazi Germany, who had lived in Russia since then). He was succeeded by Vulko Chervenkov, who took a very strong Stalinist line and dominated the party until 1954, when Todor Zhivkov became first secretary.

Under the New Economic Mechanism instituted in 1976 there was a considerable improvement in the economic situation; foreign investment was encouraged and joint ventures were established with Western multinationals like Shell Oil and Occidental Petroleum. The majority of export trade is with the USSR, but the country has had great success with exports of its wine to

the European Economic Community, particularly the United Kingdom. But the general economic situation has not really improved, particularly the availability of consumer goods. Bulgaria's reputation has not been helped by the expulsion of a large Turkish element in the population, more than 300,000 strong. The influence of Moscow has always been strong and the general liberalization in economic and social relations happening there has caused the party to accept change. On November 4, 1989 members of Eco Glasnost led huge street demonstrations against the government and Todor Zhivkov was forced to resign. He was replaced by a moderate, Peter Mladenow. General elections in Spring 1990 gave the Union of Democratic Forces (UDF) 144 seats, but the Socialist Party (formerly Communist) won 211 seats out of the 400-seat chamber and formed a government. The UDF refuses to join in a coalition.

BUND

A socialist movement of Jewish workers in Imperial Russia, it was founded in 1897. Faced with the repression of czarist days, the Bund developed skills in smuggling illegal persons and materials in and out of Russia. The Bund supported the Mensheviks from 1906 and, in the attention it paid to improving wages and working conditions, seemed to follow bourgeois goals and so separated itself from the orthodox Marxists. In 1920 the majority joined the Communist party, but a minority, which existed separately until suppressed, continued to operate in isolation in the old Jewish settlements far from Moscow and sent delegates to the Second Social Democratic Congress. The Bund was dissolved in

1921, when a Jewish section of the party was formed.

CADRES

The most important or key members of an organization at various levels, who, if selected for indoctrination, will form opinion throughout the organization. This use of cadres has been an essential part of Communist party tactics in social control.

CALENDAR

Russia officially maintained the Julian calendar long after Western Europe had changed to the Gregorian calendar. Thus by the 20th century, Russian dates in the Julian calendar were 13 days earlier than as counted elsewhere. The October Revolution on October 25 (Julian) is now celebrated on November 6 (Gregorian). On February 1, 1918, the Gregorian Calendar was adopted.

CAMPS

In 1918, as a preventive measure against potential enemies of the new state and under the guidance of Lenin and Trotsky, camps were set up to gather old bourgeois politicians, non-Bolshevik Social Democrats, Socialist Revolutionaries, anarchists, or the rebels of Kronstadt; and as early as 1919, they were also for the corrective treatment of all offenders against the regime's decrees. Soon there were tens of thousands of prisoners in the camps, many of which were situated on the islands of the White Sea. It was prisoners' labor that built the White Sea Canal, completed 1931–33.

In 1934 the detention system was organized by the NKVD under Gulag (Chief Administration of Corrective La-

bor Camps and Settlements), which at its peak had 10 million prisoners at work. The NKVD in this respect resembled the SS in Nazi Germany: it controlled a vast industrial empire and became a major element in the Soviet economy. After its workers had built the White Sea Canal, they built the Moscow-Volga Canal (1932–37), started the Baikal-Amur Railway in 1934, and were responsible for one in ten of the electrical power stations built. Whole towns in remote parts of the USSR were built by the NKVD. The Gulag system had, as with the rest of Soviet society, a plan to fulfill and it achieved its high output by offering adequate food rations only to those teams that achieved the goals set for them. By thus establishing a common motivation for groups, the Gulag reduced the risk of mutiny by prisoners.

The collectivization program increased the number of camps and changed the character of the inmates. The purges of the mid–1930s added city dwellers, the highly educated, party officials, and army officers to the old guard and the peasants already in the camps. The increasing supply of prisoners was largely due to these purges, but it was the Great Purge ordered by Stalin in 1936—without the party's authority and carried out by Nikolai Yezhov, known as the "Yezhovshchina"—that brought in prisoners by the million.

There were camps of various levels, from the katorga, or hard labor camps from which few prisoners ever came out alive, to camps like the one where Andrei Tupolev and his aircraft design team lived and carried on their work. The world knows of the camps through the novel authorized for publication by Nikita Khrushchev, *A Day in the Life of Ivan Denisovich* (1962), and later *The Gulag*

Archipelago (1973–75) both by Alexander Solzhenitsyn.

CENTRAL COMMITTEE. See POLITICAL STRUCTURE.

CENTRAL COMMITTEE SECRETARIAT. See POLITICAL STRUCTURE.

CENTRAL EXECUTIVE COMMITTEE

Elected at the first All-Russian Congress of Soviets of Workers' and Soldiers' Deputies in July 1917, it was the inner "cabinet" to which the congress delegated executive powers. In 1922 similar committees were formed in the republics of the USSR. The 1936 Constitution passed this role to the Supreme Soviet (see POLITICAL STRUCTURE).

CHEKA. See POLITICAL POLICE.

CHERNOBYL

The atomic power station near Kiev, which exploded on April 26, 1986. During tests of its functions the graphite core in Unit 4 of the station caught fire and burned for 10 days. Nine tons of the fuel went into the fallout cloud, one ton of which fell back on the site while the rest was distributed westward over Europe by the wind. Increased levels of radiation were recorded in most of Europe. Two hundred kilometers away in Belorussia, there were still seriously affected areas to be found three years later.

The USSR was condemned for its delay in admitting to the disaster and its slow response in dealing with it. A Soviet press conference on August 21, 1986, blamed human error and disregard of safety rules; six managers were given jail sentences. Thirty-one of the staff were killed in the explosion and one man died while fighting the fire; over 200 suffered from acute radiation sickness. A 30-mile exclusion zone has been created around Chernobyl and 135,000 people were evacuated from 100 villages within it. Mutations of vegetation have been observed and some seeds apparently resisting the heavy radiation have been noted for possible use in contaminated land.

The need for electricity in the area meant that in 1988 Units 1, 2, and 3 were recommissioned, but that type of reactor, RBMK, of which 15 were built, is now being closed down and no new ones built. Unit 4 was buried in a mountain of concrete.

CHERVONET

A gold coin, the first Soviet hard currency, of 3-, 5-, or 10-unit denomination; it was in circulation from 1922 to 1947.

CINEMA

There was a flourishing film industry in Russia under the czars, starting with the 1908 production *Cossacks of the Don*, made by The Pathé Company. By 1910 there were 15 companies making pictures, many of them historical subjects and some of real artistic merit, such as Vsevolod Meyerhold's *Dorian Gray* made in 1915.

The October Revolution caused many of the veteran film directors and technicians to flee to the West, and the harsh conditions during the civil war made cinema production and exhibition diffi-cult. In 1919 the industry was national-ized, and Lenin, who was great believer in the cinema as a propaganda tool, put it in the hands of the State Department of Education with his wife Nadezhda Krupskaya in charge. During the civil war, Agit Trains, as they were called, complete with projection equipment were sent out to deliver the political message to the country, and also to shoot fresh footage. Sergei Eisenstein, his future cameraman, Edward Tisse, and director Dziga Vertov all learned their business on these trains. By 1921 the economic crisis had closed all but 10 of the cine-mas in Moscow and production was down to almost nothing. With the semi-capitalist New Economic Policies intro-duced later that year production again expanded, from 11 films in 1921 to 157 in 1924.

The Sovkino Trust was set up in 1925 to control and coordinate produc-tion and distribution in the USSR, though ideological decisions still lay with the education department. At first there was little experimentation with new tech-niques, but the Politburo decision in 1925 for nonintervention by the state in matters of artistic style led to a period of great creative excitement in the industry.

High points in this period, the last years of silent cinema, were Eisenstein's *Strike* and the *Battleship Potemkim*, Vsevolod Pudovkin's *Storm over Asia*, and Dziga Vertov's *A Sixth of the World*. But this period of freedom soon came to an end under Stalin and at the All-Union Party Conference on the cinema in March 1928, it was stated that "The basic criterion for evaluating the art qual-ities of a film is that . . . it can be under-stood by millions."

The sympathetic Sovkino was replaced by the authoritarian Soyuzkino, headed by Boris Shumyatsky. The result was a period of sterility for the cinema. How-ever, following Shumyatsky's visit to Hollywood, production was enormously increased, and such musicals as *Moscow Laughs* by Grigory Alexandrov and lit-erary adaptations such as Mark Donskoy's production of Gorky's trilogy were pro-duced. Several actors made a good liv-ing playing Lenin and Stalin in "cult of personality" pictures like *The Man with the Gun*.

Eisenstein suffered under the new regime. His *October: Ten Days That Shook the World* was criticized for for-malism, that is too great a concentra-tion on style and the use of abstract elements, and he was only allowed to direct *Alexander Nevsky* after he had made a public recantation of his errors.

During World War II the Soviet cinema was almost entirely concerned with heroic documentaries like Leonid Varlamov's *Stalingrad*. The high point of feature film production was Eisenstein's *Ivan the Terrible*, shown in 1945. After the war the censorship of film produc-tion was, if anything, tightened. Sergei Yutkevitch's *Light Over Russia* was banned in 1947 and the second part of *Ivan the Terrible* was not shown until 1958. Many of the films made in this period were straightforward anti-Western propaganda, but there were notable ex-ceptions such as Alexander Ptushko's *The Stone Flower* and Vsevolod Pudov-kin's *Vasili's Return*.

In the more liberal atmosphere that followed the death of Stalin a much greater variety of subjects was allowed in films. Such films as Kalatozov's *The Cranes are Flying* in 1957 and Heifitz's *The Lady with the Dog* in 1960 would have been impossible before Khrushchev, and new talents such as Andrei Tarkovsky were also emerging. But the fall of Khrushchev once again imposed limits on the artist. And although self-expression was easier than in the Stalin era, many pictures like Tarkovsky's *Andrei Rublov* were held from distribution for ideological reasons. Tarkovsky seems to be the outstanding talent to have emerged since the war and his recent death has been a great loss for world cinema.

There are now 43 film studios in the USSR and feature output is roughly 140 films per year.

CIVIL WAR

The civil war in Russia, 1918–1920, was a complex affair consisting of a number of separate campaigns against the Bolsheviks, not coordinated by any central command on the White or anti-Bolshevik side, and took place over a vast area.

After the Bolshevik Revolution's success in Petrograd, Moscow, and elsewhere in October 1917, a number of local anti-Bolshevik provisional governments were set up. In January 1918, although the war against Germany was still in progress, the Bolsheviks set out to take control of these bodies, and the civil war began.

The Red Army, under its commissar for war, Leon Trotsky, took Kiev in the Ukraine and caused the collapse of the Don Cossack government. Then the White Volunteer Army formed by two czarist generals, Lavr Kornilov and Anton Denikin, was pushed back into the Kuban.

The war with Germany, however, continued and the German armies resumed their attacks in February 1918, obliging the Bolsheviks to accept the terms of the Brest-Litovsk Treaty. This allowed anti-Bolshevik forces to act under German protection. General Carl Mannerheim crushed the Reds in Finland, the Ukraine formed an independent government under the German puppet General Pavel Skoropadsky, and while German troops reached Rostov in May their Turkish allies moved into the southern Caucasian territories of Armenia and Azerbaijan. The Don Cossacks rose again, the Volunteer Army returned from the Steppes, and in the Far East another czarist general, Grigori Semenov, with Japanese backing, began anti-Bolshevik operations on the Manchurian border.

In May 1918 the 40,000-man Czechoslovak Legion, formed by Thomas Masaryk with the assistance of the Allies, was spread out over 5,000 miles of the Trans-Siberian Railway. They were making their slow way eastward out of Russia, when the Allied High Command ordered them to rejoin the war against Germany. In self-defense against local soviets, they revolted and became a powerful anti-Bolshevik force in the center of Russia. Their presence permitted the formation of new non-Bolshevik governments in Samara and further east in Omsk. The threat of their advance was the direct cause of the murder of Czar Nicholas and his family.

To protect their own interests in Russia and to check the further expansion of their German enemies, the Western Allies decided to intervene. The British landed troops in the north at Murmansk and Archangel, where they supported the Russian general, Eugene Miller, and in the Caspian area where they supported the regime of Nikolai Chaikovsky, blocked the Turkish advance and encouraged a nationalist Azerbaijan government in Baku. They also conducted a general blockade of Russia in the Baltic from October 1919 to January 1920. Some 40,000 British troops were involved. In August 1918, 10,000 U.S. troops and a much larger Japanese contingent landed at Vladivostok.

The arrival of the Allied forces gave impetus to the Whites, and in the south the Volunteer Army took the Black Sea naval base of Novorossisk, although the Red Army consolidated its hold on the center by taking Kazan in October. That month the White admiral Alexander Kolchak seized power in Omsk and had himself declared Supreme Ruler of All Russia. In January 1919 the French landed 30,000 troops in Odessa on the Ukrainian coast of the Black Sea, and the peasant army of Nestor Makhno, fighting against Pavel Skoropadsky and his German-backed forces, benefited from their intervention. The war with Germany had ended in November 1918 with victory for the Western Allies, and in March 1919 they decided to pull out of Russia. That March Kolchak's offensive westward from the Urals faltered and was followed by Red Army counterattacks. In May Anton Denikin opened offensives on the South and Southeast fronts, taking Kharkov in June and Poltava in the Ukraine in July. While the Red Army retreated in the south, they continued to advance against Kolchak.

The White Armed Forces of Southern Russia (the joint armies of the Cossacks and the Volunteer Army) under Denikin continued their offensives, taking Kiev and Odessa in August, Kursk in September, and Orel in October. This was the peak of White success. On the Baltic, General Nicholas Yudenich advanced toward Petrograd and then was halted by the superior force of the Red Guards and the Red Army, with Trotsky

himself engaged in the fighting. The Red Army also counterattacked at Orel.

In November Kolchak was forced to evacuate Omsk and came under the protection of the Czech Legion. Antagonized by the Whites' brutality under Kolchak's leadership, they handed him over to a revolutionary government in Irkutsk in January 1920 who executed him, and the power of the Whites east of the Urals was at an end.

In the north the White rule in Murmansk ended with the departure of the British forces and the Red Army took the town in March 1920.

In January 1920, Baron Peter Wrangel, a dashing cavalry leader, took command of the White forces in the south, but the retreats continued and the Red Army soon entered Kiev, the capital of the Ukraine. However, the new Polish republic, on behalf of the Ukrainian separatists, retook the city and in April 1920 the Bolsheviks found themselves at war with an invading Poland. Neither the Poles nor the Bolsheviks were able to put together strong enough armies to inflict a decisive defeat on the other. The Red Army brilliantly led by Mikhail Tukhachevsky pushed back the Poles to the gates of Warsaw. This was a tactical error, overextending their lines of communication, carried out at Lenin's urging and against Trotsky's advice. The Poles, helped by French military advisers, launched a savage counterattack, defeating the Red Army and driving them back into their own territory. There was disagreement, perhaps amounting to disloyalty, among the Bolsheviks at this time, and blame has been attached to Stalin and Simeon Budyenny for failing to support the Warsaw Front. International arbitration brought an armistice, and the advancing Poles were required to withdraw to the Curzon Line, a proposed frontier named after the British foreign secretary. The outcome of the Russo-Polish War was that the Poles, by the Treaty of Riga in 1921, were able to claim land in Lithuania, Belorussia, and the Ukraine.

In June Wrangel, benefiting from the diversion of Red Army troops to the Russo-Polish War, broke out of the Crimea. But with the full strength of the Red Army turned against him, he was driven back into the Crimea in October and forced to evacuate all his men from Russia in November 1920. The civil war was ended, though the Japanese had 60,000 troops in the Maritime Province until 1922 and occupied Sakhalin until 1925.

The Russian civil war was not fought on broad fronts with the trench and tank warfare of World War I, but in a much more fluid series of campaigns. These were often more like raiding parties following railway routes, with the armored train taking the part of the tank. Cavalry played an important part in the battles, but the airplane had a very minor role. The greatest Red Army leader in terms of inspiration and organization was undoubtedly Trotsky, but in the field the cavalryman Budyenny was outstanding (just as the most successful White general was the cavalryman Wrangel). Peasant armies played a part, notably those of the Ukrainian Nestor Makhno and the Red Army's Vasily Chapayev.

The effect of the fighting was catastrophic: harvests were spoiled or not collected, and food often rotted because it could not be moved from country to town. There was famine and the Bolshevik's immediate answer was the emergency measures of War Communism—that is, seizure of crops, often using the most brutal methods. The use of terror tactics was justified by White atrocities, which, in turn, justified the growth and the powers of the Cheka, or political police. This led within a few years to the setting up of the centralized and repressive regime that became the main feature of Stalinism. A generation brutalized by World War I followed by the civil war was more easily able to accept the horrors of the Great Purges of the 1930s, and by extension also to stand up to the rigors of World War II.

COLD WAR

The term used in 1947 by the U.S. statesman Bernard Baruch to describe the rivalry between the USSR and its allies and the United States and the Western nations. (See also DÉTENTE and IRON CURTAIN.)

COLLECTIVIZATION

The Communist party in 1929 ordered the amalgamation of individual peasant holdings into collective farms. (See AGRICULTURE and KOLKHOZ.)

COMECON

Council for Mutual Economic Assistance, founded in 1949 with the USSR, Bulgaria, Czechoslovakia, Poland, and Rumania as members. Albania ceased to be part of COMECON in 1961, but East Germany (1950), Mongolia (1962), and Cuba (1972) joined later. COMECON acts as a clearinghouse for problems of trade and industrial development for its members. A mutual recognition pact was signed with the West European Community in June 1988.

COMINFORM

The Communist Information Bureau founded by Andrei Zhdanov and Georgy Malenkov in 1947, with its offices in Belgrade to coordinate the Communist parties of the world. It replaced the Comintern, dissolved in 1943. The break with Yugoslavia in 1948 caused it to move to Rumania. It was dissolved in 1956.

COMINTERN

The Communist International was founded in 1919 to establish the leadership of communism in world socialism. This was the Third International, which broke off from the nonrevolutionary Second International (formed in 1889), which had collapsed with the world war. The Comintern was formed when expectations of world revolution were high. Outside the Soviet Union it was much feared, but it followed events rather than led them. Stalin ordered the Comintern to pursue objectives in the Soviet Union's interest rather than for the furtherance of a truly international movement. The 1934 Congress which urged a Popular Front of Socialists against Italian and German fasçism was the last occasion when the Comintern was effective. The treaties between Stalin and Hitler in 1939 brought disillusion to supporters throughout the world. The Comintern was dissolved in 1943, partly because its functioning had ceased and partly as a token of goodwill to the Soviet's U.S. and British allies.

The Comintern Congresses were:
1st. March 2–6, 1919—Moscow
2nd. July 19–August 26, 1920—Moscow and Petrograd
3rd. June 22–July 12, 1921—Moscow: "United Front"
4th. November 5–December 5, 1922—Moscow
5th. June 17–July 8, 1924—Moscow
6th. July 17–September 1, 1928—Moscow: "Ultra Left Faction"
7th. July 25–August 20, 1935—Moscow: "Popular Front"
See also INTERNATIONAL.

COMMISSAR

The head of a commission, the title was used by the heads of government departments set up by the February 1917 Provisional Government and the regional governors they appointed, and used by the succeeding Bolshevik rulers. People's commissars were the heads of ministries (and became known as ministers from 1946). Military commissars were party officials attached to supervise army commanders.

COMMUNIST PARTY

In 1917 this was the Bolshevik part of the Social Democrats (RSDLP) and, effectively, a separate party; in 1918 Lenin urged the Bolsheviks to rename themselves the Russian Communist Party (Bolshevik); in 1925, this became the All-Union Communist Party (Bolshevik), or CPSU(B). The term Bolshevik was not officially dropped until 1952.

COMPROMISERS

Socialist Revolutionaries and Mensheviks who would have gone into a coalition with the Kadets or the Provisional Government in 1917.

CONSTITUTION

On July 10, 1918, the Russian Soviet Federal Socialist Republic at the Fifth All-Russian Congress of Soviets adopted a constitution that laid down the dictatorship of the proletariat as the basic instrument for enforcing the rule of the revolution. This was replaced in 1924 by a federal constitution that provided for the constituent republics of the USSR, in theory allowing them self-determination and their joining the USSR to be of their own volition.

In 1936 Stalin presented the Soviet Union with a new model. Although largely drafted by Nicholas Bukharin and Karl Radek before their arrest, it became known as the Stalin Constitution. The constitution instituted the election of delegates by all citizens rather than by nomination from within the local branch of the party. It created a Supreme Soviet with one chamber elected by a direct one-man, one-vote system in equally sized electoral districts, and a second chamber made up of representatives from the different nationalities in the Union. The delegates were now not necessarily Communist party members.

It confirmed a federation of Soviet republics, with the union government in Moscow controlling matters of defense and foreign policy. All-union commissariats (later ministries) dominated parallel commissariats in the republics, but the republics had their own jurisdiction in some fields (such as primary education). On paper, it was a healthy decentralized democracy. But, while it set a liberal framework, in reality the Politburo or the NKVD could override anything they saw as an obstacle. The purges were already beginning, and, in effect, decentralization was out of the question.

After 40 years, the principles of the 1936 Stalin Constitution were polished up again with the new constitution adopted on October 7, 1977. It confirmed the role of the Communist party as the principal force in Soviet society and added statements on the rights of citizens. This constitution was amended as a result of the 19th Party Conference, "Implementing and Promoting Perestroika," in June and July of 1988. From this conference's amendments came the Congress of People's Deputies, which came into being in 1989. (See also POLITICAL STRUCTURE.)

CONSTITUTIONAL DEMOCRATS.
See KADETS.

COSSACKS

The Cossack of legend—the fur-capped horseman, the flashing saber, the wild dances to the music of the balalaika—is balanced by the image of dark riders with lead-weighted whips, slashing at demonstrating crowds in the city. They were people of southwest Russia, descended partly from Tatar peoples and mixed with Slavs who had escaped from serfdom. They lived in independent bands led by an ataman. In return for their military services they were given land and privileges by the Russian rulers. Cossacks were used to repress uprisings against the state, but their very independence always made them a danger to central authority.

By the 20th century the Cossacks were a mainstay of the czarist empire. The Don Cossacks, with their capital city of Novocherkassk and land stretching to the Black Sea, had a thriving agricultural industry with corn, grapes, and tobacco. Settlements of Cossacks ran south of the Urals, through Orenburg and Omsk and along the border with China to the Amur River. They guarded the empire's frontier and provided it with soldiers.

In 1905 Cossacks played a major part in saving the empire from revolution, but already there were signs of rebellion among them and there was an increasing number of incidents when Cossacks sided with workers rather than the authorities. In the Duma, Cossack representatives were largely liberals and began to call for more local self-government. The war of 1914 called 360,000 Cossacks to the army, but the cavalry were no match for German machine guns, barbed wire, and artillery barrages: Cossack casualties were heavy.

Called to put down revolution in Petrograd in 1917, Cossack regiments began to mutiny and their defection was a key to the revolution. The Cossack communities elected their own atamans and called congresses in Petrograd in March and June 1917. In June in Novocherkassk the Don Cossacks' Krug, their ruling body, elected general Alexei Kaledin as their ataman and a regional government was set up.

The Don Cossacks and Kaledin, 1917—
The July 1917 attempt by the Bolsheviks to take power in Petrograd was put down largely by Cossacks loyal to the Provisional Government. There were few Bolsheviks among them at this time. But Lavr Kornilov's attempt to use Cossacks in his August move on Petrograd precipitated a split between the Kerensky government and the Don Cossacks; as more Cossack troops began to side with the Bolsheviks, Kerensky found his military support quietly slipping away.

Kaledin's authority in the Don was established and Cossack independence

seemed to be a possibility as other Ural and Orenburg Cossack communities joined a Southeast Union of Cossacks. The example of the independent rada of the Ukraine was to be followed. But in December 1917, Kornilov, Anton Denikin, Mikhail Alekseev, and other generals came to the Don to build the Volunteer Army and Kaledin's moderation was swamped by the extremist Whites. The Cossacks did not flock to join the new army; many of them had had enough of war and had returned to their homes.

Don Cossacks on their own, 1918—
When Red units appeared on the Don in January 1918, Kaledin called in vain for his people to fight against them. On February 11, 1918, Kaledin, in despair, committed suicide. On February 25, the Red Cossack Colonel Golabov led his men into the assembly building and dispersed the Krug. The Cossack communities of the Urals, Orenburg, and Omsk were soon siding with the Bolshevik soviets.

Anarchy came to the Cossack country and partisan or bandit groups fought for their own survival. Kornilov's Volunteer Army, retreating to the Kuban, found the Cossacks there unhelpful, although by April 1918 the White Army felt strong enough to attack the Red Army there (and it was in this fighting that Kornilov was killed). Denikin made sure that his soldiers treated the Cossacks with care, and gradually he turned their opinion against the Bolsheviks. The Germans were advancing across the Ukraine and the Red Army was in retreat and foraging through Cossack land. As the Germans reached the Black Sea, Cossacks retook Novocherkassk and a new Krug was convened in May.

Krasnov's Cossacks in the Ukraine—The new ataman, General Petr Krasnov, took dictatorial power, approached the Germans for help, made an alliance with the Skoropadsky government of the Ukraine, called back the Volunteer Army, and raised a force of 40,000 Cossacks. By August 1918 the Red Army and the Bolsheviks were driven out. Krasnov encouraged a counter-Bolshevik terror and preached "Don for the Don Cossacks." The Ural Cossacks, too, rose against Bolshevik rule and killed everyone they suspected of being a Red.

Krasnov's rule became unpopular with the substantial non-Cossack population and with his rivals in the Krug. The tide began to move against Krasnov as food shortages increased. In December 1918 whole regiments began to desert to the Red Army. In February 1919 Krasnov resigned. While Denikin advanced on the Kiev-Tsaritsyn line, Lenin's Cossack department in Moscow sent agitators into Cossack lands calling for peace. Denikin took Tsaritsyn in June and the Don Cossacks raided deep behind the Red Army lines and Orel was taken in October. However, the Red offensive restarted, retaking Orel and then sweeping the Whites into retreat. The Krug tried to disassociate themselves from Denikin, but the prospects were poor. Denikin resigned and was succeeded by Baron Peter Wrangel. In 1920 there was another White resurgence, but Wrangel and his army were beaten back and fled from the Crimea that November. The Don and Kuban Cossacks sank back to banditry. The survivors were starving in a wrecked land, subject to searches by the Cheka looking for antirevolutionaries or stores of food.

The End of Cossack Power—The Bolshevik government set out to destroy the Cossack privileges conferred by the czarist empire, and in 1929 the 15th Party Congress decreed that collectivization of the Don and Kuban should be carried out within a year. The opposition to this brought hunger again in 1930, and there were armed risings that were put down ruthlessly. Some of the surviving Cossacks from these episodes took to the hills until the Germans came in 1941.

From 1941 to 1945 many captured Russian soldiers who agreed to put on German uniforms called themselves "Cossack" to avoid the use of "Russian," so that there was the illusion of a substantial pro-Nazi Cossack force on the German side.

Krasnov had gone to Germany, where his anti-Semitism and nationalism made him a natural recruit for Hitler's New Order and he was nominated as head of a puppet Cossack state. The old man was rounded up with other Cossacks in Austria in 1945 and handed over to the Russians; after a trial he was executed in January 1947.

COUNCIL OF NATIONALITIES. See POLITICAL STRUCTURE.

COUNCIL OF PEOPLE'S COMMISSARS. See SOVNARKOM and POLITICAL STRUCTURE.

CRIME

National crime statistics have been collected but not published since 1933. The official story has been that organized crime is "a form of criminal activity carried on in bourgeois countries, primarily the U.S." However, in 1989 Major-General Anatoly Smirnov of the interior ministry announced the 1988 figures, reflecting the changes over the previous year:

> Premeditated murder: 16,710 (an increase of 14 percent over the previous year)
> Violent robberies: 12,916 (an increase of 43 percent)
> Break-ins and hold-ups: 67,114 (an increase of 45 percent)

Total crime had risen by 3.6 percent since 1984 to nearly 1.9 million. Major cities such as Moscow have major crime: drug addiction has increased as one result of the Afghanistan war, and there are estimated to be 4,500 prostitutes working in Moscow.

CRIMEAN TATARS

Muslim descendants of the Mongol and Turkic Hordes, who invaded Eastern Europe from Central Asia in the 13th century. In the 15th century the Crimean Tatars established an independent state. Their Khanate of the Crimea came under Ottoman rule in 1475 and passed in 1783 into the Russian Empire. Under Russian rule the Tatar people were regarded as inferior and their lands were taken by Russian and Ukrainian settlers. By the start of the 20th century they numbered less than 200,000.

The Crimean Autonomous Soviet Republic was established in October 1921. After the German occupation of the Crimea in World War II, the Tatar population was accused of collaboration and treason. They were sent, under penal conditions, to Kazakhstan and Uzbekistan in 1944. The half-million survivors were "rehabilitated" in 1967 in a decree that referred to them as "formerly resident in the Crimea." The Crimean

ASSR was disbanded in 1946 and was incorporated into the Ukrainian Soviet Socialist Republic and the land resettled. Crimean Tatars were only able to make their first publicized protest in Moscow in 1987.

CURZON LINE

The Polish-Soviet armistice line of 1920. In July 1920 the Polish armies were 125 miles east of the 1919 frontier between Poland and Russia, and the Allies demanded that they retire to a line proposed by British Foreign Secretary Lord Curzon. This did not become the eastern frontier of the Polish republic, but it was used by Stalin in 1939 to justify the extension of the Belorussian and Ukrainian republics westward.

CZECHOSLOVAKIA

Area: 49,365 square miles
Population: 15,661,000
Capital: Prague; population, 1,200,000

Under former presidents Thomas G. Masaryk and Edward Benes, between the wars Czechoslovakia was a model democracy with a high standard of living. In 1938 Hitler demanded the bordering Sudetenland, which had a considerable German-speaking population, and added it to Germany with the agreement of the British and French at a meeting in Munich that year. Then in 1939 the Nazis occupied Czechoslovakia, and the nation suffered the repression and exploitation Nazis inflicted elsewhere in Europe. In 1944 the Red Army drove the Germans out of the country, although Prague, the capital, was liberated by the German-formed Vlasov army.

In March 1945, Benes, who had spent the war years in England, went to Moscow to negotiate setting up a postwar government. Klement Gottwald, the leader of the Czech Communist party, insisted on 8 of the 25 cabinet posts, but in the elections held in May 1946, the Communists only got 38 percent of the votes. Gottwald became premier nonetheless, and in 1948, in a skillfully executed bloodless coup, seized power.

Gottwald was succeeded by Antonin Zapotocky in 1953 and Antonin Novotny in 1957. The latter, under pressure for reform of the doctrinaire political and social thinking of the last 20 years, was removed from office in January 1968. He was replaced by Alexander Dubcek during the brief period of liberalization known as the Prague Spring, but the attempt at reform did not last. In August, troops from the USSR, Bulgaria, Poland, and East Germany moved into the country and Dubcek and his committee were taken unceremoniously to Moscow. In April 1969 he was succeeded by Gustav Husak and subsequently expelled from the party.

With a population of 15 million and a party membership of 1.5 million, virtually all industry is in state hands and more than 90 percent of agriculture is in either collectives or state farms. Under Husak Czechoslovakia was the scene of considerable and vicious religious persecution.

On Friday November 17, 1989, inspired by the events in Hungary and East Germany there was a massive anti-government demonstration in Prague. The crowd was mostly composed of students and the demonstrations were broken up by the police with some brutality. This caused fierce reactions throughout the country and mass demonstrations followed. On November 24 Milos Jakes, the party leader, resigned, and on November 30 the Czech Communist party announced that it was giving up its leading role.

On December 28, Alexander Dubcek was declared chairman of the Parliament and on December 29, Vaclav Havel, the playwright recently released from prison and a prominent member of Civic Forum, the citizens' movement for democracy, was elected president. General elections were announced and took place on June 8, 1990; Civic Forum won the elections, but the Communists won 13 percent of the vote.

CZECH LEGION

Czechoslovak soldiers, who were trying to leave Russia after the Bolshevik Revolution, played an extraordinary role in the civil war, making possible anti-Bolshevik uprisings in Siberia and were, in fact, the indirect cause of the czar's death.

There had been large numbers of Czech and Slovak emigrés from the Austro-Hungarian Empire in Imperial Russia for centuries, the majority of them craftsmen, small businessmen, or clerical workers. During World War I, Russia recruited many of them into a Czech Brigade. At the same time in France, a special Czech unit of the French Foreign Legion was formed that became the Czech National Army: there was a similar legion in Italy. These legions played an important part in the establishment of a new nation, created out of the wreckage of the Austro-Hungarian Empire at the Treaty of Versailles.

In Russia the Czech Legion became

a significant military unit of about 40,000 men in the Provisional Government's army. It distinguished itself in Alexander Kerensky's July 1917 offensive against the Germans, growing to the strength of an army corps. The Provisional Government agreed that the legion in Russia should now be regarded as officially part of the Czech National Army. After the Bolshevik revolution, Thomas Masaryk, the president of the Czech National Council, affirmed that the Czech army would be neutral in the civil war. He made an agreement with the new Bolshevik regime in the person of the people's commissar for nationalities, Joseph Stalin, that the legion should be brought out of Russia to join the rest of the Czech army. On March 27, 1918, the first Czech group began to leave by rail across Siberia to Vladivostok.

But on March 31, the Germans mounted a major offensive on their Eastern Front. The Allied governments first asked the Czechs to stay and fight, but then the Allied Supreme Command issued a further command to send them to France and ordered that all Czechs still to the west of Omsk should be re-routed via Murmansk and Archangel. However, the Czechs, who were for the most part nationalists and revolutionaries themselves and had nothing to fear from the revolution, preferred to continue with their original evacuation plan through Vladivostok. The Soviet administration authorized this, although there were vain attempts to persuade them to join the Bolshevik cause.

When, on May 14, there was a fight between some Hungarian ex-prisoners of war and soldiers of the legion, the local soviet arrested the Czech delegation who had come to them to protest the incident. The Czech soldiers came armed, forced the release of the comrades, and set up a Provisional Committee to run their affairs. Trotsky, as people's commissar for war, ordered the Czechs to disarm. The Provisional Committee replied by affirming its support for the Russian revolution, but saying that the Czechs chose to keep their arms, since the Soviet government had no power to ensure their transport. The French Military Mission, in fact, supported Trotsky's decree, which he reinforced on May 25 with an order that any armed Czech found on the Penza-Omsk Line was to be immediately shot.

Some of the Czechs were supporters of the Bolsheviks; more were followers of the older Czech independence movement and tended to side against the Red Army (one battalion fought with Denikin in the Ukraine), but the majority were more interested in their own survival and in returning to a newly independent Czechoslovakia. They were well equipped, well trained, and had high morale; they were one of the most effective fighting bodies in the world. When Red Army units tried to oppose them or disarm them, they replied by disarming the Soviet troops.

Using their military superiority, by early June the Czechs had taken control of almost the whole Trans-Siberian Railway. When they seized Penza, the Socialist Revolutionaries persuaded them to move on into the provincial capital of Samara (now Kuibyshev). The Czech's success encouraged anti-Soviet groups. In Samara the officers' associations opened the prisons, while the Menshevik railwaymen declared neutrality. The Bolshevik forces prepared to defend the town, but the Czechs took it on the night of June 7–8, 1918. The Socialist Revolutionaries declared a new government and began to celebrate. They fully expected the arrival of Allied interventionist forces, but these were nowhere near and had no plan to relieve them.

Czech-supported troops moved on to take Ekaterinburg on July 25 (their approach had alarmed the defenders who had immediately killed the czar and his family). The Czechs next took Simbirsk and, on August 7, Kazan.

As the Czechs moved, they roused hopes among minority peoples as well as landowners of putting down the Bolsheviks. On September 8 an all-party anti-Bolshevik conference declared an All-Russian Provisional Government. But on November 17 a group of officers overthrew it and called on Admiral Kolchak to be Supreme Ruler of All Russia and commander-in-chief of the armed forces. The Czechs protested, but the British and French Allies began sending supplies to Kolchak through Vladivostok via the railway.

The Czechs were disillusioned. The world war was over. They had fought for democracy for four years and were now tired. The Czechoslovak Republic had been declared: it was time for them to go home. In early 1919 the Czech Legion was withdrawn from fighting and was used only to guard the railway. Transport and supplies were insufficient, and the Czechs could not move as a body, whereupon they effectively took over part of Siberia and used their civilian skills. A bank was opened by a colonel (formerly a Prague banker): a daily newspaper was printed at several stations on the railway; their companies bought and sold commodities. The Czechs prospered economically in the middle of a chaotic, decaying world.

Kolchak was losing the battle against the Red Army. He was taken under Czech guard to Irkutsk, which was shortly after taken by the Bolsheviks, and Kolchak was shot on February 2, 1920. The Czechs agreed to release the imperial gold reserves that had come into their custody. On March 1 the last Czech train left and the gold was handed over.

The Japanese were the Allied power patrolling from Lake Baikal to Vladivostok, and although they halted their train at Chita to search for Bolsheviks, the Czechs made no objection: they were glad to be out of Russia and the evacuation went on from May to December 30, when the Allies declared the operation ended. One of the ships used, the *Legie*, had been bought by the legion's own bank and became land-locked Czechoslovakia's first merchant ship.

DACHA

A summer house, usually in the country or at the seaside. For Soviet officials a villa is allocated to them, sometimes for life.

DASHNAK

The anti-Russian revolutionary Armenian Federation, founded in the 1880s and the leading party in 1905 and from 1917 to 1920.

DECEMBRISTS

Members of the anti-czarist revolt of 1825, whose uprising failed, but the tradition of Decembrist conspiracy contributed to the 1905 uprisings.

DEFENSE COUNCIL

This body was founded at the beginning of December 1917 by the Sovnarkom, shortly after the Petrograd Soviet's Military Revolutionary Committee (MRC) was dissolved. (See also MRC.)

DEFENSISTS

Socialist politicians who agreed with World War I as a "Defense of the Fatherland."

DEMOCRATIC UNION

A movement that arose in 1988, styling itself as the opposition party, but it remains unrecognized since political pluralism is not yet tolerated in the Soviet Union.

DÉTENTE

A relaxation of tension, particularly attempts to end the cold war.

DIRECTORATE (COUNCIL OF FIVE)

Alexander Kerensky's proposal for governing Russia after the "Kornilov affair," and set up September 1, 1917.

DUMA

The elected legislative assemblies that were created as a result of the demands of the 1905 Revolution. At first, the electorate was to be all adult men, but property restrictions were made. The First Duma met for 73 days in 1906 and the Second Duma for 102 in 1907, but their liberal demands were unacceptable to the czar's government. With an even more restricted electorate, a Third Duma ran from 1907 to 1912 and supported the czarist government's policies, but the Fourth Duma, from 1912, grew critical of the czar's regime and of the war. When the czar abdicated in 1917, the Duma formed a provisional committee and asked Prince Georgy Lvov to form the Provisional Government.

EMPLOYMENT

Unemployment, it used to be claimed, disappeared from the Soviet Union in 1931 and was only to be found in the capitalist world. Under the 1977 Constitution, Article 40, Soviet citizens have the right to "guaranteed employment and pay in accordance with the quantity and quality of their work, and not below the State-established minimum.

With the openness of the Gorbachev era, official figures for 1984 revealed severe unemployment in some parts: Azerbaijan 27.6 percent, Tajikistan 25.7 percent, Uzbekistan 22.8 percent, Turkmen Soviet Socialist Republic 18.8 percent, Armenia 18 percent, and Kirghiz Soviet Socialist Republic 16.3 percent. These are people capable of work, but not of earning an official wage (thus housewives and small-holding farmers are included). Central Asia's high birth rate, the single-crop economy (cotton) in Uzbekistan, and tighter management of enterprises are contributory factors. While there are areas with employment vacancies, such as Siberian industrial plants, the cutback in the armed forces and the inevitable decline in the numbers of the bureaucracy will inevitably lead to colossal retraining programs.

A social security system with payments for those left unemployed by the newly recognized market forces was still, in 1989, being contemplated.

ENVIRONMENT

In the building of new heavy industry and the expansion and mechanization of farming under the five-year plans, little heed was paid to the long-term effects of these policies. Industry and agriculture have brought pollution to the Steppes—an outcome quite unexpected in the 1930s or even in the 1950s. Combined with the heavy use of pesticides and chemical fertilizers to boost agricultural production that is now showing its poisonous results, the immense and rapid plowing of land for the Virgin Lands campaign has brought erosion. Ecological disasters have taught the planners terrible lessons. It is estimated that 20 percent of Soviet citizens live in ecological disaster zones, where life expectancy is reduced by seven years and infant mortality is unacceptably high.

The coal-mining cities of the Kuzbas region in western Siberia are among the most polluted in the world. Novokuznetsk's 700,000 inhabitants have over 800,000 tons of effluent poured back down on them from their metallurgical works. The demand for coal has led to vast acres of virgin land being stripped of soil and vegetation as near-surface coal is scooped out.

The Aral Sea has been used to irrigate the cotton of Uzbekistan. Since 1960 the sea has contracted by one-third and its level has dropped by 40 feet. A salt desert has been born from which poisonous salts blow over the surrounding country. Without urgent remedies the sea will disappear by the year 2010 and the desert will have grown to cover its area. In Aralsk, once a port on the sea but now mired with stranded fishing boats, infant mortality is now

one in ten. Typhoid has increased 29 times and hepatitis 7 times.

The development of nuclear power has brought disasters, even before the Chernobyl explosion. It is said that in 1957 a large area of about 1,500 square kilometers, between Sverdlovsk and Chelyabinsk, was severely contaminated after an explosion in a nuclear waste dump and that an atomic fast breeder reactor leaked at Shevchenko in 1974. (See CHERNOBYL.)

On June 3, 1989, the natural gas pipeline from western Siberia to the industrial center of Ufa, built in 1985, leaked a cloud of gas. Two passing railway trains sparked an explosion and over 400 passengers were killed.

The Congress of Deputies set up a commission on ecology in 1989 led by Professor Yablokov, associated with the international Greenpeace organization. An awareness of ecological dangers led to a protest against the building of a nuclear waste storage site near the city of Krasnoyarsk, which would take the waste from all of Eastern Europe. No such protest would have been conceivable in previous years. In 1988 and 1989, ecological protest has led to the abandonment of a hydroelectrical scheme, a phosphate mine in Estonia, the banning of certain defoliants, and attempts to save Lakes Baikal and Ladoga. Most important has been the decision to discontinue work on diverting the flow of Siberian rivers flowing from north to the south.

ESTONIAN SOVIET SOCIALIST RE- PUBLIC

(See also BALTIC STATES.)

Population: 1,571,000; 65 percent Estonian, 28 percent Russian, 5 percent Ukrainian and Belorussian.

Area: 17,413 square miles

Capital: Tallinn; population, 478,000

For the earlier history of Estonia, see BALTIC STATES. In November 1988 the Estonian Communist party leader called for a reform program. The Estonian Supreme Soviet amended its constitution to give the republic the right to refuse all-union laws. Estonia demanded that its own language replace Russian as the official tongue and that it have its own citizenship laws. A Popular Front voiced these demands and more. It also proposed Estonia's own currency for 1990, the Korus, with its own international exchange rate. The Estonian Supreme Soviet has also recognized the right to own private property; declared land, air, water, minerals, forests, and natural resources to be the exclusive property of Estonia (the USSR previously claimed these as belonging to the whole Soviet Union); and determined that banks and major enterprises are owned by Estonia (previously under the Soviet Union's jurisdiction). Later, Indrek Toome, the prime minister, announced more plans—less drastic than earlier proposals, but including a new form of income tax and the legalization of forms of private enterprise, the return of collective and state farms to farmers, and control over immigration.

On February 24, 1989, Arnold Ruutel, the "suave and diplomatic" president, raised the Estoninan flag—blue, black, and white—over the government building at Tallinn on the old Independence Day (1918). To counter the Popular Front, an International movement, called the Yedinstvo, was formed to represent the interests of Russians living in Estonia. In August 1989 many Russians went on strike in protest against discrimination.

In March 1989 the Popular Front candidates were elected to the All-Union Congress, but four of the successful candidates were of the Yedinstvo. In May a Baltic Assembly of the Popular Fronts of Estonia, Latvia, and Lithuania was held in Tallinn. It rejected a Moscow plan that would have conceded control over the production of food and consumer goods in the 15 Soviet republics, but would have retained control over energy and heavy industry. The deputies to the All-Union Congress agreed on a united stand. This unofficial Congress met again in March 1990 with 499 delegates elected by over half a million Estonians to prepare for the forthcoming elections in Estonia.

FELLOW-TRAVELERS

Intellectuals who, although not Communists, sympathized with the party. It's a term (*poputchiki*) coined by Trotsky in 1925 and much used in the United States during the McCarthy period.

FINLAND

Area: 130,119 square miles
Population: 4,990,000
Capital: Helsinki; population, 487,000

1905–1920—The 1905 Revolution in Russia regained for Finland some of the independence that it had lost to czarist Russia at the end of the 19th century. It established, within the czarist empire, its own legislature elected by both women and men. It was the first elected assembly in Europe to have both men and women delegates.

During World War I, many Finns chose to be pro-German because this expressed their hostility to Russian rule. In January 1915, 200 Finns went for military training in Germany; by May 1916 their numbers had reached 2,000 and they had formed the 27 Königliche Preussische Jäger battalion, deployed on the Eastern Front near Riga.

In March 1917 Russian troops in Helsinki, as elsewhere, rose against their officers and the Provisional Government in Petrograd gave Finland self-government, with its legislature headed by a Social Democrat minister. But in July 1917 the Provisional Government dissolved this legislature and elections in October 1917 gave the Social Democrats 92 seats (less than the 103 they had had in 1916) and the non-socialists 108. In November 1917, with the Bolsheviks in power in Petrograd, the new Finnish Parliament decided to stand alone and Lenin recognized the independent Finnish state in December. This was followed by recognition in January 1918 by Germany, France, and the Scandinavian nations.

In January 1918 Carl Mannerheim, a czarist general of Swedish-Finnish background, started training a Finnish army at Vaasa, just as a left-wing revolt broke out in Helsinki. The Finnish government fled to Vaasa, but Mannerheim led a campaign (with some German help, in the form of their Finnish battalion of Jägers) against the uprising and headed a victory parade in Helsinki in May 1918. The Soviets regarded this as a Finnish civil war, and they accepted the Mannerheim reaction. In October 1920 Finland and Russia signed a peace treaty at Tartu (Dorpat).

1939–45—In October 1939, anticipating war with Germany, Stalin and Molotov demanded that Finnish territory in the Leningrad area be ceded for the defense of the Soviet Union. But the Soviet-Finnish talks broke down, since the Finnish Parliament would not trust its emissaries to deal with the Soviets. In November, after declaring that Finland was threatening them, the Soviet Union bombed Helsinki and invaded Finland. Stalin set up a Finnish Democratic Republic that would have become, joined with the Karelian Autonomous Republic, a Karelo-Finnish Soviet Republic within the USSR.

Mannerheim assumed supreme command of the Finnish forces. The world looked on Finland with admiration, but without any ability to help. In December the USSR was expelled from the League of Nations for the assault on Finland, without any nation voting in its support.

The Soviet 7th Army proved to be ill trained and ill equipped for a winter attack on the Finnish defense positions, and in January 1940 the Red Army Commander Kyril Meretskov was removed from overall command of the Finnish war and replaced by Simeon Timoshenko. An attack on the Mannerheim Line, preceded by a heavy artillery barrage, allowed Soviet tank forces to sweep around the defenses and drive back the Finnish troops. After Norway and Sweden had refused passage of a small Anglo-French force, on March 12, Finland stopped fighting against the Soviet Union and signed the treaty demanded in 1939, to which extra demands were now added. The Finnish army lost 25,000 men, but the Red Army casualties were much greater, possibly 200,000, reflecting their appalling military miscalculation.

Following the German attack on Russia, on June 25, 1941, Finland declared war on the Soviet Union and its troops advanced to the old 1939 frontier on the Karelian Isthmus and to the Svir River between Lakes Ladoga and Onega, where the line stayed until 1944. In spite of a strong German presence, the Finns only carried out military operations that were in their interest. Marshal Mannerheim would not take command of the German troops in Finland, since that would have reduced him, in effect, to being merely one of Hitler's generals. In December Britain declared itself at war with Finland after long diplomatic attempts to persuade Finland not to align with Germany.

In February 1944 Finland began secret discussions on peace terms with the Soviet Union through its ambassador in Sweden, Alexandra Kollontay. The war continued, however, and in June an attack drove the Finns back to their 1940 lines on the Karelian Isthmus. In August the Finnish president resigned and was replaced by Marshal Mannerheim, who got Sweden's promise of food supplies. Thus able to act independently of Germany, Finland sued for peace and an armistice was signed in September 1944; after some fighting, German troops were expelled. Mannerheim declared war on Germany in March 1945 and, his work completed, resigned as president a year later. In February 1947 Finland signed a peace treaty with the Soviet Union and its independence was assured.

FINLAND STATION

The Petrograd railroad station in the north of the city at which Lenin and his fellow Bolsheviks arrived in April 1917. See also SEALED TRAIN.

FIVE-YEAR PLANS

While the idea of planning was fundamental to socialist thinking, it was Lenin's observation of the wartime economies of the Western powers that led to adoption of similar measures in the Soviet Union during the period of War Communism. Of course, Lenin's plans went much further and included the elimination of markets and the nationalization of industries. In agriculture it included the detested methods of requisition and confiscation of grain crops.

The New Economic Policy, the policies introduced by Lenin after War Communism had failed, did not dismantle the basic structure of state planning organization introduced after the revolution. They were: (1) the VSNKh, or Supreme Council of the National Economy, established in December 1917; (2) the VTsIK, or All-Russian Central Executive Committee of the Soviets; and (3) Gosplan, or the Committee for a General State Plan, established February 22, 1921.

Under VSKNh were local organizations called Sovnarkhoz and Glavki, or Central Administrations, who looked after nationalized enterprises. The boundaries of their authority were not always entirely clear and they varied with time and circumstance.

The reason a five-year period was chosen was that it fitted quite neatly the cycle of construction for major works such as power stations, rail links, and canals. In agriculture it helped to average out the variations caused by climate. **First—April 1929**—The plan called for a 250 percent increase of investment in the economy. It assumed no crop failures, and a growth in foreign trade and credits. The real situation was quite different. Agriculture was being ruthlessly collectivized, and the kulaks, the most efficient agricultural producers, were being wiped out. This led to the appalling famine of 1933. On the international scene, the Wall Street crash signaled the beginning of worldwide recession. Under these circumstances the achievements of the plan were remarkable, and, in many cases, the targets, particularly on the industrial front, were substantially exceeded.

Second—February 1934—This plan called for more realistic growth rates than the first, but it still asked for a doubling of industrial production, which was achieved. Agricultural output was well below the target, as were all sections of consumer goods production. There were some impressive construction achievements: the Magnitogorsk and Stalinsk steel works were built, and the Dnieper dam was completed.

Third—This plan was prepared in 1937–38, in the period of the Great Purge. It called for an increase in industrial output of more than 90 percent but increased defense expenditure, and the removal of many of the better managers by the purge left most of the targets unfulfilled. Output was also affected by the Finnish War of 1939–40, and in June 1941 the Nazi invasion put the entire economy on an emergency footing.

Fourth—This covered the years 1945–50 and was therefore largely concerned, initially, with reconstruction of the shattered economy. Huge efforts were made and the modest goals, by Soviet standards, were achieved. Using 100 as an index for 1940, industrial production was 173 by 1950, for instance. Overall production reached prewar levels for producer goods in 1948 and for consumer goods in 1951. Agricultural production,

particularly the grain harvest, did not reach 1940 levels until 1952.

Fifth—The new plan covering 1951–55 was supposed to begin in 1951 but was finally presented to the 19th Party Congress in October 1952. It called for an increase in industrial production of 70 percent and large increases in agricultural production, though no provision was made for increases in farm prices. The plan had been in operation for less than a year when Stalin died.

Sixth—The 1955 plan was prepared with great thoroughness. Nikita Khrushchev, who had replaced Stalin as general secretary, had divided Gosplan (State Committee on Planning) into two parts: one for current, the other for long-term planning. The plan, passed by the 20th Party Congress, famous for Khrushchev's denunciation of Stalin, called for large increases in industrial output including the creation of a third metallurgical base in Kazakhstan and Siberia, for the production of pig iron. However, this plan had only been in existence for a year when it was decided, on December 20, 1956, that a revision was required. This coincided with Khrushchev's battle for survival against his rivals Vyacheslav Molotov, Georgy Malenkov, and Lazar Kaganovich.

Seventh—Essentially a revised sixth, it covered the years 1959–1965. The plan called for an increase in industrial production of 80 percent based on 1958 levels, which was achieved, but the output of consumer goods was well below the set target and the grain harvest, planned for 180 million tons, was less than 120 million, despite the enormous area of new planting in the Virgin Lands campaign. In part this was caused by Khrushchev's confused attempts to reorganize the structure of agriculture, but also by the continuing growth of bureaucracy and muddle.

Eighth—The plan covering the years 1966–70 was adopted by the September 1965 Plenum of the Central Committee. It called for an increase in industrial output over the whole period of 50 percent, and in agriculture of 21 percent. During the period of the plan the integrated power grid of the USSR was completed.

Ninth—The plan ratified in 1971 and covering the years 1971–75 had as its proclaimed main drive the improvement of living standards within the USSR. After only four years it was announced that national income had increased by 24 percent, industrial output by 33 percent, and agricultural by 15 percent. One of the main projects completed during the plan was the Baikal Railway line. During this period there was a very large increase in defense spending.

Tenth—This plan covered the period 1976–80, and partly as a result of high oil prices caused by the OPEC price squeeze, the economy was doing well. It was positive enough for Brezhnev to postpone the intended measures of reform that had been planned to increase the efficiency of industry. Industrial output was scheduled to rise by 36 percent while that of consumer goods by an unheard of 32 percent; even agriculture was planned to rise by 24 percent. The targets were not achieved, and defense spending had increased to some 11 percent of the GNP by the end of the period.

GENERAL ARMY COMMITTEE

The central committee governing committees, or soviets that soldiers formed in February 1917.

GEORGIAN SOVIET SOCIALIST REPUBLIC

Population: 5,297,000; 69 percent Georgian, 5 percent Azerbaijani, 7 percent Russian
Area: 26,911 square miles
Capital: Tbilisi; population 1,194,000
Abkhazian Autonomous Soviet Socialist Republic: capital Sukhumi; area 8,600 square kilometers; population 536,000.
Adzhar Autonomous Soviet Socialist Republic: capital Batumi; area 3,000 square kilometers; population 386,000.
South Ossetian Autonomous Soviet Socialist Republic: capital Tskhinvali; area 3,900 square kilometers; population 99,000.

Georgian nationalism developed strongly in the 19th century. Among Georgian political groups the so-called Third Group (*Mesami Dasi*), the first of the Marxist radical groups, was formed in 1892; one of its members was the young Stalin. Georgian politics in the early 20th century was dominated by the Social Democrats, largely Mensheviks.

In 1917 Menshevik revolutionaries proclaimed a republic, though first Turkish and then German troops moved in, prompting the Western Allies to intervene. After the Brest-Litovsk Treaty the Georgian Soviet Democratic Republic was proclaimed on May 26, 1918, and recognized by Germany, Turkey, and by the Moscow Soviet in August; 22 nations recognized independent Georgia. A treaty was signed between the Soviet Union and Georgia in May 1920, agreeing on the border between the countries. But then, on February 25, 1921, the Red Army, headed by Sergo Ordzhonikidze, marched into Georgia and forced it to become a Soviet socialist republic. It was made part of the Transcaucasian Federation in 1922, until that was abolished in 1936, when Georgia became one of the USSR's constituent republics.

Georgians have played a leading role in the Soviet Union with Stalin, Ordzhonikidze, and Lavrenti Beria being particularly prominent. After Stalin's death, the party was purged and Vasily Mzhavanadze took over as party secretary until he was removed and replaced by the head of Georgian Internal security, Eduard Shevardnadze in 1972. A further purge took place, aimed at curbing Georgia's reputation throughout the Soviet Union for unorthodox freewheeling trade methods. The February–April 1973 meeting of the Georgian Communist party was devoted to exposing "nationalist deviations"—there had been anti-Russian riots in 1956, and in 1978 there were further demonstrations against the use of Russian as an official language equal to Georgian.

The Georgian Church was incorporated into the Russian Orthodox Church when Georgia was taken into the empire, but it declared its independence in 1917, although the Russian Orthodox Church would not recognize this until 1943.

The Georgian language (a distinct language of the Caucasus) and culture have been retained with independence and vigor, and the people have their own tradition of poetry, music, and dance.

Georgia, with a large Russian population, is not as fervently nationalist as are other republics, partly because of its people's fear of their neighbors Armenia and Azerbaijan. However, in common with other Soviet republics, there have been nationalist movements. A recent one is called Ilya Chavchavadze, after a 19th-century poet and patriot, a saint of the Georgian Orthodox Church. In 1989 a Popular Front put forward candidates for the People's Congress; its radical leader, Zviad Gamsakhuria, had previously been jailed for his views on nationalism. The Rustaveli Society is a further nationalist group represented at the congress.

In November 1988, a rally of 200,000 people insisted on an end to Russification and called for Georgia's withdrawal from the Soviet Union. On February 25, 1989, (on its "Independence Day") a meeting of 15,000 in Tbilisi demanded independence for Georgia. More serious events began in April. In Sukhumi, the Abkhazi capital, there were riots as Abkhazis called for secession from Georgia and the establishment of an Abkhazi republic within the USSR. Then on April 9 in Tbilisi, after demonstrations by about 10,000 calling for greater Georgian autonomy, 19 Georgians including 12 women were killed and hundreds were injured by Soviet troops imposing order on demonstrators in the city. It was admitted that tear gas and anti-riot gas were used, but video film showed troops moving into the gas and hitting with shovels and clubs. As a result Shevardnadze flew to Tbilisi, a curfew was imposed, and arrests of over 400 people were made.

In July there were more ethnic clashes between Georgians and Abkhazians, with Georgians calling for the abolition of the Abkhazi republic and its absorption into Georgia. In Sukhumi, riots between Abkhazians and Georgians broke out over quarrels about the quota for each group to gain admission to a proposed new university and 16 people were killed. Similarly in the Ossetian ASSR there have been demonstrations, some in favor of leaving Georgia and joining with North Ossetians in the RSFSR.

GERMAN DEMOCRATIC REPUBLIC (GDR)

Area: 41,768 square miles
Population: 16,664,000
Capital: East Berlin; population, 1,236,000

The Allies agreed on dividing conquered Germany into occupation zones in 1945. With the realignment of the Polish frontiers to absorb what had been part of Prussia, the Soviet zone took in the land to the west of the Oder River and included Berlin, which was controlled by all the Allies. West Germany grew out of the U.S., British, and French zones, while the GDR was established in 1949 from the Soviet. Berlin became a contentious issue, and the attempt in 1948–49 to blockade it from the West led to the massive Berlin Airlift. The next crisis came when the Soviet Union sought to have the Western sectors of Berlin incorporated into a demilitarized free city: no agreement was reached and in 1961 the Western sectors were sealed off when Soviet and East German troops put up the Berlin Wall around them. This, with strict border controls between the two Germanies, made the Iron Curtain concept a reality.

Effective political power lay with the Communist Socialist Unity party (SED), which controlled a national front of other parties, all of which have withered away since 1949, leaving the GDR as a one-party state. The GDR has been economically successful among the Eastern Bloc countries, although in common with other Eastern Bloc countries there have been constant shortages of consumer goods.

One reason for the strict border controls has been to prevent a drain of skilled workers from the GDR to the West. However on May 2 1989, Hungary which with Poland was in the forefront of the pro-democracy movement in Eastern Europe tore down the iron curtain on its borders with Austria and allowed East German workers to cross into Austria and thence to the West. Honecker's government protested strongly but to no avail and finally a ban was imposed forbidding travel into Hungary.

By now more general protest meetings inspired by the movements for *perestroika* and *glasnost* in the Soviet Union and in Poland, had started, centered on the city of Leipzig. A political movement linked to the evangelical church, New Forum, came into existence while a new exodus of citizens began through the West German embassy in Prague. The government reacted by ordering the border to be closed. On October 9 there were mass demonstrations leading to arrests and beatings by the hated security police, the Stasi. This led to further demonstrations and on October 18 Erich Honecker was replaced by Egon Krenz (Honecker, accused of corruption, was found too sick to stand trial). On October 31, the Czech border was reopened, and on November 9 the newly appointed Politburo declared that the Berlin Wall, the hated symbol of division, would be opened, and free passage was to be allowed for all East Berliners. Much of the wall has now been demolished and pieces are being sold off as souvenirs.

Egon Krenz was replaced by Hans Modrow, a man more acceptable to the people because he had been out of favor with Honecker. German reunification is the biggest single issue in Europe at the moment. There is an overwhelming demand for it in both the Germanys, and, though generally regarded as inevitable, it has produced mixed reactions everywhere and particularly in the Soviet Union.

The Soviet Union approved the GDR's actions, but the developments call into question the status of the Warsaw Pact, COMECON, and NATO.

GERMANS IN THE USSR

In the 17th century, German settler farmers became a recognized part of Russian society. They were grouped in a German Autonomous Republic on the lower Volga from 1924 until 1941, when with the outbreak of war with Germany, the inhabitants were rounded up as potential traitors and sent east to Kazakhstan and Siberia. There are now estimated to be 1.8 million people described as German in the Soviet Union, over half in Kazakhstan with other substantial groups in the Kirghizia and Tajikistan. There is no provision for German-language education, and the proportion of German speakers has been on the decline for years. However, an All-Union Society of Germans has called for a rebirth of the German Autonomous Republic, claiming that emigration to West Germany would increase otherwise. In 1988, 74,000 Germans left the Soviet Union (most to West Germany, which has a constitutional requirement to accept them).

GLAVISKUSSTVO

The Central Directorate for Artistic Affairs.

GLAVLIT

The Soviet Censorship Office established in 1922: all publications are passed through this body for approval.

GLASNOST

The practice of "openness" and honesty about official matters and Soviet history, associated with *perestroika* in the 1980s.

GORKOM

Gorodskoy Komitet, or the party committee of a town or city.

GOSAGROPROM

The All-Union Ministry of Agriculture.

GOSBANK

The state bank.

GOSIZDAT

The state publishing house.

GOSKINO

The state cinema industry.

GOSPLAN

The State Planning Commission, founded on February 22, 1921, which produced the First Five-Year Plan. From then on, Gosplan was directly controlled by the party. (See FIVE-YEAR PLAN.)

GPU. See POLITICAL POLICE.

GREAT PURGE. See YEZHOVSHCHINA.

GRU

Glavnoye Razvedyvatelnoye Upravleniye, or Chief Intelligence Directorate of the General Staff. It operates from 19 Znamensky Street, once the Moscow home of a czarist millionaire, and acquires military intelligence mainly through the legitimate operation of military attachés in embassies throughout the world.

Although it was founded by Leon Trotsky in 1919 as the army's source of intelligence, distinct from the civil government's Cheka, the GRU is today subordinate to the Cheka's descendant, the KGB. Its successes in running agents overseas have been the atomic energy spies Klaus Fuchs in England and the Rosenbergs in the United States. The GRU also organized Gordon Lonsdale in England to obtain naval secrets and Rudolf Abel in the United States. Abel's career was acclaimed as a success by the Soviets after he had been exchanged for U-2 pilot Gary Powers, but his achievements are still under question in the United States. However, the defection of the GRU Colonel Oleg Penkovsky damaged the reputation of the organization severely. Penkovsky, while on missions to Britain in 1960 and 1961, revealed details of the state of Soviet military preparedness, which helped U.S. President John F. Kennedy outface Nikita Khrushchev during the 1962 Cuban missile crisis. After return to the USSR, Penkovsky was uncovered and shot.

The KGB now claims credit for all espionage success and has recently publicized the case of "Glenn Souther,"

alias Mikhail Orlov, who, while serving in the U.S. Navy under the full cover of U.S. citizenship, had engineered espionage in the United States until 1986; fearing exposure he returned to the USSR, where he killed himself in a depression at the age of 32. They are also proud of the exploits of the British agent Kim Philby, who retired and died in 1988 in Moscow as a KGB general. (See also POLITICAL POLICE, KGB.)

GUBERNIA

A czarist administrative territory, or province. The term was replaced by oblast or kray in 1929.

GULAG

The Chief Administration of Corrective Labor Camps and Settlements, a function of the KGB whose name became familiar through the writings of Alexander Solzhenitsyn. (See CAMPS.)

GUM

Gosudarstvenny Universalny Magazin, the large department store in Red Square, Moscow.

HEAD OF STATE. See PRESIDENT.

HELSINKI ACCORD

The Human Rights Final Agreement signed in Helsinki in 1975.

HELSINKI GROUPS

Formed in 1976 and 1977 in several parts of the USSR to monitor the effects of the Helsinki Accord, often to further the rights of would-be emigrants—Germans, Jews, and, to a lesser extent, Armenians—and to urge disarmament. They operate through small meetings and the distribution of *samzidats* (newsletters). The groups were subjected to close police surveillance and their members often imprisoned, put under restriction orders, or subjected to psychiatric treatment.

HETMAN. See ATAMAN.

HUNGARY

Area: 36,000 square miles
Population: 10,658,000
Capital: Budapest; population, 2,104,000

After World War I there was a short-lived Communist regime set up by Bela Kun, who later died in the Soviet purges. This was followed by a right-wing regime under Admiral Miklos Horthy, who allied himself with Nazi Germany. Hungary was occupied by the German Army in March 1944 and liberated by the Red Army in April 1945. In October 1945 free elections were held; the Communists led by Mátyás Rákosi obtained only 17 percent of the votes. The largest group, the Smallholders party under Bela Kovacs, was soon put under attack by the Communists who arrested him on trumped-up charges. By June 1948 Rákosi and his Soviet masters had imposed a one-party system on the country. Agriculture was gradually collectivized and most of industry nationalized.

In 1953, under Nikita Khrushchev's influence, Rákosi was replaced by Imre Nagy, who proceeded to introduce more liberal economic and social measures. In early 1955 Rákosi returned to power, and he removed Nagy from the party and reimposed strict controls. This led to a popular uprising in October 1956, during which some of the hated Secret Police (AVH) were lynched. Soviet troops intervened and there was fierce fighting—tanks and armored personnel carriers against lightly armed freedom fighters. The outcome was never in doubt. Imre Nagy was arrested by a trick, tried, and executed in June 1958. He has since been "rehabilitated" and, indeed, given a proper burial.

In November 1956, Janos Kadar was appointed party leader, and from 1962 onward he instituted social and economic reforms. Since 1968 the New Economic Mechanism has allowed more decentralized decision making than in other Eastern Bloc countries, restoring a degree of capitalism to small enterprises such as bars, cafés, and small holdings.

Perestroika reached Hungary in November 1988 when the Communist Party without any massive pressure from outside announced that it planned to move to a multi-party system. Janos Kadar had already been removed from office and replaced by Karoly Grosz. In the spring of 1989 the party, who was shedding confidence as a result of losing arguments with reforming elements, was prepared to admit that they might well lose power.

In the elections in 1945 the Communists only got 16 percent of the vote compared to 57 percent for the Smallholders. In the general elections to be held on March 25th the leading contenders for power are The Alliance of Free Democrats or SzDsz, and the Democratic Forum or MDF. Both parties are in favor of a market type economy but the Free Democrats want to move more quickly in this direction.

INDUSTRY

Before the Revolution—Russia has always been a country rich in natural resources, including coal, iron, gold, and oil. Under Sergei Witte, the minister of finance from 1892 to 1904, great strides were made in exploiting these resources in order to build an industrial base. There was direct state investment in the railway network and encouragement of foreign investment in mining, chemicals, and textiles while Russian industry was protected by high tariffs. The growth of the economy under Witte was over 5 percent per annum, and by 1913 Russia was the fifth largest industrial producer in the world.

The outbreak of war in 1914 caused an almost total dislocation of the economy and this, with the military defeat, produced the revolutionary situation that had first surfaced in 1905 and was now to be exploited by Lenin and the Bolsheviks.

Following the October Revolution the new government embarked upon an immediate but confused policy of nationalization, which included the land, larger factories, and the banks. In December the Supreme Economic Council (VSNKh) was created. In 1918 civil war broke out.

War Communism—The newly established government, fighting for its life, brought in a series of Draconian measures that came to be known as War Communism. They included total nationalization of industry, the outlawing of trade, and the virtual exclusion of money from the economy. Industrial production fell by 70 percent, coal production by nearly 80 percent, and agriculture by 40 percent. There was serious famine. Grain was seized from the peasants by force, and there were riots in the countryside and the towns. The climax was a mutiny by the sailors at Kronstadt in March 1921. The government had to act to save the revolution.

The New Economic Policy NEP—Despite the nationalization of all factories employing more than five people and the banning of private trade, at this time the urban population obtained as much as 70 percent of its grain and as much as two-thirds of all consumer goods through private channels.

In February 1921, at the 10th Party Congress and partly in response to the Kronstadt rebellion, measures were introduced to substitute taxes for requisitions of grain, while other harsh measures taken against the peasants under War Communism were also dropped. The number of collective farms declined quite sharply and shortly thereafter the reintroduction of private trading and manufacturing on a small scale was begun.

Monetary reforms were introduced, including a new unit of currency, the chervonet, to deal with the collapse of the ruble, but the budget was not balanced until 1923. The inheritance of private property was allowed in order to encourage business people to invest rather than spend their profits. In October 1921 Lenin said, "By attempting to go straight to Communism we suffered an economic defeat by the spring of 1921 worse than any defeat at the hands of Kolchak, Denikin and Pilsudski." However, at other times, he claimed that War Communism was simply a policy produced by an emergency situation.

Over the next two years private trade and manufacturing were actively encouraged, and private credit organizations were allowed to exist. Lenin talked of using the NEP and its active constituents, the Nepmen, as they were called, to help the growth of socialism by teaching "Communists how to become businessmen." On ideological and emotional grounds this was a dangerous policy and, as can be seen in the cartoons of the time, Nepmen were portrayed as greedy, vulgar, and, ominously, as Jewish. They were blamed for rising prices and were attacked as capitalist leeches.

After Lenin's death in January 1924 there was a sudden shift in policy. The Nepmen's life-style, often lavish and accompanied by the opening of casinos, race tracks, expensive food shops, and hotels, made many Bolsheviks wonder what the revolution had been for. Many businesses were closed, the banks reduced credit to the private sector from 42 million rubles to 17 in one year, and swinging increases in taxation indicated a general feeling of hostility to the New Economic Policy.

But in 1925 NEP became, at least in part, a marker in the power struggle within the party leadership. The left wing led by Trotsky, Zinoviev, and Kamenev was opposed to a right wing led by Bukharin, Rykov, and Tomsky with whom Stalin's group had formed a temporary alliance. The left was totally opposed to NEP and proclaimed that it was the path back to capitalism. Bukharin and the right were just as committed to Communist doctrines but believed that gradualism was necessary. "Grow rich with the peasant" was Bukharin's battle cry. Stalin accepted Bukharin's ideas in order to defeat the left, and when this took place in 1927, he attacked Bukharin's support for NEP.

In the meantime, with Bukharin's enthusiastic support, NEP was once again

in favor and 1925 saw the full flowering of the policies. Taxes were reduced once more, and bank credits were increased by 200 percent during the year.

INDUSTRIAL OUTPUT 1913–1925

Product	1913	1921	1925	1925
				as % of 1913
Coal[1]	29.1	9.5	16.5	57
Oil[1]	9.2	3.8	7.1	77
Peat[1]	1.7	2.0	2.7	159
Pig iron[1]	4.2	0.1	1.3	31
Steel[1]	4.2	0.2	1.9	45
Rolled Steel[1]	3.5	0.2	1.4	40
Cement[1]	1.5	0.06	0.9	60
Paper[1]	0.2		0.2	107
Sugar[1]	1.3	0.05	1.1	85
Fish[1]	1.0	0.3	0.7	70
Electricity[2]	1,975	520	2,925	150

[1]In million tonnes
[2]In million kWh
SOURCE: Adapted from Munting, *The Economic Development of the USSR*, 1982.

This brief but brilliant period was already threatened by Stalin, who at the 15th Party Congress in December 1927, after the final defeat of the left, declared that the right wing underestimated the dangers of NEP to the state.

The poor grain collections of that year led Stalin to reintroduce War Communism methods of grain collection in Siberia. From then on attacks on Nepmen were stepped up. Businesses were closed down. They were forbidden to hold public office and many were driven from state housing. Shock brigades were formed to seize goods from anyone suspected of making money by illegal trading activities and even street traders were driven from the streets again.

The attack on the "new bourgeoisie," heralded by Stalin's speeches at the 15th Party Congress, was almost complete, and in December 1929 the "Right Deviationists" made a public confession of their errors.

An American visitor to Moscow in December 1929 recorded: "On the streets the shops seemed to have disappeared. Gone was the open market. Gone were the Nepmen."

In March 1930 Stalin's article "Dizzy with Success" signaled the end of the whirlwind campaign against NEP and reined in the extreme reaction of those party officials who were closing street markets all over the USSR. But from now on private trade was confined to the margins of the economy.

THE 1st AND 2nd FIVE-YEAR PLANS					
	1928 (plan)	1932/33 (out-turn)	1932 (plan)	1937 (plan)	1937 (out-turn)
National income[1]	24.4	49.7	45.5	100.2	96.3
Gross industrial production[2]					
industrial goods	6.0	18.1	23.1	45.5	55.2
consumer goods	12.3	25.1	20.2	47.2	40.3
Workers in state employment (millions)	11.3	15.8	22.9	28.9	27.0

[1, 2]Thousand million Rubles at 1926–27 prices.
SOURCE: Adapted from Munting, *The Economic Development of the USSR*, 1982.

1934–1939—The Second Five-Year Plan, approved in January 1934, called for a 250 percent increase in investment over the first plan and 52 percent of this was to be in industry. This enormous investment in industry meant that by 1937 nearly 80 percent of industrial production was taking place in either new or completely refurbished factories and workshops. Growth was dependent on a huge increase in input of both labor and capital, not on the more efficient use of resources.

Because of the huge new labor force recruited from the agricultural sector and the shortage of consumer goods, there was a considerable degree of inflation. This was not absorbed by income tax—only 3.5 percent at the time—but by the sale of state bonds to the public.

The bonds paid 10 percent interest but had no redemption date. Businesses paid a turnover tax, which was the main source of state income, and a tax on profits.

World War II—The Third Five-Year Plan was affected both by the Great Purge of 1937 and also by war preparations. Defense expenditure jumped from 3.5 percent of the budget in 1933 to 18.6 percent in 1937. Although Soviet defenses were unprepared for the German assault in 1941, there had been a great deal of preparation for conflict. Tractor factories had been built with an eye to converting them to tank production, and some industrial complexes had been moved for strategic advantage—to Stalingrad for example. A comparison of Soviet and German wartime production demonstrates that although German industrial production was considerably higher than the USSR's, the number of weapons manufactured—tanks, military aircraft, and guns—was considerably fewer. The USSR, like the United Kingdom, was far more committed to a total war economy. The effects of the war were shattering on the economy; towns and villages were destroyed on a massive scale, more than half the steel-making capacity was lost along with 50 percent of the electrical-generating ability and 60 percent of coal output. In addition there had been a huge loss of population—something like 20 million dead—which represented a sizable fraction of the industrial and agricultural work force.

Postwar Reconstruction—The Fourth Five-Year Plan, 1946–1950, aimed at an increase in industrial output of nearly 50 percent, seeking to achieve in five years the increase planned for a 10-year period before the war. In general targets were met except in consumer goods. Despite the state of the Soviet economy Stalin would not accept the offer of Marshall Plan aid from the United States and instead insisted on large-scale reparations from the defeated Germany and its allies, including those parts of Europe under its domination. Rationing was ended in December 1947 and subsidies to heavy industry in 1948. To benefit the consumer there was a policy of price reduction in industry. An attempt to emphasize the importance of the consumer at the expense of heavy industry was brought to a halt when Nicholas Voznesensky, the head of Gosplan, was tried and executed for suggesting just this.

The Khrushchev Reforms—When Stalin died in 1953, Nikita Khrushchev showed interest in increasing the supply of consumer goods but was more concerned, because of his background, with the agricultural sector.

ECONOMIC INDICATORS, 1950–1964

	1950	1958	1963	1964
National income (index)	100	229	311	339
Gross industrial production				
industrial goods	100	263	487	475
consumer goods	100	225	320	332

SOURCE: Adapted from Munting, *The Economic Development of the USSR*, 1982.

Nevertheless, between 1953 and 1958 there was an increase in the GNP of 6.7 percent. In 1957 Khrushchev made a dramatic industrial reform with the introduction of regional economic councils, or Sovnarkhoz, which were to take the place of the ministries. It was also decided to abandon the Sixth Five-Year Plan and introduce a Seven-Year

Plan starting in 1959. The targets were optimistic and Khrushchev made a confident prediction that the economy would overtake the United Kingdom and West Germany by 1965 and the United States by 1970. In fact, although industrial production was on target, consumer goods were well below, and agriculture achieved a 15 percent rather than a 70 percent increase. At the same time the USSR was funding a military expenditure at 12 percent of GNP and a space program whose achievements, although impressive, were eating up valuable resources. In 1963 the long-term planning body VSNKh reappeared, but after Khrushchev's downfall in the following year the Sovnarkhoz were closed down and the ministries were restored to their old function.

The Brezhnev era—Under Leonid Brezhnev as party secretary with Alexei Kosygin as prime minister, reforms were introduced that were intended to give more autonomy to industry and instill a more commercial attitude.

ECONOMIC INDICATORS 1965–1975, EIGHTH AND NINTH FIVE-YEAR PLANS

	1970 (1965 = 100)		1975 (1970 = 100)	
	Plan	Real	Plan	Real
National income	140	141	138.6	127.5
Gross industrial production				
industrial goods	149–52	151	146.3	145.4
consumer goods	143–46	149	148.6	137.4
Agricultural production	125	121.4	121.7	101.8
Labor productivity				
industry	130	132	138.8	133.8
construction	125	122	137	128.5
collective farms		136	138	107
state farms		138	138	102
Real income per capita	130	133	130.8	123.9

SOURCE: Adapted from Munting, *The Economic Development of the USSR*, 1982.

Although the Eighth Five-Year Plan met most of its targets, bar agriculture and construction, the Ninth Five-Year Plan was well below planned output, particularly serious in that for the first time in the history of the USSR consumer goods were given a higher priority than producer goods. Despite the reforms, the bureaucracy was reluctant to give up its control of the economy.

Under both the Ninth and Tenth Five-Year plans, 1970–80, there was considerable emphasis on investing in Siberian resources, which in turn led to further investment in infrastructure: gas pipe lines, roads, and railways. The Soviet Union is one of the few countries currently investing heavily in rail transport. Oil has become more important than coal as an energy source, but the actual output of both has declined. There is a large nuclear power program, though how viable this will prove to be after the Chernobyl disaster is unpredictable. Despite the investment in Siberia and the east, the major industrial power is still in the west, in the Ukraine and, significantly now for the USSR, in the Baltic States. Estonia is the most industrially developed republic in the USSR.

To tackle the demand for consumer goods, deals have been made with companies in the West, such as the Fiat plant at Togliatigrad, which was producing more than a million private cars a year in 1978. The chemical industry, also in collaboration with Western companies, has vastly expanded, more than six times between 1960 and 1980.

Perestroika and Plans for the Future—
In his book *Perestroika*, Mikhail Gorbachev says, "Many things are unusual in our country now: self-financed factories and plants, encouragement of individual enterprises in small-scale production and trade, and closure of non-paying plants and factories operating at a loss." This represents far more than a continuation of the changes introduced under Brezhnev; it is more reminiscent of the policies introduced under Lenin's NEP program of the 1920s. It is a high-risk economic strategy and, although initially greeted with huge enthusiasm, it has now run into difficulties. Promises of improved conditions for groups of workers, miners, and others have not been kept and there have been extensive strikes. Troubles with the nationalities have caused disruption in the rail system, leading to shortages at the workplace and in the shops. More important, the supply of consumer goods seems to be getting worse rather than better. A recent statement in the Congress of Deputies announced a budget deficit of 120 billion rubles. The Soviet Union has enormous resources but there must be some danger that relaxation of the old controls may plunge its economy into the same state as some Third World countries such as Brazil.

In 1990 the system of taxes will be altered to fit the changes in society. A powerful central bank will begin operation and businesses that are habitually loss-making will be forced out. In the next two years the large loss-making kolkoz will be closed, and private farms will be encouraged in their stead. In this stage the foreign exchange currency auction will be well established, as will commodity auctions and the foundations of the first Soviet stock exchange.

By 1995, if the plans progress, there should be a market regulated by interest rates and credit controls, and there could be a partially convertible ruble. There would then be a balanced consumer market with true competition. The country might have the fruits of *perestroika* at last.

INTERNATIONAL

The international association of socialist parties, founded to coordinate their policies. The First International was founded by Karl Marx in 1865, the Second International was established in 1889, and the Third, or Communist International, split from this and became the Moscow-based Comintern, while the Second International continued for a few years as an association of moderate socialist parties. In 1936 a number of small radical parties formed, under Leon Trotsky in exile, a Fourth International that never amounted to an effective body.

The International is celebrated in the song, often heard at socialist gatherings: "The *Internationale* unites the human race."

INTERNATIONAL TRADE

Stalin's "Socialism in one country" policy effectively meant that the USSR was to rely on its internal market to achieve its economic aims. There has always been resistance to becoming involved in the international marketplace, subject as it is to unpredictable forces. This resistance was increased after the war by the extension of the Soviet Empire into Eastern Europe and it was formalized by the founding of COMECON in 1949. Essentially a free-trade area though tilted quite strongly in favor of the USSR, COMECOM has the major advantage of trading within the entirely artificial "credit ruble" currency area.

The main exports to the West are primary products—oil and ores—though there is growing trade in industrial products such as the Lada car and scientific instruments. The main imports consist of the sophisticated technological products not available in the country but that are needed to develop its own industry. Food, particularly grain, is also imported when the harvests are poor. The overall position on trade is not dissimilar to what it was in the time of the czars, though under the new policy of *glasnost* a trade deficit of 50 billion rubles was acknowledged recently, the first time such an announcement had been made.

INTERVENTION

The intervention of the Allied forces in the civil war in Russia, from 1918 to 1920 or in 1925 in the civil war in the east. (See also CIVIL WAR.)

The Western Allies first landed at Murmansk, Archangel, Odessa, and Batum to secure communications with the anti-Bolshevik governments and to dislodge the Germans and Turks from territory they had gained as a result of the collapse of the Russian armies and the Brest-Litovsk Treaty.

Britain sent 40,000 troops to the northern ports and the Caspian and placed some along the Trans-Siberian Railway. The British conducted a blockade of Russia from October 1919 to January 1920, and brought supplies to Anton Denikin, including some tanks.

France had 30,000 troops, mainly based at Odessa, concentrating on the Crimea and southern Ukraine. A French military mission helped the Poles against the Soviet Russians.

Greece had 30,000 men in areas of

Turkish control, which led to war with Turkey. Under Kemal Ataturk's revived nationalism, the Greeks suffered severe defeats.

The United States provided some 10,000 soldiers who worked beside British and Japanese forces.

Japan, keen on exploiting the collapse of czarist Russia, had 60,000 troops in the Maritime Province until 1922 and on Sakhalin until 1925.

IRON CURTAIN

A phrase used by Winston Churchill in a speech at Fulton, Missouri, in the United States, March 5, 1946, to describe the political and military barrier dividing Eastern and Western Europe: "From Stettin on the Baltic to Trieste on the Adriatic, an iron curtain has descended across Europe." Earlier in 1945 Churchill had referred to an "iron fence" being put about Bucharest by the Soviets. (See also COLD WAR.)

JEWS IN THE SOVIET UNION

The Jews of the USSR are a nationality without a home republic. They settled in Eastern Europe before the first century A.D. In the seventh and eight centuries they settled among the Turkic Khazars between the Black and Caspian seas, on the trade routes from the East to Byzantium. They were so successful that the Khazars adopted the Jewish faith. In the 14th century, Jews settled widely in Poland, moving into Lithuania and the Ukraine, their skills as craftsmen and traders welcomed. However, since they were often forbidden to own land, they became associated with the ruling classes as their financiers and tax collectors, and were correspondingly hated.

In the mid-17th century, Cossack and Muscovite insurgents killed hundreds of thousands of Jews as an expression of their hatred of oppression by their rulers.

The fortunes of the Jewish people in Russia seesawed through the 19th century, moving between encouragement and suppression. A period of officially organized persecution started with the assassination of Czar Alexander II in 1871 and continued until 1917. Brutal pogroms became an accepted part of their life and drove many Jews into revolutionary activities or to emigrate to Western Europe, the United States and Palestine. Pogroms were not only officially encouraged, but officially carried out through the so-called Black Hundreds.

In 1917 many of the revolutionary leaders were Jewish, some experienced in conspiracy through the Bund and some trained in radical thinking by their alienation from bourgeois society. They included Yuli Martov, the Menshevik leader, as well as Leon Trotsky, Yacov Sverdlov, Lazar Kaganovich, Karl Radek, Grigory Zinoviev, and Lev Kamenev. In the course of the civil war, more massacres took place as Ukrainian nationalists, Cossacks, and others took advantage of the situation to revenge themselves. The Bolshevik regime, too, found that Jews could be an enemy, for many were prosperous capitalists. The propaganda against exploiters of the NEP often depicted the villainous Nepmen with grotesquely "Semitic" features. Stalin undoubtedly employed anti-Semitic tactics in his campaigns against Trotsky and then against Zinoviev and Kamenev.

In 1928 it was announced that a territory would be set aside for Jews in the Far East and a Jewish Autonomous Province was proclaimed in May 1934. Few settled there, but the Jewish subdivision of Birobidzhan remains an autonomous region in Russian Soviet Federal Socialist Republic.

There are several Jewish communities in the USSR. The best known are the Ashkenazi Jews living in the Baltic States, Belorussia, the Ukraine, and Moldavia and RSFSR. These are the people who suffered directly from the anti-Semitism of the Nazis and of the later anti-Zionist campaigns. Many are actively religious and Zionist, and many were the early Bund members and socialists. The Oriental Jewish communities are the long-standing groups of Georgia (some 50,000), Bokhara (about 100,000 Persian speakers who settled centuries ago along the Silk Road from China to the West), and the Mountain Jews of Dagestan in the Caucasus (some 20,000 speaking a Persian dialect called Tat). Jews total between 2 and 3 million on a broad count, but officially there are 1.8 million in the Soviet Union.

The synagogue was the center of Jewish life, but after the decree of January 23, 1918, the Soviets began closing synagogues and suppressing Jewish culture. There was a further campaign in 1927–28 and the Jewish commissar for foreign affairs was removed by Stalin during his dealings with Nazi Germany in 1939.

The Jewish people fought willingly and well for the Soviet Union during World War II. On the other hand, in the occupied areas of the Ukraine, Belorussia, the Baltic States, and in the Russian Soviet Federal Socialist Republic, Jews were the target of Nazi extermination teams, often abetted by anti-Soviet local inhabitants who reverted easily to anti-Semitism. One of the great tragedies of the war was the failure of Soviet authorities to realize the intensity of Nazi anti-Semitism and to evacuate or at least to warn Jews of their danger. The mass killing of Jews in Kiev was the subject of Yevgeny Yevtushenko's poem "Babi-Yar" (1962). In the German occupied areas all synagogues were destroyed and few were rebuilt after liberation.

The postwar era saw a new wave of anti-Semitism. Although during the war Jewish citizens had been encouraged to maintain a high profile as evidence of patriotism, Stalin saw their fund-raising ability from the United States as evidence of the infiltration of U.S. anti-Soviet ideas. In 1948 famous actor and leading member of the Jewish Anti-Fascist Committee, Solomon Mikhoels, who had had great success in fund-raising, was killed in a traffic accident arranged by the KGB, possibly on the instructions of Andrei Zhdanov. The peak of Stalin's pathological fear of Jews came with the "Doctors' Plot" of 1953, exposed only by Stalin's death. It seemed again that life for Jews in the Soviet Union might become secure.

On February 12, 1989, the first Jewish Cultural Center was opened in the presence of Edgar Bronfman, president of the World Jewish Council and Elie Wiesel, the 1986 Nobel Peace Prize winner. The center is dedicated to Solomon Mikhoels, the actor and community leader killed in 1948.

The number of synagogues has been variously reported from 100 to as few as 60. Official Soviet figures put the numbers who attend synagogues as very low (and point out that, in general, religious attendance is higher in rural areas and that 98 percent of Jews are city dwellers). However, in Tbilisi, Georgia, in the mountains of the Caucasus, and in Bokhara, Uzbekistan, synagogue attendance is admitted to reach 20 percent of the registered Jewish population. Soviet law and order demands that every "church" have a head, so the rabbi of the Moscow synagogue is usually quoted as the official voice of the Jewish religion.

While Soviet relations with the state of Israel were fairly good until June 1967, the Six-Day War altered matters. Soviet friendship with the Arab Middle East produced official hostility to Zionism, and in 1968 the issue of visas for Soviet Jews wishing to go to Israel began to be restricted. Jews held demonstrations of dissent and sit-ins, and appeals circulated within and outside the USSR, especially to the United States and the foreign press. To counter this the KGB harassed, suppressed, or arrested protesting groups. Harsh penalties were imposed on a group that attempted to hijack a plane in 1970.

Emigration has been at an average of 50,000 Jews a year, particularly reducing the number of surviving Baltic Jews and the Georgians. After 1970 the numbers were cut and in 1987 about 8,000 emigrated, with an increase in 1988 to nearly 20,000. A core of 9,000 people remain with permits refused year after year on the ground that they have knowledge of state secrets. The causes célèbres have been of the intellectuals from the old Russian communities.

A paradox has often been that some applicants for visas to emigrate to Israel have little feeling for Zionism, but strong feelings for the freedom of Western-style democracy. Also, emigration itself can lead to terrible frustration: working to build Israel is not the same as enjoying the fruits of U.S. democracy.

JULY DAYS

On July 3, 1917, soldiers, sailors from Kronstadt and workers, over 30,000 in all, demonstrated in Petrograd against the war and low wages, and to show their detestation of the Provisional Government. They had been called out by activists of the Petrograd Soviet to overthrow it, with the slogan "All Power to the Soviets." The Bolshevik leadership did not appear and some of the march was led by the Left Socialist Revolutionary Maria Spiridonova. Although there were rank and file Bolsheviks marching, Lenin and the Bolshevik leadership thought it premature. Leon Trotsky tried in vain to stop them, but the workers were dispersed by troops loyal to the Provisional Government. Troops and workers who followed the first wave found there was no general uprising and the day ended in disorder. Bolshevik leaders, including Zinoviev and Lenin went into hiding, Lenin taking refuge in Finland. The next day, after further disorders, the Provisional Government issued warrants for the arrest of the Bolsheviks, partly on the grounds of their supposed support of Germany.

On July 9, Prince Lvov resigned and Alexander Kerensky became prime minister. On July 12 the Provisional Government reintroduced capital punishment and court-martials for the army at the demand of Lavr Kornilov. The immediate result of the July Days was a hardening of the government's attitude toward the left.

KADETS

Constitutional Democrats, first named the Liberation party, were founded in Stuttgart in 1902, and renamed the

Kadets in 1905. It was a middle-class liberal party that would have fought the war against Germany to the end. In their eyes the revolution of 1905 had successfully transformed Russia. They saw a democratic parliamentary future with liberal capitalist economic policies ahead. They opposed the October Revolutionaries and were outlawed by the Bolsheviks at the end of 1917, particularly for their support of anti-Soviet activity in southern Russia.

Leading personalities of the Kadets were Prince Georgy Lvov (chairman of the Union of Zemstvos and Towns and head of the Provisional Government from February to July 1917), Prince Trubetskoy, Grigori Konovalov, Vasily Maklakov, and on their left, Viktor Nekrasov and right, Pavel Milyukov (a minister in Lvov's Provisional Government) and Fedor Kokoshkin.

KGB. See POLITICAL POLICE.

KAZAKH SOVIET SOCIALIST REPUBLIC

Population: 16,470,000; 36 percent Kazakh, 41 percent Russian, and 6 percent Ukrainian; there also are Uighur, German, and Korean settlements.

Area: 1,049,200 square miles (including 880 square miles transferred from Uzbekistan in 1971)

Capital: Alma-Ata; population, 1,108,000

This enormous area, rich in pasture and minerals, was taken into Imperial Russia late in the 19th century and colonized with Russians. Russians at that time called the Kazakhs "Kirghiz" (to distinguish them from Cossacks), and the Kirghiz they called "Kara-Kirghiz."

The 1916 wartime decree that extended conscription to all peoples (previously the subject peoples of the empire had not been included) led to the July 1916 revolt of the Kazakhs. It was put down with the loss of 150,000 local people, some killed by the punitive force sent there and some by the Russian colonists, many thousands of whom were also killed.

The 1917 February Revolution unleashed a Kazakh nationalist movement, the Alash Orda, which threatened to throw the new Russians out. There were three Kazakh conferences, in April, July, and December, but they attracted no outside support. The Kolchak government claimed power, but by the end of 1919 Moscow-equipped troops were gaining control. On July 10, 1920, Lenin signed a decree creating a Kirghiz Revolutionary Committee and, with Red Army help, liquidated all its nationalist opponents. These events combined to force large numbers of Kirghiz to move into Chinese territory. A Kirghiz Autonomous Soviet Socialist Republic was formed on August 26, 1920. The republic became the Kazakh Autonomous Socialist Republic in 1925 and on December 5, 1936, it became a full Soviet socialist republic within the USSR.

Kazakh Bolsheviks were very rare and many Kazakhs moved with their herds away from the new power, into Chinese Turkestan or Afghanistan. The depredations of Russian settlers, the White Army, and the Red commissars caused famine and about 1 million deaths from 1921 to 1922.

One of the most dramatic developments under Soviet rule was the completion of the Turksib Railway, started in 1913 but completed with the five-year plan in 1930. It linked the industries of Tashkent with the Trans-Siberian Railway through Orenburg.

Russification and collectivization ran into serious difficulties in the 1930s, and Lazar Kaganovitch was sent there in 1932 to clear up the situation. As a result, nomadic peoples, once they joined the collective system, were officially allowed to own flocks of sheep, goats, horses, and camels. Official collectivization was not completed until 1937. Purges took a great toll of all Kazakh leaders. During World War II large numbers of Germans, Jews, and Chechens were evacuated (or deported) to Kazakhstan. The resentment against this influx caused continual unrest and in 1954 Pantelimon Ponomarenko was sent as party first secretary from Moscow. Brezhnev was also there as second secretary and then as first secretary, 1955–1956.

Khrushchev's 1954 Virgin Lands policy for grain production was most vigorously followed in Kazakhstan. Twenty-five million hectares of the 42 million plowed between 1954 and 1960 were in Kazakhstan, where intensive farming has threatened the land with erosion.

Riots in 1986 in Alma-Ata have foreshadowed a growing nationalist sentiment against immigrant labor to the oil fields. In 1989, oil workers' caravans were burnt by Kazakh rioters. In September 1989 there were interracial riots at Semipalatinsk; shortly afterwards a political movement there demanded the end of nuclear testing. In recognition of the growth of nationalism, the Kazakh language was given status as the official language of the republic.

KIRGHIZ SOVIET SOCIALIST REPUBLIC

Population (1988): 4,238,000; 48 percent Kirghiz, 26 percent Russian, 12 percent Uzbek, with other peoples, including Ukrainians, Germans, Tatars, and Kazakhs
Area: 76,642 square miles
Capital: Frunze; population, 632,000

Czarist Russia encouraged Russian immigration into the Kirghiz area, the khanate of Kokand. The practice continued under Soviet rule, the very capital being renamed after a Russian.

The Kirghiz, known then as "Kara-Kirghiz" (while the Kazakhs were called "Kirghiz" by the Russians) were included in the Turkestan Autonomous Soviet Socialist Republic controlled from Tashkent until 1924, when, still part of the Russian Soviet Federal Socialist Republic, it was made the Kara-Kirghiz Autonomous Province. In 1925 this became the Kirghiz Autonomous Soviet Socialist Republic and on December 5, 1936, the Kirghiz Soviet Socialist Republic was made a full union republic.

Attempts by the Kirghiz to establish their national identity started with the commandant of the Kokand garrison rallying forces to oppose the Red Army in 1919; these forces became the Basmachis, or anti-Bolshevik partisans. The revolt ended with the killing of Enver Pasha in 1922, and the Basmachis fought only as small local bands until 1929 when they gained strength in opposition to land collectivization.

Soviet economic policy required the traditional nomads to settle, with the result that their herds of cattle, sheep, and goats declined catastrophically. A group of Kirghiz Communists, "The Thirty," presented the party with a list of criticisms, principally against the importation of Russian officials. They were removed from all posts, expelled from the party, and some exiled. Any survivors were later victims of the purge.

KOLKHOZ

Producers cooperatives formed by combining the land of formerly independent peasants or from confiscated estate lands. They were the main instrument used by Stalin in his mass collectivization program begun in 1929, which took the number of collectivized peasant households from 1.7 percent in 1928 to 90 percent in 1936. The Kolkhoz Congress of 1935 defined it as: "A voluntary cooperative whose members had pooled their means of production in order to produce in common. Members ran their own affairs, and elected their management committee." However, in practice this democratic element was curtailed because the kolkhoz had to obey instructions from the local party organization. Payment of members depended upon the *trudoni* (workday units) worked by each man. At this stage roughly two-thirds of the produce went to the state either in direct procurements or in payment to the Machine Tractor Stations (MTS). Payments in cash to the members were dependent upon prices paid by the government, usually low, and were subject to taxes, insurance, and so on.

The Kolkhoz Congress gave legal recognition to the right of the kolkhoz household to hold and farm a private plot limited to approximately a half-hectare, on which they could keep a cow, a pig, and four sheep. Some of this produce could be sold in the marketplace. In practice, as much as 60 percent of all Soviet meat and vegetable produce has traditionally been produced from this private-sector agriculture since the time of the 1917 Revolution.

The number and size of the kolkhoz grew steadily throughout the time of Stalin and reached a peak of 125,000 units in 1950. By 1965 their number had declined to 36,000, partly by amalgamation but also by conversion to sovkhoz. (See also SOVKHOZ.)

KOMSOMOL

The All-Union Leninist Youth Organization founded in 1918. It now covers 18- to 28-year-olds. Apart from receiving intensive political education, the Komsomol are called on to act as responsible citizens and are sometimes used as an auxiliary force, patrolling on special occasions. Enrollment is voluntary but membership, which was over 40 million in the 1980s, can lead to party membership and the possibility of a career through the party. Younger children are members of the Pioneers, a politically oriented organization not unlike the scouts in other countries.

KORNILOV AFFAIR

General Lavr Kornilov, appointed commander-in-chief of the army in place of Alexei Brusilov in July 1917 by Alexander Kerensky and greeted as a hero and savior by many, had insisted on an end to Kerensky's wasteful offensive against the Germans. In August he demanded extra powers to control the anarchic situation after the July Days. On August 27–29 troops were observed moving toward Petrograd, and Kerensky suspected them to be part of a coup de'état. The reason for the moves remains obscure, but Kerensky ordered the arrest of Kornilov and other generals. Kornilov claimed he was acting in the defense of the Russian people, with no political ambition. As Kornilov's cavalry approached Petrograd, the people began to see the Red Guards as their defense against a military counterrevolution. But Kornilov submitted to arrest and along with other generals was moved to a barracks in Bykhov. Their detention lasted from September to the beginning of December, when Kornilov and his fellow officers made their escape and went south to join the new anti-Bolshevik Whites; Kornilov himself was killed the next year.

The effect of the affair was to remove army support from the Provisional Government and to open the way for the October Revolution.

KPK

Commission of Party Control, set up in 1934 to replace the TsKK, or Central Control Commission. In 1952 it was reorganized under the party's Central Committee.

KREMLIN

The term for the main fortress of a Russian city. The Moscow Kremlin, built in the 15th century and added to continuously since then, with a cathedral and a mid-19th-century palace, has been the seat of government since 1918. Red Square is on one side of the Kremlin.

KRESTY PRISON

The St. Petersburg prison used, for example, for the Kronstadt sailors taken in the July Days.

KRONSTADT

This fortified city on an island 30 kilometers west of Leningrad was the principal base of the czarist Baltic fleet. In 1917 there were some 80,000 people there—sailors, garrison soldiers (mostly artillerymen), officials, and artisans. There were several minor mutinies during the war and in February 1917, hearing the news of the Petrograd revolution, the sailors seized and shot 80 hated officers and policemen. The sailors, in the hands of a Soviet of Military Deputies, supported the Socialist Revolutionaries, the Mensheviks, and the Provisional Government. Gradually the balance of political grouping in the Soviet moved from right to left. While the right wing of the Provisional Government was never represented there, initially there were only 11 Bolsheviks among the 280 deputies, but by August there were 96. Kronstadt remained an independent community; it had its own newspaper and managed to help feed itself with its socialized kitchen gardens then and during the hard years to come.

After the failure of the June 1917 offensive, the sailors became hostile to the government and on July 4, 12,000 sailors with working men and women landed at Petrograd to join in what had initially been a Bolshevik-inspired demonstration. The march turned into chaos and the Kronstadt men returned dispirited and alienated from Petrograd. In their frustration with the July Days, some Petrograd soldiers even believed that the Kronstadt sailors were in the pay of the enemy, Germany.

The Kronstadt community's dislike of and lack of trust in Alexander Kerensky grew, and the community became a major force in the October Revoluton.

On October 25, 1917, at the call of the Petrograd Military Revolutionary Committee, some 5,000 sailors and soldiers landed in the city, occupied key posts, and stormed the Winter Palace, the seat of the Provisional Government. A further 3,000 men were landed in the next four days. Kronstadt became the October Revolution's major source of troops, ammunition, and even food.

Felix Dzerzhinsky ordered Kronstadt's prisons to be used for prisoners of the revolution, and Lenin ordered hoarders and saboteurs to be sent there. Loyal and secure as it was, Kronstadt was not a Bolshevik town. "All Power to the Soviets" was its slogan, and its ruling coalition included Bolshevik, Menshevik, and Left Socialist Revolutionaries.

Between June 14 and 20, 1918, the Menshevik and Right Socialist Revolutionaries were expelled from the Kronstadt Soviet, as they were from all Russian Soviets after the Mirbach assassination. Its multiparty democracy faded, and about 300 officers were summarily executed.

In June 1919 the advance of General Nicholas Yudenich's northwestern White Army forced the evacuation of over 16,000 women and children. In the panic the mainland fortress of Krasnaia Gorka, part of the Kronstadt garrison, mutinied and defected. It was recaptured on June 16, and a purge began of Kronstadt; hundreds of the garrison were shot after brief court-martials. The Bolshevik party grew in numbers and took firm control.

By January 1921 Kronstadt still had 50,000 inhabitants and was regarded as a loyal stronghold of the regime. It was organized and well fed. Petrograd, in contrast, was starving. On February 27 a delegation of Kronstadt sailors visited the city and returned to report the failure of the Bolshevik rule and to demand a nonparty conference. The next day the sailors of the battleship *Petropavlovsk* passed a resolution calling for free elections of new soviets, freedom of speech, the liberation of all socialist political prisoners, equal rations for all, and full rights for land-holding peasants and small industrialists who were not employers. On March 1 Mikhail Kalinin, the nominal head of state, went to the island to appeal to the sailors and to warn them. The outcome was a mass meeting that elected a non-Bolshevik Revolutionary Committee. Kronstadt was at once blockaded.

On March 8 an attempt to take the island failed, and Mikhai Tukhachevsky and Lev Kamenev mobilized a force of upwards of 50,000 men that, on March 17–18, under heavy machine gun and artillery fire, went over the ice to enter the fortress. Eight thousand sailors escaped to Finland, thousands others were drafted to other naval units or labor camps, and hundreds were rounded up and shot. It was the end of Kronstadt as a revolutionary force.

KRUG

A Cossack council, similar to a soviet or a rada, many of which were formed in the emergencies of 1917–1919.

KULAK

Literally "fist," a term used for a wealthy peasant. Kulaks were encouraged by the New Economic Policy from 1921 to the fury of old-guard Bolsheviks, but with the support of Stalin, who saw them as an element in building "Socialism in one country" and by Bukharin, who wanted their integration into the economy without force as the only ones who were producing a surplus. However, with the program of collectivization, the kulaks again became objects of hatred, and many were sent to camps or executed when their lands were taken. (See also COLLECTIVIZATION.)

KURSK, BATTLE OF

The biggest tank battle in the history of warfare took place in and around Kursk, a town in central Russia, southwest of Moscow, from July 5 to August 23, 1943.

By the winter of 1942 the German forces had formed a salient around Kursk and had consolidated their positions. To regain the initiative, Hitler had decided on a massive offensive in the summer of 1943 on the Central Front, using the salient as a springboard. The offensive was code-named *Operation Citadel* and the German forces earmarked for it were the 9th and 2nd armies of Army Group Center, commanded by Field Marshal Gunther von Kluge and the 4th Panzer Army and the Battle Task Force of Army Group South, commanded by Field Marshal Erich von Manstein. The German forces consisted of 900,000 men, 10,000 guns, and 2,700 tanks, including the latest Tiger and Panther models and the new, heavily armored Ferdinand tank-hunters—nearly all the tanks available. Among the 2,000 aircraft were the powerful Focke-Wulf 190 fighters.

The Soviet armies were under the overall command of Marshals Georgi Zhukov and Alexander Vasilevsky, though naturally all important decisions were cleared with Stalin as commander-in-chief.

Von Kluge's forces on the north face of the salient were opposed by Marshal

Konstantin Rokossovsky's Central Front armies, while von Manstein's forces in the South were confronted by General Nikolai Vatutin's units.

The total Soviet forces consisted of 1.3 million men, 20,000 guns, 3,600 tanks and self-propelled guns, and 2,800 aircraft. The armor consisted of the latest versions of the T34s, the SU medium, and the heavy KV tanks. The aircraft included YAK-9 and LA-7 fighters and IL-10 ground-attack planes.

At the Battle of Kursk the German Luftwaffe was to have swept the sky clear for the army's advance, but the Red Air Force withstood this and attacked the German air bases while harassing the assembling troops. On the day of the German attack, July 5, the Soviets sent in a wave of ground-attack planes but these were countered by a prepared massive force of Messerschmitt and Focke-Wulf fighters, shooting the Red Air Force down in hundreds and claiming over 600 in two days. But the Germans found the pace difficult to maintain, and the Soviets continued to attack the German Panzers with IL-10 Stormoviks en masse. By the start of the counterattack on July 12, huge air reserves had been brought in and the Soviet armor rolled forward. The Luftwaffe's command of the sky had been only local and temporary.

Von Kluge's 2nd and 9th armies launched a powerful offensive at the north face of the salient on July 5, but succeeded only in creating a limited wedge between the Soviet armies. The 9th Army lost two-thirds of its tanks and had to switch to a defensive role. On the southern face, von Manstein made more progress; advances up to 35 kilometers were achieved quite rapidly and heavy casualties were inflicted on Vatutin's forces, but Stalin agreed under pressure to allow Rotmistrov's 5th Guards Tank Army consisting of 800 T34s to go to his rescue.

From July 9 to 12, in the area around Prokhorovka a huge tank engagement took place. More than 1,500 tanks and self-propelled guns were in action, and the fighting close in was not to the advantage of the German Tigers and Ferdinands, which were faced with the Russian antitank artillery, their ground-attack aircraft, and the massive blasts from their Katyusha rocket launchers. Over 350 tanks and 10,000 of von Manstein's 4th Panzer Army were lost and his advance halted.

The force of the German advance was spent, and now General Vatutin's armies from the Voronezh Front and Ivan Konev's men from the Steppe Front strongly counterattacked and drove them back to their start line. This attack was followed by Generals Vasilii Sokolovski and Markian Popov, who attacked on the Orel Front and penetrated to a depth of 25 kilometers. The Soviet offensive then developed on a broad front and included Marshal Rokossovsky's Center Front forces. By July 16 the Germans were forced to desert their Orel base.

By August 3, a further counter-offensive was developed by Marshal R. I. Malinovsky's units. German forces amounting to 18 divisions, including four Panzer divisions were forced to retreat and the 1st Tank and 6th Guards armies together covered 100 kilometers and took the town of Bogodukhov. By August 11, the Voronezh Front forces under General Vatutin had cut the Kharkov-Poltava road. The Germans counterattacked but without success. By August 22 Kharkov had been cleared of enemy forces and the whole southern wing of the German forces was threat-

ened, thus allowing the Soviets to go to a general offensive. This permitted them later in the year to liberate the left flank of the Ukraine and reach the Dnieper River.

The Soviets were much assisted by the action of partisans in the rear of the German armies, who destroyed locomotives and derailed military trains in large numbers. Their activities obliged the Luftwaffe to keep its supply and repair bases far behind in Poland, letting the Soviets obtain air supremacy.

Kursk was the last major German offensive of the Russo-German war and the beginning of the end for the Wehrmacht as a triumphant military machine.

LABOR CAMPS. See Camps.

LATVIAN RIFLES

The First Latvian Rifle Regiment was formed in 1915 during World War I, when the battle front was in that territory. From this, two battalions of former czarist soldiers were formed by the Provisional Government as a locally employed force. They held part of Latvia against German occupation in 1917 and prevented a German advance on Petrograd. A number of them were in the Smolny Institute guard in the October Revolution and many joined the Red Army.

LATVIAN SOVIET SOCIALIST REPUBLIC
(See also Baltic States.)

Population: 2,673,000; 54 percent Latvian, 33 percent Russian, 8 percent Belorussian and Ukrainian
Area: 24,695 square miles
Capital: Riga; population, 900,000

For the earlier history of Latvia, see
BALTIC STATES. The most Russianized of
the three Baltic States, in November
1988 its Supreme Soviet decided not
to push for full autonomy as the Estonians
had. However, in March 1989 a demonstration by independent groups outside party headquarters was broken up
savagely by the militia. In the election
to the All-Union Congress, the Popular
Front candidates and their allies took 26
of the 30 seats. The prime minister was
among the defeated candidates, but the
party secretary, Janis Vagris, was elected
a delegate, as was Anatoli Gorbunov,
the Supreme Soviet president, backed
by the Popular Front, and a former
general in Afghanistan, Fiodor Kuzmine.
The largest majority went to the nationalist leader Dainis Evans and another
large majority to Yuri Dobelius, who
had campaigned for outright independence for Latvia.

The population's split is exemplified
by the two extremist groups: the LNNK
(National Independence Movement of
Latvia), claiming the illegality of the
Soviet takeover in 1939, and the opposing Russian organization Interfront, which
has strong support among the immigrant workers.

LEAGUE OF NATIONS

The international body formed after
World War I, which the USSR regarded
as a capitalist-imperialist body. The
USSR joined the league in 1934 but
left it at the end of 1939, after it was
condemned for its invasion of Finland.

LEFT DEVIATIONISTS

The name given by Stalinists to the
party group led from 1918 by Bukharin
and from 1923 by Trotsky, which believed
in world revolution, opposed the New
Economic Plan, and was against Stalin's
policy of building "Socialism in one
country."

LEND-LEASE

Supplies given to the USSR during
World War II by the United States on
credit terms. After the war the USSR
refused to make the token payments that
the United States demanded.

LENIN PRIZES

Prizes on the model of Nobel Prizes,
given annually since 1925 to outstanding scientists, artists, and other people.
Thirty prizes are awarded every two
years. While many winners have been
meritworthy, the prize has frequently
been awarded to politicians. Leonid
Brezhnev awarded himself the prize
and the hardline Ukrainian Vladimir
Shcherbitsky, who was dropped from
the Politburo in 1989, was given the
prize in 1982.

LENINGRAD AFFAIR

The purge of 1950. To honor the hero-
ism of the people of Leningrad after the
World War II siege, a suggestion was
made that the capital of the Russian
Soviet Federal Socialist Republic be
moved there from Moscow. Stalin, always uneasy about the party in Leningrad,
thought this might be a challenge to his
national power through a "Leningrad
faction." When Andrei Zhdanov, Leningrad's wartime leader, died in 1948, he
sent Georgy Malenkov there on the pretext of investigating the election of city
officials. The new mayor, Markian Popov,

and his predecessor, Kuznetsov, were accused of plotting to set up a separate Russian Communist party, tried by a special tribunal, and shot in September 1950. At least 200 others who had been prominent in Leningrad's siege were also shot. This was one of the disgraceful episodes exposed by Nikita Khrushchev in his address to the 20th Party Congress.

LIBERALS

The party in the Duma particularly associated with the zemstvo (local elected assemblies with limited administrative powers) and the large bureaucratic class who strove for constitutional change and political liberty.

LITHUANIAN SOVIET SOCIALIST REPUBLIC
(See also BALTIC STATES.)

Population: 3,682,000; 80 percent Lithuanian, 9 percent Russian, 7 percent Polish, 2 percent Belorussian
Area: 26,173 square miles
Capital: Vilnuis; population, 566,000

For the earlier history of Lithuania, see BALTIC STATES. On October 23, 1988, Cardinal Vincentas Sladkevicius celebrated mass at Vilnius cathedral, newly opened after over 30 years' use as an exhibition gallery. Vilnius had been regained from Poland by Lithuania as a result of boundary changes made by the Soviet Union after World War II. Kaunas, the former capital, is now the second city with a population of 450,000.

Sajudis, the Lithuanian Movement to Support Perestroika, had held its inaugural congress the day before and 200,000 people assembled, singing patriotic songs, waving the old Lithuanian flag of yellow, green, and red, and chanting "*Lietuva, Lietuva*" (Lithuania, Lithuania). On September 28, 1988, 10,000 people had turned out and been faced by riot police acting under orders of the party secretary; the next month he was replaced by Algirdas Brazauskas, Sajudis has 1.5 million names on its petitions urging total sovereignty.

A more extreme nationalist group, the Lithuanian Freedom League, demanded full independence at the rally, but the Sajudis, committed to working with the party, stopped short of secession from the USSR, preferring a looser federation with economic independence for each republic. Lithuania, however, feels less threatened by Russification than do the other two Baltic States.

In March 1989, Sajudis won a clear majority of the 39 seats in Congress, with both Brazauskas, the party secretary, and his deputy elected, while the sitting president and prime minister were defeated. The Sajudis chairman Vytautas Landisbergis also was elected.

The government under Brazauskas has agreed to consider reopening the University of Kaunas (closed by Stalin in 1950). It would operate in the Lithuanian language and would concentrate on modern subjects such as information technology and ecology as well as subjects otherwise neglected, including sociology and psychiatry. Other Baltic States have agreed to ensure its functioning.

In November 1989, the Lithuanian Supreme Court passed a bill enabling a referendum on matters of vital public interest, to be held at the request of either half the republic's parliament or 10 percent—300,000—of its citizens. This was seen in Moscow as a step toward secession.

In elections to its new congress in March 1990 Vytautis Landsbergis defeated Algirdas Brazauskas, the leader of the break-away Communist party, for the post of chairman by 91 votes to 42 and Sajudis obtained two-thirds of the seats. Although the head of Gosplan warned that the USSR might demand the repayment of seven billion rubles, on March 11 the congress declared its independence, by 124 votes to nil. The USSR Congress of Deputies immediately voted, by a heavy majority, that this declaration had no legal force.

MACHINE TRACTOR STATIONS (MTS)

These units had no land of their own to farm. Their purpose was to service the kolkhoz with tractors and other machinery. Devised by A. M. Markevich, manager of a state farm near Odessa in 1927 who perished in the purges, they were under the jurisdiction of the commissariat of agriculture and were normally divided into a number of tractor brigades. At their peak in 1954 there were nearly 9,000 MTSs employing an average of 3,000 workers each.

Until 1934 each MTS had a political department that kept watch over the orthodoxy of the kolkhoz it serviced, but these were then abolished. In 1958 Khrushchev abolished the MTSs and ordered the kolkhoz to purchase their equipment. It was a part of his policy to make the kolkhoz more self-reliant and therefore more productive. (See also AGRICULTURE.)

MARINSKY PALACE

The office of the Provisional Government in Petrograd until it moved to the Winter Palace in August 1917.

MARSHALL PLAN

The U.S. secretary of state, General George Marshall, proposed on June 5, 1947, a plan for U.S. aid for postwar European recovery. Under Anglo-French leadership, plans were made that led, in 1948, to a $17 billion program and the Organization for European Economic Cooperation. The Soviet Union suspected the terms meant the economic dominance of the West and refused offers to take part, adding to the growing East-West split in Europe. It was the Yugoslav acceptance of Marshall Plan aid terms that led to that country's break with the Soviet Union.

MARXISM IN RUSSIA

Karl Marx never carried out a detailed study of conditions in Russia but, in general, he and Engels seemed to have believed that it was the absence of private property in Russian villages that was the basis for the tyrannical government in the country.

The populist view, held by the Narodniks and their heirs, the Socialist Revolutionaries, was that the "commune" formed the basis for a special kind of Russian socialism. This idea had been entirely rejected by the Liberation of Labor group, founded in Geneva in 1883 by Georgy Plekhanov, Pavel Axelrod, Lev Deutsch, and others. Marx's views on this matter were not entirely clear, though he seemed to favor the Socialist Revolutionary view. To avoid difficulties, he said that his predictions were based on an analysis of fully capitalist societies.

Both Engels and Marx seemed to have held to the conviction that whatever form it took, revolution was what

Russia really needed and certainly would have.

Plekhanov and his group believed that Russia would have to pass through a capitalist stage before a revolution would be possible. In contrast, Lenin, who had been converted to Marxism in Kazan while at the university, had quite early come to the view that capitalism existed in the Russian village because of the exploitation of poor peasants by richer ones. This being the case, there was no necessity for Russia to pass through a more complete capitalist phase of development. This was all spelled out in *What Is to Be Done*, published in 1902, as are also the Leninist additions to Marx, which called for the awakening of a revolutionary consciousness in the masses by trained professional revolutionary leaders. Lenin's subsequent writings formed a canon that is the basis of so-called Marxist-Leninism.

MAXIMALISTS

A splinter group of the Socialist Revolutionaries. They believed in terrorism in political action, and many were arrested and executed when they attempted to kill Peter Stolypin, the minister of interior in 1907. They were usually identified as being near to the Bolsheviks with whom they collaborated in 1917, but were later persecuted as enemies and the party ceased to exist by 1920.

MENSHEVIKS

The non-Leninist "minority" faction of the Social Democrats in 1903 when Lenin divided the party (see BOLSHEVIKS), but later they were in fact the majority of the Social Democrats. They were divided into three groups: Internationalists,

who were against the war on the principle that it was not in the people's interest and agreed with the Bolsheviks on many issues; the Right, who took part in the Petrograd Soviet and in Lvov's Provisional Government in May 1917; and the "Defensists," who supported the war patriotically and thus stood to the right of most Mensheviks.

Prominent among the Mensheviks, were: Internationalists Yuli Martov and Nikolai Sukhanov (a journalist who had left the Socialist Revolutionaries and joined Martov in 1917); Right: Nikolai Chkheidze, (chairman of the Petrograd Soviet), Fedor Dan and Irakly Tsereteli (both prominent in the Petrograd Soviet, the latter taking a post in Lvov's Provisional Government in May 1917); and "Defensists" Georgy Plekhanov, Lev Deutsch, Vera Zasulich, and Breido.

The Mensheviks formed a separate party in August 1917. They included followers of Trotsky, who led their Internationalist wing. The party was suppressed in 1922 and survivors figured in a show trial in 1930.

METROPOL HOTEL

The temporary seat of the Bolshevik government in Moscow in 1918.

MGB. See POLITICAL POLICE.

MILITARY REVOLUTIONARY COMMITTEE (MRC)

An ad-hoc committee set up by the Petrograd Soviet on October 12, 1917, to control troop movements. It was dissolved on December 18, having been superseded by the Defense Council under the Sovnarkom.

MILITIA

The civil police, so-called from February 1917 in preference to the term "police," which had been made unpopular by their support of czarist rule, under the MVD (Ministry of Internal Affairs), and under the immediate control of the local soviet.

MOLDAVIAN SOVIET SOCIALIST REPUBLIC

Population: 4,224,000; 64 percent of the inhabitants speak Rumanian, 14 percent are Ukrainian, 13 percent Russian, and the remaining 9 percent are a mixture of Jews, Germans, Bulgarians, and Turkic Christian Gagauzians.
Area: 13,012 square miles
Capital: Kishinev; population, 663,000

A full Soviet republic since 1944, previously part of Bessarabia, Moldavia was a disputed Rumanian-speaking area on the edge of the Russian Empire, which, as with the Baltic States, was included in the secret protocols of the Russo-German pact of 1939 as part of the Soviet sphere of influence.

There was a small Moldavian Autonomous Soviet Socialist Republic within the Ukrainian Soviet Socialist Republic, but modern Moldavia was annexed and added to it by the Soviet Union on August 2, 1940. But when Rumania joined Hitler's 1941 invasion, the area was made part of Rumania and there were mass deportations.

Since its formation, Soviet policy in Moldavia has worked to distinguish it from its Rumanian neighbor and to emphasize its historical authenticity. The Cyrillic alphabet has been imposed on the Moldavian language, which is a dialect of Rumanian.

In 1988 the small Democratic Movement in Support of Perestroika, led by Yuri Rozhka, was accused of stirring up ethnic tension and merely imitating movements in the Baltic States. It also called for re-latinization of the Moldavian language.

Other recent movements include: the Green Movement, which argues against insensitive central planning from Moscow; the Alexei Mateyvich Movement (named after a Moldavian author), which demands the deportation of non-Moldavian "undesirables"; and the League of Students, whose pro-*perestroika* meeting in November 1988 was savagely broken up. The latter meeting was followed by another meeting at which 6,000 or more Moldavians demanded the rewriting of Moldavian history, the revision of the alphabet, and the return of university buildings from government use. The Moldavian Popular Front, formed in May 1989 under the auspices of the Writers' Union, aroused a contrasting pro-Russian Yedinstvo International Movement, urging the retention of the Russian language and Cyrillic script.

In January 1989 the authorities gave way to the growing pressure and recommended that Moldavian be made the official language and that consideration be given to using the Roman alphabet; in September this was put into effect. To add to national demands, the 140,000-member Turkic Christian Gagauzian minority are asking for autonomous status.

There was violent rioting in November 1989 followed by more riots demanding the release of nationalist protesters who had been arrested earlier. As a result of the disturbances, the former party secretary was replaced with a younger, Moldavian man.

MONARCHISTS

The Duma party that supported direct rule by the czar led by men such as Vasily Shulgin, who left Russia in 1918 but with patriotic emotion returned at the victory of World War II in 1945 and was sent to a labor camp.

MONGOLIA

Population: 2,093,000
Area: 604,247 square miles
Capital: Ulan Bator; population, 488,000

The plateau region in East Central Asia that was the original home of the Mongols, whose 13th-century empire reshaped Asia and eastern Europe. After the decline of the Mongol khanates, the area became subject to the Chinese Empire. In the 19th century the Russians moved in as Chinese central power decayed, and Mongolia and Manchuria became regarded as part of Russia's rightful sphere of influence.

In the turmoil of the Russian Revolution, an area of Mongolia administered by the czarist empire but abandoned by officials was declared the People's Republic of Tannu Tuva. The territory of Mongolia, after Baron Ungern-Sternberg had used it as a base for his own imperial ambitions, was established as the People's Republic of Mongolia under Soviet protection in July 1921. The religious city of Urga was renamed Ulan Bator and became the capital.

When the Japanese penetrated beyond Manchuria in 1938, there was a brief clash, but in 1939 another confrontation resulted in an undeclared six-week war. The Red Army was superior to the Japanese, causing the Japanese to gain a respect for the Soviets that added to their determination to stay out of the 1941–1945 war; it also provided the Soviet Union with an experienced army that would come to the rescue of the nation in the winter of 1941–42.

The postwar agreements included holding a plebiscite that confirmed the country's independence as Outer Mongolia, and a series of Sino-Soviet treaties have maintained this. Tannu Tuva (one of the postage stamp collector's joys) became an autonomous region in 1944 and since 1961 is Tuva Autonomous Soviet Socialist Republic in the Russian Soviet Federal Socialist Republic.

Mongolia has remained firmly under Soviet control, and although the nomads have been formally collectivized, the country is still thinly populated (1.9 million people in 600,000 square miles) with nomad cattlemen and with little industry. However in March 1990 crowds in Ulan Bator demonstrated demanding the resignation of the party. A revised Communist party, the Mongolian People's Revolutionary Party, was formed, but other groups, including the Mongolian Democratic Party have emerged and elections have been promised.

In 1989 the Soviet Union began withdrawing its troops from Mongolia, aiming to have the bulk, but not all, out during 1990.

MOSCOW TRIBUNE

A group formed in 1988 by intellectuals, among them Andrei Sakharov, to urge radical political reform in the USSR.

MRC. See Military Revolutionary Committee.

MUSAVAT

The socialist-nationalist political Equality party, founded in Azerbaijan in 1911.

MUSIC

In 1907 a Festival of Russian Music was staged in Paris by Sergei Diaghilev. He was a brilliant impresario and in 1909 he put on a production of Alexander Borodin's *Prince Igor* in which the dancers attracted as much attention as the singers. Over the next four years he scored an incredible success with his ballet company, for which he commissioned works by Igor Stravinsky such as *Firebird*, *Petruska*, and the *Rite of Spring*. He also introduced the sensational dancer Vaslav Nijinsky in Claude Debussy's *Après Midi d'un Faune*. Largely through Diaghilev's efforts, Russian music and ballet had achieved an international reputation.

The October Revolution and the civil war at first produced chaotic conditions for Russian music, with no fuel for concert halls and no money to pay the salaries of staff at the conservatories. But under the policies of the NEP and the flexible and imaginative guidance of Anatoly Lunacharsky, commissar of education and the arts, there seemed to be a real future for freedom and imaginative experimentation in music. The Association for Contemporary Music, set up in 1923 by Nikolai Miaskovsky, Victor Belayev, and Pavel Lamm, encouraged all this. But by 1932 Lunacharsky was gone, the association was dissolved, and the Union of Soviet Composers was established with its requirement that

music have a socialist content and be expressed in a mode readily understood by the masses. Thus the work of Arnold Schönberg, Paul Hindemith, and Richard Strauss were banished. This step effectively cut Russian music off from the developments that were taking place in the rest of the world and led to a certain provincialism, of which Sergei Prokoviev had warned before he went to America.

During the years of repression under Stalin and his cultural henchman Andrei Zhdanov, conventional composers such as Dmitry Kabalevsky, Vissarion Shebalin, and Nikolai Miaskovsky were content to turn out approved works, but all the major talents—Sergei Prokoviev, Dmitry Shostakovich, and Aram Khachaturian— had difficulties with the authorities. Prokoviev had returned to Russia in 1933 but although his *Love for Three Oranges* was tremendously popular, his *Cantata for the 20th Anniversary of the Soviet Revolution* was not performed until 1966. His successes, like the score of *Alexander Nevsky* and the *Second Violin Concerto*, were undoubtedly more accessible musically.

Shostakovich, by no means a rebel, was attacked in *Pravda* a few days after Stalin had seen a performance of his opera *Lady Macbeth of Mtsensk District*. Khachaturian had fewer problems in that his naturally folk-based musical language was in little danger of being attacked for formal elements.

After Stalin's death the loosening of political control of the arts made no enormous difference to the musical world. Nikita Khrushchev himself said in a speech in 1963, "We stand for melodious music with content, music that stirs people and gives rise to strong feelings, and we are against cacophony." It was clear that the Soviet Union was no place for dodecaphony or serialism. Today, there are contemporary composers in the Soviet Union who are more in touch with the musical idioms of the West, such as Rodion Shchedrin, whose *Second Symphony* was enormously popular. In Moscow avant-garde composers such as Denisov and Volkonsky are highly thought of critically, but little of their music is played in the West.

MVD

Ministry of Internal Affairs, which controls the ordinary police. (See also POLITICAL POLICE.)

NARKOMFIN

The People's Commissariat of Finance.

NARKOMINDEL

The People's Commissariat for Foreign Affairs.

NARKOMNATS

The People's Commissariat for Nationalities.

NARKOMPROD

The People's Commissariat of Food Supply.

NARKOMVNUTORG

The People's Commissariat of Domestic Trade.

NARODNAYA VOLYA

"The People's Will", a revolutionary group formed in 1879, which believed in violent means to seize power and the killing of senior officials. They were responsible for the assassination of Czar Alexander II in 1881. Lenin's elder brother was a member and his section attempted the murder of Czar Alexander III. Most of its members joined the Socialist Revolutionaries, but some joined the Social Democrats.

NARODNIKS

"Men of the People" (see also NARODNAYA VOLYA), the name used beginning in the 1870s for socialists who appealed directly to the people and hoped for a peasant revolution, rather than the orthodox Marxist expectation of a capitalist-industrialist transitional phase on the road to communism. In 1874 some 2,000 young men and women throughout Russia put on peasant clothes and went to live among the peasants, hoping, in vain, to start a political move toward democracy; but they were seen as a threat to established society and were arrested by the police. Some Narodniks then turned to terrorism and succeeded in 1881 in killing Czar Alexander II. Other parties such as the Socialist Revolutionaries, Trudovik, and Narodnye Sotsialisty (People's Socialists) continued to press Narodnik policies, but more radical elements turned to Marxism and founded the Social Democratic party.

A veteran Narodnik leader, Nikolai Chaikovsky, returned to Russia in 1917, opposing the Bolsheviks and heading a government in Archangel until 1919.

NATIONAL BOLSHEVIKS

A non-Communist party that supported Bolshevism after 1917 in the belief that they were the best solution for the nation's problems.

NAVAL ACADEMY

On Vasilevsky Island in Petrograd, the building used by the All-Russian Congress of Soviets in June 1917.

NAVY

The disastrous performance of the Imperial navy in the 1904–05 war with Japan, and its indifferent effect in either the Baltic or Black Sea in World War I, was balanced by the reputation the sailors gained as revolutionary activists in 1917, taking control of the fleet base of Krondstadt on the Baltic and their fighting role in the October Revolution and the following civil war. In 1922 a decision was made to rebuild the navy, but serious recruitment of naval cadets from the ranks of the Komsomols began only in 1927. The navy had then in commission: 3 battleships, 2 cruisers, including the *Aurora*, 10 destroyers, and 19 submarines, all survivors of World War I.

Between 1927 and 1941 there was a considerable shipbuilding program. Kliment Voroshilov, as Stalin's commissar for Defense, planned for a deep-sea fleet policy, as well as 18 cruisers; 4 battleships were laid down, but never completed.

The military purges, in which Stalin liquidated senior officers in fear that they might rise up against him, started with the navy in July 1937, when the fleet commander was arrested and shot. The top command was almost totally eliminated in the next year.

World War II saw part of the navy idle in the Pacific, part taken or destroyed in the Baltic, and the remainder fighting desperate coastal actions in the Black Sea and the Arctic. In spite of the urgency of bringing munitions from Britain and the United States through the German blockade, the escort of convoys was done almost totally by the Western Allies, the Soviet navy being unable to help. The most successful naval work was on inland waters—the Caspian, the Don and Volga rivers, and Lake Ladoga, where supplies were taken to the beleagured city of Leningrad.

The Soviet navy (*Voyenno-Morskoy Flot*, VMF) in 1945 comprised about 220 warships, many of them obsolete and confined to coastal operations. Postwar expansion increased the navy to 1,400 ships, including 630 warships by 1962. Under Admiral Sergei Gorshkov, commander of the navy from 1956, its growth continued and by the mid-1980s this strength was approximately doubled. The navy was transformed from a coastal force into a blue-water force.

The Soviet navy has four fleets: Northern, based at Severomorsk; Baltic at Baltisk; Black Sea at Sevastopol; and the Pacific at Vladivostok. There is also a Caspian flotilla based in Baku.

The most striking development of the Soviet navy was in submarines. Diesel-electric engined submarines were converted to carry and fire long-range missiles in the early 1950s, and in 1960 nuclear-powered submarines began to be built. In 1973 submarines carrying missiles with a maximum range of 4,200 miles and capable of reaching targets in any part of the United States came into operation; several of these were kept permanently deployed in the North Atlantic and North Pacific. With the more sophisticated submarines introduced in 1978, there were also the highly accurate MIRV (multiple independently targeted re-entry vehicle) missiles. In 1984 the first of a new class of 13,600-ton submarines capable of carrying 16 long-range missiles and of staying hidden under the Polar ice cap for long periods was launched.

With all its northern seaports liable to become ice-bound, the Soviet navy places a great reliance on icebreakers. The world's first nuclear-powered ship was the *Lenin*, 1960, a 16,000-ton merchant ship capable of breaking through Arctic ice 12 feet thick. The *Lenin*, however, disappeared (perhaps the result of an accident with its reactors) in 1967.

The Soviet navy no longer sends submarine patrols close to the U.S. Atlantic seacoast and is sending fewer surface ships on world ocean cruises. This may be because it has better weapon technology that does not require standing patrols; because Western navies have responded with more aggressive counter-patrols; and because of budgetary restraints. A big fleet is no longer necessary when submarines with intercontinental missiles can hit the United States without leaving port. Under Gorbachev new economies have been introduced and the world role of the Soviet fleet has been allowed to diminish.

After the rapid expansion of the 1960s and 1970s, Red Navy ships are now plagued with mechanical faults. In October 1986 a Yankee-class submarine (a class of 10,500-ton missile-carrying boats, built in 1963–1968 with two nuclear reactors for power) ran into difficulties. Nuclear disaster was averted by a crew member who, in shutting down the power plant, was himself entombed in the reactor compartment. By 1989 the total number of nuclear-powered submarines

lost was six. On April 7 a 9,700-ton Mike-class hunter-killer was the sixth of these, losing 42 from its crew of 80 as it sank off Norway. On June 26, 1989, a 1960s-built Echo-class nuclear-powered submarine broke down and was taken in tow to Murmansk; this happened again in July to an Alfa-class submarine.

NEPMEN

The derogatory term used for those who took advantage of and profited from the New Economic Policy (NEP).

NEW ECONOMIC POLICY (NEP)

Economic policies introduced by Lenin in 1921 when the harsh measures of War Communism had alienated the peasants and failed to achieve necessary industrial production in the country. Monetary reforms were introduced and the inheritance of private property was allowed. Private trade and manufacturing were actively encouraged, and those involved became known as Nepmen. Lenin talked of using the New Economic Policy to "teach communists how to be good businessmen." The peasants were encouraged to produce surpluses by paying their taxes in goods and being allowed to sell in the marketplace. Essentially, their relationship to the state was as taxpayer only. The policy was so effective that by 1927 less than 2 percent of the land was in the hands of collective or state farms. Although the policies continued after Lenin's death in 1924, there was always opposition from the left of the party and from the public, who resented the Nepmen. Stalin's speeches at the 15th Party Congress in 1927 sounded the death knell for NEP.

NEWSPAPERS

Pravda ("Truth")—The leading Soviet newspaper with a circulation of 9.7 million in 1989 and the official organ of the Central Committee of the Communist Party of the Soviet Union. The newspaper was founded by Lenin in 1912, and he was its editor, with Maxim Gorky as its literary editor, until 1914. The paper was hounded by the czarist government and during the revolution its offices were destroyed by military cadets.

Pravda is essentially an organ of information and education, reporting on scientific, economic, and cultural topics. It contains no sensational or scandalous news items and aims to stress and interpret the party line. Stories concerning international relations are, in general, left to *Isvestia*, which is the official Soviet government newspaper. *Pravda* carries a staff of more than 100 full-time correspondents. The editorial staff is headed by a board approved by the Central Committee of the party.

Pravda was first published as a daily in St. Petersburg by the party in 1913. Appearing in various forms, it settled into publication from Moscow on March 3, 1918.

Pravda's editor Victor Afanasyev was removed on October 18, 1989, after 13 years in the post and replaced by Ivan Frolov of *Komsomol*. The newspaper had been criticized for tendentious coverage of nationalist movements and a crude attempt to smear Boris Yeltsin. Frolov was faced with a drop in circulation from 10 million to an estimated 5.5 million.

Isvestia ("The News")—The first issue came out on February 28, 1917. Now published by the Presidium of the Supreme Soviet, and thus under the strong influence of the new Congress of People's Deputies, its illustrated Sunday supplement is *Nedelya*, first issued in 1960. The circulation was 10 million in 1989.

On January 2, 1989, *Isvestia* published two pages of advertising—the first Soviet daily ever to do so; a full page for a French industrial concern and a second with advertisements for Soviet, West German, and Belgian companies and a bank. *Isvestia* is trying to attract readers with human interest stories rather than the traditional issues of official communiqués.

Krasnya Zveda ("Red Star")—The daily paper of the ministry of defense, first issued on January 1, 1924.

Literaturnaya Gazyeta ("Literary Gazette") —The weekly paper of the Writers' Union, from 1929, now with a circulation of 3.1 million. Its political pronouncements were until recently the voice of the party's ideology specialists.

Moskovskiye Novostni ("Moscow News") —A weekly published in Moscow by Tass, the Soviet news agency, since 1930, directed at a foreign audience. At present it is published in seven languages with a total circulation throughout the world of 1 million.

Trud ("Labor")—The official organ of the trade unions, with a circulation of nearly 20 million in 1989. It has shown little urge to move with the times and a projection for 1990 suggests a drop in circulation to 17 million.

Argumenty I Fakty ("Arguments and Facts") —Edited by Vladislav Starkov, a popular weekly with a circulation that has risen to 22 million, the biggest selling weekly in the USSR. First published in 1979 from a basement on the outskirts of Moscow, it retains the appearance of an underground bulletin. It is the organ of what was originally a strict party-based ideological group, but under *glasnost* it has found a hungry market. The paper gives facts without the traditional verbal padding of the official press. It prints scoops and reveals scandals. *Argumenty I Fakty* went too far in publishing a poll that suggested opposition figures such as Andrei Sakharov might be more popular than Mikhail Gorbachev; the remarkable thing is that the editor survived the government's fury. It is suggested that its circulation could reach 30 million in 1990, if enough newsprint were to be allotted.

Komsomolskaya Pravda ("Komsomol Truth")—The Communist youth organization paper. As with other official papers, it suffers under *glasnost* and is losing circulation, from an estimated 17 million in 1989 to a probable 13 million in 1990.

NOMENKLATURA

The list of posts in the party and state to which appointment requires higher party approval. Those on the list are likely to be reelected to their posts or promoted to similar or higher positions in other parts of the USSR. Under Leonid Brezhnev there were perhaps over 2 million people on the nomenklatura, constituting a new, secure social class.

NKGB. See POLITICAL POLICE.

NKVD. See POLITICAL POLICE.

NUCLEAR POWER

The first nuclear-generated electricity in the world came from Obninsk, near Moscow, in 1954. In the 1970s the USSR began a nuclear energy program, and in the 10th Five-Year Plan, 1976–1980, installed capacity was to be expanded from 5.5 to 19.4 million kilowatts. Volgodorsk on the Don-Volga Canal was opened in the five-year plan as a center to manufacture equipment for nuclear power stations. Nuclear power stations in the Soviet Union are of two types: graphite-water and water-moderated.

Operational nuclear energy stations by 1984 were as follows:

1,000 megawatt or more
　　Leningrad (two stations)
　　Chernobyl (where the reactor exploded in 1986)
　　Kursk
Less than 1,000 megawatts
　　Beloyarsk (three stations, in the Urals)
　　Troitsk (in the Urals)
　　Bilibino (in the north of the Far East)
　　Rovno
　　Dmitrograd
　　Obninsk
　　Shevchenko (east of the Caspian)
　　Metsamor
　　Novovoronezh (four stations)
　　The nuclear energy station at Razda in Armenia was closed as a safety measure after the December 1988 earthquake.

NUCLEAR WEAPONS

Semipalatinsk in Kazakhstan is a nuclear-weapon testing site.

OBKOM

The Communist party committee of an oblast.

OBLAST

A province or region. After 1929 the term replaced gubernia for an administrative unit. There are also nine autonomous oblasts in the USSR, including Nagorno-Karabakh in Azerbaijan.

OCTOBRISTS

A political party founded in 1905 to ensure the success of the Duma and the continuance of the czarist régime. They represented large commercial interests, supported the czar's 1905 manifesto, and were a majority party in the Third and Fourth Dumas. In 1915 they suggested a coalition to the Kadets in order to form an effective war government, and in 1916 they entered into a conspiracy with senior army officers to overthrow the czar. In March 1917 they joined with the Kadets in Prince Georgy Lvov's Provisional Government. Leading personalities were Alexander Guchkov (a minister in Lvov's Provisional Government), Mikhail Rodzianko (president of the Fourth Duma) and Savich.

OGPU. See POLITICAL POLICE.

OKHRANA. See POLITICAL POLICE.

ORGBURO

The Organizational Bureau of the Central Committee, a key group with the Secretariat. Stalin joined the Orgburo in 1920. It drafted the 1922 constitution.

OVIR

The MVD (see POLITICAL POLICE) department of visas, which arranges emigration or private foreign trips.

PAMYAT

Meaning "memory," a current anti-Semitic Russian nationalist group, which often opposes the call of the Soviet republics for greater autonomy.

PARTISANS

There had been a tradition of irregular fighting bands in parts of Russia, especially among the Cossacks of the south, who remembered their 18th-century uprising under Emelyan Pugachev. The origins of the Red Army lie in part in these traditions. Consequently, in World War II, when civilians or soldiers found themselves overrun by the rapid advance of the Germans, it was natural to consider forming guerrilla units. Early Red Army thinking had included Mikhail Tukhachevsky's "Doctrine of Proletarian War," which was hostile to centralized control and made use of partisans. When the tide of the 1941 German advance had swept over whole regions and armies, there were left behind arms and men waiting to rise again. At first, looting and pillaging were their main activities and all contact with the army was lost. The Nazis added to the impetus to go underground with their savagery and exploitation of all local resources. However, the institutions that survived, such as collective farms, became the focus for anti-Nazi resistance movements. The terrain was an important element in determining where partisan groups thrived; neither the cold Northern Front nor the open plains of the Ukraine offered the necessary cover, while the forests and marshes of Belorussia and the mountains of the Caucasus and the Crimea were well suited to partisan bands.

A partisan headquarters was set up in Moscow in 1942 to direct units and to organize radio contact and parachute drops; they became an effective part of Soviet strategy from 1943. The partisans developed different roles. In areas near the fighting lines they became the Red Army's advance guard, most markedly at the Battle of Kursk, where they destroyed the German lines of communication and created their own by building bridges and providing, in effect, a corridor for the Red Army's advance. Around Bryansk the forests held major units that could sweep an area behind the German lines, denying them control. In 1943 the Germans estimated there to be 80,000 partisans in Belorussia, and in the Ukraine some 220,000. As the Red Army advanced, partisans lost their function and were either incorporated into the army or deployed as security forces behind the lines.

To counter the partisans, who were subject to Hitler's merciless decree to be shot on sight, mass hunts were organized, but with little success in the forests. Around Bryansk the Germans armed and encouraged anti-Soviet civilians to attack the partisans. This had some success, but the bands themselves took to banditry for their own, rather than the German, good. Another approach was to use prisoners who volunteered for the work, usually Lithuanian, Ukrainian, or Tatar, but as soon as they saw who was winning, they often deserted the German cause.

Parallel to the Soviet partisans were the national groups that formed with

Soviet encouragement in Hungary, Rumania, and Bulgaria and which paved the way for Soviet takeover. The same would have been true of Tito's partisans in Yugoslavia, but their victory bred a sense of self-reliant achievement and led to Yugoslavia's independent attitude toward Russia. In Poland, the Home Army grew from a coalition of small groups but was never acceptable to Moscow and led to the tragedy of their 1944 uprising in Warsaw.

PARTY CONGRESSES

Parallel to the Supreme Soviet, the Communist party of the Soviet Union has as its supreme body, the party congress, which meets only rarely to discuss its Central Committee's report, the new five-year plan, and changes in the party rules and program. The congress elects the Central Committee, which discusses policy proposals and decisions. Party congresses have been held at irregular intervals, but since 1971 they have been held every fifth year.

Between the congresses, party conferences have been held which have a similar attendance but customarily are not used for vital policy decisions.

The following are the party congresses held:

1st. March 1898. Held in Minsk, attended only by nine; announced the formation of the Russian Social Democratic Labor party.

2nd. July 1903. Held in secret in Belgium, then moved to London; it led to the Menshevik-Bolshevik division.

3rd. April 1905. Held by the Bolsheviks in London while the Mensheviks held their congress in Geneva.

4th. April 1906. The "Unity congress,"

in Stockholm, with a Menshevik majority.

5th. May 1907. Held in London, with a small Bolshevik majority.

6th. January 1912. Held in Prague, the Bolsheviks constituted themselves a separate party, finally splitting with the Mensheviks and electing a central committee. Lenin, Sergo Ordzhonikidze, Yacov Sverdlov, Grigory Zinoviev, and (in his absence) Stalin were the leading members. They now constitute the Russian Social Democratic Labor Party (Bolshevik).

7th. March 6–8, 1918. "Extraordinary" congress, dominated by the problems of the Brest-Litovsk Treaty. The majority voted for Lenin's argument for its necessity and a minority for the Left Communist call for a revolutionary war. The party's name was altered to the Russian Communist Party (Bolshevik).

8th. March 18–23, 1919. Met under the threat of intervention and immediately after the founding of the Communist International. Questions of attitudes toward the peasantry and of the building of the Red Army were discussed. Stalin obtained control of the Orgburo.

9th. March 1920. Lenin announced his 10-or 20-year program for the electrification of the country. A faction labeled Democratic Centralists advocating collective management was rejected.

10th. March 8–16, 1921. Lenin announced the New Economic Policy. Congress was interrupted by the Kronstadt rebellion. The Secretariat included Molotov.

11th. March 17–April 2, 1922. The newly elected Central Committee

voted to establish the post of general secretary to run the Secretariat, to which Stalin was appointed. Frunze and others put forward the "Doctrine of Proletarian War," formulated by Tukhachevsky, which advocated a decentralized and territorially raised army with no supreme command and reliance on a trained and armed people, fighting as partisans.

12th. April 1923. Lenin being ill, Zinoviev gave the general report (Stalin had suggested Trotsky, who had declined.) Stalin reassured the party that there was no leadership split and expanded the Politburo, bringing in his nominees.

13th. May 1924. Krupskaya handed Lenin's "Testament" to Stalin, who put it to a committee, and an edited version was issued. Zinoviev demanded Trotsky's recantation of his theory of permanent revolution.

14th. April 1925. Stalin presented his "Socialism in one country" thesis. The Leningrad delegation, under Zinoviev's influence and holding to ideals of world revolution, voted against Stalin's report and Zinoviev himself attacked it in public the following December. The new Central Committee was expanded from 51 to 63, with fewer opponents of Stalin in its membership.

15th. December 1927. Congress was preceded by "discussion sheets" in *Pravda* and its resolutions were carried out by a rehearsed group of Stalinists who drowned with shouting any attempt at opposition. The five-year-plan to expand heavy industry was ratified. The term "Thermidorean" was used to describe the Trotskyite opposition.

16th. June–July, 1930. The First Five-

Year Plan and its modifications were the main item. The slogan "Fulfill the Five-Year Plan in Four Years" was used to urge the party to economic success.

17th. January–February 1934. "The Congress of the Victors." The authority of the party and its leader, Stalin, was now unquestioned.

18th. March 1939. There were 2,035 delegates, but only 59 of those from the 17th Party Congress attended; 1,108 of its 1,966 delegates had been arrested. The congress is to restore the party after the "Yezhovshchina," through promotion to the many vacancies.

19th. October 1952. After a 13-year break, a new Central Committee was elected. Malenkov gave the Central Committee report and Khrushchev put forward the new party statutes; among the changes were dropping the *B* for "Bolshevik" from the party name. The Sixth Five-Year Plan was announced, which called for increases in food production. Stalin proposed that the Politburo be replaced with a new Presidium, but this was only a maneuver to unsettle the top members of the party.

20th. February 1956. Marked by the "secret speech" of Nikita Khrushchev, in which he revealed to the party for the first time the "illegal" activities and excesses of Stalin.

21st. January 1959. The congress was called to launch the Seven-Year Plan.

22nd. October 1961. Khrushchev failed to get support for his educational reforms and to check the use of resources by heavy industry, in spite of the congress's treating him with

the greatest respect. A new party program was announced that would further the "withering away of the state." Shelepin made further disclosures of Stalin's misdeeds; it was outspokenly anti-Stalinist and, as a result, Stalin's embalmed body was removed from Red Square.

23rd. March–April 1966. Organized by Suslov, but Brezhnev survived the power struggles and was formally appointed party general secretary.

24th. April 1971. Emphasized the need for a new European security settlement and ruled that congresses should be held at five-year intervals.

25th. February 1976. Dominated by Brezhnev. The 10th Five-Year Plan was announced, turning the goals away from consumer goods.

26th. March 1981. Organized by Chernenko, it revised the system of leadership.

27th. March 1986. The "Reforming congress." Gorbachev presented a new edition of the party progam, laying down the principles of *perestroika*. This was followed in 1988 by a specially convened 19th party conference (one had not been held since 1966). The Central Committee's report was used as a basis for debate, and not, as in all previous congresses, simply accepted. The congress passed resolutions on *perestroika*, to ensure that deputies had power and responsibility, and on greater independence of regions. The next party congress was brought forward from 1991 to October 1990.

PERESTROIKA

Meaning "restructuring." The process of restructuring society and the state, dismantling the "command and administer" system, following the 27th Party Congress in 1986.

PIONEERS

The national organization for 10- to 15-year-olds. (See also KOMSOMOL.)

PLANNED ECONOMY

A planned, or "command," economy is one in which the main drive is not consumer demand or choice, as in a market economy, but a plan drawn up by government by which the national resources are allocated in accord with political and social policies.

As early as December 1917 there were schemes for economic development, such as the plan to increase steel production using iron ore from the Urals and coal from the Kuznetsk Basin. At the first meeting of the Council of Sovnarkhoz, an outline plan for the economy of the whole country was discussed. The civil war soon put an end to this kind of global thinking, but practical plans for the supply of fuel, metals, cotton, and other basic materials were put into operation. No doubt an important link was established in the mind of the planners during the period of War Communism between the idea of planning and the use of coercion. At the Ninth Party Congress in April 1920, the preparation of an overall plan covering the whole country was adopted as official party doctrine, and, in December, with Lenin's blessing, a plan for the electrification of the Russian Soviet Federal Socialist Republic was presented. It was to carry out this plan that Gosplan was created. A similar plan to organize the metal industry was produced in 1923.

In the same year Ivan Killinikov, an engineer and chairman of Gosplan's industrial section, put forward a plan that covered most of industry and by which output was to increase by 182 percent. The targets were reached, but the investment needed was vastly in excess of that planned.

Similar plans were prepared for transport and agriculture. The agricultural plan was devised by the economist Nikolai Kondratiev, a member of the Socialist Revolutionary party

In 1925 Gosplan started work on the first fully comprehensive five-year plan, the final version of which was not accepted until May 1929.

THE FIRST AND SECOND FIVE-YEAR PLANS

	1928 (plan)	1932-33 (out-turn)	1932 (plan)	1937 (plan)	1937 (out-turn)
National income[1]	24.4	49.7	45.5	100.2	96.3
Gross industrial production[2]					
industrial goods	6.0	18.1	23.1	45.5	55.2
consumer goods	12.3	25.1	20.2	47.2	40.3
Workers in state employment (millions)	11.3	15.8	22.9	28.9	27.0

[1], [2] Thousand million rubles at 1926–27 prices.
SOURCE: Adapted from Munting, *The Economic Development of the USSR*, 1982.

Party resolutions concerning the plan were very firm on the need to expand defense and the socialist sector, that part of the economy in full public ownership, but were moderate concerning agriculture and on the balance between producer and consumer goods in industry. Of the major authors of the plan, the best known is S. G. Strumilin. Like most of the planners of this time he disappeared in the purges of the 1930s.

The 1929 plan called for extremely high growth rates in all areas of the economy but especially in industry and agriculture. However, by the time the plan was fully in operation, Stalin had effectively assumed power and his concept of planning was very different from that of the economists.

Stalin said: "We need a plan that will ensure a systematic preponderance of the socialist sector of our national economy over the capitalist sector. For a five-year plan in which this was forgotten would not be a five-year plan but a five-year imbecility." Considering that in 1928 approximately 75 percent of industrial production and only 2 percent of agricultural production came from collective or state farms, kolkhoz, or sovkhoz, it was obvious that huge changes would have to be made to satisfy Stalin's ideals.

There was nothing cautious about his thinking and nothing humanitarian, either. He had decided that the industrial sector would be funded by agriculture. Since the peasants would not cooperate, they would be forcibly collectivized, including the ruthless destruction of the kulaks. In the industrial sector, he was not interested in the careful balancing of resources or the gradual evolution of labor productivity by training programs. He believed in the vast heroic gesture. Huge construction projects were embarked upon, to be carried out by team leaders inspired by the white heat of socialist fervor. He formally denounced ideas of carefully sustained growth as "bourgeois deviationism." He said, "We bring tremendous changes to every aspect of human life . . . we penetrate the forces of nature and human relations in society."

The planners had allowed for minimum and maximum versions of their goals, but Stalin was interested only in the latter. In almost all areas of the economy the plan called for at least a 100 percent increase in output; in some vital sectors such as tractors, it called for output to increase by a factor of 50. The actual results, insofar as they can be realistically determined, were uneven. Producer goods achieved 127 percent of target, consumer goods reached only 80 percent. Agriculture was the most disappointing production of all; in 1932, agricultural products reached only 57 percent of target.

However, it must be said that even using the most pessimistic Western evaluation, an annual rate of growth of at least 10 percent per annum was realized. Even when considering the low starting base, this was an impressive achievement whatever one may feel about the human cost.

POGROM

Meaning "destruction." In the Russian Empire, these attacks on Jews became officially condoned and mob assaults were common in the 19th and 20th centuries.

POLAND

Population: 36,745,000
Area: 128,628 square miles
Capital: Warsaw; population 1,641,000

The ancient kingdom of Poland was divided among the Prussian, Austrian, and Russian empires in 1795. Russian Poland was fought over in World War I and its territory taken from the empire under the Brest-Litovsk Treaty. A republic of Poland was founded in November 1918 and guaranteed independence by the Treaty of Versailles. The new republic and Soviet Russia became engaged in war in 1919 as Polish troops, with French military advisers, attacked the Ukraine. The Red Army counter-attacked and were gaining the upper hand when, in August 1920, they were defeated outside Warsaw. Poland consolidated its victory with territorial gains, taking Vilnius (Wilno) from Lithuania and parts of the Ukraine and Belorussia.

In 1939 Poland was caught beween Stalin and Hitler, hated and despised by both. When in March Stalin proposed a conference to discuss ways to stop Hitler, Poland refused for fear of provoking Hitler. In August Stalin, ignoring Poland as a power, signed a treaty with Germany in which spheres of influence were secretly included, dividing Poland on the Vistula River and giving back to the Soviet Union those parts of the Ukraine and Belorussia lost in 1920. Assured that the Soviet Union would not interfere, on September 1, Germany invaded Poland.

On September 17 the Red Army moved into Poland, taking the agreed parts of the Ukraine and Belorussia—78,000 square miles of land and over 12 million people. Between 180,000 and 250,000 Polish soldiers surrendered to the Red Army. Most were sent east for detention. Soldiers found in civilian dress were arrested and sentenced to hard labor; from these a new Polish army was later recruited. Estimates of the numbers removed vary from a half-million to 1.5 million. Of 15,000 army officers arrested, 4,000 probably were shot in 1940.

Some of the Polish government escaped and formed a government in exile in London. In April 1943, Stalin broke off diplomatic relations with this government in protest of its accusations that Polish army officers had been mas-

sacred in the Katyn Forest. Later that year, at the Allied conference at Teheran, the Soviet Union was promised that its borders would be at least those of June 1941, and that Poland would not have any part of the Ukraine or Belorussia. The Curzon Line was suggested as a border, westward toward the Oder River.

In 1944, when the Red Army advanced across the Vistula River, followed by units of the Soviet-created Polish army, Vyacheslav Molotov asserted that the people of all Belorussia and the Ukraine had chosen to join the USSR and that the Poles must agree with the Soviet Union on new frontiers. He also attacked the anti-Soviet tone of statements by Polish generals and leaders of the underground. In July the Soviet Union set up a rada, or a Committee of National Liberation, in Lublin. Stanislaw Mikolajcek, the head of the Polish government in London, flew to Moscow, hoping to make some agreement with the Soviet Union in the belief that it needed his coooperation with the Polish underground. There was already a large non-Communist underground army in Poland organized from London and commanded by General Bor Komorovski, known as the Home Army.

On August 1, as the Red Army reached the outskirts of Warsaw, the 35,000-strong Polish Home Army rose up against the German occupiers. The army wished to take Warsaw itself and not be liberated by, or in debt to, the Soviets. But the Soviets declared that it was not a true uprising but rather a group friendly to the Germans, and a waste of Polish lives. On October 2 the last of the Home Army in Warsaw surrendered. The uprising was put down with terrible brutality, and Mikolajcek went back to London.

In January 1945 the Soviets entered Warsaw and set up a Government of National Unity, including Mikolajcek's Peasant party. In June Poland signed a treaty agreeing to the new borders, thus moving the country west into Germany and causing large deportations of Germans. But Soviet pressure led to an election in 1947 that put the Communist-Socialist alliance in power and drove Mikolajcek out of Poland. A constitution in 1952 modeled the country along Soviet lines.

Internal unrest persisted and, after riots in Poznan in 1956, forced the government to release Stefan Cardinal Wyszynski from arrest and return Wladyslaw Gomulka, who had been expelled in 1948, to the secretaryship of the party. Gomulka was removed in 1970 in the face of popular unrest, but it was not until 1980, when food shortages brought industrial workers out on strike, that substantial change appeared.

The independent trade union movement, Solidarity, led by Lech Walesa made public demands of General Jaruzelski's government, which, at first were answered by martial law, but this was lifted in 1983. The economic difficulties of the country persisted and Solidarity, encouraged by international support, particularly from the Vatican headed by a Polish-born Pope, edged towards multi-party elections. These were held in June 1989 and Solidarity candidates won in a landslide victory. In August Tadeusz Mazowicki, ex-editor of the Solidarity weekly paper, became prime minister. Local elections are to be held in May 1990. Although Poland now has a democratically elected government—with Soviet approval—they are still faced

with a disastrous economic situation, appalling ecological difficulties and a huge foreign debt. Lech Walesa visited the United States early in 1990 to appeal for investment and technical assistance.

POLICE

The term "police" became tainted by association with the repressive czarist police and was dropped after February 1917. The civil police are the Militia. (See also POLITICAL POLICE.)

POLITBURO. See POLITICAL STRUCTURE.

POLITICAL PARTIES

The main political groups prior to 1905 were: Liberals, Narodniks, and Trudoviks.

Parties and other political groups by 1917 were (1) on the left: Anarcho-Communists, Social Democrats (Mensheviks, Bolsheviks, and regional social Democratic parties in Latvia, the Ukraine, and Russian Poland), Socialist Revolutionaries (founded in the 1890s from Narodnik groups), Left Socialist Revolutionaries (formed by Boris Kamkov and Maria Spiridonova in 1917), Center-Left and Center-Right Socialist Revolutionaries, Socialist Populist (Trudoviks), and Socialist Revolutionary Maximalists; (2) in the center: Kadets (Constitutional Democrats), People's Socialists, Progressives, Octobrists; and (3) on the right: Monarchists, and the Union of the Russian People.

POLITICAL POLICE

Prerevolution—Okhrana—After the assassination of Czar Alexander II in 1881, the rising number of active antimonarchist terrorist groups caused the Russian government to strengthen the national gendarmerie by setting up a department for "the protection of public security and order"—the Okhrana. The Okhrana relied on a mass of paid informers and on fear. It had a reputation for beating confessions out of suspects, or simply arranging for their murder. Elements of the Okhrana continued to work up to 1920 for the various White governments in Russia.

1917–1922—Cheka—Even the most liberal of revolutionaries had the lesson of the Paris Commune in their minds: in 1871, when the Commune took over Paris, they killed one officer, but when the officers retook Paris, over 30,000 Communards were executed. They feared any counterrevolution. From the start of the revolution, to protect the Bolsheviks against subversion and to combat the Okhrana, Lenin employed Felix Dzerzhinsky, whom he had known in exile, to organize a political intelligence unit that became the Special Commission for the Struggle Against Counter-Revolution and Sabotage, or Cheka. It was unusual among secret police organizations in being directly responsible to the center of government and not to a ministry of the interior, as had been the case with the Okhrana.

In March 1918 the Cheka transferred its headquarters to Moscow, where political action was becoming centered in the course of the civil war. In November its powers were modified by representatives from the commissars for justice and internal affairs, for up to then its Red Terror had been administered by three-man tribunals responsible to no

higher authority. In 1917 Dzerzhinsky had had no more than 100 operatives, but by 1921 there were probably 30,000. He employed informers and guards, often from nationalities whose cultural differences would make them indifferent to their prisoners.

1919—GRU—To counterbalance the Cheka's power Trotsky, as commissar for the army, set up a Department of the Red Army General Staff, the Chief Intelligence Administration, or GRU. Its first chief was General Jan Berzin, later executed in the 1937 purge. In 1921 Cheka opened a foreign department, INO, which in its turn watched over Trotsky's GRU.

1922–1934—GPU and OGPU—In February 1922 the Cheka was abolished and replaced by the GPU, (State Political Administration) and it was brought under the control traditional for political police, the People's Commissariat for Internal Affairs (NKVD), with Dzerzhinsky as head of both. The GPU was renamed the OGPU (Unified GPU) in November 1923.

Dzerzhinsky died in 1926 and was succeeded by Vyacheslav Menzhinsky. He found that the Soviet spy networks overseas had collapsed, starting with the arrest of their agents in Prague in 1926 and in Poland and Switzerland in 1927. Menzhinsky at once appointed Genrikh Grigorevich Yagoda as assistant chief of the NKVD's General Section for Terror and Diversion, SMERSH. Yagoda created the new overseas networks, this time ensuring that they were supervised by a reliable Soviet resident.

1934–1943—NKVD—In 1934 OGPU was abolished and its functions fully absorbed into the NKVD, or People's Commissariat for Internal Affairs. The power of the NKVD grew and it developed paramilitary forces, including armored units, capable of crushing any sign of resistance.

Labor camps had been set up as early as 1919 for the corrective treatment of offenders. In 1934 the system was organized by the NKVD under Gulag (Chief Administration of Corrective Labor Camps and Settlements). (See CAMPS.)

After the assassination of Sergei Kirov in December 1934, Stalin immediately decreed that the NKVD could carry out sentences of imprisonment or death as soon as its tribunal had judged a person guilty.

In 1936 Stalin ordered Yagoda's arrest and he confessed to poisoning Valerian Kuibyshev, Menzhinsky (thus taking over his post as head of NKVD), Maxim Gorky, and Gorky's son Maxim Peshkov; Yagoda was shot in the Lubyanka prison. His successor, Nikolai Yezhov, who had been a member of the party's purge commission since 1933, in two years raised the intensity of the purge to a peak, even purging the staff of the NKVD itself, before being removed himself (he vanished from Soviet history without trace). Yezhov was replaced in 1938 by Stalin's fellow-Georgian Lavrenti Beria, the people's commissar in the NKVD, who halted the policy of mass arrests.

1943–1946—NKGB—The reorganized People's Commissariat for State Security under Lavrenti Beria, the NKGB was responsible for seeking out the unreliable elements, while the NKVD continued to administer the camps.

1946–1953—MGB and MVD—The NKVD was replaced in name by the MVD when all the people's commissariats were replaced by ministries, hence NKVD became MVD. But the MGB, Ministry of State Security, existed from 1946 to 1953. Beria remained in control of the State Security organs until shortly after Stalin's death in 1953 and then he, too, was shot.

1954–on—KGB—In 1954 the MVD and MGB were reorganized, the former taking responsibility for all criminal matters and the latter becoming the KGB, or Committee of State Security, restricted to state security. The prosecutor general, who had been subject to the authority of the NKVD, was confirmed as being in charge of all law enforcement in the USSR and of being accountable to the Central Committee of the party. Under his authority were the prosecutors of republics, oblasts, towns, and raions. The Special Boards, which had been able to pass sentence on cases presented by the NKVD and MGB, were abolished. This was followed in February 1955 with a change of personalities in the Supreme Court.

From its headquarterrs in the palatial building on Dzerzhinsky Square, the KGB controls an immense organization including the 23,000 uniformed Border Guards and, with the MVD, the Internal Troops, both part of the Armed Forces, but not under the Ministry of Defense. Although its latest chairman has given time to public relations, including the creation of a film explaining the work of the KGB, the Congress of Deputies in 1989 was still unable to get figures on its budget.

The chairmen of the KGB since Beria's elimination have been:

1954–1958 Ivan Serov
1958–1961 Alexander Shelepin
1961–1967 Vladimir Semichastny
1967–1982 Yuri Andropov
1982–1988 Viktor Chebrikov
1988–   Vladimir Kryuchkov

POLITICAL STRUCTURE

Up to 1988, all voters elected their district soviets and republic supreme soviets. They also voted for members of the USSR's Supreme Soviet, or All-Union Supreme Soviet of the USSR. This had two chambers: the Soviet of the Union, with about 750 members, one member for every 300,000 electors; and, to provide a regional balance, the Soviet of the Nationalities, of about 630 members, with 32 delegates from each republic, 11 from each autonomous republic, and one from each autonomous area.

The delegates to both of these bodies were elected every four years. They were not necessarily party members, nor were they necessarily of the nationality they were representing in the body; they were screened, however, by the party-appointed electoral commissions and presented on an approved list. These bodies met for only a few days twice a year to pass major items of legislation, but they appointed commissions to study proposals for legislation, and to carry on its functions throughout the year; they also elected the Presidium of the Supreme Soviet. This Presidium (or standing administrative committee) consisted of about 40 people elected by the Supreme Soviet to run the affairs of the nation; it included the chairmen of the 15 Soviet republics with senior party officials and others who might also be members of the republics' soviets. Its chairman was the nominal head of state.

Parallel to the Supreme Soviet, the Communist Party of the Soviet Union has as its supreme decision-making body the Party Congress. It appoints the Central Committee and also its Presidium and Secretariat. The Central Committee functions between the party congresses, carrying out its decisions. From 1917 to 1934, it acted as the party's parliament. In 1957, under Nikita Khrushchev, the Central Committee became a decisive body, ending the assumption that only the small group in the Politburo held final power. It was the Central Committee that provided the majority that voted him out of power in 1964.

The party's Secretariat of 10 members was established after the Sixth Party Congress and was first headed by Yacov Sverdlov. In March 1919 the post of responsible secretary was established and held by Vyacheslav Molotov until 1922, when Stalin was appointed general secretary. He held this post, developing its great powers, until his death in 1953. The Central Committee elects from its members the Politburo, which is responsible for the running of the party between plenary sessions of the Central Committee; it usually has 14 full and 8 candidate members who attend but have no voting right.

The Council of Ministers (originating in 1917 as Sovnarkom, the Council of People's Commissars) is appointed by the Politburo or, when the Politburo is not in session, by the Presidium of the Supreme Soviet. The members are the heads of ministries or departments running the nation, chairmen of key committees, and heads of industries. The council has its own Presidium composed of its leading ministers and the chairmen of the republics' Councils of Ministers. In theory, the Council of

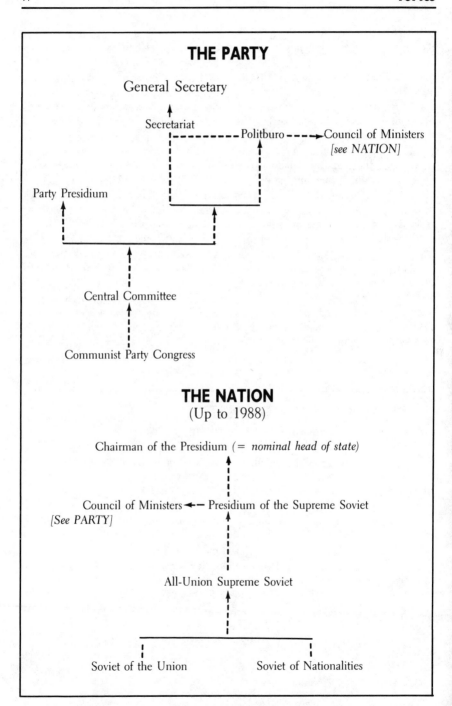

Ministers implements the policies of the Supreme Soviet; in practice, it exercises its power by issuing decrees that have the force of law. The council usually meets only once or twice a year, hence its Presidium carries great weight, although its decisions are subject to the Politburo's scrutiny.

In 1988 the political-administrative structure of the nation was changed by the introduction of the Congress of People's Deputies, comprising 2,250 deputies. One-third—750—of the congress seats are from the major all-union public organizations (the Communist party, Komsomol, trade unions, public committees, scientific academies, trade unions, artists' unions, women's councils, and so on). The party itself has only 100 reserved seats, although party members are likely to be in considerable numbers among the remaining 1,500 seats shared among the republics and regions. The congress replaced the party's rubber stamp, the Supreme Soviet.

Under the reformed constitution announced in 1988, after March 26, 1989 there would be a variety of parliamentary candidates for the voter to choose from. Mikhail Gorbachev ruled out multiparty elections, and said that the party would remain the "huge integrating force" of the Soviet Union. In February, a Party Central Electoral Commission vetted the list of 8,300 candidates, producing a final short list for each republic's constituency seats. A quarter of the seats were single, unopposed candidates and many contested by only two candidates, with a few having three or more candidates. In some, particularly in Lithuania, there were as many as eight candidates. For the 750 seats for public organizations, there were 880 nominations.

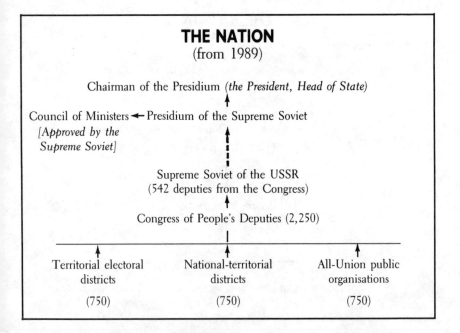

THE NATION
(from 1989)

Chairman of the Presidium *(the President, Head of State)*
↑
Council of Ministers ← Presidium of the Supreme Soviet
[Approved by the
Supreme Soviet]
↑
Supreme Soviet of the USSR
(542 deputies from the Congress)
↑
Congress of People's Deputies (2,250)

Territorial electoral districts	National-territorial districts	All-Union public organisations
(750)	(750)	(750)

The Congress of People's Deputies elected from its numbers a working parliament, still called the Supreme Soviet of the USSR (of two chambers: the Soviet of Nationalities, presided by Rafik Nishanov, and the Soviet of the Union, with 271 deputies each). One-fifth of the Supreme Soviet's 542 members stand down every 12 months, and there are elections from the deputies to the congress. The Supreme Soviet chose as its president Mikhail Gorbachev and as its vice-president Anatoly Lukyanov. The Supreme Soviet in 1989 set to debating an unprecedented heavy program, from deciding its own rules of procedure to coping with the nationalist demands of the constituent republics.

POPULATION

The USSR gained land and people as a result of treaties made after World War II.

Territory	Square Miles	Population (est. 1945)
Lithuania		
Latvia	62,000	6,100,000
Estonia		
East Prussia	3,500	400,000
East Poland	68,000	10,000,000
Bessarabia and Bukovina	19,000	3,700,000
Moldavia	13,000	2,200,000
Carpathia	5,000	800,000
Karelia Petsamo	20,000	500,000
Tanna Tuva	64,000	60,000
Kurile Islands and southern Sakhalin	18,000	400,000
		24,160,000

The birth rate in the USSR has declined since 1950 from 26 births per thousand people to 18 births per thousand in 1975. It is higher among non-Slav peoples; Russians now constitute less than 50 percent of the population of the country.

POTSDAM CONFERENCE

The conference of the Allied heads of state held shortly after the end of the war in Europe, July 17–August 2, 1945. It was attended by Joseph Stalin, Harry S Truman, and Winston Churchill (whose place was taken during the conference by Clement Attlee, who had become British prime minister, defeating Churchill in a general election). Although there was a deadlock over most subjects, particularly on the matter of political control in Soviet-occupied territories, Poland, Czechoslovakia, and the Balkans, there was some agreement on the reparations each country could exact from its respective occupation zones of Germany. The Oder-Neisse Line was agreed to as the western frontier of Poland. Truman told Stalin that the Allies had in their possession a bomb greater than anything used before. Stalin presumably thought this was some kind of bomb with a heavier load of explosive; he was not told it was the atomic bomb.

Truman asked Stalin formally to cooperate in joint action against Japan, and the Allies issued a final summons to Japan to surrender. From then on it was a race to see whether the Soviet troops could mount an offensive and gain a credible victory over Japan or whether the use of the atomic bomb would end the war before this.

PRAVDA. See NEWSPAPERS.

PRESIDENT

Until 1988 the head of state of the Soviet Union was, nominally, the chairman of the Supreme Soviet. Yakov Sverdlov, until his death in 1919, was the first president. Mikhail Kalinin held the post in the war years from 1938 until his death in 1946. But the effective head of state has been the man who held the post of first secretary or general secretary of the Communist party, a post first created by Stalin. Holders of this or equivalent posts have been:

Joseph Stalin: 1927–1953
Georgy Malenkov: 1953–February 1955
Nikolai Bulganin: 1955–1957; head of government in concert with Khrushchev
Nikita Khrushchev: 1955–October 1964; head of party—preferred the title First Secretary
Leonid Brezhnev: 1964–November 1982; revived the post as general secretary in 1966; also chairman of the Presidium of the Supreme Soviet
Yuri Andropov: 1982–Februry 1984
Konstantin Chernenko: 1984–March 1985
Mikhail Gorbachev: 1985–; He became president of the Supreme Soviet in October 1988.

The chairman of the Presidium of the Supreme Soviet has ranked as head of state in post-Stalin times:

Leonid Brezhnev: 1960–1964
Anastasy Mikoyan: 1964–1965
Nikolai Podgorny: 1965–1977
Leonid Brezhnev: 1977–1982
(The post was vacant from November 1982 until June 1983)
Yuri Andropov: 1983–1984
Konstantin Chernenko: 1984–1985
Andrei Gromyko: 1985–1988

PRESIDIUM. See POLITICAL STRUCTURE.

PRIME MINISTER

The prime minister has been the chairman of the Council of People's Commissars (Sovnarkom) or Council of Ministers since 1946, the body nominated by the Supreme Soviet as the government. The postholders have been:

Vladimir Lenin: 1917–1924
Alexei Rykov: 1924–1930
Vyacheslav Molotov: 1930–1941
Josef Stalin: 1941–1953
Georgy Malenkov: 1953–1955
Nicholas Bulganin: 1955–1958
Nikita Khrushchev: 1958–1965
Alexei Kosygin: 1965–1980
Nikolai Ryzhkov: 1985–

PROGRESSIVE BLOC

From 1915 to 1917, during World War I, the liberal center of the Third and Fourth Dumas, which was the overall majority, excepting the Social Democrats and Trudoviks on the left and the parties of the right, Monarchists, and the Union of the Russian People demanded that the czar have a government that would have the confidence of the people.

PROGRESSIVES

A party in the Third and Fourth Dumas representing landowners and the established middle classes. The party held a political position between the liberal Kadets and the conservative Octobrists.

PROVISIONAL GOVERNMENT

The government formed by the Duma upon the collapse of the czar's regime in February 1917. The Petrograd Soviet agreed to support the Duma's temporary committee headed by Prince Georgy Lvov, with the Kadet leader Pavel Milyukov as minister of foreign affairs, the Octobrist Alexander Guchkov as minister of war, and the Socialist Revolutionary Alexander Kerensky as minister of justice. When the Soviet opposed the continuation of the war against Germany in May, Milyukov and Guchkov resigned, Kerensky became minister of war, and five more socialists came into the government. The Soviet mistrusted the Kadets, and in July pressure from the Soviet forced Prince Lvov to resign and Kerensky became premier of the Provisional Government.

Although the Provisional Government issued decrees on political and personal freedom, abolishing censorship and the existing police organization, and promised elections to a new constituent assembly with universal suffrage, Kerensky tried to continue the war. The Petrograd Soviet, however, held greater power and, from the July Days on, popular demonstrations and declarations centered on its activities rather than on the Provisional Government. The army commander-in-chief Lavr Kornilov demanded firm action against the left, but in Petrograd, factory workers, Kronstadt sailors, and the Bolshevik Red Guards came out against such action and in defense of the Soviet. By October the Provisional Government had little control and the Bolsheviks seized their opportunity to overthrow it. Kerensky and the other ministers fled.

PURGES

During the revolution and afterward during the civil war, terror was used as a conscious tool of policy by the Bolsheviks, to some extent in direct revenge for White terror tactics. During this time party purges were a different matter, intended to cleanse the party of undesirable elements. Those purged simply lost their membership or party posts. It was only later that purging implied imprisonment or killing. The first purge took place in 1921, after the 10th Party Congress. But in 1922 Lenin wrote, "We are living in a sea of illegality" and Stalin's ruthless treatment of the party in Georgia made Lenin realize how dangerous Stalin as general secretary could be. He could not have foreseen what was to come.

In the struggle for power after Lenin's death it took Stalin six years of complex and vicious political maneuvering to defeat his opponents on the left and right. Trotsky was expelled to Turkey in January 1929, and his leading followers were removed from the party and exiled. The Right Opposition led by Nicholas Bukharin and Mikhail Tomsky was defeated in the Central Committee, and both men were dismissed from their posts in April. Shortly after that they published recantations of their views. A second party purge followed to weed out their supporters. In 1929 Stalin launched the collectivization of land and the war against the kulaks. This climaxed in the famine in the Ukraine and Kazakhstan in which perhaps 5 or 6 million people died, and another 10 million kulaks were either mass deported in appalling conditions to Siberia or were executed.

Stalin was imposing his will on the party and the country, but there was still opposition. In 1930 two members of the Central Committee circulated a memorandum criticizing Stalin for his authoritarian attitudes. They were expelled from the party and one of them, Vissarion Lominadze, killed himself in

1935. Then in 1932 Nikolai Ryutin and some followers issued a platform specifically naming Stalin as "the evil genius of the revolution" and calling for his removal. Stalin called for the death penalty but obtained little support. Sergei Kirov, Grigory Ordzhonikidze, Valerian Kuibyshev and Stanislav Kossior are recorded as having spoken against him and he was only supported by Lazar Kaganovich. There seems in fact to have been a moderate bloc unwilling to use terror tactics against such respected members of the party, and many of Stalin's moves from 1932 until he launched the Great Terror in 1936 can only be understood in these terms.

In 1933 and 1934 a general purge of the party was launched by the end of which nearly a million members had been expelled; at the end of the year, Ryutin was jailed.

In January 1934, the 17th Party Congress—the "Congress of the Victors" —was held, at which Stalin proclaimed that while at the last congress it had been necessary to finish off certain anti-Leninist groups, now "there is nothing to prove and, it seems, nobody to beat." Of the 1,966 delegates to the congress, 1,108 (nearly 60 percent) were to be executed and of the 139 members elected to the Central Committee at the congress, 98 were to be shot during the peak years of the terror.

Stalin had already assembled his political supporters, such as Molotov, Ordzhonikidze, Kirov, Kaganovich, Zhdanov, Khrushchev, Malenkov, and Mikoyan. He now assembled his machine of repression. In April 1933 a new Central Purge Commission, with Nikolai Yezhov and Matuel Shkiryotov, had been set up. This was followed by the Special Sector of the Central Committee headed by Poskrebyshev, and the State Security Committee with many of the same personnel. In July 1934 the OGPU was subsumed by the NKVD, and Yagoda was put in charge of the NKVD.

The Murder of Kirov—On December 1, 1934, Sergei Kirov, a member of the Politburo and secretary of the Leningrad party, left his office to attend a conference being held in a room in the same corridor. He was shot in the back by a young party member, Leonid Nikolaev, and died almost immediately. Kirov was normally heavily guarded but on this occasion his chief bodyguard, Borisov, was nowhere to be found. The party made an instant announcement claiming that the assassin was a supporter of Grigory Zinoviev and the leftist elements in Leningrad. It now seems certain that the plot to kill Kirov was directed by Stalin through Yagoda, and that its purpose was to provide a basis for the total destruction of all opposition to his rule. Certainly everyone involved in the plot, including the NKVD men who killed Borisov in a faked car accident, were themselves disposed of—most of them immediately, all within a few years. Stalin himself went to Leningrad to conduct an inquiry into the killing and immediately issued a decree that became one of the legal planks for the conduct of the Terror. It stated that:

1. Investigative agencies were to speed up the cases of those accused of acts of terror.
2. Judges were not to hold up execution of death sentences to consider the possibility of pardon because they would not be granted for these offenses.
3. The NKVD were to carry out the

death sentences immediately after the sentence was awarded.

There was an instant wave of arrests in Leningrad and Moscow. Declared to be counterrevolutionaries, the prisoners were quickly tried, sentenced to death, and executed; many others were simply shot out of hand in the NKVD cellars. Throughout the country thousands more people named on NKVD lists as suspect were arrested.

In December 1935 Kamenev and Zinoviev were arrested and, later in the month, it was alleged that Nikolaev and some of the other accused were part of a Leningrad center for terrorist activities. On January 15, Zinoviev, Kamenev, and 17 others were brought to trial, accused of having given political encouragement to this group. They admitted moral responsibility for having encouraged opposition to the regime but denied any connections with the crime. Zinoviev was sentenced to 10 years, and Kamenev to 5 years. The others were given similar sentences. This confession of moral responsibility was part of the process by which denials of responsibility by the accused for specific acts were devalued, and the outside world was led to believe that the charges were justified. Changes in Soviet law at this time all seem to indicate preparation for the massive purge that was about to be unleashed. In June 1935 a decree was issued that provided a five-year exile for any adult member of a family one of whose number had fled abroad. All penalties, including the death penalty, were now extended down to 12-year-olds.

The Show Trials—Stalin now prepared to destroy the Zinoviev-Kamenev group and set out to obtain the confessions necessary for a public trial. Pressure was exerted on the accused, sometimes by prolonged interrogations and deprivation of sleep accompanied by brutal bullying, sometimes by threatening their families, sometimes by straight torture or beatings by specially trained thugs known as "boxers." But in the case of Zinoviev and Kamenev, although they were subjected to severe interrogation, the main reason they agreed to provide confessions to crimes of which they were totally innocent was Stalin's promise not to execute them or their followers. He agreed to give this promise in the presence of the whole Politburo. In the end it was given in front of a closed session consisting only of Stalin, Voroshilov, and Yezhov. Members of the Zinoviev-Kamenev group were accused of having joined with a Trotskyite group, including Trotsky's son Sedov, for the purpose of assassinating Stalin and his close associates, Voroshilov, Kaganovich, Kirov, and Zhdanov. At the trial, which was held in the little October Hall of the Trade Union House on August 19, 1936, the accused with two exceptions pleaded guilty. Vyshinsky in his speech for the prosecution talked of the Kirov murder in the following terms: "These mad dogs of capitalism tried to tear limb from limb the best of the best of our Soviet land. They killed one of the men of the revolution who was most dear to us, that admirable and wonderful man, bright and joyous as the smile on his lips was always bright and joyous. . . ." He ended by saying, "I demand that these dogs gone mad should be shot—every one of them." The accused then made their pleas, most of them condemning themselves, some saying that they deserved to be shot as traitors. Kamenev was more dignified, saying, "No matter what my sentence will be, I, in advance consider it just."

The prisoners were taken back to prison and, despite Stalin's promises, immediately executed. According to reports Zinoviev pleaded for his life when he realized that they had been tricked, whereas Kamenev went to his death maintaining his dignity.

The names of Bukharin, Rykov, and Tomsky had been mentioned at the Zinoviev trial in connection with terrorist activities, and there is no question that Stalin was aiming the next major phase of the Terror against them. But there was opposition to the idea of a trial on these grounds, and instead Stalin turned on Yagoda, who had been chief of the NKVD since 1934, accusing him of slackness. Yagoda joined others on trial in 1937 and was executed as a member of an "anti-Soviet bloc of rightists." In his place as head of the NKVD Stalin appointed Yezhov in September 1938.

The "Yezhovshchina"—In November there was a trial of Trotskyite saboteurs in Siberia, and in December another connected with sabotage on the railways. In January 1937 another group, described as the Anti-Soviet Trotskyite Center, of whom the main figures were Karl Radek and Grigory Pyatakov, were tried. Most of the accused were sentenced to death; Radek was given a 10-year jail sentence, but was later killed in prison by a criminal. In February 1937 Ordzhonikidze died under suspicious circumstances; it is not clear whether he was murdered or forced to commit suicide. He had resisted Stalin in the past and his elder brother had recently been shot after being tortured. At the February—March Plenum of the Central Committee the direct attack on Bukharin and Rykov was made. Despite attempts by remaining moderates like Pavel Postyshev to dissuade Stalin from proceeding with the purge, the two men were arrested at the meeting and removed to jail. In March Yezhov cleared the NKVD of all Yagoda's men—3,000 are reported to have been executed in the year. One of them, Chertok, who had interrogated Kamenev, jumped from his 12th-floor flat rather than face interrogation.

Purge of the Red Army—On June 11, 1937, Marshal Mikhail Tukhachevsky and eight other senior army officers were tried and executed for "breach of military duty and oath of allegiance, treason to their country, treason against the peoples of the USSR, treason against the workers and peasants Red Army."

This revelation of treachery on the part of these eminent soldiers was as startling to the Soviet people as it was to the world outside. Until then there had been every sign that Stalin looked on the military with considerable favor.

Stalin's campaign started with the arrest of Dmitri Shmidt, an old veteran and commander of a Kiev tank unit in July 1936. He was accused of involvement in a Trotsky-inspired assassination attempt. In May 1937, Tukhachevsky and Yan Gamarnik were both relieved of the office of deputy commisar of defense and Tukhachevsky posted to the Volga Military District.

The basis of the treason charge against the men surfaced in mid-May in the form of a dossier "proving" that Tukhachevsky was preparing to betray his country's defense secrets to the German High Command. The documents were prepared with great care by Reinhard Heydrich of the Sicherheitsdienst, or SS intelligence, as part of a plot to destroy the High Command of the Red Army. The suggestion is that Stalin was fully aware of the origins of the material.

Tukhachevsky and the others were soon arrested and, after a purely formal trial and despite appeals to Stalin, were shot, probably in the courtyard of the NKVD building in Dzerzhinsky Square.

Many explanations have been given for Stalin's actions against the army, including personal grudges. According to Trotsky, Tukhachevsky's attack on Warsaw in 1920 (leading to a severe defeat for the Red Army) was undermined by Stalin's attack on Lvov. The marshal had not hesitated to make his views known about this, which had led to bad feelings between the two men.

Stalin, like all dictators, went in constant fear of a coup d'état, and although there is no proof that such a thing was ever contemplated by the accused men, Stalin may have genuinely believed it.

Following the execution of these dominant figures, the NKVD, at Stalin's behest, started the wholesale slaughter of any "dissident elements" in the Red Army. Soon after, 20 younger generals from the Moscow headquarters were executed and the entire command of the Kremlin Military School was arrested. The campaign culminated in 1938 with the execution of Marshal Vasili Blyukher, who had led the 1937 counterattack against the Japanese in Manchuria. By the outbreak of World War II the purge had accounted for 3 of the 5 marshals, 14 of the 16 army commanders, all 8 admirals, 60 of the 67 corps commanders, 136 of the 199 divisional commanders, and 221 of the 397 brigade commanders. It has been estimated by Soviet sources that about half of the officer corps—perhaps 35,000 men—were shot.

As a result of this purge the 1939–40 Finnish war was a disaster for the Soviet Union. Similarly, the feeble response made to the German attack in 1941 can be directly attributed to lack of adequate preparation and poor leadership. The situation was saved only by the survival of two good generals, Georgi Zhukov and Simeon Timoshenko, and some excellent staff officers. Stalin's appointees, mostly part of his old civil war group such as Voroshilov and Budyenny, were often disastrous, and at best mediocrities. In 1940 German intelligence came to the conclusion that it would take the Red Army four years to recover from the effects of the purges and get back to its 1937 level of efficiency.

That the Red Army survived the assaults of the Wehrmacht and the Luftwaffe is remarkable but perhaps even more so is that it survived the damage inflicted on it by the head of state. It may be that the unexpected result of the purge was to produce generals who were on average 20 years younger than their German opponents and that much more adaptable to new tactics.

The Provinces—Now it was the turn of the provinces to feel the full effects of the Terror. Stalin's most trusted and most ruthless henchmen were sent to accomplish his intention, which was by now to crush any spark of resistance in the party. Zhdanov took charge in Leningrad where virtually the whole leadership, both political and industrial, was removed. Beria was sent to the Caucasus, Malenkov to Belorussia, and Kaganovich to Smolensk. Khrushchev, Molotov, and Yezhov were sent to the Ukraine to deal with what was described as the "National Fascist Organization" headed by the party chairman there. On August 30, alerted by Molotov's suggestion that a visit to Moscow would be in order, the chairman shot himself and his wife. In January 1938 Khrushchev was appointed first secretary of the Central Committee of the Ukrainian party replacing Kossior, who was arrested in April 1938, and Khrushchev proceeded to replace the entire Ukrainian party structure. The purge proceeded at all levels and produced an atmosphere of fear that struck at the roots of political and social life. Denunciation was one weapon; there was a well-known case in Odessa of a man who denounced 230 people. The writer, Isaac Babel, who himself died in a camp in 1941, wrote, "Today a man only talks freely with his wife, at night, with the blankets pulled over his head." One woman was sentenced to 10 years for saying, after his arrest, that Tukhachevsky was handsome.

The Last Show Trial—On March 2, 1938, the last great show trial took place in the October Hall. Bukharin, Rykov, and Nikolai Krestinsky were the most important party figures, but there was also Yagoda, the disgraced NKVD chief, Rakovsky, and 20 others. They stood accused of spying, of sabotage, of provoking a military attack on the USSR, of being responsible for the deaths of Sergei Kirov and Maxim Gorky. Bukharin was charged with plotting to seize power and to kill Lenin and Stalin in 1918. Andrei Vyshinsky conducted the prosecution.

Krestinsky startled the court by withdrawing his confession but, after a night in the Lubyanka, once again adhered to it. Bukharin had agreed, threats having been made against his wife and young child, to pleading guilty to all charges; but he withdrew his confession before

the trial started and only agreed after he had been severely interrogated, though not tortured. In court he defied Vyshinsky and denied all charges. Vyshinsky's final summary produced his usual abusive rhetoric. Bukharin was that "damnable cross of a fox and a swine." The others "must be shot like dirty dogs." "Our people are demanding one thing: crush the accursed reptiles." Bukharin made a spirited defense of himself in his final speech. He denied the charges in detail, but agreed in general that he had degenarated into an enemy of socialism, and attacked Western commentators who suggested that the confessions were not voluntary. Aside from attempting to save his family, the only explanation for this confession, as for so many others, must be something like that Arthur Koestler's provided in his *Darkness at Noon*: that loyalty to the party and the historical necessity of its triumph overrode any values based on humanism. All the accused were found guilty and, apart from three less important figures, sentenced to death.

The purge was not confined merely to the USSR; it spread its tentacles to foreign Communists from Germany, Yugoslavia, Italy, and Spain. The Polish party was probably the worst affected, with 10,000 Poles in Moscow alone shot at the time of the Bukharin trial.

In July two more important party figures, Stanislav Kossior and Robert Eikhe, were arrested and disposed of after a brief trial; in August, just after the climax of the Terror, Yezhov was dismissed from the NKVD and Beria was appointed to take his place.

At the 18th Party Congress in March 1939, only 35 of the 1,827—less than 2 percent—delegates were left from the Congress of the Victors in 1934.

Body Count—It has been estimated that at the time of the fall of Yezhov, some 5 percent of the population had been arrested, and that one of the reasons for his dismissal, and for the slowing down of the whole process of the purge, was that it was administratively impossible to keep up the supply of places in the prisons or the camps. The population of the camps is estimated at 30,000 in 1928 and 12 million in December 1938.

Casualties—During the whole period of Stalin's rule, and including deaths from the famine in 1932, the collectivization of land and the massacre of the kulaks in 1929–30, and the Terror from 1934 onward, the total number of casualties must be in the order of 15 to 16 million. According to Robert Conquest in the *Independent* (London 5/12/88), birth and death registration seems to have stopped in the Ukraine and North Caucasus during the Great Purge. Taking figures for mortality and a declining birth rate into account, there was a "population deficiency" in the USSR between 1930 and 1937 of that amount. The results of a census of January 1937 were suppressed and the Census Board was shot. The census of 1939 does not carry conviction, since Stalin announced the figures before the census had been completed, and no account was taken of deaths in the camps.

Current Soviet figures show that from 1930 to 1932, 10 million peasants were deported to the Arctic, among them 2 million able-bodied young men, of whom at least a third died. In 1937–38 there were 7 to 8 million arrests and at least 1 million executions. In the course of recent investigations of the purges and the Terror in the USSR, the Kuropaty execution site (near Minsk in Belorussia)

has been opened up. The number of bodies is estimated at 102,000, but it seems possible that the number at that place alone may approach 300,000.

RABKRIN (RKI)

Raboche-krestianskaya Inspektya, or Commission of Workers' and Peasants' Inspection, established on February 7, 1920, under Stalin's control to monitor the administrative apparatus. It functioned until 1934.

RADA

The Ukrainian term for council or soviet.

RAIKOM

The party committee of a raion.

RAION

An administrative district of an oblast.

RAPALLO, TREATY OF

The treaty ending the war between the two former empires of Germany and Russia, signed in 1922. Germany and Russia resumed diplomatic relations and renounced all claims against one another. One result of the treaty was Germany's secret use of Russia to develop weapons and military tactics otherwise forbidden by the Treaty of Versailles.

RED ARMY

The army formed by Lenin in January 1918 from the Red Guards. At first a volunteer army, conscription began during the civil war. The name Red Army

TOPICS

was dropped after World War II in favor of Soviet Army.

The war against Japan, which led to the 1905 Revolution and the following years of repression by the army saw the emergence of revolutionary tendencies even among Red Guard regiments and signs of hesitancy in the Cossacks. The disasters of World War I—with hundreds of thousands of new recruits ill trained and poorly armed, smashed by German artillery, made prisoner by the thousand or left wounded without help—led to the disintegration of the czarist army. By 1917 there were 15 million men in the army. Casualties amounted to 3 million dead or seriously wounded and 2.4 million prisoners of the Germans and Austrians. In August 1915 conscription was extended to all males with few exceptions and by late 1916 mass draftings of men, some over 40 years old, were taking place, with resulting riots and desertions.

In 1917 Petrograd workers began to strike against their terrible conditions. There were 180,000 soldiers available to the authorities to control the city, and another 150,000 nearby. But many were untrained and many were recuperating wounded. Of these perhaps only 12,000, including Cossack cavalry, could be counted as reliable. On February 25 the czar ordered the military commander to put an end to the disorders. The order forced the soldiers and their officers to take sides, and many sided against the czar rather than be used to repress their own kind. On February 27 the Volynskii Regiment paraded and refused to obey orders. They shot a captain and burst into the neighboring barracks, where another regiment joined them. Soon 20,000 armed men were on the streets of Petrograd.

The Great Mutiny shook the czarist army. The Duma hoped it could control the army and Alexander Kerensky, then minister of war, called on the soldiers for support and to express their loyalty to the Duma. Most of the generals also preferred loyalty to Russia rather than to the czar. The army, in general, greeted the revolution but accepted the continuation of the war against Germany and the replacement of the czar by Mikhail Alekseev as commander-in-chief.

Order No. 1 of the Petrograd Soviet (addressed to the Petrograd garrison) was issued on March 1, 1917. It decreed that soldiers' representatives should be chosen and report to the Duma; that the military was subordinate to the soviet; that the Duma's orders should only be obeyed if not in conflict with the soviet; that while discipline should be maintained, standing at attention and saluting were abolished; and that elaborate czarist titles were to be abandoned in favor of "Mr. Captain." The order reached the whole army and was greeted enthusiastically in the ranks, but it effectively destroyed the czarist army.

The October Revolution put the Petrograd Soviet into Bolshevik hands. The remnants of the Stavka would not accept the new soviet's orders, and had no interest in continuing the war, allowing the advance of the German army to continue steadily with little resistance. The Bolsheviks needed an army if only to defend themselves against counterrevolution. Lenin issued a proclamation, "The Soviet fatherland is in danger," and on February 23, 1918 (now considered the birth date of the Red Army), men flocked to enroll in the new army. In Petrograd, 60,000 joined and 20,000 were sent to face the Germans. At the same time the Soviets began to make peace through negotiations at Brest-Litovsk, but appointed the commissar for foreign affairs, Leon Trotsky, as commissar for war. On March 4, 1918, Trotsky made a Higher Military Council (VVS), which drew up a plan for an army of 1.5 million men. Lenin passed the instructions to Yakov Sverdlov's Central Executive Committee, the All-Russian Central Committee of the Soviets, which on March 29 ordered compulsory military service.

1918–1925—The new army was built out of the old. Old regular officers in the field, in headquarters, and in the ministry became part of the Bolshevik army. They were invited, then ordered, to volunteer; in 1918, over 20,000 officers were enrolled. But they were called military specialists, since the concept of officer had been banned. Political commissars—trusted Bolsheviks—were appointed to every unit down to the regimental level, in conformity with the Provisional Government's practice (which derived from a similar usage in the early Napoleonic armies). The commissars led a Revolutionary Military Council at each army headquarters, of which the military commander was a member, and the council conducted that army's campaign. The history of the civil war on the Red Army's side was written by these commissars, and they often depicted themselves as the generals. Many, of course, had no previous experience—Trotsky, Stalin, Mikhail Frunze, and Kliment Voroshilov being notable examples. Fewer cavalry officers had come over and their places as commanders were taken by sergeants such as Simeon Budyenny.

By 1920 the Red Army had expanded to 5.5 million men, of whom at least 48,000 were former czarist officers and 214,000 former noncommissioned officers. There had been defeats and chaotic routs, but in the long run it was gaining the upper hand in the civil war with the Whites. By 1922 the intervention was over and the last substantial White Army under Wrangel had been driven out.

In 1922 Frunze put forward his "Doctrine of Proletarian War," which emphasized mobility, the use of offensive strategies, and guerrilla activity in a war that would liberate the workers of the world. Frunze and Tukhachevsky, with Voroshilov's support, put this to the 11th Party Congress. Trotsky opposed it and, with Lenin and other Bolsheviks, wanted to end the regular standing army and replace it with a militia (which would have been based on the urban worker and not the peasant guerrilla-cavalryman). In 1923 the Central Control Commission of the party set up an inquiry that went against Trotsky and resulted in Frunze's appointment, first as chief of staff in 1924 and then in January 1925 to replace Trotsky as commissar for military and naval affairs.

Frunze started on a program of reform. By 1925 he had reduced the army from 5.5 million to 562,000 and he established a pattern of compulsory military service, a small regular army, and a militia. Frunze had ousted Trotsky but he died, conveniently for Stalin, within the year; Voroshilov became commissar and chairman of the Revolutionary Military Council. The Red Army now belonged to Stalin.

1925–1937—Kliment Voroshilov was Frunze's heir. The Red Army had gained a corps of professional officers and a program to train them. The relationship between the army and the party had been defined: while the politicization of the soldiers decreased, the power of the political commissars was maintained. The 15th Party Congress, which formally expelled Trotsky, included in the First Five-Year Plan a commitment to develop an economic base that would ensure the nation's defense.

In 1928 the Revolutionary Military Council gave Red Army commanders a rank and benefits they would retain into retirement, and in 1935 officers were given new personal ranks, ranging from lieutenant to marshal. In the face of fascism and Nazism in Europe and the spread of war in the Far East, the standing army was increased by 1935 to 1.3 million, the Revolutionary Military Council was abolished and replaced by a less powerful Military Council, and a General Staff was created. In 1937 the army felt strong and clear of the unpleasant purges in the party and the rest of Soviet Russia.

1937–1941—In April 1937 newspapers began to criticize the Red Army leadership, and Tukhachevsky cancelled a planned visit to Britain. The commissar system in the army was reinforced and the purge started in the Red Army. (See PURGES.)

The purges wiped out the skilled professional soldiers at the top and middle ranks and halved the lower levels. Commands were taken over by young, ill-prepared officers, by Komsomol reservists, and by recalled retired middle-level officers. Even the loyal Voroshilov reported to Stalin that morale and discipline in the army and navy had crumbled.

The first campaign of the Red Army in Europe was the occupation of Poland

from the east in 1939. Cracks in the logistical services began to show, but when Stalin launched the Red Army into war against Finland, the deficiencies were clear and he reversed his policy. The Red Army was again allowed a professional corps of officers without intrusion from political doctrinaires. On May 8, 1940, Voroshilov was replaced by Simeon Timoshenko and the titles General and Admiral were restored. Military commissars were abolished and a new harsh military code was introduced, which included severe punishments and instant obedience to officers, symbolized by saluting. The 1918 decrees were abandoned.

1941–1945—The shock of the German attack in June 1941 caused Stalin to revise the High Command. A State Committee for Defense, the Stavka, and newly empowered commissars were created to stiffen the military will by threats. A number of senior party men were sent to supervise the different fronts, coordinating the military, industrial, and civilian activities. Voroshilov was commander of the Northwest and Zhdanov was political supervisor; the Western theater was commanded by Timoshenko, with Bulganin as his shadow; the Southwest had Budyenny and Khrushchev.

In 1942, faced with further German advances, Stalin continued to strengthen the army. On the Stalingrad Front he put Khrushchev in charge of the overall political effort, and sent his most trusted Stavka generals to command in the field. He redefined the status of the officer corps, reintroducing epaulettes to emphasize and give weight to rank, and making the General rank a higher category. The families of the military were to have special privileges. Morale was further raised by designating specially successful units as Guards Regiments and so on, recalling the glories of the old Russian army.

1945–1953—With the end of the war in Europe, Stalin reasserted party control over the army. Heroes like Marshal Zhukov were transferred out of public view and credit for the victory was given to Stalin and the party. Zhdanov, the political head of the Leningrad victory, was deputed to bring strict party discipline to all fields—cultural, scientific, and military. A trusted military elite was established, with the experienced and victorious posted out of public view to the provinces. But after his death, Zhdanov's Leningrad associates were purged and again Stalin seemed to favor the military as a balance to the party.

1953—Malenkov curbed military expansion by stressing the importance of nuclear deterrence, for by now the Soviet Union's scientists had developed thermonuclear weapons and the military's budgets were cut. Malenkov used the extra funds to speed up his consumer program. Military discontent coincided with the rise of Khrushchev. The day of Malenkov's resignation, Marshal Zhukov was made minister of defense.

On March 11, 1955, 11 generals were promoted to marshal and Zhukov led a move to loosen party hold and to revise strategic thinking. But in October 1957 Zhukov was dropped (accused of "Bonapartism") and replaced by Marshal R. I. Malinovsky: this was a victory for Khrushchev and the party, but also for other army factions. The army was against reduction to a nuclear-missile support role and pressed for a large army that would be able to repulse an attack, with a strong regular cadre able to cope with the technological complexity of new weapons.

The Brezhnev Doctrine, in which the Soviet Union maintained its dominance over the Eastern Bloc, intervening overtly in Czechoslovakia and Hungary and able to show local superiority to China, was central to strategy in the sixties and seventies. It was maintained by successive ministers of defense, while the army gradually improved its weapons systems. The Soviet position remained unchanged until the lack of success in Afghanistan, a minor local war, caused dissatisfaction in both the nation and the army.

In January 1986 the new leader Mikhail Gorbachev stated the objective of total elimination of nuclear weapons. On December 7, 1988, at the United Nations Gorbachev announced a cease-fire in Afghanistan beginning January 1, 1989, and cuts in the Soviet armed forces. Then on March 21, 1989, he signed a decree to reduce ground forces by 530,000. One officer in six (or perhaps five) were to go, including officers from the two armored divisions being returned from Germany and disbanded. The overall reductions were planned as: Europe—240,000, Far East—200,000, and southern USSR—60,000.

From Germany, 4 of the 19 divisions stationed there in 1989 would go, as would one each from Czechoslovakia and Hungary. In the Far East the cuts would mean about half the troops facing China and the bulk of the 65,000 troops in Mongolia would be withdrawn.

RED GUARDS

Armed bands of workers in Petrograd in

1917 became officially recognized as Red Guards and were the model for workers in other cities.

In industrialized Russia, young workers often lived in barracklike accommodations provided by the factory or in overcrowded apartment buildings. The needs of the war had led to an increase in the number of young workers in Petrograd, not only because of production requirements but also because the frequent drafting of workers to the army drew more recruits to industry from the countryside. Housing conditions were terrible and food shortages constant; strikes and consequent police repression were common.

The 1905 Revolution had led to both workers' soviets and armed groups: in Helsinki they had been called Red Guards. The situation in 1917 brought both of these into action again. On February 25, striking workers armed only with sticks and knives began fighting the police. The military governor found he could not rely on the army—not even the Cossacks—to support the police and units of the army began to mutiny. Weapons now came into the workers' hands.

By mid-March 20,000 men were under arms in Petrograd, organized in many different ways, and the groups began to use the name Red Guards. They were not aligned to political parties, but with the confrontation in April between the Provisional Government and the antiwar factions, the Red Guards showed their strength in demonstrating against the prowar ministers. At first the Mensheviks opposed them, since they might be a rival to the revolutionary groups of soldiers and seemed to be a power base for Lenin's Bolsheviks. A Red Guard conference in April failed to establish them as revolutionary institutions.

The Petrograd City Duma organized a militia, effectively a police force, that was to be paid by the factories' managements. Lenin and the Bolsheviks saw the city militia as policemen rather than as armed workers and opposed it, encouraging a Council of the Petrograd People's Militia instead. On June 10 the Bolshevik Central Committee called for street demonstrations against the war and against the Provisional Government, but these were abandoned after Nikolai Chkheidze organized another demonstration on June 18 that turned out to be dominated by the Red Guards.

In July, soldiers, sailors from Kronstadt, and Petrograd workers—in all certainly over 30,000—demonstrated against the war, against low wages, and in hatred of the government. The day ended in disorder; Irakly Tsereteli called on the Provisional Government to disarm the Red Guards, and the Council of the Petrograd People's Militia was raided and its officials arrested. The Provisional Government published a general militia law for Petrograd, Moscow, Kiev, and Odessa to bring workers' armed squads under control, which provoked further antagonism. The factory managements began to refuse to pay the militiamen, adding to the confusion.

By August the Bolsheviks were building a new Red Guard organization based on factories, in 13-man units grouped in companies and battalions (of 480 riflemen) under district commands. The structure allowed Red Guards also to have representatives in each district. At this point Alexander Kerensky, leader of the Provisional Government, dismissed Lavr Kornilov, the army commander, who then seemed about to launch a military coup against Petrograd. The Red Guards rallied to the defense of the Petrograd

Soviet and no Kornilov attack materialized. The Red Guards drew encouragement from this and, despite the Provisional Government's opposition, began to grow in number and weapon strength. In September there were between 20,000 and 30,000 Red Guards in Petrograd, mostly armed with rifles but also with machine guns and some artillery.

When the Bolsheviks saw their opportunity for a takeover in October, they underestimated the Red Guards' size and power. Although not necessarily Bolshevik themselves, they were a force to be reckoned with in Petrograd and took many local initiatives in seizing key points. They turned out to be the most dependable support for the Bolshevik seizure of power.

In other industrial cities, including Moscow, a similar pattern of soviets and workers' militias had developed since February and, similarly, after the "Kornilov affair" the city militias decayed and were replaced by the Red Guards. Everywhere they were factory-based young men, ready in October to take power even before Bolshevik soldiers arrived or to send forces to help in the seizure of nonindustrial areas. Workers who had been with the Red Guards and returned, unemployed, to their villages were often the leaders in forming village Red Guards.

The Red Guards defended the revolution from immediate counterattacks and protected stores and food supplies from looting. They enforced new decrees and many became the first members of the Cheka. Detachments were sent to fight the Don Cossacks and the Ukrainian Rada, to Finland, and to the Urals. When the German army advanced in December, Red Guards were sent to the front. Yet they were basically factory

workers on part-time volunteer duty, and this made their next role ambiguous.

On January 15, 1918, the Workers' and Peasants' Red Army was decreed. Many of the Red Guards were enrolled as soldiers, and they brought into the army their collective spirit and acceptance of political organization. But at senior levels, professional soldiers could not accept their amateur colleagues in positions of command. The two—Red Army and Red Guards—existed side by side until, at the Ninth Party Congress in 1920, Trotsky proposed territorial militias based on industrial enterprises or the like. But since in essence the Red Guards were a spontaneous organization of workers, the regular soldiers, who were led by Frunze and were used to a central command structure, objected. With the end of the civil war the idea of and the need for the Red Guard faded, just as Trotsky's influence had.

RELIGION

On November 2, 1917, a Declaration of the Rights of the Peoples of Russia abolished all national religious privileges and restrictions. This was aimed at the Russian Orthodox Church, the state church of the czarist empire, and by removing its privileges it relieved oppressed religious groups, Jews, Armenians and others, by putting them on equal footing. Other decrees put church schools and teaching institutions under the authority of the Commissariat of Education, gave only civil marriages legal status, and cut all state funding of churches.

In the constitution of July 1918 clergy were condemned with the capitalists, ex-police, and criminals, being deprived of the right to hold office and to vote; it also limited the clergy's right to housing or food rations. However, the state and religion were firmly separated and religious freedom was guaranteed. This was followed by an ordinance that specified the churches and cults as Russian Orthodox, Old-Believers, Georgian, Catholic, and Protestants (all as one), Judaism, Islam, and Buddhism—or any cult not listed.

The Eighth Party Congress of 1919 declared the need for a program of scientific antireligious propaganda, and the 1921 10th Party Congress urged a massive campaign. During the 1922 famine church possessions were often seized by the state to help meet the emergency, thus intensifying the struggle. In May, Patriarch V. I. Tikhon was arrested after protesting against the seizures; in June a state-approved "Living Church" established a supreme church administration; and in July the Metropolitan of Petrograd was executed.

The disestablishment of the church proceeded with varying degrees of vigor. Abuses were later officially criticized, such as closing a house of prayer when a group of 20 citizens were prepared to take responsibility for it, stripping religious objects of their ornamentation if they were used by a proper group, searches of priests carried out at a time when they were ministering to a group, and priests given unseemly forced labor such as cleaning the streets. Interpretations of the laws followed, and in 1921 the teaching of religion was confined to seminaries and the like. In 1924 it was laid down that children could only have religious teaching at home.

The 12th Party Congress of 1923 said the New Economic Policy had allowed bourgeois clerical-nationalism to grow, meaning pan-Islam, Zionism, Roman Catholicism among the Poles and Baptist evangelism in the northwest. However, crude antireligious tactics were warned against at this congress and the next in 1924.

In 1929 the law was further tidied. Citizens over 18 years old had the right to form "religious societies" or "groups of believers," but these were restricted to religious activities (there could be no charities, pilgrimages, or reading rooms, for instance). The society had to be registered, its funds only to be collected within the group and not as fees or charges, meetings to be held only in the registered buildings or elsewhere by specific permission. The public display of rites, ceremonies, or cult objects was forbidden. Religion was in the hands of the state.

In August 1929 the continuous working week was introduced throughout the USSR with varying days of rest, which were in contradiction to established religious feast or rest days; absence from work could result in loss of rations or housing rights.

The principle of religious freedom was modified in Stalin's 1936 Constitution as the right to profess but not to propagate religion. Stalin demolished the Christ the Savior Church in Moscow in 1930s, but in the patriotic fervor of the war of 1941 the Orthodox Church regained something of its old national importance, and the Jewish community gained great sympathy in the face of Nazi persecution. Apart from the recognition of the Orthodox Patriarch as a national figure, there was little change in the official attitude to religion. Nor did the post-Stalin era bring change beyond minor technical revisions of the laws. In 1953 there were 15,000 churches, reduced through Khrushchev and Brezhnev, to 6,794 by 1986.

Gorbachev appointed a new head of the Government Council for Religious Affairs, Konstantin Kharchev, in November 1984. He agreed to the reopening of churches and mosques, ended the persecution of minor sects like the Hari Krishnas, and oversaw the government's part in the millennium of the Russian Orthodox Church (from A.D. 988). Thirty-five churches were acquired by the Russian Orthodox Church and three monasteries returned, including the Danilov in Moscow, to be the church's administrative headquarters. A new cathedral was to be built in Moscow and six churches, used as warehouses, to be restored. However Kharchev's enthusiasm was excessive for a career party man. He had supported a plan of Patriarch Pimen for democratic elections to the church leadership, and was accused of meddling with the church's affairs. He tried to reduce the KGB's influence on religious committees. But worst of all he espoused the cause of the banned Ukrainian Uniate Church. Kharchev was removed from his post in mid-1989 and replaced by the more cautious Yuri Khristoradnov.

The Uniate Church, or Byzantine Rite, of the western Ukraine uses Orthodox liturgical forms but gives its allegiance to Rome, although it is distinct from the Roman Catholic Church. It was a Polish creation of 1595 to lure Christians away from the Russian Orthodox Church. As a Ukrainian nationalist church it suffered persecution under the czars.

Their leader, the Metropolitan of Lvov, had been a noted patriot for many years, standing up to Polish repression in the 1920s and 30s and to the Germans during their occupation. The party secretary in the Ukraine, Nikita

Khrushchev, attended his funeral in 1944, but in 1946 the church was accused of wartime collaboration and ordered to merge with the Russian Orthodox Church. Thousands of obstinate adherents were deported, and yet 4 million continued in an underground fashion with masses said secretly in forests and cellars. They complained of persecution, citing the beating of members and of disruption of Christmas celebrations (celebrated by the Old Style calendar on January 7). Their churches have been blocked by police who try to force Orthodox priests to take services. In 1986 at an ecumenical meeting in Assisi, Italy, the Uniate Cardinal (who lives in Rome) and the Orthodox Metropolitan of Kiev were the only two clerics who refused to shake hands.

The True Orthodox Christians have been in schism from the Russian Orthodox Church from 1925 with the death of Patriarch Tikhon, who they said was murdered because of resistance to communism and was succeeded by Metropolitan Sergei, who they thought to be involved with the OGPU. They were the object of purges in 1937, and the survivors are fervently against ecumenism, which they suspect to be a plot against true churches. They survive in the shadows without official recognition, which is not surprising since they canonized Czar Nicholas in the 1980s.

The Catholics of the Armenian Rite are found in the Armenian and Georgian republics, and number well over 100,000.

Newer Christian sects of Western origin have been enlarging their following, although figures are unreliable. Among them are the Evangelical Christian-Baptists with, in 1987, 5,000 communities uniting over a half-million people with 49 new prayer houses opened since

Gorbachev took office. Seventh-day Adventists flourish, and there are also secret adherents to the banned sects of Pentecostals and Jehovah's Witnesses.

Islam had been seen as a force in opposition to czarism by the Bolsheviks of 1917; in 1916 many had risen in protest against a widened conscription order. However, traditional Muslims were suspicious of the Russian Bolsheviks and the application to them of decrees on churches gave rise to hostility. There was a Commissariat for Muslim Affairs between 1918 and 1920, but this was abandoned and a less conciliatory attitude adopted. The 12th (1923) and 13th (1924) Party Congresses recognized that the great mass of Muslims retained their "medieval prejudices" and that stronger campaigns against them were needed. In the Great Purge of the 1930s, many Muslims were accused of being in the pay of Japan as spies and saboteurs. In 1930 it was admitted that Islam dominated among the Chechen and Ingush: these Sunni Muslims were accused of collaboration with the Germans during the war and their communities broken up. By 1941 it was reckoned that there were only 1,312 mosques served by 8,052 mullahs in the whole of the Soviet Union.

In spite of the deportations from the Caucasus, the status of Islam in the Soviet Union improved with the war and the number of recognized mosques doubled; in 1945 a group was permitted to make the Haj pilgrimage to Mecca, though it was years before another pilgrimage was permitted. Gradually the party reverted to an anti-Islamic attitude that, before it came to a head, was dampened by the Central Committee's November 1954 decree condemning antireligious excess. By 1959 official fig-

ures suggested that there could be 30 million Muslims in the Soviet Union; with Moscow's awareness of its neighbors in Asia and of Communist China's mishandling of its Muslims, softer approaches began.

Jews number about 2 million officially and their religion is among those officially recognized. (See JEWS IN THE SOVIET UNION.)

REPUBLICS

The USSR is the Union of Soviet Socialist Republics. The union consists of 15 equal union republics, the largest of which is the Russian Soviet Federal Socialist Republic. Some of the union republics contain within their boundaries autonomous republics, autonomous provinces (oblast), and autonomous regions (okrug).

Autonomous republics inside a union republic have their own constitution that takes their special circumstances into account. Similarly, autonomous provinces and regions are fitted into the constitutions of their republics and have their own range of special features. There are 15 union republics (SSR); within four of these are 20 autonomous republics (ASSR).

Republics	Capital	Population (1988 est.)
1 Russian SFSR	Moscow	146,450,000
2 Ukrainian SSR	Kiev	51,377,000
3 Uzbek SSR	Tashkent	19,569,000
4 Kazakh SSR	Alma-Ata	16,470,000
5 Belorussian SSR	Minsk	10,141,000
6 Azerbaijan SSR	Baku	6,921,000
7 Georgian SSR	Tbilisi	5,297,000
8 Tajik SSR	Dushanbe	4,969,000
9 Moldavian SSR	Kishinev	4,224,000
10 Kirghiz SSR	Frunze	4,238,000
11 Lithuanian SSR	Vilnius	3,682,000
12 Armenian SSR	Yerevan	3,459,000
13 Turkmen SSR	Ashkhabad	3,455,000

| 14 Latvian SSR | Riga | 2,673,000 |
| 15 Estonian SSR | Tallinn | 1,571,000 |

RIGHT OPPOSITION (ALSO KNOWN AS RIGHT DEVIATIONISTS)

The name given by Stalinists to those led by Nicholas Bukharin, Alexei Rykov and others in 1928 to 1929 when some of the party urged compromise with non-Communists. (See also LEFT DEVIATIONISTS.)

RKI. See RABKRIN.

RMC

Revvoyensoviet, or Revolutionary Military Council of the Republic, the top military command, 1918–1934.

ROMANOV

The family dynasty of czars of Russia from 1613 to 1917.

RUBLE

The old unit of Russian currency, with 100 kopecks to the ruble, used by the Soviet Union. The gold-based chervonet was introduced in 1922. In 1988, the official rate of the ruble was U.S. $1 = 0.60 rubles, but the black market gave five rubles to the dollar. In November 1988, hard-currency auctions were officially held, with major importers or exporters being allowed to participate. The first result was to devaluate by 90 percent the official tourist rate for Soviet citizens, making the rate per U.S. $1 = 6.26 rubles. It is proposed that in 1991 there will be a new system of convertible currency, ending the artifi-

cially high rate that has been maintained for years to the detriment of foreign trade.

RSDLP

The Russian Social Democratic Labor party.

RSFSR

The Russian Soviet Federal Socialist Republic, the official name of Bolshevik Russia until 1922, when the USSR was formed; now it is the name of the largest Soviet republic.

Population: (1988); 146,450,000
Area: 6,593,391 square miles
Capital: Moscow; population, 8,614,000

The RSFSR covers three-quarters of the Soviet Union's area and over half its population are in it. The RSFSR is in effect the core of the old Russian Empire, from the Baltic to the Pacific, including Siberia but without the Polish and Ukrainian provinces to the west and without the Central Asian conquests of the mid-19th century. Eighty-three percent of its people are Russians, but there are about 100 other nationalities. In the RSFSR, there are 16 autonomous republics (ASSR):

ASSR	Capital	Population (1987)
Bashkir	Ufa	3,894,000
Tatar	Kazan	3,564,000
Dagestan	Makhachkala	1,765,000
Udmurt	Izhevsk	1,586,000
Chuvash	Cheboksary	1,329,000
Komi	Skytyvkar	1,246,000
Checheno-Ingush	Grozny	1,235,000
Buryat	Ulan-Ude	1,030,000
Mordovian	Saransk	964,000
Karelian	Petrozavodsk	795,000
Mari	Yoshkar-Ola	738,000
Kabardino-		

Balkarian	Nalchik	732,000
North Ossetian	Ordzhonikidze	619,000
Kalmyk	Elista	329,000
Tuva	Kyzyl	290,000
Yakutsk	Yakutsk	278,000

There are also 5 autonomous regions and 10 autonomous areas (containing nationalities insufficiently large to form separate republics), among them being the Jewish Autonomous Province in Birobidzhan close to China.

Eleven RSFSR cities have populations over a million: Moscow, Leningrad, Gorky, Novosibirsk, Kazan, Kuibyshev, Sverdlovsk, Chelyabinsk, Omsk, Perm, and Ufa.

After the civil war, industrialization under the five-year plans changed the population pattern of the RSFSR. Much of the redevelopment was in Siberia—where the czarists exiled revolutionaries, and, under Stalin, the camps were set up for the victims of collectivization and the purges. The iron and steel industry in the Urals was redeveloped, partly at the new town Magnitogorsk and partly around the coalfields of the Kuzbas, where Kuznetsk became called Stalinsk (and is now Novokuznetsk). Oil and gasfields in western Siberia, beyond the Urals, have provided half the annual Soviet output.

It is in the Soviet east that discontent has been shown. In the March 1989 elections to the Congress of People's Deputies, with a high turn-out of electors, party secretaries failed to be elected in many places, including the Karelian ASSR, the Jewish Autonomous Region, Sakhalin, and Khabarovsk.

The coal mines of the Kuzbas, the second largest producing fields after the Ukrainian Donbas, were said to be underfinanced and with productivity well below international standards, with 50 percent of underground work still done by hand. Its coal-mining cities are among the most polluted in the world. In July 1989, 12,000 Kuzbas miners went on strike, and the numbers soon increased to 100,000. In October Vorkuta miners also went on strike, claiming that the promised benefits had not reached them.

In the Yakutsk ASSR, with over 3 million square kilometers but only a quarter of a million people, elections to the Congress of People's Deputies were dominated by local issues of housing, food, and consumer goods and the party candidates suffered heavily. There is no movement for independence in these deprived territories, but there are powerful feelings of dissatisfaction with centralized control, although the local popular front, The Democratic Union, has been gathering support.

In December 1989 the party central committee set up a "Russian Bureau" to look after the RSFSR's interests in the Soviet Union. The elections in March 1990 for the republic's congress had a fairly high turnout, 70 percent in Moscow. But even in supposedly conservative Leningrad Gorbachev's reforms were looked at critically and the radicals of the Popular Front gained over the party nominees.

RUMANIA

Population: 22,553,000
Area: 91,600 square miles
Capital: Bucharest; population, 1,834,000

Rumania is a predominantly agricultural country and was a monarchy. In 1940, under German pressure, King Carol ceded land to Bulgaria and Hungary and then Bessarabia (which became part of the Soviet republic of Moldavia). It allied itself with the Axis during the war in the hope of saving itself and the king abdicated in favor of his son. In 1944 King Michael attempted to take the country out of the war and ordered his army to put itself under the command of the Red Army. In February 1945 Andrei Vyshinsky ordered King Michael to appoint a Communist, Petru Groza, as premier. The government formed had several parties, but by 1948 King Michael had been forced to abdicate and the Communist party, combined with the Left Social Democrats, had a firm grip on the country.

By the time Nicolae Ceausescu came to power in 1965 more than 90 percent of the land was either in state farms or as agricultural cooperatives. He built up a very personal dictatorship that included more than 30 members of his family and in particular his wife, Elena, who was appointed deputy prime minister. He played a maverick role within the Soviet Bloc, failing to support them on the invasion of Hungary and remaining friendly with the Chinese.

Domestically, Ceausescu's rule was both brutal and disastrous. He established the Securitate, the most feared secret police in Eastern Europe, and reduced the economy to penury by insisting on repaying debts to the United States, which had been built up by extravagant and pointless developments. He preferred to be known as the "Conducator," and at the end of his reign was planning to destroy 13,000 villages and replace them with agrotowns. When the momentous changes began in Eastern Europe in the spring of 1989, and had even reached Bulgaria in November, it was generally assumed in the West that Ceausescu was entrenched enough to hold out.

But on December 17 there was rioting in the provincial city of Timiosoara, which was brutally suppressed by the army and the Securitate. According to the Rumanian government, more than 600 people were killed and many more disappeared. On December 21, Ceausescu appeared before a vast crowd in Bucharest and was greeted by howls of derision. He and his wife fled by helicopter but were captured, speedily tried, and executed.

Rumania is now being governed by the National Salvation Front, but elections are to be held on May 20, 1990, and there are several parties expected to contest the first properly democratic elections to be held in the country since 1937.

RVS

Revvoyensoviet; see RMC.

SAJUDIS

The Lithuanian party of democratic activists who support *perestroika*. See also DEMOCRATIC UNION.

SAKHALIN AND THE KURILE ISLANDS

The Russian Empire reached the islands north of Japan and east of Manchuria in the 1850s. Southern Sakhalin (Karafuto) was acquired from Japan in exchange for the Kurile Islands in 1875, but retaken by Japan in the Treaty of 1905. After World War II the Soviet Union took both southern Sakhalin and the Kuriles back, gaining only 18,000 square miles and less than half a million people. But the resulting territory was of great strategic importance in the north Pacific and gave the Soviets control of a valuable fishing area.

Sakhalin—When Anton Chekhov visited the island in 1890, studying the large czarist penal colony there, he called it "the end of the world." The northern part of Sakhalin became an NKVD corrective camp and part of the Gulag empire. After World War II the Soviets reinforced it heavily as a defensive frontier. It was from Sakhalin in 1983 that the Soviet fighters took off to destroy the Korean airliner that had strayed from its flight path.

The original islanders, the Nivhi people, still live there, but the camps, the mineral exploitation, and the cement factories have made the island a dismal place. In the 1989 elections to the Congress of People's Deputies, the party secretary was voted out and a young journalist voted in. With Gorbachev's dream of developing the Far East region, there are glimmers of hope for Sakhalin among the young.

Kurile Islands—The four islands to the north of Hokkaido, Japan, annexed by the Soviet Union in 1945. Japan refuses to sign a peace treaty until they are returned, but the settled inhabitants—Russians, Ukrainians, and Belorussians—are determined to remain and develop the local fishing industry. They also argue that the islands were explored and taken hundreds of years before by Russians.

SAMZIDAT

Meaning "self-publication," there are newsletters or single issues of works of literature or politics produced outside the official publication and censorship system. They are typed, stenciled, or photocopied and distributed by individuals, usually clandestinely. The word was formed by analogy from Goszidat, the state publishing house. Works published outside the Soviet Union were sometimes called *tamzidat*, or "over there" publications.

Switches in policy and practice have meant that some authors have their work published both openly and as *samzidat* literature, or that sometimes *samzidats* become public. Particularly from 1966, when more effective controls were imposed after the Khrushchev "thaw," there was a proliferation of *samzidats*. Alexander Solzhenitsyn is a good example; after the authorized publication of his *One Day in the Life of Ivan Denisovich*, he found it impossible to get his following works, such as *Cancer Ward*, published in the Soviet Union, so the works were irregularly published abroad and, in 1974, he was expelled from the USSR.

Although the *samzidats* of the sixties were typically anti-Stalinist or liberal, there have also been ultra-nationalist writers whose unapproved works have appeared by these means.

SCISSORS CRISIS

The economic crisis of 1923–24, when two divergent economic trends shown graphically resembled a pair of scissors. The price of food went down and the price of industrial products went up. Peasant income went down and their costs went up. The result was the discontent that the New Economic Policy tried to appease.

SEALED TRAIN

The train on which Lenin and his companions arrived at the Finland Station in Petrograd in 1917. On April 10 (in the calendar used in Western Europe), a train left Zurich, Switzerland, taking a party of revolutionaries into Germany, which was then at war with czarist Russia. A railway carriage was prepared for them and was locked by the railway authorities (technically called a "sealed train") to carry them through the Rhineland, via Berlin, to the Baltic port of Sassnitz, where they were ferried across to Trelleborg in Sweden. By night train they went to Stockholm and thence into Finland, unloading their baggage at the Russian frontier and boarding another train that took them to Petrograd.

Here they were greeted by large crowds. All day Bolshevik agitators had been touring the city, displaying slogans and putting up posters to say "Lenin Arrives Today. Meet Him." At the station were not only the crowds the party had called for but also a deputation from the Petrograd Soviet (which had made it a practice to greet all returning revolutionaries). Nikolai Chkheidze, the chairman of the Soviet, a Menshevik and opposed to the Bolsheviks, was obliged to greet Lenin at the station.

A list of the 30 passengers made at the start of the journey was as follows:

Lenin and his wife, Krupskaya
Georgy and Valentina Safarov, a Bolshevik who had attended the Zimmerwald conference and who would later serve on the All-Russian Central Committee of the Soviets
Grigory Ussievich
Helene Kon
Inès (or Inessa) Armand
Nikolai Boitsov
F. Grebelsky
A. Konstantinovich
E. and M. Mirinhov
Abraham Skovno
Grigory Zinoviev, his wife, Zena Radomyslsky, and their son
D. Slussarev
B. Eltchaninvf
Grigori Brillant (or Sokolnikov, his revolutionary name)
M. Kharitonove
D. Rosenblum (probably of the Bund)
A. Abramovich
S. Scheinesohn
Mikha Tskhakaya (or Barsov, a Georgian who had been a delegate to the Third Party Congress before Stalin)
M. Gobermann
A. Linde
M. Aisenbud (probably of the Bund)
Pripevsky (the assumed name of Radek)
David Souliachvili
Olga Ravich

SECRET POLICE. See POLITICAL POLICE.

SMOLNY INSTITUTE

Formerly a girls' school in St. Petersburg, it became the offices of the Petrograd Soviet and, in September 1917, the headquarters of the All-Russian Congress of Soviets.

SNK. See SOVNARKOM.

SOCIAL DEMOCRATS

The All-Russian Social Democratic Labor Party (RSDLP), the Marxist party founded at Minsk illegally in 1898, when all the delegates were arrested. The second congress was, therefore, held in

Brussels and London in 1903, where the Lenin-led (majority) Bolsheviks gained a vote over the (minority) Mensheviks. The Bolsheviks saw the future state as one where only workers and peasants ruled, while Mensheviks wished to include middle-class liberals as well for the sake of steady social development. By 1917 the two groups were effectively separate parties, and in 1918 the Bolsheviks adopted the name Communists. There were also regional Social Democratic parties in Latvia and the Ukraine.

SOCIALIST REVOLUTIONARIES (SR)

A political party, founded in the 1890s from Narodnik groups; it consisted of radical intellectuals who looked to the peasants rather than industrial workers as a revolutionary base. Early in the century the Socialist Revolutionaries had a "combat section" devoted to the assassination of key czarist officials. During World War I, the SRs were mainly "Defensists," agreeing that the war was necessary as "Defense of the Fatherland." Although weakly represented in the Fourth Duma, the SRs had a considerable following in the country, more so than the Social Democrats.

SR Maximalists split from the SR in 1905 and were similar to the Anarcho-Communists in urging revolution. This group believed in terrorism in political action, and many were arrested and executed after 1906, when they attempted to kill Peter Stolypin, the minister of the interior in 1907. They were usually identified as being near to the Bolsheviks with whom they collaborated in 1917, but were later persecuted by them and the party had ceased to exist by 1920. The Center-Left was led by Viktor

Chernov and the Center-Right by Abram Gots, Nicholai Avksentiev, and Ekaterina Breshko-Breshkovskaya.

The Left Socialist Revolutionary party, an internationalist wing formed by Boris Kamkov and Maria Spiridonova, split from the SRs in October 1917, joining the Bolsheviks in the Military Revolutionary Committee until March 1918 when, opposing the Brest-Litovsk Treaty with Germany, they withdrew. In July 1918 they took part in an armed revolt against the Bolshevik government.

SOCIALIST POPULIST. See TRUDOVIKS.

SOCIALIST REALISM

The doctrine by which Soviet arts were judged. It was first publicly defined in the statutes of the Writers' Union in 1934 as "the basic method of Soviet imaginative literature and literary criticism," demanding from the artist "a truthful, historically concrete depiction of reality in its revolutionary development." The doctrine was then extended to all arts. Socialist realism was given a historical foundation, crediting Maxim Gorky and other Russian writers with conforming to it before its formulation, as were Vladimir Mayakovsky, Michael Sholokov, and Alexander Fadeyev, for example. Great international writers were also named as practitioners of socialist realism, including the German Bertolt Brecht, the Frenchman Louis Aragon, and the Spaniard Pablo Neruda. Socialist realism in the theatre was deemed to be practiced by Konstantin Stanislavsky, in the cinema by Alexander Dovzhenko, and in music by Dimitri Shostakovich. In pictorial art and sculpture, socialist realism was produced by mediocre artists and bore a striking similarity to the contemporary art of Nazi Germany, idealizing the human body—male or female—in relation to industrial effort.

A characteristic of socialist realism was its willingness to conform to the party line: that, for instance, collectivization was popular and that any depiction of a peasant who did not like it (or any worker who did not praise a five-year plan) was untypical and therefore not part of socialist realism. This gave party officials an entry to literary or artistic criticism, and was the basis of Andrei Zhdanov's campaign, from 1946 until his death in 1948, against intellectuals.

After Stalin there was a relaxation in the witch-hunt of writers and artists, but Andrei Sinyavsky's critique of socialist realism published abroad in 1956 was the eventual cause of his arrest and trial with Yuli Daniel in 1965.

SOVIET

Meaning "council." The term was commonly used in Russia prior to its adoption by the Communists.

SOVIET ACADEMY OF SCIENCES

Originating from the academy founded in 1724 by Czar Peter the Great, with 270 full and 540 corresponding members, it is potentially the largest single concentration of scientific talent in the world.

SOVKHOZ

State farms formed originally from land confiscated from the large estates. They were managed and staffed by paid workers, and it was hoped that they would serve as model farms to instruct the peasants in proper farming methods. Sovkhoz were always preferable to kolkhoz ideologically because they represented the ideal method of socializing agriculture.

In 1940 they numbered 400; by 1962 their number had grown to 8,500 and they included a total area of 250,000 hectares. When the Virgin Lands program got under way in 1954, the sovkhoz was the model chosen to undertake the vast agricultural expansion. Despite the sovkhoz's theoretical advantages and some practical ones—there were none of the complications often found in dealing with the kolkhoz—the results were continuously disappointing. Perhaps this was because they lacked the personal involvement conferred by the private plot.

SOVNARKOM (SNK)

Soviet Narodnikh Kommissarov, or Council of People's Commissars. This was the all-Bolshevik body elected by the second All-Russian Congress of Soviets in October 1917 that (with some Left Socialist Revolutionary members), after November 8, 1917, became in effect the government of the nation exercising legislative powers, with Lenin as its chairman. In 1946 this became the Council of Ministers.

SOVNARKOZ

Local economic councils set up in 1957 to replace centralized ministries.

SPANISH CIVIL WAR

In 1936 the Spanish left was dominated by the two general trade unions: the CNT, dominated by the anarchism of

Mikhail Bakunin; and the UGT, Marxist but not Bolshevik. The Spanish Socialist party had formally disassociated itself from the Comintern and from Russian Bolsheviks in 1921, and a separate Spanish Communist party had been founded. The Communist party was small in 1933 and had been torn apart over the expulsion of Trotsky. One group had formed the Workers and Peasants' Alliance, which became the central group in POUM (Partido Obrero de Unificación Marxisto). For the elections of February 1936 the left came together, at the suggestion of the Communists, in a Popular Front. The outcome gave them 278 seats against 55 of the center and 134 of the right; of the 278 Popular Front seats, the Communists held 17.

When General Francisco Franco led a military rising against the government in July 1936, the reaction of Stalin and the Soviet Union was dictated more by their fear of the growth of the Nazis and their anti-Comintern pact with Italy than by the opportunity to promote a Communist Spain. The Comintern was brought into play, and Communists from other countries were encouraged to participate. In August they accepted a noninterventionist agreement with France and Britain and officially banned the export of weapons to Spain. At the same time the USSR established diplomatic relations with Spain and sent an ambassador with a formidable staff. This staff included Yan Berzin, who had just left his post as head of the GRU, or Military Intelligence; as consul-general in Barcelona came Vladimir Antonov-Ovseenko, a leader of the October Revolution but who had since been thought a Trotskyite.

The Spanish Civil War gave the Red Air Force an opportunity for combat experience and the first 18 I-15 fighters were unloaded at Cartagena on October 13, 1936. Probably up to 1,500 planes were sent to Spain and up to 770 air crews served for some time during 1936 to 1938. The Soviet aircraft outmatched the first German aircraft they met, giving the Republicans air superiority until the Messerschmitt BF-109 altered the balance in mid-1937.

At the time, socialists throughout the world saw Spain as a microcosm of world politics: fascism was being fought by the popular fronts of the world. Disappointments were bitter. From the left-wing point of view, the policy of nonintervention meant that France and Britain were allowing Germany and Italy a free hand against the Republican government. The activities of the Soviet Union seemed as much directed against its allies as against Franco and the fascists, judging by the betrayals and purges of the Anarchists and Social Democrats in Spain. Most of the Soviet officers sent to Spain were executed on their return, because Stalin feared them to have been corrupted by exposure to Western values.

SR. See SOCIALIST REVOLUTIONARIES.

STALINISM

The model of socialism in the Soviet Union questioned openly since the 20th Party Congress and attacked under the leadership of Mikhail Gorbachev. Its main features were:

1. An official ideology drawn from Marx and Lenin and used as the only measure of the correctness of any policy, law, or tactic.
2. The insistence on a one-party sys-

tem with decisions made at the top and binding on all lower organizations.

3. Common ownership of the means of production, whose meaning was extended to mean state ownership and central planning of the economy and thence to party control of all institutions, the courts of law, trade unions, the press, and cultural organizations.

4. The belief that citizens can be converted to conform to a collective pattern and that individualism should be strictly controlled, hence criticism of the regime became punishable.

5. A "cult of personality," assuming that the leader of the Soviet Union must be not only great but perfect.

STAVKA

Army Supreme Headquarters, a term used both in czarist days and in the Soviet Union, when it was reestablished on July 10, 1941.

STRIKES

Strikes in industry, when they occurred, have never before been publicized, but in July 1989 newspapers reported that the nation's coal miners had gone out on strike, losing 3 billion rubles' worth of production and threatening fuel supplies for the winter. The number of strikes in the first half of 1989 was given as 100. In April a new draft law on trade unions was published, reaffirming the unions' duty to defend the workers' interests, but not stating clearly if there was a right to strike. This was followed in October by a decree from the Soviet Congress outlawing strikes in essential industries. However, the decree established the right to strike as an extreme measure, and the right was not confined to unions but could be exercised by a work-floor group, allowing management found to have mismanaged to be dismissed.

SUPREME SOVIET. See POLITICAL STRUCTURE.

TAJIK SOVIET SOCIALIST REPUBLIC

Population: 4,969,000; 59 percent Tajik, 23 percent Uzbek, 10 percent Russian
Area: 54,019 square miles
Capital: Dushanbe; population, 582,000 Gorno-Badakhshan Autonomous Region, high in the Pamirs

The Tajik people differ from others of Central Asian Soviet republics in being Persian rather than Turkic speakers, although in Gorno-Badakhshan, high in the Pamirs, the population is mainly Kirghiz. The region was incorporated in the czarist empire only in 1895 (under a treaty with Britain, which at that time was much concerned with Afghanistan) and taking part of the territory of the emirate of Bokhara. Bokhara was declared a Soviet Republic on September 2, 1920, and the Red Army moved into Dushanbe on February 21, 1921. The territory then became the Tajik ASSR within the Uzbek SSR on March 15, 1925, and came into the Soviet Union as an SSR on December 5, 1929, the seventh union rebublic.

Rebel Tajiks, commonly known as Basmachis, were active in their resistance to the Soviets up to 1926, and the last armed threat to them was a brief invasion in 1931 from Afghan territory by Ibrahim Beg, styling himself as the Commander of the Islamic Army. The political unreliability of some party leaders in this affair, together with a failure to meet the collectivization targets, led to a purge of the leadership. In 1934 and 1937 the party was again purged, among the leadership being, it was declared, Trotskyites and Bukharinists. Unlike other victims of the purges, those from Tajikistan have not been "rehabilitated."

In common with other republics there was an upsurge of nationalism in the 1980s. In 1987 there were anti-Russian and anti-Uzbek riots in Dushanbe. Since then mixed marriages have decreased in number and non-Tajiks are said to be leaving the republic. In January 1990 there were further anti-Russian and anti-Uzbek riots (who were identified with the settler groups) in the capital Dushanbe. Moscow feared that this was another sign of Muslim fundamentalism, but the Tajiks are largely Sunni Muslims and not immediately affected by the Iranian Shia movement; the riots seem to be of nationalist rather than religious origin.

TATARS

There are two groups of Tatars in the USSR; the Kazan Tatars with an autonomous republic on the Volga River east of Moscow, and the Crimean Tatars.

Tatar Autonomous Soviet Socialist Republic (within the RSFSR):
Population: 3,564,000
Area: 26,000 square miles
Capital: Kazan; population 1,094,000

The assimilated Turkic-speaking descendants of the Golden Horde formed the khanate of Kazan, a rival to Moscow

until 1552, when it was taken by Czar Ivan IV, known as "The Terrible." The Muslim Tatars were subjected to religious and racial persecution, but by the end of the 18th century their right to practice their religion was recognized, as was their control of Russian trade with Asia. Further religious repression in the mid-19th century only added to their religious determination. At the same time the Tatars began to develop their education and literacy. By 1917 Turkic newspapers were widely read and printed in Ufa, Orenburg, Astrakhan, and Uralsk.

In July 1917 a united Muslim Congress was convened in Kazan and in November at Ufa, where elections were held. On November 29 the congress declared an autonomous state, which existed until the Bolsheviks dissolved it officially in April 1918, having decreed a Soviet Socialist Tatar-Bashkir Republic on March 23. The civil war prevented any realization of local governments, however on March 23, 1919, the Bashkir ASSR was established and the Tatar ASSR on June 25, 1920.

Tatars felt that by making two republics, the Soviets had reduced their status to that of other small minority peoples. Dissatisfied Tatar intellectuals were purged during the 1930s. However the survival of the Tatar language, used at party meetings and at institutes of higher education, has ensured the continued identity of the people.

Crimean Tatars—Muslim descendants of the 13th-century invading Mongol and Turkic Hordes, the Crimean Tatars had, in the 15th century, an independent state. From Ottoman rule, they passed in 1783 into the Russian Empire. Under Russian rule they were a declining subject people and there were fewer than 200,000 of them by the start of the 20th century.

The Crimean Autonomous Soviet Republic was established in October 1921. After the German occupation of the Crimea in World War II, the Tatar population was accused of collaboration and treason. They were sent, under penal conditions, to Kazakhstan and Uzbekistan in 1944; the half-million survivors were "rehabilitated" in 1967 in a decree that referred to them as "formerly resident in the Crimea." The Crimean ASSR had been disbanded in 1946 and incorporated into the Ukrainian SSR and the land resettled.

TAURIDE PALACE

The building in St. Petersburg that housed the czarist Duma and in 1917 the Petrograd Soviet.

THAW

The sense of cultural freedom that followed the death of Stalin.

THEATRE IN THE SOVIET UNION

The prerevolutionary theatre of Russia was dominated by the Moscow Art Theatre, founded in 1898 by Vladimir Danchenko and Konstantin Alexeyev (Stanislavsky), who in 1902 produced one of Maxim Gorky's first plays *The Lower Depths*, as well as justly celebrated productions of Chekhov, Ibsen, and Hauptmann.

After the revolution and under the generous and enlightened rule of Anatoly Lunacharsky, the resolution made at the Eighth Party Congress "to open and make accessible to the working masses the treasures of classic art" was imple-

mented. Numerous theatres already in existence—the Moscow Arts, the Alexandrinsky, and the Theatres for the People in Petrograd—were absorbed into the system, as well as the Bolshoi in Moscow and the Kirov in Leningrad, which specialized in opera and ballet. Many new ones—the Lenkom, the Lensoviet, the Meyerhold, for example—were established. In addition to these the nationalities and the republics established their own theatres; in 1938 Georgia had 39 theatres.

In Stalin's time the usual problems of censorship existed as much in the theatre as elsewhere, and as a result there are not many Soviet dramatists of note. Ivanov's *Armoured Train* was a success, as were Afinogenov's *Fear* (1931) and *Distant Point* (1934); Mikhail Bulgakov's *Day of the Turbins* saved the author from acute disfavor, if not worse—Stalin liked it so much he saw it 14 times. It was even produced in London in 1938 under the title *White Guard*.

During World War II there was, of course, little new theatrical activity, though there were plays by Simonov and Rozov on popular patriotic themes.

Following Stalin's death there was, as in the other arts, a considerable loosening of official restraint on the theatre. Several new theatres have opened in the last 20 years, of which the most notable are the Taganka, the Theatre of Satire, and the Meyerhold. This latter is a gesture toward the rehabilitation of the theatrical martyr of the Stalin era. What really separates the Soviet theatre from the rest of the world is the degree of security given to the actor. Each theatre has a permanent company and performs a changing repertoire of plays. Actors, directors, and designers have a job for life.

THIRD WORLD (USSR INVOLVEMENT)

1917–1924—The Bolsheviks' success in 1917 and their survival and victories in the civil war sent tremors throughout the world. An international revolution was a threat that seemed real. On March 2, 1919, 52 leading revolutionaries met in Moscow to establish the Third International, known as the Comintern. (The First International had been founded by Marx in 1864 and was dissolved after a split with Mikhail Bakunin in 1876; the Second International was a nonrevolutionary movement formed in Paris in 1889 that collapsed in 1914 with the outbreak of world war). They believed that Europe weakened by war would soon go up in flames and their time would have come. The second Comintern Congress of 1920 produced Lenin's *Theses on the National and Colonial Question*, which stressed the need to support anticolonialist forces to undermine the imperialist world. This was the height of Zinoviev's influence as head of the Comintern. In September 1920 at a congress in Baku, he was host to 1,800 delegates of some 20 nationalities from the Middle East and Central Asia. The Red Army under Mikhail Frunze succeeded in ejecting the traditional rulers from the subject states of the former czarist empire in Khiva and Bokhara and brought them under Bolshevik rule. In August 1920 Lenin saw the chance of carrying the revolution into Western Europe, where the Red Army was advancing into Poland, but world revolution was not at hand and the Polish workers did not rise to meet their would-be liberators. The Red Army was beaten and driven back.

The development of Stalin's "Socialism in one country" policy, as against Trotsky's theory of permanent revolution, culminating in the 13th Party Congress in 1924, put the interests of the USSR first; from the mid-1920s there was an isolationist stance toward what is now called the Third World.

1953–1962—The Comintern's early dreams of world revolution had faded, but the turmoil of the post-World War II period gave new hope to dreamers of a socialist future. By the 1950s the Soviet Union had the new governments of Eastern Europe on one frontier and Communist China on the other. To the south, independent India and Pakistan gave evidence of friendship. There was hope that further political advances might be made.

The main stages in Russia's involvement with the Third World were:

1. 1955—Bandung Conference. Twenty-nine states of Asia and Africa (including Communist China, but excluding the USSR) met at Bandung in Indonesia. The main theme was their dissatisfaction with the domination of international politics by the quarrel between the two superpowers—the USSR and United States—and the danger of a Sino-American war. But this was also the year in which the USSR started supplying arms to a "nonaligned" Egypt, which was also the adversary of America's ally, Israel.

2. 1958—The West African state of Guinea turned down France's offer of independence within a French-controlled economic pact, and at once all French aid was cut off. Ghana offered political support, and the USSR made loans to support the economy.

One item of totally inappropriate aid is said to have come when an entire airport and all equipment was shipped to Guinea—down to the snow plows for the (Russian) winter.

3. 1961—Belgrade Conference. Thirty-five Mediterranean and Afro-Asian countries met and agreed on the principles of Bandung and declared nonalignment. This conference was an embarrassment to the Soviets, since the dissident Communist leader of Yugoslavia, Marshal Tito, was the host. However, the Soviets were able to make tactical use of the principle of nonalignment as a tool against U.S. influence, and it provided them with an important voting bloc in the United Nations General Assembly.

Advances were made in relations with the Third World, but not with the full success hoped for. Often military aid was asked for rather than economic, and the regimes supported did not turn out to be the friends that the Soviet Union desired. In the case of Somalia, an aid recipient turned out to be an enemy. In Afghanistan, increasing economic aid turned into political intrigue and involvement that culminated, in 1979, with a war from which the Soviets pulled out in 1988 in some disarray, with damage to their international reputation.

In 1961, Kwame Nkrumah, the president of Ghana, toured the Soviet Bloc after the Belgrade Conference and was impressed by the state-owned corporations he saw. He returned to Ghana and within five years had created some 50 state corporations, obtaining various forms of international aid for all of them. The Soviets gave particular help to the state farms and the gold mines. The refinery for the gold was, however, already obsolete by the time of its delivery and added neither to Ghana's riches nor to the USSR's reputation as a donor. Other offers were to train 400 military specialists and a large number of doctors. The former offer made the old officer corps nervous and was a major cause of the military coup that toppled Nkrumah in 1966. The medical training disturbed the medical profession, and returning graduates were subjected to severe testing and required to take further training, discouraging subsequent students from going to the USSR.

TRUDONI

Units of a day's work.

TRUDOVIKS

The Socialist Populists. A large group in the First Duma, of Narodnik origin. They campaigned mainly for land distribution. At first many of them sided with the Kadets, while others leaned toward the Social Democrats, although they did not associate with the revolutionary aspect of socialism. Alexander Kerensky was a Trudovik from 1912 to 1917, but then joined the Socialist Revolutionaries as minister in Prince Georgy Lvov's Provisional Government. The Trudoviks then ceased to have independent political significance.

TsIK

Tsentralnyi Ispolnitelnyi Komitet, or the Central Executive Committee elected by the Congress of Soviets.

TsKK

The Central Control Commission. It is the top controlling party body, elected by the party congresses, from 1920 to 1934. See KPK for after 1934.

TURKMEN SOVIET SOCIALIST REPUBLIC

Population: 3,455,000; 68 percent Turkoman, 13 percent Russian, 9 percent Uzbek
Area: 188,417 square miles
Capital: Ashkhabad; population, 382,000 (subject to earthquakes, Ashkhabad was completely destroyed in 1948 and then rebuilt)

A battleground for many Asian empires, the land lost much of its fertility and by the 19th century was inhabited by Turkic-speaking Sunni Muslim peoples, centered on the oases and along the rivers. The rulers were the Persians or the khanates of Khiva. In the last quarter of the century the Russian Empire extended itself beyond Kazakhstan, taking Khiva and Merv and meeting, on the Amur-Darya River, the British sphere of influence in Afghanistan.

In 1916, as in the rest of the Russian Central Asia, the attempt to conscript indigenous people (formerly exempt) for military service caused riots in the towns. But when the Bolsheviks tried to take power in 1917, mainly through the efforts of railwaymen in Ashkhabad, they met hostility and a Russian White Provisional Government of Transcaspia and a Turkmen Congress were formed. When the Turkmen Congress tried to form an army from returned Turkmen cavalry, the Red Army sent units to Ashkhabad to disperse them. A Turkestan Autono-

mous Soviet Socialist Republic was proclaimed as part of the Russian Soviet Federal Socialist Republic on April 30, 1918, but in July the congress with some Mensheviks and Socialist Revolutionaries, and help from a British army group from Persia, established themselves in Ashkhabad. This threatened the city of Tashkent, in Bolshevik control, but when the British withdrew, the Red Army under Mikhail Frunze's command took the area early in 1920. In 1924 the Central Asian Republics were redefined and the Turkmen SSR came into being on October 27, 1924, with its congress formally declaring its formation and entry ino the USSR on February 14, 1925.

Collectivization attempted to force nomads into farms, and there was open rebellion from 1928 to 1931. The purges of the 1930s were directed particularly against those who gave signs of nationalist opposition or who objected to the vast cotton schemes imposed from Moscow.

When in 1958 the first secretary of the party, Babayev, argued that leading posts should be filled by Turkmen, he and others of the party were dismissed and expelled.

In 1989, after the May Day parade, 200 students rioted. The shortages of food and goods were an immediate cause, but there has been a growing Muslim-nationalist feeling against the small Russian population.

U2

The U.S. spy plane shot down near Sverdlovsk in May 1960. The Lockheed U2, first flown in 1955, was designed to fly at a great height, over 80,000 feet, for clandestine reconnaissance. The Soviet Union went to great lengths to shoot it down, and thereafter the U2 was used for other lawful purposes. The pilot, Gary Powers, was put on a show trial.

UFA CONFERENCE

At Ufa, an industrial center in the Urals, on September 23, 1918, an anti-Bolshevik government was established by dissident members of the Petrograd Constituent Assembly. Alexander Kolchak disbanded it in December 1918.

UKAZ

Also *ukase*. A state decree of the czarist days, the term was revived in the 1936 Constitution.

UKRAINIAN SOVIET SOCIALIST REPUBLIC

Population: 51,377,000; 74 percent Ukrainian, 21 percent Russian, 1 percent Jewish, 1 percent Belorussian.
Area: 233,100 square miles
Capital: Kiev; population, 2,544,000

1917–1921—The first distinctive appearance of Ukrainian nationalism was in the 19th century with the poetry of Taras Shevchenko, but in its political forms it emerged only after the establishment of Soviet Russia and the Treaty of Versailles, which divided its people into citizens of the Soviet Union to the east and of Poland, Rumania, and Czechoslovakia to the west. Political attitudes to the Soviet Union were ambiguous. On one hand there were strong Russian Pan-Slavist sympathies; on the other, strong feelings of a Ukrainian identity that stressed the importance of the sepa-rate language, and the fact that the majority of the population belonged to the Greek rather than the Russian Orthodox Church.

In April 1917 the first Ukrainian rada (or council, the equivalent of a soviet) was established by an academic, Mikhailo Hrushevsky. In July an administration in the city of Kiev was started under Vladimir Vinnichenko, a Marxist writer, and Simon Petlyura, a journalist and amateur soldier (all "a ridiculous farce of a few university professors and students," according to the German Communist Rosa Luxemburg). They declared a Ukrainian People's Republic after the pattern of the Bolsheviks in Petrograd, but the Germans, whose armies controlled the region, threw them out and put in a government based on the landowning aristocracy in power, as part of their new Eastern Order.

Early in 1918, Bolshevik troops invaded and set up another Soviet Ukrainian government. But on March 3, 1918, the Brest-Litovsk Treaty recognized Ukrainian independence. Soviet troops withdrew and the rada returned to Kiev, though powerless in the economic and political chaos. The Germans appointed General Pavel Skoropadsky as hetman (ataman) of the Ukraine, but chaos prevailed as peasant groups fought to protect their crops with arms taken from the disintegrating Russian army, and the Germans carried out bloody reprisals to defend their supporters.

When the German Empire collapsed in November 1918, the nationalist Directorate emerged again with Vinnichenko as president and Petlyura as commander-in-chief; armed forces grew rapidly to 100,000. Petlyura entered Kiev on December 14 and Skoropadsky fled to Berlin, disguised as a German officer.

On one side of the Ukraine was the new republic of Poland, anxious to extend its influence to the Dnieper River, and on the other side, the new Soviet state threatened by the White anti-Bolsheviks. A succession of Ukrainian governments came and went supported by either one of these powers. For a time a West Ukrainian Republic was formed in Galicia, but this came under Polish rule. The Red Army finally won the military struggle for the Ukraine, and the last of the nationalist governments went into internment in Poland after a final raid into the Soviet Union in October 1921.

In spite of Stalin (commissar for nationalities), who would have brought the Ukraine into the Soviet state as an autonomous republic, a soviet socialist republic was established in December 1920. The Bolshevik leaders were opposed to the old "Great Russian Chauvinism" and encouraged an independent cultural life in the Ukraine. Hence, although there was a permeation of Russian, Ukrainian sentiment was allowed to be identified.

1921–1959—Collectivization at the end of the 1920s hit the Ukraine heavily, where the peasant ways of land use ran counter to the large-scale farming being introduced, and large numbers of peasants were deported from the Ukraine.

Ukrainians in Poland and Czechoslovakia began to identify themselves as minority groups there, and a Ukrainian Military Organization and a Union of Ukrainian Nationalistic Youth were formed and joined in 1929 together as the OUN (Organization of Ukrainian Nationalists). In 1938, as Czechoslovakia was occupied and dismembered by Nazi Germany, the OUN began to see its opportunity. One faction declared Ukrainians to be Aryan and became the willing tools of the German Nazis. The inheritors of the Ukrainian People's Republic, the UNR had by this time strong links with the Polish government and many of its members moved west toward the Germans when the Soviets took half of Poland in 1939 and became the unwilling pawns of the Germans.

The World War II underground in the Ukraine has usually been described in terms of Khrushchev's partisans (he was party secretary there from January 1938) and an underground Central Committee; there were nationalists and anti-Communists, and some who cooperated with the Germans, especially in the western Ukraine. There was the Ukraine Insurgent Army (the UPA); the Banderists (followers of Stefan Bandera, a Ukrainian nationalist released in Poland in 1939); Bulba's men, led by Taras Borvets; and the OUN folloers of Col. Andrew Melnyk, a former Austrian officer and Ukrainian nationalist. Melnyk had moved to Rome and led the OUN from there until, during the war, he was taken into Nazi custody for attempting to set up a government in Kiev.

The OUN survived as a relatively powerful underground organization during the Soviet occupation of eastern Poland, as parts of that territory were taken into the Soviet Ukraine. As the Red Army retreated in 1941, Ukrainian nationalists claimed that the NKVD shot all prisoners with long sentences and, in some towns, burned the prisons with their inmates inside. The OUN members tried to establish Ukrainian nationalist governments in Lvov (Bandera) and Kiev (Melnyk), but the Germans dispersed these and jailed the leaders. They were released in 1944 in order to lead the OUN against the Soviets, but the OUN were at war with both Stalin and Hitler.

Many of these groups continued after the Soviet reentry into the Ukraine in 1944 and carried on a civil war until some time in the 1950s. They may have hoped that the defeat of Nazi Germany would mean the reestablishment of small independent nations and the OUN kept hoping for a popular insurrection. The UPA forces, mainly in the western Ukraine, had been hotly nationalist and had in their campaigns killed Jews, Poles, and Slovaks; there were claimed to be as many as 20,000 UPA fighters by 1944, some operating in the eastern Ukraine and as many as 6,000 in Polish territory. Brezhnev played a part in the elimination of the UPA. The famine conditions of 1947–48 brought more support for insurgents and more attempts to suppress or reeducate people. It was under these circumstances that the Uniate Church was banned in 1946.

The destruction of the nationalist underground was completed in 1959 with the assassination in West Germany, where he then lived, of Stefan Bandera.

1953——The death of Stalin brought immediate changes to the party in the Ukraine. Khrushchev said that he had restrained Stalin in his fight against the Ukrainian intelligensia after the war, and claimed that Stalin would have deported them all to the east. Alexei Kirichenko was sent as party secretary, and was succeeded by Nikolai Podgorny in 1957. Both were Ukrainians with considerable power in the USSR and both gave a feeling of self-esteem to the Ukraine.

At least three underground political movements were uncovered in the western

Ukraine between 1958 and 1961, and their leaders either executed or given long sentences. In spite of this there has been a continual current of dissent, particularly among academics urging the use of the Ukrainian language.

Although in the Gorbachev era, the Ukraine still lived in the Brezhnev climate. The party secretary, Vladimir Shcherbitsky, was the last of the Brezhnev-era men on the Politburo of the Soviet Union, appointed in 1972. Although he expressed commitment to *perestroika*, the Ukraine was still without the reforms of the Baltic States. Shcherbitsky attempted to stop the publication of a Ukrainian *Narodny Rukh* Popular Front program before the 1989 elections. This, supported by nationalists, members of the Uniate Church, and human rights campaigners, was the strongest group outside the party. Shcherbitsky was replaced by Ivashko, a party worker in Kiev, and dropped from the Politburo in 1989.

In Kiev new organizations were formed, including Zelenje Svit (Green World), Hromada (Gathering) at the University, the Ukrainian Cultural Club, the Ukrainian Helsinki Union, and the Ukrainian Democratic Club. In Lvov, in the western Ukraine, annexed from Poland in 1939, there are many who can remember a pre-Soviet Union society; there, a Lion Society was formed in 1987 to preserve Ukrainian culture.

In the March 1989 elections to the All-Union Congress, while many voters spoiled their ballot papers as a protest against the party's ban on their election meetings, many party candidates failed to get seats. With insufficient votes they were not declared elected. Thus in Kiev the party secretary and the mayor, although unopposed, were not elected.

In November 1989 Rukh put through changes in the election laws of the Republic scrapping the Communist party's fixed quota of parliamentary seats. There are strong environmental concerns in the Ukraine not least because of the Chernobyl disaster, and the fact that ten more nuclear stations are planned for the republic. The new political movements also claim that the Dnieper and the Black Sea are becoming badly polluted and they wish to exercise control of the chemical works that are causing the damage.

UNION OF THE RUSSIAN PEOPLE

A political party established in 1905, avowedly nationalistic, monarchist, and anti-Semitic, the open front for the Black Hundreds, who in the period up to the revolution, with approval of the czarist authorities, carried out pogroms and murders of radicals.

UZBEK SOVIET SOCIALIST REPUBLIC

Population: 19,569,000; 69 percent Uzbek, 11 percent Russian, and others including the Kara-Kalpak Autonomous Soviet Socialist Republic (capital: Nukus; population: 1,140,000)
Area: 172,700 square miles
Capital: Tashkent; population, 2,124,000
The city, of largely Russian creation, was nearly destroyed by an earthquake in 1966 and has since been reconstructed.

A former protectorate of the Persians, which language is widely used in the towns of Bokhara and Samarkand (which the inhabitants wish to be considered an enclave of the Persian-speaking Tajiki-

stan), Imperial Russia conquered its dominant khanate of Khiva in 1873 and controlled the emirate of Bokhara and the khanate of Kokand. With Samarkand and Tashkent a large Russian province was carved out. The revolts of 1916 were widespread in the area, but the 1917 Revolution gave the opportunity for Russians in the towns to take over. Largely Menshevik but with Left Socialist Revolutionary and Bolshevik railway workers and soldiers in Tashkent, provisional governments were formed. The Muslims of Turkestan were observers of the revolution.

Among the early campaigns of the Red Army were those to bring the land under Bolshevik control. Mikhail Frunze arrived in November 1919 with instructions from Lenin to this end, and found strong Muslim and nationalist attitudes there. To the Bolsheviks these were lumped together as anti-Communist bandits—Basmachis—and, therefore, not to be tolerated. Moscow's power was maintained from the largely Russian city of Tashkent. The Turkestan Autonomous Soviet Republic was formed in 1918 and, with the Red Army's victories, the Bokhara and Khorezm People's Soviet republics in 1921.

A version of the New Economic Policy was introduced to Turkestan, in an attempt to fit the local economic patterns. In 1924–25, Turkestan was divided into national units (partly as a counter to pan-Turkic claims that the peoples of Central Asia were one, united by Islam and Turkic culture). The major republic of Uzbekistan was formed in 1925 and from 1928 it featured largely in the Soviet Union's five-year plans.

Collectivization of agriculture from 1931 meant intensive growing of cotton, using the best irrigated land for this. Uzbekistan was to give the USSR independence from foreign cotton markets. But even after the de-Stalinization process from 1953, cotton remained the center of its planned economy.

A cotton fraud of 3 billion rubles was uncovered in 1983 and led to years of investigation. As a result Inamzhon Usmankhodzhayev was removed from post of party leader in January 1988 (for "reasons of health"), as was Akil Salimov, president of Uzbekistan's Supreme Soviet. The party leaders of Samarkand and Bokhara were sacked in October 1988. The most spectacular of the accusations was against Yuri Churbanov, son-in-law of Leonid Brezhnev, accused of taking 650,000 ruble bribes while deputy interior minister from 1980 to 1983. He was arrested, tried, and sentenced on December 30, 1988.

But worse than the fraud, in the long term, has been the result of intensive cotton planting: irrigation that has wrecked natural water supplies, fertilizers that have chemically polluted the countryside, and a monoculture that has deprived the markets of the traditional abundant varieties of fruit.

The Muslim peoples of Uzbekistan have retained their languages and customs while outwardly conforming to Soviet practices. In spite of official disapproval, combined with controlled toleration, Islam is strong. The Tashkent Islamic Board, responsible for 30 million mostly Sunni Muslims in Uzbekistan, Kazakhstan, and Central Asia, sacked its Mufti Shamsuddinkhan ibn Ishan Babakhan on February 6, 1989, after appeal to the party secretary, Gairat Kadryov. This was a demonstration of their rejection of party-appointed toadies.

The 160,000 Meshketian Turks, deported from southern Georgia to Uzbek-

istan in 1944, were the subject of racial attacks beginning June 3, 1989, and 15,000 were evacuated to the safety of military camps in the Ferghana Valley where most of them live, and later taken out of Uzbekistan. Cars were burned and the party headquarters attacked; 87 deaths were declared, although other estimates exceeded 100, among them Tajiks and a Russian. Mesketians are seen to be active in street markets and are held responsible for shortages. A few have returned to Georgia, only to find their lands long occupied by other Georgians. Some of the blame for the Ferghana riots was put on Holy Uzbeks, a group of religious Sunni Wahabis. Ethnic riots erupted again when Uzbeks rioted against the police demanding the release of 400 of their number arrested in Kokand by KGB troops.

The new party secretary, Rafiq Nishanov, is associated with those who feel that Uzbekistan has been treated as a colony, supplying raw materials to Russia. The nationalist Birlik ("Unity") movement, founded in 1988, has condemned the anti-Meshketian riots and told how rumor was used to spread dissension among Sunni Muslims (who have little in common with the Shiite fundamentalists of Khomeini's Iran) and destabilize the new regime's efforts at *perestroika*. Anti-Meshketian riots continued in 1990, as part of the expression of Uzbekistan's economic grievances, resentment of corruption, and hatred of settlers.

VEKHI GROUP

A group of young philosophers who had broken both with Marxist thought and with other radical traditions of Russian thinking in the 1860s and '70s. Influenced by Peter Struve, they published a book of essays in 1909 under the title of *Vekhi* ("Landmarks"). Their thinking stressed the need for the intelligentsia to break away from outworn revolutionary traditions, for government to be based on the concept of law, and for the state and nation to combine into a whole. There was also a strongly religious element in their arguments.

Apart from Struve, the other members of the group were Nikolai Berdiaev, Serger Bulgakov, Semen Frank, B.A. Kistiakovsky, Mikhail Gershenzon, and A.S. Izgoev.

The book, which quickly went into five editions, attracted violent criticism from the Kadets, from the Socialist Revolutionaries, and, of course, from Lenin, who accused it of being typical of the Kadet outlook. After the revolution, of which they profoundly disapproved, some of them produced another volume of essays under the title of *De Profundis*. In one of the essays, Struve calls for the overthrow of the Bolsheviks for the salvation of the state. He made a direct contribution to this idea by joining the White Army under the leadership of Anton Denikin. The majority of the Vekhi group, Struve included, emigrated during or after the civil war.

VISHESINSKAYA MANSION

The Petrograd headquarters of the Bolsheviks in July 1917.

VOLOST

A rural district.

VSNKₕ

Vesenkha, or the Supreme Council of the National Economy. It chiefly managed industry, established in December 1917 and operated until 1934.

VTsIK

Vserossisski Tsentralnyi Ispolnitelnyi Komitet, All-Russian Central Executive Committee of the Soviets, formed in February 1917 mainly of moderate socialists, Mensheviks, and Socialist Revolutionaries. In October a new VTsIK was elected by the second All-Russian Congress of Soviets with a Bolshevik majority. It was the top law-making and executive body of state power in the Russian Soviet Federal Socialist Republic from 1917 to 1936. This became the Presidium of the Supreme Soviet.

WAGES

There are considerable wage differentials in Soviet industry, with the highest wages going to miners and workers in the oil industry. Wages are low by Western standards, but housing, though of rather poor quality, is available at very low rents. The party elite (nomenklatura) get not only better wages but also privileges such as access to special shops, better housing, cars, chauffeur driven cars for high party officials, holidays in special resorts, and no difficulty obtaining higher education for their children.

WAR COMMUNISM

The term used to describe the policies adopted during the confusion or nearanarchy of the first years of Communist rule, beginning in mid-1918. The decree on nationalization led to the wholesale takeover of factories and businesses and, in reaction, a chaotic decline in industry and in food distribution. Grain requisitioning was carried out by Cheka squads going out to villages; food rationing in towns was done with social discrimination against the bourgeoisie. Inflation (multiplying some 1917 costs by 4 million in 1922) was welcomed by War Communism enthusiasts as "the dying out of money" and the breakdown of society as its replacement by a Communist society.

WHITES, WHITE RUSSIANS

The name given to the anti-Bolshevik forces in the civil war. The color white (as opposed to red) is often associated with monarchist, loyalist, or legitimist movements. It derives from the color used by the French Bourbon monarchy. "White" in this sense is not to be confused with Belorussian "White" Russia.

WHITE ARMIES

The Armed Forces of South Russia (AFSR) as a coalition of White forces, consisting of:

1. The Volunteer Army, set up by Mikhail Alexseev in the Don Cossack region in 1917, notable for the Don campaign under Lavr Kornilov and the "Ice March," or first Kuban campaign; it was then commanded by Anton Denikin.
2. The Don, Kuban, and Terek Cossack armies, formed by local provisional governments.
3. The Northwestern Army, the smallest of the White armies, formed in October 1918 at Pskov, under German protection. In May 1919 it was in Estonia; in July, under Nicholas Yudenich, it advanced

toward the Petrograd suburbs, but with only 14,400 men it was much inferior to the Red Guards who faced it. In November 1919 the army was disarmed and interned in Estonia.

4. The army formed by the All-Russian Directorate at Omsk in September 1918, led by Admiral Alexander Kolchak. At Samara another army was formed under Viktor Chernov. It was with these armies that the Czech Legion collaborated.
5. Jäger battalion (see FINLAND), or Finns trained in the German army who took part in holding Finland against the Soviet atttacks.

At Archangel, the Russian General Eugene Miller tried to raise a force, but met with no local enthusiasm, and on February 21, 1920, he evacuated himself and his followers. In Murmansk there was no White Army at all and the only opposition to the Red takeover was the presence of the British army.

At Vladivostok an army formation took charge, under Japanese occupation. In eastern Siberia, also under Japanese control, the Cossack commander in Transbaikal, Gregory Semenov, had authority over troops. (See also INTERVENTION.)

WINTER PALACE

An official home of the czar, and after August 1917 the seat of the Provisional Government.

WORLD WAR II

Always referred to in the Soviet Union as the Great Patriotic War. The Russo-German pact signed in September 1939, and Stalin's belief that Hitler could not possibly fight a campaign on two fronts, seems to have deluded him into believing that the Nazis would not move against the USSR, at least not in the immediate future. The massive German attack, which they code-named Operation Barbarossa and launched on June 22, despite numerous reports both from intelligence sources and from his own generals in the field, took Stalin completely by surprise.

The German attack was launched on three fronts simultaneously: Army Group North driving for Leningrad via the Baltic States, Army Group Center aiming for Moscow on the line of Minsk and Smolensk, and Army Group South for Kiev and the Ukraine. Over 3,000 Soviet aircraft were destroyed in the first 10 days of fighting, and the Red Army, many of its best commanders killed in the purges and with inadequate tanks and aircraft support, was in no posititon to resist. Leningrad was under siege within a fortnight, and on the Central Front the German army had reached more than 350 miles beyond Smolensk by early August, with 850,000 Soviet troops captured.

In the south, though there was stronger resistance at first, 1.5 million men were captured at Kiev and at Uman in the Ukraine. By October 15, Rostov and Kharkov had been captured. By October 20, Operation Typhoon saw the German troops 40 miles from Moscow.

In December, General Georgi Zhukov, who had been brought in to defend the city, counterattacked, and the Red Army launched other attacks at Rostov and to relieve Leningrad. Although these were not notably successful, the temperature on the Center and Northern fronts had dropped to minus 40 degrees and

the Nazi forces, unable to make further progress, fell back from the capital.

In the spring of 1942 Hitler launched his offensive in the Caucasus, partly to seize oilfields supplying fuel to the Red Army, but it became increasingly concentrated on the capture of Stalingrad. Spearheaded by General Friedrich von Paulus, with his 6th Army Group, a direct attack was launched in August. The city was defended street by street, and then in November General Georgi Zhukov in overall command of armies under Generals Konstantin Rokossovsky, Nikolai Vatutin, and Andrei Yeremenko led an attack to retake the city. Despite desperate attempts by the German High Command to reinforce von Paulus, he was captured in February 1943 with 90,000 of his men and 250,000 in total casualties. This was effectively the turning point of the war.

The second great German defeat was the Battle of Kursk in August 1943 (see KURSK), the biggest tank battle ever fought. This was followed by an overall Soviet offensive in which the Red Army captured Smolensk at the end of September and Kiev in early November.

By 1943 the situation of the Red Army had improved enormously. Counting on the neutrality pact signed with the Japanese in 1941, Stalin had brought reinforcements in from the Far East; also, the newly expanded industries beyond the Urals were turning out new and improved tanks and aircraft. After 1942 the USSR had received vast quantities of war matériel including aircraft, particularly motor transport from the United States and Britain. The supplies came overland through Iran and by sea to the Arctic port of Murmansk and some through the eastern port of Vladivostok. At the same time younger and better commanders had replaced those relics of the civil war such as Marshals Kliment Vorshilov, Simeon Budyenny, and Simeon Timoshenko. The German situation was precisely the reverse: they had suffered huge losses, partisans were tying down large numbers of German troops, and Hitler continually interfered with his High Command. All in all, German morale was very low. By January 1944 the Red Army was attacking on all fronts, and by now the Soviet High Command had a superiority of more than two-to-one in men, tanks, and aircraft. Furthermore, the U.S. and British landings in Italy in 1943 and in France in 1944 diverted all German reserves from the Soviet Front.

At the end of 1944 German Army Group North was trapped in a huge pocket in the Baltic States, and in August an offensive in the Balkans had led to the capitulation of Rumania together with the majority of the German armies there. By February 1945 Bulgaria, Hungary, and Yugoslavia had all fallen to the Red Army. In April Marshal Rodion Malinovsky's men reached Vienna.

On April 25, the 2.5 million men of the eight Soviet armies in the central sector launched an all-out attack on Berlin. They entered the Reichstag on April 30. Hitler committed suicide in his bunker on the same day, and on May 9 Field Marshal Wilhelm Keitel signed the document of unconditional surrender that ended the war in Europe.

The Soviet Union had suffered enormous casualties, perhaps approaching 20 million dead and missing and the destruction of much of its industry. The Great Patriotic War had started only a few years after the terrible purges of the 1930s. But the effect, encouraged by Stalin's radio speeches, was to revive an intense patriotism that enabled the country to triumph in face of appalling odds.

WRITERS' UNION

The sole professional organization of writers in the Soviet Union, established in 1934 on the basis of a party decree of April 23, 1932.

In the comparatively liberal atmosphere that flourished in the immediate aftermath of the revolution, writers were allowed to criticize the regime to some extent. But by the time Stalin assumed power the situation had changed. In 1934 at the first All-Union Congress of Soviet Writers, Andrei Zhdanov laid down the doctrine of socialist realism as the fundamental criterion for Soviet literature and literary criticism. It was adopted as a charter by the meeting, and from then on all writers wishing to be published—for expulsion meant not being published at all—had to follow the line.

The Writers' Union is structured on the pattern of other Soviet political institutions. It has several thousand members and a board of several hundred elected from them. The board elects its Secretariat of several dozen members, with a president and first secretary. The Secretariat has its core, its Bureau, which effectively runs the union.

From 1934 to 1936 the board controlling the union was headed by Maxim Gorky. Anna Akhmatova and Mikhail Zoshchenko were expelled in 1946, but after Stalin's death there was some relaxation of the rules; however, Boris Pasternak was expelled in 1958, and Alexander Solzhenitsyn in 1969. The board monitors its own members—approximately 8,000—and actively encourages high standards of writing and publishes several magazines, of which the best known is *Novy Mir* ("New World") and the newspaper *Literaturnaya Gazyeta*. Although it can be seen as a repressive instrument, its positive function is to allow writers an economic and personal freedom for doing their work.

YALTA CONFERENCE

February 4–11, 1945. The last meeting of the war between Roosevelt, Churchill, and Stalin, at which they sorted out the political future of the world. Stalin agreed to end the Russo-Japanese neutrality pact of 1941 and declare war on Japan two or three months after Germany's surrender, providing: (1) the Mongolian People's Republic was maintained; (2) the 1904 gains by Japan against czarist Russia including Sakhalin were returned, Dairen was internationalized, the Soviet Union would have a naval base in Port Arthur, and the railways would be brought back under Sino-Russian control; (3) the Kurile Islands given to the Soviet Union.

However Stalin's demands for a seat in the United Nations for each of the USSR's republics was turned down, though the seats for the Ukraine and Belorussia were conceded.

YEZHOVSHCHINA

The Great Purge starting with the assassination of Sergei Kirov in 1934, carried out by first by Genrikh Yagoda and then from 1936 by Nikolai Yezhov on Stalin's orders. As many as 10 million people were arrested, many exectued, millions held in camps, and only a few tried in public show trials. The intensity of the purge ended when Lavrenti Beria was appointed people's commisar for internal affairs in 1938. The Leninists and old Bolsheviks had mostly been destroyed and Stalin's power was absolute. Under Nikita Khrushchev and later under Mikhail Gorbachev the details of the "Yezhhovshchina" were made known.

ZEMSTVO

The local self-government unit set up in the czarist reforms of 1864., Each zemstvo was elected by all classes to administer education, health, roads, and welfare. Their national association, the All-Russian Union of Zemstovs, was a major force in maintaining the fabric of society during World War I. It campaigned for social reform and was part of the revolutionary action in both 1905 and February 1917.

PART TWO

BIOGRAPHIES

ABEL, RUDOLF IVANOVICH. 1902?–1971

A Soviet intelligence officer. He was convicted in the United States and sentenced in 1957 to 30 years in prison for handing over secrets to the USSR, but was exchanged in 1962 for Gary Powers, the U.S. pilot of the U2 reconnaissance plane shot down over the Soviet Union in May 1960.

ABRAMOV, FEDOR. 1920–

Writer. Born in Archangel and a member of the Communist party since 1945, he gradutated from Leningrad State Unviersity with a degree in philology and, from 1950, was head of the department of Soviet literature there. His works are leading examples of the 1950s school of "village prose" and include *Brothers and Sisters* (1958); a novel about northern peasants during World War II, *Fatherlessness* (1961); and *In Severnaya Zemlya* (1962), which deals with life on the kolkhoz. He has also written critical works, notably his study of *The Kolkhoz in Post War Prose* (1954).

AKHMATOVA, ANNA (ANNA ANDREYEVNA GORENKO). 1889–1966

A prerevolution poet who was officially disapproved of until 1940. She chose the pen name "Akhmatova" from her Tatar great-grandmother. With Osip Mandelstam she was a member of the Acmeist group, which sought precision in poetic expression and a place in the tradition stemming from Graeco-Roman literature. After her husband was executed in 1921 her poetry was refused recognition until 1940, though again banned in 1946, when she was, with Mikhail Zoshchenko, the star victim of the Zhdanov witch-hunt that involved imprisonment of her son; she was condemned for "bourgeois-aristrocratic aestheticism" and called "part nun, part harlot." She continued to write. Among her works was the cycle of laments entitled *Requiem*, on the Stalinist Terror, and included the experience of standing in line to find news of her jailed son. Expelled from the Writers' Union but rehabilitated in 1959, she was able to travel abroad for the first time since 1912; she revisited Italy and also received an honorary doctorate from Oxford University.

ALEKSEEV, MIKHAIL. 1857–1918

Soviet army general. He gained promotion by his administrative talent, without any influence from other quarters. A successful commander in 1914 and 1915, he was made chief of staff at the Stavka (Army Supreme Headquarters) when Czar Nicholas assumed command of his armies in August 1915. His ignorance of social etiquette (such as leaving the table before the czar in order to return to his desk) did not endear him to the aristocrats on the staff. He was commander in chief until briefly replaced by General Alexei Brusilov in 1916. He attempted to serve the Provisional Government but found the intrusions of the Petrograd soviet intolerable. As a result of the "Kornilov affair," he was forced to retire from the Stavka and, in November 1917, he quietly went south to Novocherkassk, where he tried to form the Volunteer Army in the Don Cossacks Territory under General Alexei Kaledin. He fought for a while under Anton Denikin, until he died exhausted and ill from cancer in October 1918.

ALTMAN, NATHAN. 1889–1970

Artist. He studied at Odessa Art School and in Paris. His early influences were cubism and futurism, but he soon turned to more respresentational styles. In 1920 he did a bust of Lenin in bronze and then took up portrait painting; he did a well-known portrait of Anatoly Lunacharsky. He was also involved in graphic design and did sets for Nadimir Mayakovsky's *Mystery Bouffe* in 1921 and Shakespeare's *Hamlet* in 1954.

ANDREYEV, ANDREI. 1895–

A Communist party member since 1914 and a member of the Presidium since 1953. He started as a member of the Metal Workers' Union and progressed through a number of party posts, being a member of the Politburo from 1926 until 1950, when Stalin, apparently by caprice, emoved him from that office.

ANDROPOV, YURI VLADIMIROVICH. 1914–1984

Soviet leader, 1982–1984. He was born in Ngutskaya, the son of a railroad official. Rising from Komsomol organizer and leader, he became "first secretary" of a number of party organizations from 1940. He was ambassador to Hungary in 1953–57, the time of the Soviet suppression of the Hungarian uprising, then head of the party's liaison committee with overseas parties. He rose through the ranks of the party's Central Committee, as Mikhail Suslov's protégé, to the Politburo Central Committee in 1967,

becoming chairman of the KGB in May. He gained a public reputation for attacking bureaucracy when he gave the Annual Lenin Birthday Speech in 1976.

Andropov also started an anti-corruption campaign bringing charges against Nikolai Shchelokov, former minister of internal affairs, and Sergei Medunov, both members of the Central Committee. In 1984 he had the director of the largest food store in Moscow tried for corruption and executed. He put new men into the Politburo, among them his protégé Gorbachev. In May 1982 he became general secretary of the party and, on Leonid Brezhnev's death, November 10, 1982, he was made general secretary of the Central Committee. In December, he became a member of the Presidium, for which he was president until his death from kidney failure two years later.

ANTONOV, ALEXANDER. ?–1922

A former Socialist Revolutionary politician who led the uprising in the Tambov area, 1919–1921, with 50,000 peasants and Red Army deserters. The uprising was suppressed only by implementation of the New Economic Policy. The slogan of the uprising was "Down with Communists and Jews."

ANTONOV-OVSEENKO, VLADIMIR A. 1883–1939

A regular infantry officer who joined the Social Democrats in 1903. He was jailed for his political activities but escaped in 1907 and reached Paris in 1910. Here, despite his Menshevik sympathies, he became friendly with Lenin and joined the Bolsheviks in May 1917.

A slim, handsome man, more like a poet than a warrior, Antonov-Ovseenko played a leading role in the October Revolution as a member of the Military Revolutionary Committee, and was responsible for the capture of the Winter Palace. He was a Red Army commander, most notably leading the February 1919 move into the southern Ukraine, which caused the French troops, which had landed at Odessa, to withdraw from the civil war.

After Trotsky's fall in 1925, Antonov-Ovseenko was removed from his posts and sent as ambassabor to Czechoslovakia and then to Lithuania. He published a declaration in favor of Stalin (refuting Lenin's Testament) and became ambassador to Poland in 1928. He was made Soviet consul-general in Barcelona upon the outbreak of the Spanish Civil War in 1936, but, like many others sent there, was recalled in 1937, supposedly to become people's commissar for justice in the Russian Soviet Federal Socialist Republic, but actually was put on trial and, because he refused to confess at a show trial, was shot.

ARMAND, INESSA OR INÈS (b. STEFAN). 1874–1920

Paris-born daughter of a French actor and an Anglo-French mother, she became tutor to the family of French industrialist Eugène Armand in Russia, one of whose sons, Alexandre, she married. In 1903 she joined the Social Democrats and was arrested but escaped from detention. She met Lenin in Paris in 1909 and settled there. She was sent back to Russia, illegally, in 1912 to help with the elections to the Fourth Duma, but was again arrested and again escaped, reaching Switzerland in 1913.

She spent the war there, returning with Lenin on the "sealed train."

Armand played little part in the October Revolution and was part of the left-wing opposition to the Brest-Litovsk Treaty. Her main work for the Bolsheviks was directed to improving the conditions of women factory workers. She died of cholera after a visit to the Caucasus, and was buried in the Kremlin wall. Lenin clearly was attracted to her and was deeply affected by the news of her death. However close their friendship, there is no evidence that they were lovers.

AVILOV, MIKHAIL. 1882–1954

Painter. Born in St. Petersburg and studied at the Academy of Arts from 1904 to 1913. An academic painter known for his battle scenes, such as *A Breakthrough on the Polish Front by the 1st Cavalry Army in 1920*. He was made People's Artist of the Russian Soviet Federal Socialist Republic in 1953 and was awarded the Red Banner of Labor.

AVKSENTIEV, NIKOLAI. 1878–1943

A right Socialist Revolutionary, a minister in the provisional government. He moved from Petrograd to help organize the Omsk government in Siberia, and was a member of the Ufa Directorate with Alexander Kolchak. But when he was arrested as a socialist by the Whites, he left Russia from Vladivostok in December 1918.

BABEL, ISAAC. 1894–1941

A novelist (*Red Cavalry*, 1924), short story writer (*Odessa Tales*, 1923–34), and playwright (*Sunset*, 1928, *Maria*, 1935). Babel served for a time in a Cossack military unit, which gave him the unusual experience of being a Jew working equally among a people of long-standing anti-Semitic tradition. Although much acclaimed, his polished prose and his highly individual ironic standpoint, combined with his description of the horrors of anti-Semitism and of the Polish-Soviet war of 1920, made him politically suspect. He was arrested in the "Yezhovshchina"—another irony since Nikolai Yezhov was a personal friend—and died in a concentration camp.

BAKST, LEON. 1866–1924

Painter and scenic designer. Born in Grodno and studied at the St. Petersburg Academy of Art and in Paris. Returning to Russia, he became a member of the World of Art group. His illustrations and paintings of the time were strongly influenced by the art nouveau movement. He was one of Diaghilev's most important designers, doing sets and costumes for *Firebird* and *Daphnis and Chloe*. His art used themes from both classical Greece and the East. After leaving Russia in 1909, he worked in Paris, London, New York, and Rome.

BAKUNIN, MIKHAIL. 1814–1876

International revolutionary and anarchist. A man of imposing appearance, born to the Russian landed gentry, he went to Germany to study Hegel and became engrossed in radical politics. In 1848 he joined in the uprisings, first in Paris and then in Germany. He took part in a revolt in Prague and then went to Dresden, where he was arrested and

sentenced to death for his part in the uprisings there, but, instead, he was handed over to the Austrians, who deported him to Russia in 1852. He prospered in exile in Siberia, and in 1861 escaped, through America, to Europe. He became his own sort of International Socialist, but was disowned by Marx's International. Fascinated by Sergei Nechaev, he collaborated on the "Revolutionary Catechism." This finally alienated him from Marx, but he had a long-lasting influence on Italian and Spanish anarchists.

BARKHIN, GRIGORY. 1880–1969

Architect. Studied at St. Petersburg Academy of Arts and after graduating taught there. From 1930 to 1967 he was professor at the Moscow Architectural Institute. An excellent example of a completely establishment Soviet architect, he is remembered for his Izvestia building in Moscow, built in 1925, and also for the restoration of Sevastopol, rebuilt between 1943 and 1946.

BENOIS, ALEXANDR. 1870–1960

Painter and scene designer. Born in St. Petersburg, the son of an architect, he worked in Paris before World War I. When he returned to Russia, he became the ideologist of the World of Art group. He was against purely formalistic trends in painting and, from 1918 to 1926, was director of the Picture Gallery at the Hermitage Museum. His early work showed an interest in the world of privilege, such as *The Last Promenades of Louis XIV*, painted in 1897. In 1908 he designed the sets and costumes for Stravinsky's ballet *Petruska*. In 1921 he did the same for the Bolshoi's production of Goldoni's *Servant of Two Masters.* From 1926 he lived in Paris and was involved in theatre design work.

BERDYAEV, NIKOLAI A. 1874–1948

A philosopher who advocated a mystical "creativity." He was expelled from the Soviet Union in 1922. He lived in France as an active anti-Marxist, although he had been a Social Democrat in 1905. His book *Freedom and the Spirit* aroused considerable interest in his time.

BERIA, LAVRENTI. 1899–1953

A Georgian follower of Stalin. He was a member of the party from 1917, working in intelligence from 1921. He was first secretary to the Transcaucasian Committee of the Party, 1932–38, acting as Stalin's agent there. In 1934 Stalin made him a member of the Central Committee and his deputy in the Caucasus. In 1938 he succeeded Nikolai Yezhov as commissar for internal affairs, or head of the NKVD, and organized the terror after the 1936–38 "Yezhovshchina" purge. From 1941 to 1953 he was deputy chairman of the Council of People's Commissars (later Ministers) in charge of security. Beria's empire included its own armed forces, armor, and aircraft. He even controlled the internationally famous "Moscow Dynamo" football team. After Stalin's death he was made minister of internal affairs, but he was arrested in the post-Stalin power struggle in June 1953. He was shot in December, after a trial in which he refused to plead guilty, went on a hunger strike, and begged on his knees for mercy.

According to Khrushchev, Beria was a notorious womanizer, indeed a rapist and an alcoholic. He once said to Khrushchev, showing his overweening pride and confidence in his power "Listen, let me have a man for one night, and I'll have him confessing he's the King of England."

BERZIN, YAN K. 1889–1937

Head of the 4th bureau of the GRU (Soviet military intelligence, founded by Trotsky) from 1920 to 1935. In 1905 he led an active guerrilla force at the age of 16. Captured and exiled to Siberia, he returned to join the Red Army after the 1917 Revolution. A drinking companion of Kliment Voroshilov and holding the rank of general, he was responsible for organizing the network of agents and spies beyond the frontiers of the Soviet Union. One of his main targets was China, where the political victories of the Chiang Kai-shek nationalists of 1927 had removed all main contacts. Among his emissaries was the famous German spy Richard Sorge, who later moved to Japan. In 1935 Berzin was removed from his post and replaced by General Semion Uritski. He went to Spain as military attaché, using the names "Goriev" and "Starik." He played a major part in the defense of Madrid, but with other Soviet advisers he was recalled to Moscow in 1937. Both he and Uritski were shot in 1937 and both "rehabilitated" in 1964.

BIRYUKOVA, ALEXANDRA. 1929–

Central Committee secretary for consumer goods. She joined the Politburo as a candidate member in 1988, the first woman appointed for over 20 years. She trained and worked as a textile engineer until 1968, when she became secretary to the Central Council of Trade Unions.

BLYUKHER, VASILI K. ?–1938

Marshal of the Soviet Union and commander-in-chief in the Far East. After fighting in the civil war, he became commissar for war for the Far Eastern Republic in 1921, until it joined the Russian Soviet Federal Socialist Republic in 1922. From 1924 to 1927, he was one of the principal advisers to Sun Yat-sen, the Chinese republican, using the cover name "Galin." He formed the Special Red Banner Far Eastern Army in 1929, taking action against the Chinese when they seized the Manchurian Railroad. His deeds became legendary in the Soviet Union.

On August 6, 1938, Blyukher was suddenly replaced as commander in the middle of battle, reassigned to Moscow, arrested, tried, and, on November 9, shot. It was the year after the other generals and Marshal Mikhail Tukhachevsky had been shot, but he was one of the first to be "rehabilitated" after Stalin's death.

BOGDANOV (MALINOVSKY), ALEXANDER A. 1873–1928

A philosopher and writer on economics and scientific topics. He graduated from Kharkov in medical science but became involved in revolutionary politics and supported the Narodniks in 1899. In 1904 he became a Social Democrat and went to Switzerland, where he met Lenin. In his philosophical writings he attacked Nikolai Berdyaev and impressed many of the Bolsheviks by his arguments. He served on the editorial boards of Bolshevik publications including Vpered, and then became involved in the school on Capri founded by Maxim Gorky.

Although elected to the Central Committee at the Third Party Congress, Bogdanov led a non-Leninist leftist splinter group after 1905, which Lenin outmaneuvered. He was expelled from the party for factionalism in 1909. In Russia during the revolution, he undertook the directorship of what became the Communist Academy. He refused to become involved in party quarrels, retained his post under Stalin, and devoted himself to scientific pursuits. He was the author of several books, including two science fiction novels. His death was apparently the result of an ill-conceived medical experiment.

BONCH-BRUEVICH, VLADIMIR D. 1873–1955

A journalist and revolutionary. Born in Moscow and a graduate of the Kursk Surveying Academy, he became an active Marxist in 1892 and emigrated to Zurich in 1896. There he continued his studies and met Lenin and the Liberation of Labor group. Returning to Russia he helped set up Bolshevik publications and ran a bookshop in St. Petersburg. He was on the board of Pravda from 1912. After the July Days, it was in Bonch-Bruevich's dacha in Finland that Lenin took refuge. In the October Revolution he was commander of the Tauride Palace district and later held administrative posts, including the move of Sovnarkom to Moscow and the reorganization of Moscow's water and sewage systems. His brother, Mikhail, was a czarist general recruited by Trotsky to organize the Red Army's first general staff.

In 1931 Bonch-Bruevich published his memoirs of 1917–1918; and he became director of the State Museum of Literature in 1933. From 1945 until his death, he was director of the Museum of Religion and Atheism.

BORODIN (GRUZENBERG), MIKHAIL. 1884–1951

The romantic Comintern agent of the 1920s and 1930s. Born in a Jewish village near Vitebsk, he joined the Bund and then, from 1903, became a follower of Lenin in exile. He went to Riga in 1905, from where he fled to Sweden and, in 1907, to the United States. He managed to study at Valparaiso University, Indiana, and became a teacher of English to immigrants in Chicago, mixing with U.S. socialists there under the name of Michael Berg. In June 1918 he returned to Moscow, where Lenin employed him to deliver a letter to the workers of America. He did not manage to get to America with the letter, but got it into the hands of John Reed, who published it. Next year, as a senior Comintern agent, he smuggled gold and diamonds into the United States to support Communist movements there and in Mexico. In England as "George Brown," he oversaw the reorganization of the Communist party in 1922; he was arrested and deported in 1923. About this time he began to use the name "Borodin."

That same year he went to China to establish relations between the Bolsheviks and the leader of the Chinese national revolution, Sun Yat-sen, and to stimulate the Chinese Communist party. In China, Borodin was at first spectacularly successful. His team included the future Marshal Vasili Blyukher, who worked with the military commander of the Chinese forces, Chiang Kai-shek. Michael Borodin seemed to be leading China into the communist world. When the Chinese nationalists won a victory in 1927, the world at first saw it as a gain for Borodin and the Chinese Communist party (including its leader, Mao Tse-tung). But Chiang outmaneuvered the Communist party and the nationalists gained supremacy. Borodin had to make his way back to Moscow in 1927.

In 1929 he moved out of Comintern work and set to work in industry. Then in 1930 the U.S. journalist Anna Louise Strong started the English-language weekly *Moscow News*, which he ran for the rest of his life. In 1949 Stalin had him arrested because of his association with foreigners. He died in a labor camp in Siberia.

Borodin's wife, Fanya, whom he had met in Chicago, followed him to Russia, then went with him to China, where she was imprisoned and threatened with execution, but survived him by nearly 20 years.

BRESHKO-BRESHKOVSKAYA, EKATERINA. 1844–1934

"The Grandmother of the Revolution," a Socialist Revolutionary who spent many years in prison or exile. When in 1878 she was sentenced to forced labor by the czarist government, the reports of her plight by George Kennan, U.S. journalist, made her internationally famous. She adopted Alexander Kerensky as her "political heir," but left Russia after 1917 and lived in Prague, Czechoslovakia, the star of all the liberal White emigrés.

BREZHNEV, LEONID ILYICH.
1906–1982

Soviet leader from 1964 to 1982. Born in Dneprodzerzhinsk (then Kamenskoye), a steel town in the Ukraine, where his family had been steel workers for three generations. Brezhnev was the eldest son, with an elder sister and a younger brother. He was still a child when the 1917 Revolution brought the Bolsheviks to power, and while the civil war raged in the Ukraine with Red and White armies sweeping through the town pillaging, looting, and killing.

In 1921 Brezhnev graduated from high schoool. In 1923 he took the major step of joining the Komsomol and was chosen to study surveying at the Kursk Land Technical College. On graduation in 1927 he was drafted to the Land Department of the Kokhanovksiy Rayon, in Belorussia. He was just in time for the opening of Stalin's campaign for the collectivization of the Russian peasantry.

1927–1935—During the winter of 1927 the party organizations in the rayons were told that they must use extraordinary measures to obtain the grain that the peasants preferred to hoard rather than sell to the state. The methods, earlier justified because of the civil war, included beatings and threats of deportation. There can be no doubt that Brezhnev applied such methods with enthusiasm. In 1929 the policy of liquidating the kulaks caused a split in the party and the "Right Deviationists," Nicholas Bukharin and his associates, were purged for supporting the peasantry. The purge caused gaps in the organization, and Brezhnev was promoted to fill the place of his purged superior in the Land Department. In 1929 he joined the party and next year, at the age of 24, was promoted to deputy chairman of the Land Management Board for the whole of the Urals. Before he went, and acting on "dekulakization" orders received from his headquarters, he organized meetings at the collectives at which "unanimous decisions" were taken to expel all kulaks. Depending upon their degree of resistance to change, they were to be deported, in extreme cases to Siberia and in lesser cases to remote districts of the oblast or beyond.

Shortly after his arrival at Sverdlovsk for his new job, Brezhnev was sent to the Moscow Agricultural Academy. This promotion did not last for long. He left school and returned to work in a factory in his hometown. The reason is not known but seems certain it was the result of a political argument, perhaps with an influential Bukharinite. Back at Kamenskoye, Brezhnev joined the local institute to complete his engineering studies. He did well there and became active in institute and local politics. In 1933 there was an appalling famine in the Ukraine. Once again, the fate of the peasants was not aided by the forced collection of grain that had once again been instituted, and of which Brezhnev was undoubtedly a part. The mortality rate for one town near Kamenskoye was 11,680 out of a population of 60,000. In 1935 Brezhnev graduated with honors from the institute, and in the same year he was drafted into the army and spent a year in Siberia, where he became a platoon sergeant in a territorial unit.

1936–1939—On his return from the army, Brezhnev became director of a technical college in Kamenskoye, and then was elected vice-chairman of the executive committee of the city's soviet, taking the place of another victim of Stalin's purge. The purge sharpened when Khrushchev arrived in the Ukraine in January 1938 as party secretary. He and his NKVD chief cleared out all "recidivist elements" and "cold followers of the Ukrainian party." Nationalism there remained a constant problem for the Soviet leaders. The Ukrainian party leaders Stanislav Kossior and Pavel Postyshev were executed, and by the beginning of May only two members of the party and government institutions had survived. One of the people that Khrushchev picked for his new administration was Brezhnev; he appointed him head of the Dnepropetrovsk regional party committee's Department of Ideology and Indoctrination. In other words, he had become Khrushchev's propagandist. In this role Brezhnev concentrated on Stalin's Russification policy for the Ukraine; just as Russian was to be a compulsory subject in schools, so newspapers and magazines in the Ukraine were to be printed in Russian. He had also, more importantly, found a patron. Brezhnev's career from then on was to be tightly linked with Khrushchev's.

1939–1945—When Hitler invaded Poland in September 1939, the Red Army operating under the Russo-German pact occupied eastern Poland. Brezhnev organized rallies in the territories newly added to the Ukraine to show popular support. In June 1941 the Ukraine was the first to be swept by the German advances. In October Brezhnev was appointed first deputy chief of the Political Administration of the Southern Front, the Ukraine war area. The political officer for this front was Khrushchev, and

Brezhnev worked directly under him for much of the war. Essentially Brezhnev was a military commissar, a position abolished in 1940 but reintroduced during the chaos following the German invasion. Morale was low; there were thousands of desertions. The commissars, and when necessary Lavrenti Beria's special NKVD units, were there to keep the fronts intact. Commissars and party workers were supposed to go into action first, as inspiration, and there are numerous stories of Brezhnev's having done so. The truth of these stories is impossible to establish, but it was necessary for an emerging leader to have an impeccable war record and he did.

In 1944 Brezhnev arrived in Uzhgorod in Transcarpathia to plan the takeover of the territory, which Stalin needed as a gateway to Czechoslovakia. He set up a People's Congress and organized support for a union with the Ukraine. He also, with help from the army and the NKVD, crushed the UPA (Ukrainian Insurgent Army), with a ruthlessness that equaled Khrushchev's operations in Poland in 1939. Thousands were killed, many more deported.

In June 1945 Brezhnev took part in the Victory Parade in Red Square. He ended the war with the rank of major general.

1945–1953—Khrushchev had returned to the Ukraine, and from his headquarters in Kiev was reassembling his political team. He got Brezhnev's discharge from the army, and made him party secretary in the important industrial oblast of Zaporozhye, where Brezhnev organized the rebuilding of the Dneproges dam and the Zaporozhye steel works in record time. The achievement saved Khrushchev, who was out of favor with Joseph Stalin for what was regarded as his failure to meet economic targets in the Ukraine. At the same time he was being intrigued against by Georgy Malenkov. Khrushchev returned as party secretary in the Ukraine, and in December 1947 Brezhnev was awarded the Order of Lenin personally by Stalin.

In 1950 Khrushchev, as part of his power play with Malenkov, managed to get Brezhnev appointed party secretary of Moldavia to fulfill the five-year plan that the party secretary there had bungled. There, Brezhnev launched a "dekulakization" drive on the new collective farms, which he claimed had been infiltrated by subversives, using, where necessary, the death penalty, which he had reintroduced. He turned agriculture around and then launched a Stalinist attack on the cultural front, insisting that Moldavian literature and art be ideologically strengthened. He then fought off an attack in *Pravda*, obviously inspired by Malenkov.

In October 1952, Stalin's expansion of the Central Committee found a place for Brezhnev, and he also made it into the party's Secretariat. On November 7, he made his first public appearance at the anniversary parade with Stalin above the Lenin Mausoleum in Red Square.

1953–1959—Following the death of Stalin in October 1953, the struggle for succession temporarily banished Brezhnev to the Ministry of Defense, where he became a deputy chief of the Main Political Administration, though he continued to work in Moscow. Khrushchev, as part of his maneuverings against Malenkov, became his boss again.

It is generally believed that Brezhnev was involved in the plot to destroy Lavrenti Beria, probably in coordinating the actions of the party members and the military.

Khrushchev's next ploy in his battle with Malenkov was the Virgin Lands program. Since much of the land was in the Kazakh SSR, he attempted to get his protégé appointed there as party secretary. Malenkov insisted on his own man, Pantelimon Ponomarenko, and won; Brezhnev was made his deputy. The two men fought a battle for power in the republic until Malenkov's final defeat and resignation in February 1955; by May, Ponomarenko had disappeared. Drought in the Virgin Lands caused Brezhnev and his patron trouble in 1955, but they were fortunate in 1956 with a harvest that was the best in many years. For his work there he received a second Order of Lenin. In July 1957 Brezhnev defended Khrushchev in defeating the anti-party group that had attempted to oust him and was given a place in the Presidium.

1960–1964—In June 1961 Brezhnev was awarded the title Hero of Soviet Labor for his work in the development of rocket technology and for assuring the successful flight of a Soviet man on the spaceship *Vostok*. He had been involved with Dmitri Ustinov and the scientist Mstislav Keldysh as a management team for the production and development of ballistic missiles since 1956. By the time of the manned flight in 1961, he had left the program.

In May 1960 Brezhnev succeeded Marshal Kliment Voroshilov as chairman of the Presidium of the USSR. Until now this had been a formal appointment, but he was to transform it into a vital instrument of Soviet foreign policy.

In February 1961 Brezhnev set out for Africa to put into practice the USSR's support for the "National Democratic State," a concept that in the Soviet view described many of the postcolonial countries in Africa and Asia. He visited Morocco, Guinea, and Ghana and promised them lavish aid in return for which they promised to take the socialist road or at least align themselves against the West. He also began to organize aid for the MPLA (the popular movement for the liberation of Angola). In Asia he signed an arms deal with President Sukarno of Indonesia. In India he provided more than $30 million in military equipment and, when Nehru visited Moscow in December 1961, he directly backed his move to liberate Goa, Daman, and Diu from the Portugese. He was also involved in negotiations with Cambodia, with the intention of limiting China's influence in Asia; economic assistance to Afghanistan was provided for the same reasons in 1963. His efforts in Yugoslavia were not so fruitful, nor were they with the Shah of Iran. In general Brezhnev was a more polished diplomatic performer than Khrushchev, and was adept at dealing with crowds. A great deal of money was spent by the USSR in these activities; in 1961 alone, aid worth more than $500 million was extended.

Between 1960 and 1964 there was a fresh power struggle in the party—this time between Frol Koslov, the Leningrad party chief and his associates, and the Ukrainian group headed, until his dismissal in 1960, by Kirichenko, and then by Brezhnev. The power struggle between the two groups was marked by observers in terms of appointments within various party structures or the position in lineups at official celebrations.

The situation was changed abruptly when Koslov had a severe stroke and, at the June plenum in 1963, the two candidates for Khrushchev's successor emerged as Nikolai Podgorny, secretary in the Ukraine since 1957 but new to Moscow and dependent on Khrushchev, and Brezhnev, no longer trusted by his old patron, who regarded him as too ambitious and independent. In July 1964 Brezhnev was freed from his other duties to concentrate on his job in the party's Secretariat.

1964–1967—During the last few years of Khrushchev's rule, Brezhnev's attitude toward him was a mixture of support and criticism. He supported him on agriculture until Khrushchev proposed adding an additional layer of administration and further restricting the private plots attached to collective farms. He disagreed with him about what he saw as a soft attitude toward the West about Berlin and the confrontation with China. When the plane was sent to pick up Khrushchev from his dacha on the Black Sea—crewed incidentally by KGB men—the plot to oust the party secretary had been cleared by Brezhnev not only with the KGB but also with the military— Marshals Malinovsky and Grechko were both old Ukrainian friends. By the time of the 22nd Party Congress, Brezhnev's supporters in the Central Committee, with men such as Veniamin Dymshits, Sergei Pavlov, and Nikolai Tikhonov, numbered 15. Neither Nikolai Podgorny or anybody else in the Central Committee had anything like the same support.

Having been elected first secretary of the Central Committee in October 1964, Brezhnev set about consolidating his position. He became chairman of the Constitutional Commission in December, and two years later, at the 23rd Party Congress, took the title general secretary, which only Stalin had held before. He also became chairman of the Defense Council, thus further strengthening his hold on the military. His two main rivals for power in the party were Nikolai Podgorny and Alexander Shelepin. Podgorny, as the number two man in the party's Secretariat, represented a real threat. Brezhnev attacked Podgorny's moderate policies toward the consumer industries and his foreign and defense policies; and, at the December 1965 party plenum, managed to remove him from the party's Secretariat and place him in Anastasy Mikoyan's job as chairman of the Supreme Soviet Presidium. During the same year Brezhnev's other rival, ex-KGB chief Shelepin also made something of a bid for power by attempting to obtain a meeting with Chairman Mao to discuss Sino-Soviet rapprochement. He was severely criticized for acting against the collective principle of leadership, stripped of many of his jobs, and replaced as deputy premier. In 1967 he was removed from the Secretariat. Between April and the end of the year in 1965, half of the Central Committee chiefs had been removed and replaced by Brezhnev's candidates. Two important appointments were Konstantin Chernenko, appointed head of the General Department of the Central Committee, and Yuri Andropov, who in May 1967 replaced Vladimir Semichastny as head of the KGB.

1967–1971—Both in agriculture and defense, Brezhnev charted a different course from that of Khrushchev. He called for increased capital investment, increased but stable farm prices, a reduction in income tax, and increased liberty in the use of private plots.

In defense, Brezhnev took the view expressed in a speech in November 1964 that peaceful coexistence with the West could be achieved by strengthening the military power of the USSR. To back this up, defense spending for the 1966–70 plan increased by nearly 50 percent, and for the next two five-year plans by an even greater percentage. This involved recruiting more men and reinstating the separate role of ground forces that Khrushchev had merged with the rest of the defense establishment. The number of ballistic missiles was greatly increased, by 1972 surpassing the U.S. total, and the Soviet fleet under Sergei Gorshkov was raised to superpower size and status. Malinovsky was succeeded as minister of defense in 1967 by Marshal Grechko, who was co-opted into the Politburo in 1973 at Brezhnev's personal request.

1971–1978—Prior to 1971 Brezhnev had taken a hard (i.e., anti-Khrushchev) line on foreign policy, but he had come to realize that hostility to China was pushing the Chinese toward better relations with the United States. He was also acutely aware that the expenditure called for in the next five-year plan on consumer goods and defense would not be possible without Western aid, unlikely to be granted while the USSR continued its cold war posture. He believed that with détente the USSR, as with Nazi Germany, would be able to have both guns and butter.

Brezhnev opened his campaign for détente in West Germany. He obtained recognition of East Berlin as the capital of East Germany in return for guaranteeing unlimited access of civilian traffic to West Berlin.

May 1972 produced a summit with U.S. president Richard Nixon and the signing of the first SALT treaty. The April 1973 plenum in Moscow produced complete support for the policy of détente and for Brezhnev personally. But his subsequent visits to the United States and U.S. demands on human rights somewhat soured the détente scene. The Helsinki Accord, for instance, which dealt with both economic and human rights issues, produced little in terms of action. Not much progress was made with new SALT talks under President Ford and, though a treaty was signed with President Carter in May 1979, it was felt that things had not gone quite as intended. The Soviet invasion of Afghanistan in December 1979, denounced by all Western nations, created a sudden and complete chill in the climate of détente.

Brezhnev continued to strengthen his position in the Politburo. Alexander Shelepin, already demoted, was dropped from the Politburo in April 1975. The only opponents of any stature left were Alexei Kosygin, Nikolai Podgorny, and Dmitri Polyansky. He used Podgorny as a pawn in his battles with Kosygin and did not remove him from the Politburo until 1977. Polyansky was blamed for the agricultural disaster of 1975 and was dismissed. But the battle with Kosygin was long and bitter. Kosygin held on to his "soft" doctrines on defense and industry for as long as he could, even resisting the idea of Soviet aid to North Vietnam, until the passage of his own economic reform package was threatened. Kosygin did not make the report on the 10th Five-Year Plan in 1976 and, as Andrei Kirilenko took over a large part of his economic empire in 1977, he was eliminated as a major player. At the same time Brezhnev appointed new members of the Politburo who were his allies: Marshal Grechko, Andrei Gromyko, and Grigory Romanov. In 1978, Konstantin Chernenko joined the Politburo and Nikolai Tikhonov and Eduard Shevardnadze became candidate members, while Mikhail Gorbachev, a relatively unknown figure from Stavropol, was appointed as the secretary responsible for agriculture.

1978–1982—In 1974 Brezhnev underwent major surgery for dental problems and was fitted with a pacemaker. A visit to West Germany in May 1978 had to be cut short for health reasons and his television appearances had to be extensively edited. But, as is usual in the USSR, Brezhnev showed no willingness to retire, and it was the chill he caught while attending the celebration of the October Revolution in Red Square that lead to his death in November 1982.

Judgment of his term of office has been dominated by tales of the corruption that flourished and his fondness for nepotism. His son Yuri, though a well-known alcoholic, had been made a member of the Central Committee, his son-in-law Yuri Churbanov was jailed for corruption in 1988, and his daughter Galina, whose liaison with a black-marketeering circus manager was notorious, was made a senior executive in Intourist.

BRODSKY, ISAAK. 1883–1939

Painter. Borrn in the Zaporozhye Oblast, he studied at the Odessa Art School. He started his career by painting lyrical landscapes and some portraits, but after the revolution he became well known for historical pictures of the revolutionary period, with paintings such as *The Solemn Opening of the 2nd Congress of the Comintern, 1920*. His most famous is *The Execution of the 26 Baku Commissars in 1925*. He also painted a well-known portrait of Maxim Gorky.

Brodsky was appointed professor and director of the All-Russian Academy of Arts in Leningrad and was awarded the Order of Lenin for his life's work.

BUDYENNY, SIMEON. 1883–1973

Marshal of the Soviet Union. A dragoon sergeant in the czarist army, he joined the Red Army in 1918 and during the civil war campaigned with Stalin. Starting as second in command of No. 1 Socialist Cavalry Regiment, he became the most successful cavalry commander of the civil war. He led his 1st Cavalry Army both in Poland, where he was involved in the controversial attack on Lvov, and in the final victory over Wrangel in 1920.

In 1937 Budyenny was given command of the Moscow Military District, and in 1940 made first people's commissar for defense. At the outbreak of war in 1941, Stalin appointed him to the Stavka (Supreme Army headquarters). In September he was posted to the reserve armies and later sent to the Western Caucasus theatre, returning to Moscow in 1942. In January that year Budyenny was made commander of cavalry and a member of the Supreme Military Council.

From 1947 to 1953 Budyenny was deputy minister of agriculture for horse breeding. While in the post he developed a special breed of riding horses known as the Budyenny Breed. He was known for a frank and rather coarse manner and, like some other civil war comrades

of Stalin, was not highly thought of by his professional colleagues. Ivan Konev called him "completely incompetent." He was said to have killed his first wife in a fit of temper.

BUKHARIN, NICHOLAS IVANOVICH. 1888–1938

Communist party leader and thinker. A Bolshevik from 1906, he was forced to live abroad in Western Europe from 1911, where he met Lenin and Stalin. He moved from country to country; he was in the United States in 1917, and returned that year to Russia via Japan. He joined the October Revolution in Moscow, seeing it as the beginning of a world revolution, calling for a "holy war in the name of the proletariat." His logical mind tried to fit all problems within a system and, in 1918, with Evgeny Preobrazhensky, he produced the popular *ABC of Communism* and was editor of *Pravda* in 1917. Lenin regarded him as "the greatest and most valuable theoretician in the party."

He saw War Communism as a natural step toward socialism but soon acepted and advocated the NEP (New Economic Policy). The "scissors crisis" and the failure of the German revolution in 1923 separated him from Trotsky and found him in support of Stalin's "Socialism in one country." He became Stalin's spokesman, and at the 15th Party Congress declaimed against the expelled Left Opposition, declaring that "the iron curtain of history is about to fall."

Then in 1928 his support of the peasantry and of the neo-capitalist doctrine of the NEP made him vulnerable to attack by Stalin. He was expelled from the Politburo (but left on the Central Committee). With Mikhail Tomsky and Alexei Rykov, Bukharin recanted his errors, admitting his responsibility for the Right Opposition of 1928–29. However, in February 1934 Bukharin became the editor of *Isvestia* and in August he was among the leading speakers at the First Congress of Soviet Writers. In 1936 the Politburo sent him to France to meet other socialists and collect material for the Marx and Lenin Institute.

In January 1937, Bukharin ceased to edit *Isvestia*, and in February he received notice of his forthcoming expulsion from the Central Committee, going on hunger strike in protest. With Rykov, he was accused of being a spy and saboteur and arrested. In March 1938 Bukarin, with Genrikh Yagoda, Alexei Rykov, and others, was tried for treason and of having been a party to the murders of Sergei Kirov, Maxim Gorky, and Vyacheslav Menzhinsky. He was found guilty and shot. The trial convinced the U.S. special ambassador Joseph E. Davies, who attended it with an interpreter, that Stalin had uncovered a real nest of traitors. Bukharin's last wish was to write a note to Stalin; using an old nickname, he wrote "Koba, why do you need me to die?" Stalin kept the note in his desk for the rest of his life. In 1988 Bukharin was "rehabilitated."

BULGAKOV, MIKHAIL. 1891–1940

Writer and theatrical director. Born in Kiev, he was qualified as a doctor. After the October Revolution he wrote a novel, *White Guard*, and several plays, including *Days of the Turbins*, a sequel to his novel, and *Flight*, which dealt with the fate of the intelligensia as a result of the revolution. In *Zoia's Apartment* and *Crimson Island*, written beween 1926 and 1928, he satirized the period of the New Economic Policy. His work came under increasing critical disapproval for its elements of satire, and he took to work in the theatre as a director. His salvation came in Stalin's surprising pleasure at the play *Days of the Turbins*, which he is said to have sat through 14 times in 1932.

Bulgakov wrote several more plays but they were not produced until long after his death in 1940, because they centered on the problems of art in a country ruled by a despotic monarch. His last novel, the *Master and Margarita*, which he had been working on for many years, was not published until 1965.

BULGANIN, NIKOLAI A. 1895–1975

Party leader 1955–1957. In 1918 he joined the Cheka, and, in 1922, having established a reputation for his grasp of economic issues, was appointed to the Supreme Council of the National Economy. In 1927 he was put in charge of the Moscow Electric Plant and in 1931 became chairman of the Moscow City Soviet and worked first with Lazar Kaganovich, then Khrushchev. Also on the City Committee at this time were Georgy Malenkov and Nikolai Yezhov. He continued to rise through the ranks of the party until 1938, when he became deputy premier. He was minister of defense, 1947–49 and 1953–55, gaining the rank of marshal, and had a place in the Politburo from 1952 to 1958. He was appointed chairman of the Council of Ministers (and thus head of state) after Malenkov's fall in 1955.

For a brief period he and Khrushchev

appeared to act in concert as joint leaders and traveled the world together, going to Yugoslavia in 1955 and India, Burma, and Afghanistan in 1956. In 1957 Bulganin was a member of the anti-party group that attempted to oust Khrushchev. The others were dismissed immediately; he was allowed to remain until 1958, when he was expelled from the Presidium.

BUNIN, IVAN. 1870–1953

A poet and novelist. He opposed the 1917 Revolution and went to live in Paris from 1919. He was awarded the Nobel Prize for Literature in 1933, the first Russian to receive the prize. This reflected not so much his literary quality as a demonstration of anti-Bolshevism.

CHAGALL, MARC. 1887–1985

Artist. Born near Vitebsk, he studied art at St. Petersburg with Leon Bakst, among other artists, and from 1910 to 1914 lived in Paris. At the outbreak of World War I he returned to Russia and was conscripted into a camouflage unit. After the revolution, Anatoly Lunacharsky made him commissar for fine arts in Vitebsk, where he opened an art school. His liberal views of art conflicted with Casimir Malevich and he moved to Moscow. There he worked on scenery for the Yiddish Theatre until, in 1922, he left Russia, going first to Berlin and then to Paris. He is known for his vivid use of color and the strong and unusual arrangements of figures in space. Many of his images are based on his Jewish childhood in a small Russian village.

CHAIKOVSKY, NIKOLAI V. 1850–1926

A veteran Narodnik revolutionary. He returned from exile in 1918 as a "Defensist" to join the anti-Bolsheviks in Archangel. He led the Provisional Government there and was named as one of the original five members of the Ufa conference, until he left for Paris in January 1919, announcing his support for Alexander Kolchak, but retiring from the political struggle.

CHAPAYEV, VASILY I. 1887–1919

Soviet peasant army leader. The most famous of the Bolshevik leaders of semi-independent peasant armies. A simple man capable of inspiring his unruly and illiterate followers, he had been selected for officer training in 1915 and later rose to command a Red Army cavalry division. He was the subject of a romantic Soviet film, *Chapayev*.

CHEBRIKOV, VIKTOR. 1923–

A Ukrainian security officer with the rank of colonel general. In the headquarters of the KGB from 1967, he succeeded Yuri Andropov as chairman in 1982. He was appointed to the Politburo in 1938, becoming a full member in 1985. In 1987, with Yegor Ligachev and the conservatives, he openly criticized Gorbachev's *glasnost* policy and, after the party conference in September 1988, he was moved sideways to head a commission on legal reform, being replaced as head of the KGB by Vladimir Kryuchkov. In September 1989 he was dropped from the Politburo.

CHERNENKO, KONSTANTIN. 1911–1985

Soviet leader, 1984–1985. Born in central Siberia, a Komsomol in 1929, and a party member in 1931, he was active in the purges of kulaks, probably as a member of NKVD during the 1930s. He was with the NKVD in World War II and a postwar aide to Brezhnev in Moldavia. Brezhnev was responsible for his rapid promotion from head of the Secretariat of the Presidium of the Supreme Soviet in 1964, to secretary of the party's Central Committee in 1976, then to the Politburo in 1978 and to run Brezhnev's own personal staff. In February 1984 he succeeded Yuri Andropov, on his sudden death, as general secretary and on April 11 as president of the Presidium. Chernenko was backed by the "old men," Nikolai Tikhonov, Andrei Gromyko, and Marshal Ustinov. He seemed to let affairs revert to the days before Andropov, and the campaigns against bureaucracy and corruption lapsed. His ill health, obvious at the start of his period of office, soon led to his death in March 1985.

CHERNOV, VIKTOR M. 1876–1952

The founder of the Socialist Revolutionary party. In exile in Switzerland and England until 1917, he returned to be minister of agriculture in the Provisional Government from May 1917. In the July Days the angry marchers arrested him as soon as he appeared to speak, but he was rescued by Trotsky. "Take power, you son of a bitch, when they give it to you!" growled one of the mob. But Chernov's mild, rational ways had no place in the revolution, and he continued to hope for a solution through the Constituent Assembly. When it met after the October Revolution, his presidential speech was ineffective. He moved to Samara in 1918 to head a Soviet Revolutionary government. He emigrated in 1920 to France and then to the United States.

CHICHERIN, GEORGY V. 1872–1936

Soviet diplomat. An aristocrat who served in the Communist diplomatic service, he joined the Socialist Revolutionaries in 1905, and then the Bolsheviks and, as a result, was forced to leave Russia. He returned in January 1918 and took over from Trotsky as commissar for foreign affairs in March. The U.S. diplomat Geroge Kennan described "the gigantic disorder of his office, his apparel and his working habits; his near-sightedness; his ill-health and hypochondria; his aversion to daylight and fresh air; his limitless pedantry and inability to delegate detail; his love of music in general and Mozart in particular. Aesthete and bookworm turned revolutionary, animated by faith always close to despair, slaving day and night to execute the hectic diplomacy of the young revolutionary state..." (*Soviet-American Relations, 1917–20*).

Chicherin successfully made treaties establishing the Soviet Union's relations with its neighbors; the Baltic States, Finland, Poland, Persia, and Afghanistan in 1920–21. In 1921 he achieved recognition with Britain for the Soviet Union through a trade agreement, and in 1922 signed the Treaty of Rapallo, establishing relations with Germany. Stalin was not at the time concerned with foreign affairs, and Chicherin was allowed to remain in his post until 1930 when he was succeeded by his assistant

Maxim Litvinov. He spent his remaining years in quiet obscurity.

CHKHEIDZE, NIKOLAI S. 1864–1926

A Social Democrat from Georgia who became the Menshevik leader in the Duma from 1907 and the first president of the Petrograd Soviet. He warned delegates to the All-Russia Congress of Soviets against a Bolshevik takeover in June 1917. He became president of an assembly to establish an independent republic in his native Georgia, where he had spread Marxism in the 1890s. When the Soviet Republic was established there in 1921, he escaped to France. Trotsky wrote a letter to him in 1913 with adverse comments on Lenin, and Stalin published the letter after Lenin's death as proof of Trotsky's treachery.

CHURBANOV, YURI. 1937–

The son-in-law of Leonid Brezhnev, having married Brezhnev's daughter Galina in 1971. He came to the world's attention as a militia general posted to Murmansk in 1982, but was relieved of his post and rank as general in February 1985. He was put on trial by the Soviet Supreme Court in September 1988 with others from Uzbekistan for corruptly receiving over $1 million during his period in office as first deputy minister of the interior, 1978–1982, and was sentenced on December 30 to 12 years' hard labor. He was said to have used his position to block probes into corruption in Uzbekistan during the administration of Sharaf Rashidov, the Uzbekistan party secretary, and above all to have covered up the three-million-ruble Uzbek cotton fraud between 1976 and 1983.

DAN (GURVICH), FEDOR I. 1871–1947

An early Menshevik leader. He was on the first executive committee of the Petrograd Soviet in 1917, but the Bolsheviks had him arrested in 1921 and he emigrated in 1922, first to Berlin, then Paris and, in 1940, to the United States. He was active in maintaining Menshevism overseas.

DANIEL, YULI. 1925–1988

A dissident writer. He was arrested in September 1965 and put on trial with Andrei Sinyavsky in 1966 for having published abroad without permission. They were "secret" writers of parodies of Soviet life, little known in the USSR but read abroad. The trial was in the hands of Yuri Andropov, then head of the KGB. In an unusual move in a show trial, he allowed them to plead not guilty and had them tried on the charge of libeling the state. That fiction could be judged a libel made the case a notorious travesty of justice. Daniel received a five-year sentence, but was freed in 1970 and exiled to Kaluga until 1979. He then lived in Moscow, where some of his work was published before his death.

DENIKIN, ANTON, I. 1872–1947

A leading White general in the civil war. His father had risen from serfdom in Siberia to become an army officer, and Denikin was a general commanding an army group for the czar in 1917. He first led the Volunteer Army, based in the Kuban and northern Caucasus in 1918, and defeated Gregory

Ordzhonikidze's 11th Red Army in January 1919 on the Southern Front. In June his army entered Kharkov in the Ukraine and cleared the Soviet forces out of the Don country. Hoping for victory he put himself under the authority of Admiral Alexander Kolchak, in command of the Armed Forces of Southern Russia, taking Odessa and Kiev in August. But Simeon Budyenny's Red Army cavalry outfought Denikin in October and with revolts by the peoples of Dagestan and the Kuban behind his lines, his army was driven into retreat.

Kolchak resigned in favor of Denikin in January 1920. Although he made new agreements with the Don Cossacks for the government of southern Russia, Denikin was forced to retreat into the Crimea, where in April he handed over his command to Baron Wrangel, then resigned and sailed to Constantinople and thence to England. He lived in France for many years but died in Ann Arbor, Michigan, in 1947.

DEUTSCH (DEICH), LEV G. 1855–1941(43?)

Radical politician. The founder, with Georgy Plekhanov, of the Marxist Liberation of Labor group in 1883. From 1876 he was an active terrorist and was extradited from Germany to Russia in 1884. After 16 years' imprisonment he escaped from Siberia in 1901 and became a leader of the Social Democrats, working with Lenin on *Iskra*. He was a Menshevik and a "Defensist" during the war. He left politics after 1917, living in Western Europe and the United States. He wrote several works on the history of radicalism in Russia.

DIAGHILEV, SERGEI. 1872–1929

Theatrical impresario. A flamboyant figure with an amazing talent for discovering and encouraging talent. He studied at the St. Petersburg Conservatory under Nikolai Rimsky-Korsakov, and in the 1890s was involved with Alexander Benois in founding the World of Art group. In 1907 he organized the Russian Seasons Abroad with composers such as Sergei Rachmaninov and singers like Feodor Chaliapin. In 1909 he had his first combined opera-ballet season and created a sensation by commissioning Igor Stravinsky to write the music for *Firebird* (1910), *Petruska* (1911), and *The Rite of Spring* (1913). Later he used Sergei Prokoviev, together with great choreographers such as Michel Fokine, Leonid Massin, and George Balanchine.

His most famous dancer was Nijinsky, and he also persuaded artists such as Alexander Benois and Leon Bakst to design sets and costumes for him. He had discovered that there was a huge appetite for Russian ballet in the West, and in 1913 with his Diaghilev Ballets Russes he toured the world playing in London, Rome, and the United States.

DIMITROV, GEORGY. 1882–1949

The Bulgarian head of a secret Communist network in Germany, later Bulgarian premier. He was arrested after the Reichstag Fire in 1933 and put on trial by the Nazis, who had just come to power. He defended himself so energetically against Goering, who had undertaken the prosecution, that he made Goering look like the guilty party. Although acquitted, he was held until international pressure had him released.

He went to the Soviet Union and stayed there until 1946, when he was intalled as premier of Bulgaria. He was general secretary of the Comintern from 1935.

DOBRYNIN, ANATOLY. 1919–

Ambassador to United States from 1962 to 1985. Gorbachev brought him back in 1985 to advise on the summit talks with U.S. president Ronald Reagan. In 1986 he was made head of the Central Committee's international department, until replaced in 1988 by Alexander Yakolev.

DUDINTSEV, VLADIMIR. 1918–

An author and journalist. His *Not by Bread Alone* (1956), criticizing Soviet society, was his most successful work, published by the official liberal periodical *Novy Mir* in the year of the 21st Party Congress. But it was later attacked as anti-Soviet by the government.

DYMSHITS, VENIAMIN. 1910–

An engineer and party figure. From 1931 to 1950 he was engaged in the construction of metallurgical plants, including an involvement with Brezhnev in the reconstruction of the Zaporozhye Iron and Steel Works in 1946. From 1950 to 1953 he ran the central administration for construction in the lead industry. By 1959 he had risen to first deputy chairman of the State Planning Commission of the USSR and shortly after was made chairman. At the 24th Party Congress he was elected to the Central Committee.

An ally of Brezhnev's in the power struggle for succession, he was made chairman of the newly established Council of the National Economy (Sovnarkhoz) in 1965, and was hailed in the West as the new "Economic Czar." He is the only Jewish member of the Politburo.

DZERZHINSKY, FELIX. 1877–1926

Chekist leader. Of Polish-Lithuanian aristocratic origins, he had joined the Socialist Revolutionaries as a youth and was exiled to Siberia in 1897; he escaped in 1899, was recaptured, but escaped again in 1902, this time reaching Berlin. There he joined the Social Democratic Bolsheviks and was closely associated with Rosa Luxemburg. However, he was arrested again in Poland in 1905 and was continuously in jail until the 1917 Revolution freed him. Lenin used his skills on the Military Revolutionary Committee and in December 1917 asked him to organize the Cheka (Commission for Combatting Counterrevolution and Sabotage), which in 1923 became OGPU. He was also commissar for transport in 1921 and director of the Economic Council from 1924 until his death. His political stance remained strongly to the left, opposing the Brest-Litovsk Treaty and the principle of self-determination for nationalities, which put him close to Stalin in the matter of the Russification and occupation of Georgia.

Hard, even harsh, Dzerzhinsky was generally accepted to be incorruptible, though blindly obedient to the party. He died of a heart attack at a Central Committee meeting and was succeeded as head of the NKVD and OGPU (as it had become) by Vyacheslav Menzhinsky, who was, not surprisingly, suspected of poisoning him.

EHRENBURG, ILYA G. 1891–1967

A poet and novelist. He spent much of his life in Paris after escaping there in 1906, returning to Russia only for the years 1917–1921. He returned home during the war and was for a time a member of the Supreme Soviet and twice a winner of the Stalin Prize. Several of his novels were set abroad, in France or the United States: *The Fall of Paris* (1942), *The Storm* (1947), and *The Ninth Wave* (1951). His novel *The Thaw* (1954–56), departing from the norms of socialist realism with an ideologically neutral standpoint, was the symbol of cultural liberalism of the post-Stalin 1950s. When called on by the Writers' Union to denounce Boris Pasternak, he replied, by telephone. "Ilya Ehrenburg has gone away and will not be back for some time."

EISENSTEIN, SERGEI. 1898–1948

Film director. Born in Riga, the son of an architect, he studied civil engineering and during the civil war worked on the Red Army's propaganda trains. After the war he became interested in the theatre, studied under Vsevolod Meyerhold, and directed a number of productions. in 1923 he made his first film, *The Wise Man*, and then in 1925, *Strike*, in which the masses are shown as a revolutionary force in history.

In 1925 Eisenstein made *The Battleship Potemkin*, frequently acknowledged as one of the greatest films ever made, with its theme of revolution as a struggle for freedom and dignity. In 1928 his *October: Ten Days That Shook the World* was criticized by the party as showing formalistic elements, referring to its visual style. In 1929 he made *Old and New* about the land collectivization program. Between 1929 and 1932, out of favor in the USSR, he worked in France and Mexico, where he made the uncompleted *Que Viva Mexico*. In 1938 he made a public confession of errors and was allowed to direct *Alexander Nevsky*, a patriotic film about the defeat of the German knights in the Middle Ages, for which he received the State Prize of the USSR in 1941. In 1945 he made *Ivan the Terrible*, a study of despotism and the use of power. The film was in two parts and the second could not be shown until 1958, after Stalin's death and 10 years after Eisenstein's.

ENGELS, FRIEDRICH. 1820–1895

A German businessman and political philosopher, an associate of Karl Marx. He retired comfortably from business and lived mostly in England from 1842. With Marx, he was the author of the *Communist Manifesto*, and completed *Das Kapital* after Marx's death.

ENVER, PASHA. 1881?–1922

A leading Turkish general who came to political power in Turkey but fell when Kemal Ataturk took over. He offered to take Central Asia and India for the Bolsheviks, in return for their helping to bring him back to power in Turkey. He went to the emirate of Bokhara for this purpose in November 1921, but left the Bolshevik cause and sided with their Basmachi enemies, styling himself commander-in-chief of All the Armies of Islam. He captured Dushanbe in February 1922, thus controlling the old kingdom of Bokhara. He was killed in battle on August 4, 1922, by the Red Army

EREMENKO, ANDREI I. 1892–1970

Red Army general who survived Stalin's purges and whose skills helped win the war. Of Ukrainian peasant stock, he became a cavalry sergeant, was selected for the Frunze Military Academy in 1935, and was a general at the outbreak of World War II. Transferred from the Far East in July 1941 as a deputy commander to Simeon Timoshenko, he took over the Bryansk Front in September. In the 1942 winter offensive he commanded the 4th Shock Army in the northwest. Stalin sent him in August to the new Southeast Front near Stalingrad in August 1942, soon renamed the Stalingrad Front, with Khrushchev as his political adviser. Eremenko held the southern perimeter of the besieged Germans in the city, and fought off the relief attempts from the south. His command was renamed the South Front, and after the fall of Stalingrad in 1943 he was sent, first, to take Rostov and, then, to the north of the Baltic Front to retake Smolensk and south again to the Crimea and, finally, back to the Baltic for the last attack on East Prussia. His account of Stalingrad (1961) is of importance, although he implies that he and Khrushchev were the real planners of the victory. He was promoted to marshal in 1955 and was on the Central Committee in 1956.

ESENIN, SERGEI ALEXANDROVICH. 1895–1925

An "imagist" poet. He affected the appearance of a peasant in the literary salons of the czarist empire. He welcomed (but did not understand) the 1917 Revolution. After publishing *Memoirs of a Hooligan* (1918), he left Russia. He was briefly married to the American dancer Isadora Duncan, but returned to Russia where he could not adapt to a changed world and hanged himself.

FADEYEV, ALEXANDER A. 1901–1956

Party activist and writer. He was born in Kalinin to a family of professional revolutionaries. He fought in the revolution and civil war as a Bolshevik. At the age of 19 he took part in the suppression of the Kronstadt rebellion and was twice wounded. He wrote several novels concerning the civil war, and *The Rout* (1927) was hailed by critics as portraying the men of the revolution from within. He wrote *Leningrad in the Days of the Blockade* about the famous siege, and in 1945, *The Young Guard*, a romantic tale about a group of underground members of the Komsomol and their gallant exploits against the Nazis. It received the State Prize of the USSR and was filmed in 1948.

Fadeyev was a member of the party's Central Committee from 1939 to 1956 and from 1954 to 1956, secretary of the Writers' Union. He led campaigns against unorthodoxy in literature and was implicated in the purges of writers in the 1930s. His best-known book, *The Young Guard*, was itself criticized for failing to show the party's leading role.

Fadeyev was a dedicated alcoholic and prone to taking exaggerated positions. As a result of Khrushchev's revelations about Stalin and his crimes at the 20th Party Congress, he killed himself.

FEDIN, KONSTANTIN. 1892–1977

A prolific novelist from a middle-class background. After release from being held as a prisoner in Germany in World War I. During the civil war he edited a newspaper and joined a group of young writers disclaiming ideological purpose. He changed his ways and wrote several novels about Soviet life that conformed to the later doctrine of socialist realism. He wrote *The Desert* (1923), *The Peasants* (1925), and between 1928 and 1940, *The Rape of Europe*, which concerned the falsity of the world of bourgeois values.

During World War II, he wrote the tetralogy *First Joys* and *An Unusual Summer* and, between 1961 and 1965, *The Bonfire*, which deals with the origins of the revolution and its psychological effects on those involved in it. He was first secretary of the Writers' Union from 1959 and its chairman from 1971. Fedin was responsible for the attacks on Boris Pasternak and for the suggestion that Andrei Sinyavsky be tried (according to Alexander Solzhenitsyn).

FEOKOTISTOV, KONSTANTIN P. 1926–

A designer of spacecraft, from the first Soviet satellite to Yuri Gagarin's flight and later developments. He flew and carried out experiments in *Voshkod I* (1964) and has made other space flights himself.

FOTIEVA, LIDIA A. 1881–1975

Lenin's secretary. Involved in revolutionary politics before the age of 21, she emigrated to Switzerland in 1904 and helped Lenin's wife, Krupskaya, with work for the party. After the revolution she became Lenin's devoted private secretary until his death in 1924. She was also on the Secretariat of the Council of People's Commissars of the Russian Soviet Federal Socialist Republic until 1930. From 1938 she was on the staff of the Central Lenin Museum.

FRUNZE, MIKHAIL V. 1885–1925

Red Army commander. He joined the Social Democrats in 1904, while a student at the St. Petersburg Polytechnic, siding with the Bolsheviks. That year he was arrested and banished from the city. He continued his political activities and was a leader of the Moscow uprising in December 1905. He had been a delegate to the 1905 Third Party Congress in London in 1905, and was a delegate to the Fourth in Stockholm in 1906. From 1907 to 1914 he was imprisoned. Rearrested in 1915, he escaped to Chita and joined the All-Russian Union of Zemstvos, working on the Western Front.

In February 1917, Frunze led revolts and military mutinies in Minsk, Belorussia, becoming the chief of staff of the armed forces there after the "Kornilov affair." He took charge of putting down the Yaroslav rebellion in July 1918 and then was put in command of the Southern Army Group against Alexander Kolchak, although dismissed by Trotsky in 1919. He became Red Army commander in Crimea and the Ukraine in February 1920. From there he immediately took command in Central Asia of the Turkestan Army Group, capturing Khiva and Bokhara, using Red Army soldiers recruited from peoples of the Caucasus. In September 1920 he led the campaign against Baron Wrangel on the Southern Front. He was then made commander of the Red Army in the Crimea and the Ukraine, where he ended both the "Petlyura" and "Makhno" affairs.

In 1924 Frunze was made deputy chairman of the Revolutionary Military Council and a member of the Central Executive Committee. He was also a candidate member of the Politburo and commandant of the Military Academy (later named after him). With Mikhail Tukhachevsky and Nikolai Gusev he was involved in the reorganization of the Red Army. Together they elaborated the "Doctrine of Proletarian War," which denounced centralism as inhibiting the army's potential for maneuver.

Frunze was a practical leader and a first-rate underground tactician with the outward appearance of a senior military man. But his championship of one-man command and his obvious ambition made the Central Committee suspicious of him, and when he died under minor surgery for an ulcer his death was strongly rumored, and asserted by Trotsky, to have been a murder ordered by Stalin. His wife committed suicide shortly afterwards. He was twice awarded the Order of the Red Banner and his ashes are interred in the walls of the Kremlin.

FURTSEVA, EKATERINA. 1910–1974

A party member from 1930 and on the Central Committee from 1952. She was on the Presidium from 1957 to 1961 and was minister of culture in 1960 until her death. She was the first woman to join the Politburo, but she was ousted as a result of Frol Koslov's intrigues. Gossip suggested that she had been Khrushchev's mistress: she certainly was one of his fervent supporters. Her later years were clouded by the scandal of the luxurious dacha she had built for herself.

GAGARIN, YURI, 1934–1968

The first man to orbit the earth in a space capsule, in 1961. He was killed in an air crash and was given a state burial.

GAMARNIK, YAN B. 1894–1937

A military leader during the civil war and chairman of the Revolutionary Military Council from 1934. He learned of the arrests of officers and on May 31, 1937, killed himself. The news of his death (or his reported absence from committees) told others of the beginning of the military purge.

GAPON, FATHER GEORGY. 1870–1906

A Ukrainian "worker priest" who led the demonstration on "Bloody Sunday," January 22, 1905. He had built a large, but loosely organized association, for a while linked to the police, which he wanted to use peacefully. He escaped to Geneva, but fame came to Father Gapon and he was courted by politicians and publishers. He now had money and he began to spend it luxuriously, visiting Monte Carlo. Back in Russia he was suspected of being an informer and was killed by the Socialist Revolutionary "combat section," their hit squad.

GINZBURG, ALEXANDER. 1936–

A dissident writer. After two spells in labor camps for his nonconformist behavior, he was charged by the KGB in 1964 with possessing subversive literature. The case was dismissed at the trial, but another arrest and trial in 1968 aroused world interest and protest over his five-year sentence.

GONCHAROVA, NATALIA.
1881–1962

Painter and scenic designer. Before World War I she was involved with the progressive art movements that produced such exhibitions as *The Jack of Diamonds, Donkey's Tail,* and *Target.* Her work was much influenced by the cubist and futurist movements, and with Mikhail Larionov she started the rayonist movement. In 1915 she moved to Paris and worked in the theatre, carrying out designs for Diaghilev and others. She died in Paris.

GORBACHEV, MIKHAIL SERGEEVICH, 1931– .

Soviet leader, 1985– . Born of peasant stock in the Caucasian village of Privolnoye in the Krasnogvardeysk district of Stavropol Krai, which lost as much as one third of its population during the artificially created famine of 1932. His maternal grandfather was a kulak, who was temporarily deported during the 1937 purge. As a youth he worked on the local collective farm, and then obtained entry to Moscow State University where, from 1950 to 1955, he studied law. He had joined the Komsomol while still at school and in 1950 became a candidate member of the CPSU. After graduating from the university, where he shared a room with Zdenek Mlynar, later one of the organizers of the Prague Spring movement in 1968, he joined the Komsomol organization in Stavropol. He spent the next six years there, being promoted to first secretary of the Stavropol Komsomol committee in 1960.

Gorbachev at this time married Raisa Titorenko, a fellow student in Moscow where she was studying philosophy. She was offered a job teaching philosophy at the Stavropol Agricultural Institute, and is obviously a remarkable and forceful woman who has had a considerable influence on her husband's career. In 1962 he joined one of the supervisory agricultural units that were part of Nikita Khrushchev's new deal for agriculture. He spent five years there and also studied for a degree in agro-economics. He qualified in 1967, and in 1970 became first secretary of the Stavropol Krai committee of the CPSU. At the 24th Party Congress in 1971 he was elected a full member of the Central Committee.

Stavropol is a fertile area and Gorbachev had considerable success with agricultural production there. In this he was helped by having the patronage of Fedor Kulakov who was then head of the agricultural department and became secretary for agriculture on the Central Committee. He had also attracted the favorable attention of Yuri Andropov and Mikhail Suslov, both of whom, suffering from kidney disorders, were used to taking the waters at Kislovodsk, a well known spa used by privileged party members, and under Gorbachev's jurisdiction. The enthusiastic young man had greeted them at the station on several occasions. So, after Kulakov's somewhat mysterious death in July 1978, it was not surprising that they backed him for Kulakov's job on the Central Committee in Moscow.

In Moscow Gorbachev set to work to deal with the complex problems of agriculture while Raisa was appointed to a readership in philosophy at the State University. There was a very bad harvest in 1979–80 which in no way affected his standing and in October 1980 he was made a full member of the Politburo. Perhaps it was felt that he needed all the available backing to deal with the layers of bureaucracy which now existed there. The harvest in 1981 was the worst since 1975 and 46 million tons of grain had to be imported. In 1982 the Food Program—a total review of agriculture—was published. It was comprehensive but contained no real elements of reform. In 1982 the harvest, though not brilliant, was adequate and Leonid Brezhnev's death drew attention away from the secretary of agriculture's possible shortcomings.

By March 1983 Andropov was general secretary and Gorbachev was generally recognized as his main assistant. Andropov had little time to pursue his campaign against corruption, for by February 1984, he was dead and the obviously frail Chernenko had temporarily taken over in the Kremlin.

Chernenko had time to repeal some of Andropov's reform measures, and there was a crack down on dissidents. It was the time in which the Nobel prize-winning physicist Andrei Sakharov and his wife Elena Bonner, the prominent Jewish activist, were exiled to Gorky. Although Gorbachev was still high in the Politburo, his only real backers were Nikolai Ryzhkov and Yegor Ligachev.

On December 10, 1984 at a Moscow conference on ideology he used the word *glasnost* for the first time to describe the condition which should accompany socialist democracy. Later in the month Gorbachev, as chairman of the Supreme Soviet's Foreign Affairs Committee, visited London to a enthusiastic welcome and made a great hit with Prime Minister Margaret Thatcher, though in practical terms he was unyielding on Afghanistan and on human rights issues. At the beginning of 1985

Chernenko died and in March Gorbachev was declared General Secretary.

General Secretary—Gorbachev's supporters on the Politburo, Nikolai Ryzhkov, Viktor Chebrikov, and Yegor Ligachev were both older and more experienced than he and did not owe their progress in the party to him. He made Ryzhkov chairman of the Council of Ministers but did nothing about the others. Grigory Romanov, an old rival, disappeared into retirement after an inspection trip Gorbachev made to his power base, Leningrad, in May 1985. At the end of 1985 Viktor Grishin also stepped down, partly it is said because Chebrikov had let it be generally known that Grishin's daughter-in-law's father was Beria. Gorbachev, at the same time, promoted Eduard Shevardnadze to the post of foreign minister, but as a Georgian, he was not an entirely popular choice.

The situation in the USSR that Gorbachev inherited was immensely depressing. The economy was in terrible shape, apart from the production of defense material and space technology, it resembled a third world state more than an industrial superpower. The standard of living was low, infant mortality high, even life expectancy was declining. He seems to have believed that *perestroika*, the restructuring of the economy and the party, and *glasnost*, openness, would right the situation.

With Leonid Abalkin, a radical economist and now deputy prime minister, he introduced The New Economic Mechanism in the summer of 1987. This introduced a new system of "self accounting" to state enterprises, related for the first time to profitability. It also gave permission for a limited form of entirely private enterprise in the shape of cooperatives. The first foundered because no attempt was made to take the more radical step of changing the system whereby 90 percent of all production was allocated to the state, nor to change the source of materials. The cooperative movement attracted savage criticism on the grounds that the cooperatives were profiteers who were charging outrageous prices. After two years the situation has, if anything, rather deteriorated. There was a good harvest in 1989, but output is stagnant, millions of days have been lost due to strikes, the money supply is increasing, and so is inflation.

The new two stage six-year plan calls for price reforms in 1991 plus increased production of food and consumer goods, and for 1993–95 an increasingly market-based economy. The new property laws coming in to effect in July 1990 under which peasants will be granted private land which they will be able to leave to their heirs, are expected to boost agricultural production, as will the end of Gosagroprom, the bloated agricultural bureaucracy set up in 1986 which failed to increase production. Over 900 joint ventures have been arranged including one with Fiat which will increase the production of cars by 25 percent. A unified tax system is also planned and even the introduction of a Stock Exchange.

Perestroika also applies to the political situation and here Gorbachev's plans have been constantly modified by the extraordinary speed of change in the satellite states of Eastern Europe and in some of the republics of the Soviet Union. The major change, the establishment of the Congress of People's Deputies to take the place of the Supreme Soviet, and the party's abrogation of its role as the "leading and guiding force of Soviet society," which

it held under Article 6 of the Constitution, have been the most striking. A crowd of 150,000 demonstrated in Red Square. Multi-party elections have been held in the RSFSR and elsewhere and party members have done very badly in many of them.

Gorbachev has dealt harshly with the internal problems in the republics, as in Georgia in April 1989 and in Azerbaijan in January 1990. Not at all like his reasoned performance in the Baltic states where in March 1990 Lithuania announced its departure from the Soviet Union.

Internationally, Gorbachev has had an easier time than at home. He has been able to make bold and decisive gestures which have earned him glowing praise around the world. This started with his speech to the United Nations in December 1988 when he said, "today the preservation of any kind of closed society is hardly possible." He declared a ceasefire in Afghanistan and at the same time began the process of disarmament, which was emphasized by a January 1989 cut of 14.2 percent in the military budget and the withdrawal of half a million men from Europe and Asia. He established warm relationships with U.S. presidents Ronald Reagan and George Bush, and in December 1989 had an audience with Pope John Paul II.

Mikhail Gorbachev's revolutionary changes have won him praise but also a great deal of criticism from both sides. From conservative elements in the Soviet Union, such as Yegor Ligachev, and Anatoly Gidaspov, leader of the Leningrad party, has come harsh criticism. They went along with him at first, but now, alarmed at the possible disintegration of the party and the Soviet Empire, as well as the loss of their long held privileges, they would like to call a halt. From the radicals, of which Boris Yeltsin is a good example, has come another sort of complaint. They believe that he has not taken radical enough steps, either politically or economically, and that the country will slip into chaos through inertia.

Gorbachev has now sought a new role for himself as president of the Republic, a position to which the Congress of Deputies voted him on March 14, 1990. This post, until it becomes elective in four years time, gives him more power than Stalin possessed. He has declared that in the power vacuum left by the apparent disintegration of the party, strong leadership is needed to prevent disaster. He has demonstrated amazing political skills in achieving what he has to date. He will need all his skill and a large measure of good luck to continue successfully "riding the tiger" of the new Soviet Union.

GORKY, MAXIM (ALEXEI MAXIMOVICH PESHKOV; "GORKY" = BITTER). 1868–1936

Writer. After a childhood as an orphan and years wandering as a poor student *Childhood* (1913), *My Apprenticeship* (1918), and *My Universities* (1923), his first collected tales, published in 1898, made him a famous writer. He supported the Bolsheviks and lived in exile (on Capri) from 1906 to 1913. In 1917, opposed to the seizure of power, he set up a non-Bolshevik left-wing group. He again lived in Italy from 1921 to 1928, then returned to Russia and headed the Writers' Union. He was called the founder of socialist realism and became a friend of Stalin. He seemed to share with Stalin a contempt for peasants; his article *On the Russian Peasantry* (1922) paints them as boorish subhumans who hoard food while the townsfolk starve. His death on June 16, 1936, was claimed to have been caused by Trotskyites or right-wing elements and was used by Stalin as a reason for the purges of the period.

GORSHKOV, SERGEI. 1910–1988

Commander-in-chief of the Red Navy, 1955 to 1985. He joined the navy in 1927 and served mostly in the Black Sea, commanding a destroyer squadron in 1945. His rise to commander of the fleet in 1956 came under Khrushchev, who had dismissed a fleet commander for resisting demands for economies. But the debacle of the Cuban missile crisis of 1962 reversed the Soviet position. Khrushchev fell from power and the new leadership felt the need for a strong navy to project their power globally. Under Brezhnev, Admiral Gorshkov was given the new rank of Admiral of the Fleet of the Soviet Union, and he planned a new Soviet naval strategy (set out in his book *The Sea Power of the State*, 1976). From a small coastal defense force using conventional naval artillery, he built a fleet of missile-launching submarines capable of striking at any point in the world. He also ensured that the Soviet Union had a massive conventional fleet with big surface ships and aircraft carriers whose world cruises and courtesy visits to Third World countries boosted Soviet prestige while striking fear into its rivals. But after Brezhnev's death, his position weakened as rivals for promotion debated his strategic concept. Why, they argued, was a big fleet necessary when submarines with intercontinental missiles could hit the United States without leaving port? Under Gorbachev new economies were introduced and the world role of the Soviet fleet was allowed to diminish. Gorshkov died three years after his retirement.

GOTS, ABRAM. 1882–1937? AND MIKHAIL. 1875–1906

Wealthy brothers who did much to organize the Socialist Revolutionaries. Mikhail died of cancer and Abram was exiled from 1906 until 1917. He returned as a Socialist Revolutionary leader in the Petrograd Soviet. He was one of the main accused in the 1922 show trials of the Social Revolutionaries. He was probably shot in a camp in Alma-Ata, in Kazakhstan.

GRECHKO, ANDREI A. 1904–1976

Marshal and minister of defense from 1967 until his death. He joined the Red Army as a youth in 1919 and was selected for training at the Frunze Military Academy and, later, the General Staff Academy. After commanding an army during World War II, he had command of the Soviet forces in East Germany, 1953–57. He rose under Khrushchev, commanding the land forces of the USSR (1957–60), then succeeding Ivan Konev as commander of the Warsaw Pact forces, 1960–67. He had joined the Communist party in 1928 and became a member of the Politburo in 1973. His study of the armed forces of the Soviet Union (published in 1974 in English; in 1977 in the USSR) describes the invincibility of Soviet arms, its record in World War II, and its abilities in a nuclear age.

GRISHIN, VIKTOR. 1914–

A surveyor by profession and party worker. He spent his early years working in the railway industry in Serpukhov, where he also became first secretary of the Committee of the Communist party for the city. In 1950 he moved to Moscow, where he ran the machine building department of the party's Moscow Committee. In 1956 he became president of the All-Union Central Council of Trade Unions. In June 1967 he was promoted to first secretary of the party's Moscow City Committee.

Grishin was elected by the 19th, 20th, and 22nd Party Congresses to membership in the Central Committee and was made a member of the Politburo in 1971. He was a serious candidate for the post of general secretary after the death of Brezhnev, but it is believed that his opponents spread rumors (generally believed) that his son's wife was the illegitimate daughter of Lavrenti Beria, thus removing him as a serious threat to Gorbachev.

GROMYKO, ANDREI A. 1909–1989

Soviet diplomat. Born near Minsk, he joined the party in 1931. As head of the U.S. department in the Ministry of Foreign Affairs and an attaché in the Soviet embassy in Washington in 1939, he began a diplomatic career unlike any other in the Soviet Union. He served as ambassador in Washington, 1943–46; he was present at the Teheran, Yalta, and Potsdam conferences. He returned to the Soviet Union in 1946 as a deputy in the Supreme Soviet. He was the USSR's permanent delegate to the U.N. Security Council, 1946–1949, where his use of the veto to stonewall Western proposals made him famous as "Mr. Nyet." Gromyko was ambassador to Britain, 1952–53; deputy foreign minister from 1953 after Stalin's death; and then foreign minister, 1957–85. He was finally made the titular president of the USSR in 1985, and held that post until 1988, when he retired. In 1989 he stepped down with other old-guard party men from the Central Committee. He was now an old, tired man whose life among the Communist elite had made him remote from life's realities. Upon his death, he was given a formal state burial, in keeping with his character—cool and passionless.

GUCHKOV, ALEXANDER. 1862–1936

The leader of the Moderate Liberals after 1905 and founder of the Octobrist party. He was the leader of the majority in the Third Duma and the Duma's chairman on military affairs, urging reform then and during World War I. He became minister of war in the Provisional Government in 1917. He went to Pskov to obtain the czar's abdication, leaving Russia for Paris in 1918 after the October Revolution.

Guchkov had a taste for dueling and fought twice while leader of the Duma; once he was jailed for wounding an opposing deputy and once he contemptuously fired in the air at a duel with a colonel he thought a spy for Germany.

HOOVER, HERBERT C. 1874–1964

The 35th president of the United States (1929–1933). His place in Soviet history arises from his work as chairman of the American Relief Administration. He headed the American Relief Committee in Europe from 1914 to 1919 during

World War I, and transferred his efforts to Soviet famine relief after this. He became U.S. secretary of commerce in 1921.

"ILF AND PETROV"—ILYA FAINZILBERG (1897–1937) AND YEVGENY PETROVICH KATAYEV (1903–1942)

Satirical writers, authors of *The Twelve Chairs* (1928), *The Golden Calf* (1931), and *Little Golden America* (1936). As satirists, they naturally fell under political suspicion, but their worldwide popularity ensured their survival.

ILYUSHIN, SERGEI V. 1894–1977

Aircraft designer famous for the IL-2 Stormovik and the later Ilyushin airliners.

ILICHEV, LEONID F. 1906–

A conservative or neo-Stalinist who was deputy chief and chief editor of *Pravda*, 1950–58. He served as head of the press department of the Foreign Ministry from 1953; as head of the KGB, 1958–61; as secretary of the party's Central Committee, 1961–65; and as deputy foreign minister, 1966–68.

IOFFE, ADOLF. 1883–1927

A Menshevik who was with Trotsky in Vienna in 1908. As a member of the Brest-Litovsk Treaty negotiating team, he struck the Germans with his naïve optimism. He had in common with Trotsky the illusion that by announcing "No peace, no war," Russia had ceased to be at war and that there would be peace. Ioffe was later ambassador to Germany, Switzerland, and China. He killed himself when Trotsky was expelled from the party.

KAGANOVICH (KAGAN), LAZAR M. 1893–

Party leader and staunch Stalinist. A Bolshevik from 1911, he moved upward through party posts, becoming secretary of the Ukrainian party in 1925 and adopting there the Stalinist policy of Russification. His zeal in the Ukraine led to the purging of many Ukrainian Communists, but Stalin bought favor there by dismissing him in 1927. A member of the Politburo from 1930 and a loyal Stalinist, he was in charge of collectivization and the 1933–34 party purge as chairman of the Commission of Party Control. He was people's commissar for railways from 1936 to 1944 and headed several other commissariats.

With Georgy Malenkov and Vyacheslav Molotov in 1957, he tried to oppose Khrushchev. He failed and was expelled from all his posts. The old Stalinist hardliner lives on in retirement into the Gorbachev era.

KALEDIN, ALEXEI. 1861–1918

A czarist general whose World War I reputation as a successful cavalry leader gave him great fame. Resigning from the army because of the revolution, he became leader of the Don Cossack state and was proclaimed ataman on October 25, 1917. His attempt at a counterrevolution failed and he shot himself in January 1918.

KALININ, MIKHAIL I. 1875–1946

Senior Communist stateman. He joined the Social Democrats in 1898 and was arrested the next year, the beginning of a series of arrests and deportations. He joined the Bolsheviks in 1906 and was elected mayor of Petrograd after the 1918 October Revolution. He succeeded Yakov Sverdlov as president of the All-Russian Central Executive Committee of the Soviets in 1919, and in 1923 became president of the Central Executive Committee of the USSR. A dummy noted only for his loyalty, he was chairman of the Supreme Soviet from 1938 and so remained for the rest of his life.

KAMENEV (ROSENFELDT), LEV BORISOVICH. 1883–1936

Revolutionary and Soviet leader. A student radical, he had been arrested many times before the 1905 revolt. In 1902 he visited Paris and met the *Iskra* group. In 1908 Lenin asked Kamenev to join him in Geneva to edit the Bolshevik paper, *Proletary*. He became a leading propagandist overseas until 1914, when he was assigned to take charge of *Pravda* in St. Petersburg. After World War I broke out he was arrested, and in May 1915 deported to Siberia, to the same settlement as Joseph Stalin.

In April 1917, back in Petrograd, he took over the editorship of *Pravda*, in which he fought against the April Theses of Lenin. In October, with Grigory Zinoviev, he voted against an armed uprising. They then demanded conciliation and a coalition with other socialists. Although Lenin was firmly opposed to their ideas he needed support and Kamenev, elected president of the Central Executive Committee, was given the chance to continue working for the Bolshevik cause. Although he was with Trotsky at the Brest-Litovsk negotiations, he was given little to do in the civil war.

Trotsky saw Zinoviev as an agitator, excited by the moment, while he saw Kamenev as thoughtful and analytical.

In 1922, during Lenin's illness, Kamenev was one of the three, with Zinoviev and Stalin, who opposed Trotsky. As Stalin took over the party machine, Kamenev lost the support of his Moscow party, which he had been running, and by the 15th Party Congress in 1927, his political career, like Zinoviev's, had sunk. Together they submitted to party discipline and denounced the Trotskyites in January 1928. They hung on until Stalin had them expelled from the party in 1932. Readmitted after self-criticism the next year, they showed their support for Stalin at the 1934 17th Party Congress.

They were arrested in 1935 after the murder of Sergei Kirov and sentenced to imprisonment. In July Kamenev was retired, and again the next year put on a public show trial with Zinoviev, accused of an alliance with the Nazis. He was executed in August 1936. His sentences were annulled by the Soviet Supreme Court in June 1988.

KAMKOV, BORIS D. 1885–1938

A Socialist Revolutionary Internationalist. One of the organizers of the Left socialist Revolutionaries in the July Days of 1917. After three years' imprisonment he left politics and worked as a statistician. In 1938 he was swept up in the purge, put on public trial, and shot.

KANDINSKY, WASSILY. 1866–1944

Abstract artist. He was born in Moscow but studied art in Munich. He moved to Berlin, but then went back to Munich where he helped to found the Blaue Reiter movement. His work developed in a more abstract direction, and he is generally recognized as a major influence on the development of abstraction in painting. He returned to Russia at the time of revolution and held posts under the Commissariat for Popular Culture. He was among the organizers of the Museum of Pictorial Culture in Petrograd. In 1921 he founded the Academy of Arts and Sciences, but after the civil war he returned to Germany, taught at the Bauhaus for a time, and, when Hitler took power in 1933, settled in Paris.

KANTOROVICH, LEONID. 1912–1986

A mathematician and economist. He was awarded, jointly with Tjalling Koopmans, a Nobel Prize in Economics in 1975.

KAPITSA, PETER. 1894–1984

A physicist. He worked at Cambridge University from 1924, where he became a professor and in 1929 the first foreigner to become a member of the British scientific academy, the Royal Society. He was detained in the Soviet Union on a visit in 1935, and was made director of the Institute of Physical Problems, continuing to do important research. He was awarded the Order of Lenin and two Stalin Prizes. For his work on low-temperature physics, he received a Nobel Prize in 1978.

KAPLAN, FANYA (ALSO KNOWN AS DORA). ?–1918

Socialist Revolutionary and exponent of terrorism. On August 30, 1918, Kaplan shot Lenin in the neck and shoulder as he left the Michelson plant in Moscow, where he had been addressing the workers. She had spent 11 years in prison for trying to kill a czarist official in Kiev. Freed in 1917, she worked as a milliner, but dedicated herself to the revolution and believed that Lenin had betrayed it by abandoning the Constituent Assembly. Taken first to the Lubyanka, she was soon taken for interrogation in the Kremlin. She had no useful information and on September 3, 1918, was shot in prison.

KATAYEV, VALENTIN. 1897–

Socialist realist writer. The son of a teacher from Odessa, he fought in the Russian army from 1915 until 1917, then joined the Red Army and fought against Anton Denikin. He wrote several short stories about this era in *Notes on the Civil War*, which contained a mixture of heroics and satire. A satirical play, *Squaring the Circle*, followed in 1928.

In the 1930s he turned toward heroic and ideological themes in such books as *I am the Son of the Working People* (1937) and *Son of the Regiment* (1945). His greatest success was the Odessa-based novel that began with the publication of the widely read *The Lonely White Sail* (1936), filmed in 1937, and developed slowly into the huge four-part novel, *The Waves of the Black Sea* (1961). His writings were based on current society, *Time, Forward* (1933) being about a construction team during the five-year plan. Katayev's other claims to fame lie in his being the first Soviet author to own a refrigerator (in the mid-1930s) and to have not joined the party until 1958. His younger brother wrote under the name Petrov with his collaborator Ilf.

KAUTSKY, KARL. 1854–1938

A German socialist. He was secretary to Friedrich Engels in London from 1881. He opposed the Bolsheviks in Russia but supported the Mensheviks in Georgia. His writings drove Lenin into a fury, who then devoted his convalescence in 1918 to a book attacking Kautsky. He lived in Austria until his last year, when he escaped from the German Nazis to the Netherlands.

KERENSKY, ALEXANDER. 1881–1970

A Russian politician and leader of the Provisional Government. He entered the Fourth Duma in 1912 as a moderate socialist, gaining some fame for his defense of the Armenian Dashnaks. He later joined and led the Socialist Revolutionaries and Ekaterina Bresho-Breshkovskaya made him her "political heir." In 1917, under the Provisional Government, he was at first minister of justice and then of war. In July he was made prime minister. He attempted a military offensive against Germany in 1918, but its failure led to disaffection in the army and the October Revolution. Although he survived an apparent attempt at overthrow by the army commander, Lavr Kornilov, he was thrown out by the Bolshevik takeover in November. He went into exile in France, Austria, and, finally, the United States.

It was an odd coincidence that both he and Lenin were from Simbirsk and that Kerensky's father should have been Lenin's schoolteacher.

KHACHATURIAN, ARAM. 1903–1978

Composer. Born in Tbilisi, he studied music at the Gresin Music Academy, which he entered in 1922, and then at the Moscow Conservatory from 1929. His *Symphony No 1*, his diploma piece, was written in 1935, and this was followed by his *Piano Concerto* in 1936 and the *First Violin Concerto*, which won him a Stalin Prize in 1940. In 1939 he was selected vice-president of the organizing committee of the Union of Soviet Composers. In 1942 he wrote the music for the ballet *Gayane*, which contains the well-known *Sabre Dance*.. Equally well known is his music for the ballet *Spartacus*. In 1947 his *Sinfonya Poema* was criticized for its formalism in the time of Zhdanov, when this implied corrupt Western influence. In spite of this he was awarded the Order of Lenin.

Khachaturian wrote numerous film scores. His music is valued for the way in which it often uses Armenian and Georgian folk tunes and his deep understanding of the Russian academic tradition as exemplified by Nikolai Rimsky-Korsakov.

KHRUSHCHEV, NIKITA SERGEYEVICH. 1894–1971

Soviet leader, 1955–1964.

1894–1941—Born on April 17, at Kalinovka in Kursk Oblast, he came of peasant stock. In 1908 his father, unable to make a living on the land, moved his family to Yuzovka (later Stalino and now Donetsk) in the Donbass Basin of the Ukraine, where he had obtained work in the coal mines. Khrushchev, at the age of 15, was taken on as an apprentice fitter in a mining facilities company. In 1912 revolutionary groups were actively fomenting strike activity in the mines and, as he was known to be involved, he was fired. However, quite soon he obtained a job as a fitter in another mining house.

During World War I, as a mine worker he was exempt from callup and married for the first time. He wife Yesofrina had two children, a boy and a girl, before dying from typhus at the end of the war.

Miners' strikes in the Donbass continued throughout the war up to the February 1917 Revolution. After the revolution, though still not a member of the Bolshevik party, Khrushchev was elected to one of the revolutionary committees. The committees had been formed to confront the various forces threatening the hold of the revolution on the Ukraine. The Cossack army of Alexei Kaledin was defeated in 1918 by the Donets Proleterian Regiment, of which Khrushchev was a member, but they were then threatened by the Germans who, after the Brest-Litovsk Treaty, had proclaimed a Ukrainian republic. At this stage he joined the Bolshevik party, but since the Germans were now occupying the area, he had to escape eastward and join the Red Army.

From then until the end of the civil war, Khrushchev was involved in minor political work in the Red Army. He fought on the Tsaritsyn Front and then joined the Army of the Kuban, which broke the White Army at Krasnodar, and was present when the White forces surrendered at Sochi in May 1920.

After the civil war, Khrushchev returned to the Donbets and became involved in the immense work of reconstruction that took place under Lenin's New Economic Policy. He was appointed political leader of one of the three major mining sections and secretary of the party cell of the recently established technical college. In two years the Donbass Basin was back to half its prewar production, and in 1924, at the age of 30, Khrushchev was elected secretary of the raikom, the party of the area. He also got married for the second time.

By 1927 Khrushchev had attended a party congress as a full delegate, and the output of coal from the Donbass had exceeded prewar levels. His ascent of the party hierarchy was about to begin. In 1928 he came to the attention of the general secretary of the Central Committee of the Ukrainian Communist party, Stanislav Kossior, and he was selected as one of the first students for the Industrial Academy that had opened in Moscow.

He quite soon came to dominate the academy politically, being responsible for its purging of "Right Deviationist" elements, supporters of Nicholas Bukharin. Among them was Nazezhda Alliluyeva, Stalin's wife who became friendly with Khrushchev, a relationship he later claimed had influenced Stalin's attitude to him. It was while he was at the academy that he encountered Lazar Kaganovich, who was now a member of the Politburo. Kaganovich wanted a competent, tough, and politically sound administrator to cleanse the party organization of any rightist tendencies. Khrushchev was appointed first secretary of one of the Moscow districts, and by 1934 at the age of 39 he was Kaganovich's deputy in the capital. When Kaganovich was made people's commissar for transport, Khrushchev took over as first secretary in Moscow in 1935. There, he was part of a group that included Nikolai Bulganin, chairman of the Moscow Soviet; Georgy Malenkov, running the Organization Bureau of the Party Committee; and Nikolai Yezhov, later to be the dreaded activist of the purges.

Khrushchev made a considerable contribution to the building of the metro in Moscow, the main section of which was opened in 1935. In carrying out this work, much of it using forced labor, he showed the determination and ruthlessness for which he was to become well known. For his work in Moscow he received the Order of Lenin, his first decoration. He also became very friendly with Bulganin, and both men were often invited to dinner by Stalin. Khrushchev himself wrote: "I was literally spellbound by Stalin, by his attentiveness, his concern . . . I was overwhelmed by his charm."

During the Terror, starting in 1934, and from 1937 when Stalin began to remove a large proportion of the old-guard Bolsheviks, their associates, and families, Khrushchev, despite his later denunciations of Stalin's tyranny, did nothing to protect his old friends. In fact there are numerous speeches on record in which he showed himself eager to denounce anyone who had fallen from Stalin's favor or who he believed to stand in his way. In 1938 he received his reward, being elected to the Presidium and becoming a candidate member of the Politburo.

In 1938 Khrushchev was appointed acting first secretary of the Ukrainian Communist party, as part of Stalin's purge of the party there. He went to work with a will. Indeed, six months after his arrival, only three members of the 1937 committee were left. He wrote: "The successful, triumphant crushing of the Fascist agents—all those contemptible Trotskyites, Bukharinites, and bourgeois nationalists—we owe to the personal efforts of our leader above all, to our great Stalin."

At the beginning of 1939 Khrushchev was concerned with developing the industry and agriculture of the region and then, later in the year, with absorbing into the western Ukraine and Belorussia parts of Poland occupied following the Russo-German pact. This involved seizing landlords' estates and collectivization on a massive scale, and the deportation of "unsympathetic" elements to Siberia and elsewhere. Much of this work was carried out by Ivan Serov, people's commissar of internal affairs for the region, who became a valued colleague and friend, as did Georgi Zhukov, who was appointed commander of the Kiev Special Military District.

On June 22, 1941, German troops crossed the border and attacked the frontier guards. The war had begun.

1941–1953—Khrushchev's role during the war, on both the Ukraine Front and at Stalingrad, was as a political commissar on the military councils of the area. His official rank was lieutenant general. He had some disagreements with Stalin, particularly at the beginning of the war, when he in common with Zhukov and others believed that Kiev should be abandoned. They were forced to submit to Stalin's will.

In 1944, when the Ukraine had effectively been cleared of German troops, Stalin once again appointed him first secretary of the Ukraine and also chairman of the Council of Commissars. It was obvious that despite his relatively low profile during the war he was still in favor. He devoted his energies to rebuilding the shattered agriculture and industry of the area, which proceeded steadily during 1945, but in 1946 agricultural output was hit by a devastating drought that caused widespread famine. Unable to meet the state's procurement demand, Khrushchev appealed to Stalin, who replied with an abusive telegram and followed this by appointing Lazar Kaganovich in his place as first secretary. Khrushchev was careful to collaborate fully with Kaganovich, and the situation was saved by a record harvest in 1947. In 1948 the harvest was even better and Khrushchev was relected first secretary. But within a year he had left the Ukraine and taken up a new role in Moscow as first secretary of the Moscow Obkom.

In Moscow for the next three years he was mostly concerned with applying his new theories about agriculture to the Moscow Oblast. He amalgamated the small collectives to form larger units and, since this was successful, he obtained the approval of the Central Committee. He then came out with a grandiose scheme for the creation of agrotowns, vast farming communities with populations of 12,000 each, complete with apartment blocks, schools, restaurants, and swimming pools. The scheme was a fantasy; there were no resources available to create it and it was ended by a critical article in *Pravda*. Shortly after this, in October 1952, the 19th Party Congress was held, and it increased the membership of the presidium to 25 plus 11 candidate members. A little later, and in contradiction to the spirit of the congress, Stalin formed a new Bureau of the Presidium consisting of Malenkov, Beria, Bulganin, Khrushchev, and himself. This was all part of the succession game that Stalin was playing, a game that became suddenly terrifying with the announcement on January 13, 1953, that State Security had uncovered the

"Doctors' Plot." Stalin even made the suggestion that Kliment Voroshilov was a British agent. There seems little doubt that Stalin was planning the destruction of the remains of the old guard, certainly Molotov and Mikoyan. On March 3, Stalin had a severe stroke and on March 6 he was dead. The battle for the succession, long flourishing underground, came out into the open.

1953–1955—All former members of the Politburo and the other powerful state organs were invited to a conference in the Kremlin. A new Presidium was elected with Malenkov as chairman of the Council of Ministers, Beria in charge of MVD and MGB (Internal Affairs and State Security), and Bulganin at the Ministry for the Armed Forces, with Khrushchev as secretary of the Central Committee in Moscow. Essentially power was held by this triumvirate until July, when Beria was arrested at a meeting of the Presidium by Marshal Zhukov, acting on their orders. He was accused of being a careerist and a traitor, tried, and shot. At the same time the MVD was neutralized by the arrest of its senior staff and Beria's confederates were dealt with in the same way.

The second triumvirate now consisted of Malenkov, Khrushchev, and Bulganin. Khrushchev had been elected to the party secretariat of the Central Committee in March, and in September he was elected first secretary of the Communist party.

In August 1954 Malenkov made his bid for power with a policy calling for rapid development of both light and food industries at the same rate as heavy industries. Khrushchev counterattacked with a speech in which he demonstrated the appalling condition of agriculture,

and in February 1954 he launched his great plan for the cultivation of the Virgin Lands. In his role as secretary of the Central Committee, he started traveling all over the Soviet Union, and attended congresses in Poland and Czechoslovakia. In December 1954 he went to China and negotiated a deal with Mao Tse-tung by which the USSR was to supply China with capital goods.

By late 1954 Malenkov's position had been heavily undermined and, in February 1955, Malenkov resigned as chairman of the Council of Ministers and was replaced in the triumvirate by Georgi Zhukov. In November Khrushchev and Bulganin flew to India, an event that received worldwide press coverage, only equaled by the detonation of another hydrogen bomb, this time in the stratosphere.

Domestically, Khrushchev's concern with agriculture continued to dominate the political scene. While 1955 was a good year for agriculture in general, the Virgin Lands program was affected by a severe drought.

1956—The 20th Party Congress opened on February 14, 1956. The trials of Beria and his associates, though only reported in outline, had caused a profound interest in the darker events of Stalin's regime. A Central Committee commission had produced a report on the cult of Stalin, and some prisoners had been released. Rebellions broke out at a number of camps and were brutally suppressed. Khrushchev suggested to the Presidium of the Central Committee that they include a section on the "cult of personality" at the Congress. The idea was rejected by members of the Politburo.

At the congress Khrushchev introduced several novel, even revolutionary ideas: that peaceful coexistence was possible and that the transition from capitalism to socialism could be a gradual one. He talked of the destruction of the Beria gang, but made no mention of Stalin.

He then proposed to the Presidium that as a delegate he should make a speech about Stalin. A compromise was reached. It was agreed that he could make the speech, but as secretary and at a closed session to be held after the election of the new Central Committee. Obviously many members were fearful of their chances of reelection. The speech was delivered on the morning of February 25 to an audience of 1,500 delegates, including a hundred party members newly released from jail and rehabilitated.

The speech revealed the conflicts between Lenin and Stalin at the end of the former's life, hinted at Stalin's involvement in the murder of Sergei Kirov, and blamed Stalin for the disasters at the beginning of the war. It blames Stalin for the repressions of the postwar period as well, and claimed that before his death he was planning new assaults on the party. The speech was carefully planned. It made no mention of the destruction of the Left and Right Opposition in the 1930s nor, more significantly, of the destruction of the kulaks and the mass deportations. Essentially it was concerned with Stalin's attacks on the party, not on the people. It also managed to implicate and therefore discredit some of his Politburo rivals, particularly Malenkov, but also Kaganovich, Molotov, and Voroshilov.

The effects of the speech on the Soviet Union and the Communist world were startling. Monuments to Stalin were pulled down all over the country, towns were renamed—Stalingrad became Volgograd—and pro-Stalin riots in Georgia had to be put down with casualties running into hundreds. Only Palmiro Togliatti, leader of the Italian Communist party, asked whether it might be possible that there was some profound flaw in the very nature of the Soviet system.

Khrushchev set up special commissions to examine cases of prisoners in the camps and, by the summer of 1956, several million prisoners had been released; posthumous rehabilitation was also declared on a similar scale. On the other hand, it was also noticeable that very few members of the NKVD-MGB were punished for their treatment of prisoners. In Khrushchev's words, "We must not carry out a St. Bartholomew's Eve Massacre." He added that if all those who had participated in Stalin's crimes were to be brought to book, more people would have to be imprisoned than had just been rehabilitated and released. Some cautious freeing of the cultural life of the nation was allowed, but he was always willing to attack anyone who went too far in this direction.

At the beginning of 1956 foreign policy dominated the agenda. Anastasy Mikoyan was dispatched to China to grant further economic aid. Khrushchev and Bulganin visited Britain and met the Queen. Relationships with Tito were improved by a visit from him to Moscow. In Eastern Europe the situation was not so happy. The speech attacking Stalin at the 20th Party Congress had caused crises in the parties of Poland and Hungary. In Poland workers were demonstrating and farms were being decollectivized. In Hungary, the unpopular party leadership had been ousted and Imre Nagy was bringing non-Communists into his government. Nagy's' government demanded the withdrawal of Soviet forces stationed there. Soviet tanks and troops crushed the Hungarian opposition and imposed a pro-Soviet government.

At the same time in Egypt President Gamal Abdel Nasser's seizure of the Suez Canal led to an attack by Britain, France, and Israel; this only ceased when pressure was exerted by the United States. The Suez situation made it hard for the West to take a firm line about the Soviet Union's action in Hungary. There is no doubt that Khrushchev's position in the Politburo was in danger after the 20th Party Congress speech and that the conservative elements were looking for an opportunity to attack him. The troubles in Poland and Hungary could be directly linked to his speech and, aside from the strategic necessities of the situation, he was involved in protecting himself.

1957–1958—In 1957 it was decided to restore to their homelands the many national groups who had been deported under Stalin. This was carried out at Khrushchev's orders despite the opposition of Vyacheslav Molotov, Georgy Malenkov, and other conservative elements in the Politburo. They were given further reason to intrigue against him when he introduced the idea of reorganizing the central administration of government by introducing Economic Councils (Sovnarkhoz) to oversee ministries. Khrushchev also, rashly, declared that the Soviet Union would, within a few years, equal the production of the United States in meat, milk, and butter. In June, at a three-day meeting of

the Presidium, a list of charges was leveled against him, including economic "voluntarism" and willful action. It was the intention of the plotters, the conservative element, to replace him with Molotov as first secretary. Khrushchev, with support form Anastasy Mikoyan, Mikhail Suslov, and Alexei Kirichenko, defended himself on the grounds that he could only be removed by a plenum of the Central Committee. It was not possible for the plotters to arrest him since he was backed by the army (Georgy Zhukov) and the KGB (Ivan Serov). The plenum was called and overwhelmingly supported him. Molotov, Malenkov, and Lazar Kaganovich lost their seats on the Presidium; Malenkov was made manager of a power station, Molotov was sent as ambassador to Mongolia, and Kaganovich was to manage a factory. Shortly after this, Zhukov, despite his support, was replaced as minister of defense by Malinovsky.

1958–1961—At the beginning of 1958 Khrushchev was in a powerful position. He had dealt with the opposition and was appointed chairman of the Council of Ministers, while still holding, like Stalin, the position of first secretary. He now concerned himself with reorganizing the educational system, and at the end of 1959 sanctioned cuts in the armed services and deprived officers of the militia and the MVD of some of their privileges. Also in 1958, and much less to his credit, he was behind the vicious campaign directed at Boris Pasternak for publishing *Dr. Zhivago* outside Russia. In May 1960 changes were made in the Central Committee and Kosygin, among others, was elected.

In foreign affairs Khrushchev quarreled with Tito again and canceled commercial credits to Yugoslavia, while relations with China cooled somewhat. In September Khrushchev visited the United States, gave a speech at the United Nations, and went to Hollywood where he was greeted with enthusiasm. In May 1960 a summit meeting with U.S. president Dwight D. Eisenhower was canceled as the result of the U2 spyflight. In September 1960 Khrushchev attended a meeting of the United Nations. He lost his temper several times and interrupted British prime minister Harold Macmillian by taking off his shoe and banging it on his desk. Macmillan asked for a translation.

Agriculture—The 1958 harvest was good, and in January 1959 an extraordinary 21st Party Congress was held to discuss the new seven-year plan. It was proposed among other things to increase industrial production by 80 percent and the chemical industry by 300 percent. There were to be massive increases in electronics, and light industry was also to be specially favored. In agriculture Khrushchev had the striking idea of closing the Machine Tractor Stations (MTS) and selling their machinery to the collective farms. Many of the farms could hardly afford to buy the machines and others had no ability to service them. The net result was less use of machinery and a decline in production.

In January 1961, because of the obstinate failure of the agricultural program to deliver the results expected, another plenum of the Central Committee was convened. The decision was now taken to reorganize the Ministry of Agriculture and those of all the republics. They were no longer to be concerned with the organization of production, but with the scientific aspect of

farming and the dissemination of information to the farms. Khrushchev and his advisers, who still included Lysenko, believed in the elimination of fallow in crop rotation, and this was put into operation throughout the country; it proved to be a mistake. Also mistaken was his action in introducing a new layer of administration into agriculture whose work would be to supervise a larger group of collectives. By the end of 1962 industrial production had increased by 9.5 percent but agricultural production had only risen by 1.2 percent, and in the Virgin Lands erosion had written off several million hectares of land. In 1963 the harvest was again very disappointing and at a plenum of the Central Committee Khrushchev asked for a huge increase in the production of fertilizers and herbicides.

1961: Berlin and Cuba—In April 1961 Yuri Gagarin circled the earth in the spaceship *Vostok* and received a hero's welcome in Moscow, while Khrushchev was again awarded the Order of Lenin. In the United States relations with the new Communist government in Cuba were tense, and President John F. Kennedy authorized a landing by Cuban émigrés—the fiasco known as the Bay of Pigs. This led to closer military cooperation between Cuba and the USSR. In June Kennedy met Khrushchev in Vienna for general discussions including the security of entry into West Berlin, which the Soviets wished to hand over to the East Germans and which led to the building of the Berlin Wall. Hardly had this crisis been solved when the infinitely more serious Cuban missile crisis occurred. In July 1962 Cuban leader Fidel Castro's brother Raoul arrived in Moscow seeking military aid that would include medium-range missiles with nuclear warheads and bombers with nuclear capacity. By October the hardware had been dispatched and the launching pads were being constructed in Cuba. Meanwhile, U.S. intelligence had reported this to the White House and Kennedy promptly issued a statement warning that the United States would not tolerate the setting up of ground-to-ground missiles in Cuba. Khrushchev ignored this and continued to send weapons. On October 22, Kennedy went on television to tell the U.S. people that he had ordered a complete blockade of Cuba and had placed the armed services on alert, ready to invade and occupy Cuba if the missile bases were not removed. On October 24, two Soviet vessels approached the line of the blockade while in Cuba work went on to prepare the missiles and the airstrip for the Soviet bombers. On October 26, Khrushchev responded to Kennedy's messages and proposed that if Kennedy would raise the blockade he would remove or destroy the missiles there. The crisis was over.

In 1962 Russo-Chinese relations also underwent a change for the worse again, starting with a series of articles in Chinese papers attacking the integrity of the Soviet Communist party. In the Chinese press Khrushchev himself was constantly referred to as the "great revisionist."

22nd Party Congress—In October 1961 at the 22nd Party Congress, Khrushchev once again raised the matter of Stalin's crimes, and this time he specified the members of the anti-party group who had attempted to prevent him from making them public. As a result a resolution was passed calling for the removal of

Stalin's remains from the mausoleum in Red Square. That night the coffin was placed in a deep hole outside the walls and several dump trucks unloaded tons of cement on top of it. There were further rehabilitations of Stalin's victims, and more freedom to discuss such matters in the media, which culminated with the Presidium's approval of the publication of Alexander Solzhenitsyn's *One Day in the Life of Ivan Denisovich.*

By 1964 there was a good deal of discontent in the USSR. The seven-year plan was not producing results. Food was scarce, as were many consumer goods, and prices had risen. The armed forces were smarting under the reductions in their pensions and privileges, and the peasants were unhappy about curtailment of their right to earn money from private plots. Khrushchev had now grown accustomed to wielding the reins of power and seemed unaware of the groundswell of discontent. In April he celebrated his 70th birthday, and it was announced that the title Hero of the Soviet Union had been conferred on him.

1964: The Final Year—Khrushchev spent much of what was to be his last year in power in travel abroad. In May he went to Hungary, and then visited Egypt to celebrate with Nasser the opening of the Aswan Dam. In June he began a three-week tour of Scandinavia and took his family. He also went to Czechoslovakia as well as welcoming endless visitors to Moscow, including New York governor Nelson Rockefeller and President Sukarno of Indonesia.

On October 12, 1964, the Presidium of the Central Committee was summoned to meet, with the objective of removing Khrushchev from all his official positions. The plot had been hatched by Mikhail Suslov and Alexander Shelepin but they were supported by both Brezhnev and Malinovsky; and by the time of the meeting only Mikoyan supported Khrushchev. He was summoned to Moscow from his holiday dacha by Brezhnev. The meeting at which he took the chair specified the reasons for their discontent and asked for his resignation. He refused at first and the meeting broke up, but the next day Khrushchev agreed and at the second meeting Brezhnev was elected first secretary and Alexei Kosygin, chairman of the council of ministers. A report was read itemizing Khrushchev's faults and shortcomings. It accused him of:

Taking hasty and ill-considered decisions

Encouraging unnecessary administrative changes in government

Taking sole credit for his country's achievements

Ignoring the authority of the Presidium and treating the members with disdain

Applying foolish theories in the field of agriculture

Treating Russia's allies in a cavalier fashion, ignoring some and being recklessly generous with others.

Many of these charges certainly were true, and such was the atmosphere of the meeting that when the resolution was put to the plenum "that N. S. Khrushchev be released from his duties because of his advanced age and poor health," it was passed unanimously. Khrushchev himself, when he returned to his home, said: "Well, that's it. I'm retired now. Perhaps the most important thing I did was just this: that they were able to get rid of me by simply voting, whereas Stalin would have had them all arrested."

His retirement was spent in a fairly modest dacha at Petro-Dalneye on the outskirts of Moscow. He was paid a pension of 400 rubles a month and an ancient car was put at his disposal. He was also alloted an apartment in Moscow, which he rarely used. He lived there with his wife and spent a good deal of time with his grandchildren. He started work on his memoirs, dictating them into a tape recorder, and they were published in the West in 1971. It is not clear by what route they got there. Khrushchev himself denied any part in it when he was summoned to explain himself to the chairman of the party's Control Commission.

On September 11, 1971, Khrushchev died of a heart attack. He was buried without the elaboration of a state funeral in the cemetery of Novo-Dyevichy. It has been said of him that at least he left his country a better place than he found it.

KIRILENKO, ANDREI. 1906–

A party member from 1931. An engineer and secretary of the Central Committee from 1966, he was considered an alternative successor to Brezhnev, but his challenge for power dwindled when Brezhnev gave his support to Andropov.

KIROV, SERGEI K. 1886–1934

Leader of the Leningrad party. A Social Democratic Bolshevik, he was jailed in 1906 and was in Siberia until 1917. He moved with the 11th Red Army to Baku and the Caucasus in 1919, and was elected as a delegate to the 10th Party Congress. From May 1920 to February 1921 he was the Soviet ambassa-

Petrograd, 1917. Members of the Red Guard at a May Day demonstration.

Lenin addressing a demonstration in Moscow, 1920. Leon Trotsky waits his turn to speak on the steps. After 1927 Trotsky was painted out whenever the photograph was used.

Military leaders of the Civil War, 1918–1920. Left to right: Simeon Timoshenko, Simeon Budyenny, and Kliment Voroshilov.

March 17, 1921. An attack on the rebels of Kronstadt, across the ice.

1927 cartoon from *Krokodil* satirizing the Nepmen, who made money from the New Economic Policies introduced by Lenin in 1921.

Anatoly Lunacharsky, commissar for education and the arts, in 1930, addressing a rally at the Young Pioneers Stadium, Moscow.

Berlin, May 1945. Soviet soldiers celebrate the capture of Berlin on the Reichstag building.

Homecoming. An old man and a boy return to their village at the end of World War II.

Party leaders surround Stalin's bier in the House of Unions, Moscow, March 1953. Left to right: Vyacheslav Molotov, Kliment Voroshilov, Lavrenti Beria, Georgy Malenkov, Nikolai Bulganin, Nikita Khrushchev, Lazar Kaganovich, and Anastasy Mikoyan.

Red Square, Moscow, 1964. Left to right: Alexei Kosygin; Marshal Malmousky; Leonid Brezhnev; Wladyslaw Gomulka, secretary of the Polish Communist party; Anastasy Mikoyan; Chou En-Lai, foreign minister, People's Republic of China; and Nikolai Podgorny.

Soviet Premier Nikita Khrushchev meets U.S. Pres. John F. Kennedy at the June 1961 summit meeting in Vienna.

An aide supports the Soviet president, Leonid Brezhnev, as he reviews an honor guard at the Budapest airport, 1979.

Soviet General Secretary Mikhail Gorbachev, in Berlin in 1989, takes part in the 40th anniversary celebrations of the German republic.

dor to Georgia, preparing the way for the invasion. In April 1923 at the 12th Party Congress he became a full member of the Central Committee.

In December 1925, he was sent to Leningrad to cleanse the party of its association with Grigory Zinoviev, a task which took several years. In July 1930 Stalin made him a full member of the Politburo. In the next few years he may have opposed some of Stalin's wishes, particularly the proposed shooting of Nikolai Ryutin, an opponent of Stalin's policies,and the special rations given in Leningrad. Also, in January 1934 the 17th Party Congress greeted his candidature for the post of general secretary with loud applause. On December 1 he was shot. A young Communist, Leonid Nikolaev, was named his murderer. Stalin used the murder as a justification for another purge of the Leningrad party, in which thousands of opponents were shot or deported to camps. The murder is a mystery and a source of speculation still. Had Kirov in fact been involved in an anti-Stalin movement? Did Stalin engineer the murder and use it to destroy others? Kirov was officially treated as a hero after his death.

KOKOSHIN, FEDOR F. ?–1918

A lawyer member of the Kadet party in First Duma. A conservative to the right of most Kadets, he was in the Provisional Government and urged Alexander Kerensky to accept Lavr Kornilov's proposals for drastic military powers. After the October Revolution, in January 1918 while a prisoner in the Marinsky Hospital, he was shot by a group of sailors.

KOLCHAK, ALEXANDER V. 1874–1920

Admiral in command of the Black Sea fleet from 1916. Overthrowing the Ufa Directorate, he led a government in Siberia, based in Omsk, as Supreme Ruler, with the blessing of France and Britain from late 1918. He failed to keep the support of his troops, the people of the region, or the strong Czech Legion and he lost power in December 1919. He was captured at Irkutsk and executed.

KOLLONTAY, ALEXANDRA. 1867–1952

The first woman ambassador in the world. Her mother was a wealthy heiress and her father an aristocratic czarist officer, both of whom had liberal and intellectual connections. Born before the marriage she was given her father's name, Domontovitch. Her marriage to Vladimir Kollontay in 1893 did not last long, but she later claimed that she became a socialist when, on a trip with him, she saw workers' housing and among the houses, unnoticed and uncared for, a dead child. A supporter of Lenin from 1901, she joined the Bolsheviks. She insisted that the Social Democrats support women workers and found her political base among St. Petersburg's female textile workers. She was part of the "Workers' Opposition," voicing popular complaints that the urban workers had not gained from the revolution.

Madam Kollontay was a feminist in a party unaware of feminism (although the Russian bourgeoisie had already accepted a great deal of the principles of women's rights, the working classes had not yet been brought to face the need for them). She was made people's commissar for social security in October 1917, and pushed through a series of decrees and declarations for women, including, in December, the abolition of religious marriage and the instituting of marriage and divorce as a purely civil matter. Her role, thereafter, became that of the token woman, and she was moved out of the center of power to become the Soviet ambassador, first to Norway in 1923, then Mexico in 1927, and then Sweden from 1930 to 1945, where her position in a neutral country had importance in negotiating peace with Finland.

Her well-groomed appearance and her declared opposition to the conventional institution of marriage led many to assume that she devoted her life to her sexual pleasure. This was not so. She stressed the "self-preservation of the individual" and that women's lives should be realized to their fullest potential.

KONEV, IVAN S. 1897–1973

Marshal of the Soviet Union. He joined the party in 1918. A taciturn and guarded man, he survived the army purges of the 1930s and, in April 1941, his 19th Army in the Caucasus was moved to the western border of the USSR to face the brunt of Hitler's June invasion. In the retreat he was given command of the Western Front, the principal defense of Moscow, and made deputy to Marshal Zhukov. His thrust into the German lines to the north of Moscow in November 1941 marked a turn in the war, followed by the great counterattacks. In the 1943 Battle of Kursk, his Steppe Front took the offensive and captured Kharkov. He commanded the Ukrainian Front, sharing (or disputing)

with Zhukov the honor of taking Berlin in 1945.

He succeeded Zhukov as commander-in-chief of the Soviet ground forces from 1946 to 1956. He was first deputy defense minister in 1956, commanded the Warsaw Pact forces from 1955 to 1960, and headed the Soviet forces in Germany during the critical period of the building of the Berlin Wall, 1961–62.

KORNILOV, LAVR G. 1870–1918

Communist general. A war hero after his daring escape from capture by the Austrians in 1915, he was made general in command of the Petrograd Military District in 1917 and was responsible for the czar's arrest. He led an army in Alexander Kerensky's 1917 offensive, and when it was broken by the Germans he retained its discipline. Kerensky made him commander-in-chief. Thinking he was acting in the best interests of the Provisional Government, he mobilized troops to remove the Bolsheviks from Petrograd, but Kerensky misunderstood his moves and had him arrested, accusing him of planning a military coup. This became known as the "Kornilov affair."

Kornilov escaped to the Don, to join Anton Denikin but was killed in action by an enemy shell shortly thereafter.

KOSLOV, FROL. 1908–1965

Party worker. He joined the Communist Party of the Soviet Union in 1926, when he was a textile worker in Leningrad, and began his party career there, becoming party secretary and associate of Andrei Zhdanov. He rose in 1957 to be chairman of the Council of Ministers of the Russian Soviet Federal Socialist Republic. Koslov mobilized the Leningrad party to support Khrushchev when he was challenged by the anti-party group in 1957, and as a reward was appointed Khrushchev's deputy. In 1960 he was appointed secretary to the Central Committee and began to mount a serious challenge to Brezhnev as Khrushchev's successor, firing a number of people from the Secretariat, including Ekaterina Furtseva, as part of his campaign. In 1961 he fell out with Khrushchev on Yugoslavia and on agriculture, and in 1963 he launched an attack on Brezhnev in the pages of *Pravda*. He suffered from a stroke in 1964 and his removal from the Politburo in the same year signaled Brezhnev's victory in the leadership struggle.

KOSSIOR, STANISLAV V. 1889–1939

Ukrainian party leader. He joined the party in 1907, and was exiled to Irkutsk in 1915, returning to Petrograd in February 1917. He was then sent to the German-occupied Ukraine, where he had charge of party work and prepared for an armed uprising. At the time of the Brest-Litovsk Treaty in 1918, he joined the left-wing Communists and led a underground party when Anton Denikin ruled the area. From 1921 he held various party posts in the Ukraine and in Siberia. Kossior was a candidate member of the Politburo from 1927 and a full member from 1930, and became general secretary of the party in the Ukraine. But his adherence to Leninism and his belief in "internationalism'" was not wanted in Stalin's day. In January 1938, when Khrushchev came as acting party secretary to the Ukraine to clear out nationalists and dissenters, his be-

liefs led to his downfall, arrest, and execution.

KOSYGIN, ALEXEI N. 1904–1980

Communist party leader. A Leningrad textile engineer and party worker who was promoted by Andrei Zhdanov in the 1938 purge to be chairman of the Leningrad Soviet. His party career prospered, and by 1952 he was a member of the Central Committee and the Politburo, and was minister of light industry, although he had lost Zhdanov's patronage at his death in 1948. He continued under Khrushchev, becoming chairman of Gosplan in 1958. In 1964 he was elected chairman of the Council of Ministers, taking Khrushchev's place, while Brezhnev took the post of party general secretary. He held this post, effectively premier of the Soviet Union, under Yuri Andropov.

KRASIN, LEONID B. 1870–1926

Revolutionary, later diplomat. An old Communist who, although he had broken with Lenin in 1909, had political importance and whose industrial expertise was used in building the Soviet economy. From 1900 he worked in Baku as an engineer in the expanding oilfields. His technical skills were also used in setting up secret printing presses.

Under the cover name Zimin ("winter," in Russian) he was the chairman of the Third Party Congress in London at which the Bolshevik faction emerged. He returned to take charge as an engineer of the St. Petersburg lighting system, but was forced to flee when the authorities discovered his political background. In 1918 he undertook to head the commission organizing supplies to the Red Army and was made commissar for trade and industry. He was twice ambassador to Britain and also to France. He died in England.

KRASNOV, PETR N. 1869–1947

The last of the Cossack romantics: a Don Cossack czarist general and novelist. With his Cossacks he supported Alexander Kerensky at the time of the "Kornilov affair" in 1917, but his men and the revolutionaries began to parlay and for a time it was uncertain who was guarding whom. Krasnov engineered Krensky's escape, which ended in the United States.

Krasnov was elected ataman of the Don Cossacks and took dictatorial power, approached the Germans for help, made an alliance with the Skoropadsky government of the Ukraine, called in the Volunteer Army, and raised a force of 40,000 Cossacks. By August 1918 the Red Army and the Bolsheviks were driven out. Krasnov encouraged a counter-Bolshevik terror and preached "Don for the Don Cossacks." Krasnov's rule became unpopular as food shortages increased. In December 1918 whole regiments began to desert to the Red Army. In February 1919 he resigned.

Krasnov left Russia for Germany. The Nazis chose him to lead the puppet Cossack state in World War II, but by then he was an elderly man leaning on a stick. The Cossack prisoners paid him little attention and called him "Granddad." He was handed over to the Soviets by the British, who found him with other Cossack troops in Austria in 1945. He was executed in January 1947, after a trial for fighting against the Soviet Union, espionage, and terrorism.

KROPOTKIN, PETER. 1842–1921

A prince and an anarchist. He had a reputation as an explorer in Manchuria and Siberia, and was secretary of the Russian Geographical Society. He was linked to extreme revolutionaries and imprisoned in 1874, escaping to Western Europe in 1876. Although he did not approve of communism or of the Bolsheviks, he returned to Russia after the revolution for the last years of his life. This act seemed to give a blessing to the revolution and he was held in great esteem.

KRUPSKAYA, NADEZHDA K. 1869–1939

A Soviet official and wife of Lenin. A teacher from the class of poor official gentry, she worked with Lenin and went with him into exile, marrying him in 1898. She later became vice-commissar of education, and a member of the Central Committee and the Presidium.

She supported Grigory Zinoviev in 1925–26, but "capitulated" to Stalin. Her humiliation by and subjection to Stalin was nearly absolute. She was obliged to stand by, in posts of minor dignity, while he exterminated the old party. Her book, *My Life with Lenin*, became her main task; the role of Lenin's widow.

KRYUCHKOV, VLADIMIR. 1924–

KGB leader. Trained as a diplomat, his first posting abroad was as third secretary to Moscow's embassy in Hungary, where Yuri Andropov was ambassador, 1955–59. He evidently impressed Andropov during the Hungarian uprising and the subsequent Soviet repression in

1956, for when Andropov became chief of the KGB in 1967 he brought in Kryuchkov, then working in the Central Committee. Kryuchkov soon rose to be head KGB man in New York in the 1970s, and head of all KGB foreign operations in 1978, with the rank of general. He became chairman of the KGB, in succession to Viktor Chebrikov, in September 1988.

Kryuchkov's style is in contrast to the KGB's past reputation. He is courteous and cultured; he was the first KGB chief to receive the U.S. ambassador in his office, and has appeared in a film showing the modern, suave KGB. Gorbachev appointed him a full member of the Politburo in September 1989.

KULIK, GRIGORY I. 1890–1950

Marshal of the Soviet Union. From sergeant in the czarist army, he rose, with Simeon Budyenny, in the Red Army. Like others of his background he was promoted beyond his abilities and training. Stalin even gave him the job of running the main ordnance directorate for the whole Red Army (having remembered his being in charge of a few guns at Tsaritsyn). An old cavalryman, he opposed the introduction of the T34 tank. He was dismissed for gross inefficiency in 1941 and was lucky to survive. From marshal he was demoted to major, but near the end of his life was promoted to major general by Stalin.

KUN, BELA. 1886–1937

Hungarian Communist. A prisoner of war from the Austro-Hungarian army in Russia, he led the Hungarian Soviet government from March to August 1919, until it was suppressed ferociously by a counterrevolutionary force that led, in 1920, to the right-wing government of Admiral Horthy. He escaped by way of Vienna to Russia. An object of suspicion to Stalin as a man with potential allies, he died in the Great Purge.

KUUSINEN, OTTO. 1881–1964

An old party member from 1904. He was a member of the Finnish revolutionary government of 1918, made head of the short-lived puppet "Finnish government" set up in the USSR in 1939. From 1940 he was chairman of the Presidium of the Finno-Karelian ASSR Supreme Soviet.

LANDAU, LEV D. 1908–1968

A physicist. He received the Nobel Prize in 1962 for his fundamental research in the superconductivity and superfluidity of liquid helium. Educated at Baku and Leningrad universities, he became head of physics at Kharkov University. A leading international figure in space technology, nuclear physics, plasma physics, stellar energy, and low-temperature physics, he also helped make the first Soviet atomic bomb.

LARIONOV, MIKHAIL. 1881–1964

Painter and scenic designer. Born in Moldavia, he went to Paris in 1906 to study and was much influenced by the fauvist and neo-primitivist movements. He returned to Russia and, with his friend Natalia Goncharova (a contemporary), helped organize the trio of exhibitions *Jack of Diamonds* (1910), *Donkey's Tail*, (1912), and *Target* (1913). He also developed the abstract theory of painting known as rayonism. In 1915 he went to Paris and worked for Diaghilev, designing for opera and ballet. He was an important influence on Soviet artists in the early days of the revolution. Later in life he returned to painting genre paintings; he died in France.

LAZO, SERGEI. 1894–1920

Bolshevik leader in the Russian Far East. A young Communist from the Amur region, who joined the Southern Maritime Province Committee formed in January 1918 to replace the overthrown Vladivostok Soviet. He was made commander of the partisans and then leader of the military revolutionary staff. The Provisional Zemstvo Government gave him charge of the military council. When the Japanese decided to attack the Provisional Government in April 1920, it was decided not to resist but that troops should take to the hills with their weapons. Lazo and other council members were captured by the Japanese, who disposed of them by burning them in a locomotive boiler.

LENIN, (ULYANOV) VLADIMIR ILYCH. 1870–1924

Childhood and Youth—He was born in Simbirsk on April 22, 1870, in the old Tatar kingdom on the banks of the Volga. Lenin's father, whose family were of nomadic Chuvash origins, was a schoolteacher, a kind and pious man who became director of the school system of the province and, therefore under the existing system, a nobleman. His mother, loving but determined, came from a prosperous bourgeois family of mixed German and Swedish descent with a fair-sized estate near Kazan. Lenin

was the third surviving child of their six children.

He was educated at the grammar school in Simbirsk, and he and his brothers and sisters led a peaceful and happy middle-class life. Everything changed when Lenin was 16. His father died of a brain hemorrhage and shortly afterward his brother Alexander, to whom he was devoted, became involved in an unsuccessful attempt to assassinate Czar Alexanader III and, despite all his mother's efforts, was hanged on May 20, 1886. On the June 22, Lenin passed his finals at the grammar school with the highest possible marks and a glowing testimonial from headmaster Fyodor Kerensky (father of the future prime minister in the Provisional Government).

Lenin entered Kazan University to read law in August 1887. Up to this point he had, despite his brother's fate, showed no interest in revolutionary politics. But in the summer he read Nikolai Chernyshevsky's *What is to be Done?*, a novel written when the author was a political prisoner. The hero of the novel is Rakhmetev, one of the "new men" who are prepared to live a life of the greatest privation in order to bring about a new society in which all men would be free. The book had an extraordinary effect on several generations of revolutionaries and Lenin was to prove no exception. Later in the year he took part in student demonstrations, was expelled from the university in December, and was placed under surveillance by the political police at his mother's estate at Kokushkino, where he studied law.

At the age of 20 in 1890, through his mother's influence, Lenin was allowed to take his finals at St. Petersburg and was awarded a first class degree. In 1893, at age 23, Lenin moved to St. Petersburg and started work in the office of a lawyer.

The Revolutionary—Contemporary accounts agree that Lenin had now changed profoundly. He seemed much older than his years and was almost completely bald. He had started reading Marx and Engels after he was expelled from university and by now had become a serious revolutionary. When he arrived in St. Petersburg he immediately sought out revolutionary circles in the city, where he was known by the name of Nikolay Petrovich.

In February 1894 he met a young girl, Nadezhda Krupskaya, who had joined one of the study circles. She came from his sort of background though her parents were now impoverished. She seems to have greatly admired him from the first and was content to act as his secretary, to code and decode his messages, and generally look after him from then until the end of his life, though they were not married until 1898.

In March Lenin wrote his first extended work, *What the Friends of the People Are: How they fight the Social Democrats*, an attack on the Narodniks.

In April Lenin went to Geneva and met Georgy Plekhanov and Pavel Axelrod, and then to Paris where he met and talked with Paul Lafargue, Marx's son-in-law. He completed his European trip by staying in Berlin before returning to St. Petersburg. In December Lenin, with many other Social Democrats in the movement, was arrested and spent a year in jail before, as a result of his mother's influence, he was exiled to Shushenskoye in southern Siberia.

In Shushenskoye he lived in the house of a well-to-do peasant, Apollon Zyrianov. He thoroughly enjoyed his time there, fishing, talking to the peasants, and endlessly reading. He wrote the important pamphlet, *The Tasks of the Russian Social Democrats*, which spelled out his ideas concerning an insurrectionary movement led by the Social Democrats among the factory workers. On March 13, the First Congress of the All-Russian Social Democratic Labor party met in Minsk and Lenin declared himself a member. In May 1898 Krupskaya and her mother arrived in Shushkenskoye, and the couple were married in July and moved into their own house.

In February 1900 Lenin returned from exile but left Krupskaya, who had to remain in exile for a further year. He returned to Psovsk but then went, illegally, to St. Petersburg, when he and Yuli Martov were arrested with their pockets full of subversive literature; Lenin was soon released.

Exile—Lenin went to Switzerland to visit Axelrod and Plekhanov with whom he quarreled about an article he had written for the new publication *Iskra*. He then moved to Munich, where he arranged for the printing and distribution of *Iskra* and where he was joined by Krupskaya in March 1901. Shortly after this he began work on his book, *What Is To Be Done?*, in which he outlined his policies and beliefs at some length. He demonstrated the influence of Sergei Nechayev when he wrote of "this powerful and secret organization rising up to destroy the autocracy." He stressed that this movement could not be democratic, that one man or a very small number of men must make all the ultimate decisions. Shortly after the book was published, the German printers of *Iskra* decided that it was unsafe to continue printing it and Lenin convinced the editorial board that they should move it to London. Lenin and Krupskaya rented an apartment at 30 Holford Square, obtained a reader's ticket for the British Museum, and found a printer for *Iskra*. They were soon joined in London by Martov and Vera Zasulich. At this point Leon Trotsky arrived from Russia at the beginning of his long exile, and he and Lenin spent some time walking around London together. He recognized Trotsky's qualities but, at this time, he and the younger man were not close.

Lenin was still arguing with Plekhanov, and when the editorial board voted to take *Iskra* back to Switzerland, Lenin had such a severe attack of shingles that he was confined to bed.

Bolshevik and Menshevik—On July 30, the Second Congress of the All-Russian Social Democratic Labor party opened in Brussels, was closed by the police, and moved to London. It was at this congress that the split in the party took place. Martov wanted a "broad" party, open to anyone who supported any of its organizations, and Lenin wanted a "narrow" party, confined to those who had worked for one of the organizations. Plekhanov and Trotsky sided with the side getting the minority vote, the Mensheviks. Lenin, though he continued the battle and was now the leader of the majority group, the Bolsheviks, was profoundly depressed and in poor health again. In November he resigned from the editorial board of *Iskra* and then, in the summer of 1904, he abandoned his revolutionary activities and with Krupskaya went off to the mountains to recover. In September they returned from their holidays, and Lenin planned a new revolutionary newspaper V*pered* ("Forward") with his new supporters, including Alexander Bogdanov and Anatoly Lunacharsky. In the first edition of the new paper he wrote an article forecasting a popular uprising in Russia. Within three weeks, "Bloody Sunday," the massacre outside the Winter Palace, had sparked off the 1905 Revolution.

The 1905 Revolution—The main events of the 1905 Revolution took place without any participation from Lenin. When Lenin finally arrived in the city in October via Sweden, he was closely shadowed by the Okhrana (the czar's secret police) and crossed the border to Finland to escape them. While he was there the uprising in Moscow took place. For the next two years Lenin and Krupskaya lived mostly in or near St. Petersburg, though he made occasional trips to Finland and Denmark for conferences or meetings. There were attempts at unifying the party from time to time, but Lenin was still determined to maintain his Bolshevik principles and also to remain in charge. At the end of the year he traveled to Tammerfors, where the first All-Russian Bolshevik Conference was held. In April 1907 he was arraigned at a special party tribunal for an article he had written against the Mensheviks. He defended himself vigorously and was not expelled from the party. Lenin proclaimed that it was permissible to use any weapons against opponents who had caused a split in the party because "every split is a great crime against the party."

Fifth Party Congress—In May Lenin traveled to London where the Fifth Party Congress took place. It was attended also by Leon Trotsky, Grigory Zinoviev,

Lev Kamenev, and—on one of his rare trips out of Russia—Stalin; also Nikolai Rykov and Kliment Voroshilov and on the Menshevik side were Plekhanov, Martov, Axelrod, and Feodor Dan. Lenin was in impressive form and attacked the Mensheviks for siding with the bourgeoisie, the Kadets, and the Duma. He accused Trotsky of being a Menshevik in disguise.

Exile Again—In January 1908 Lenin and Krupskaya once again left Russia and returned to Switzerland. They were to spend the next nine years in Europe. In Geneva he wrote *Materialism and Empirocriticism*, a philosophical study, and in December they moved to Paris. When they arrived in the French capital, the party decided to launch a new magazine called the *Social Democrat*, and in order to remain on the editorial board, which included Martov, Lenin was forced to agree to a much-modified policy that downplayed talk of armed insurrection. Then in the spring of 1910, to everyone's surprise, Lenin developed a close friendship with an attractive French woman, Inessa Armand, wife of a rich industrialist, who had abandoned her husband for the pleasures and perils of revolutionary politics. The relationship lasted for many years and was important to both. Krupskaya, who always put her husband's happiness first, was at one time quite prepared to step aside and let them marry. Lenin, at heart a domestic bourgeois, strongly resisted the idea.

In the spring of 1911 Lenin set up a school for the training of underground workers near Paris. Zinoviev and Kamenev lectured on the history of the party, while Armand lectured on political science and ran a communal kitchen in her dining room.

In January 1912 a conference of the Bolsheviks was held in Prague at which Lenin asserted his dominance over the party. In June he believed there to be signs of an insurrection in Russia, and he moved to Cracow in Austrian Poland where he hoped to be able to influence events more easily. There he met Nikolai Bukharin for the first time.

In Cracow, Krupskaya's health deteriorated and they took a cottage in the Tatra Mountains, but finally Lenin had to take her to Berne, where she was operated on for goiter. For the next two years they spent the winters in Cracow and the summers in the mountains except for occasional trips to attend conferences or meetings in Paris, Berlin, or Brussels.

World War I—At the outbreak of war Lenin was in Nowy Targ, Galicia. The Austrian authorities searched his house and arrested him. He was freed on appeal by sympathizers in Austria. He returned to Cracow and then traveled to Berne via Vienna. They were to spend the next three wartime years in Switzerland, either in Berne or Zurich, short of money as usual and living in uncomfortable circumstances most of the time.

Georgy Plekhanov and Karl Kautsky had come out in support of the war and Lenin attacked them for this. In his *Tasks of Revolutionary Social Democracy in the European War*, he called the war a "bourgeois, imperialist, dynastic war" and proposed as a slogan "For the Socialist Revolution" and as an immediate goal, "A Republican United States of Europe." Their neighbors and closest associates at this time were the Zinovievs and Inessa Armand.

At Zimmerwald in September 1915 Lenin declared that the task was to turn "the imperialist war between peoples into a civil war" but his motion was defeated. On March 15 after lunch Lenin was getting ready to return to the library as usual when a friend ran in to announce news of a revolution in Russia.

Revolution—Lenin's initial reactions to the February Revolution were much concerned with the possibility of a counter revolution headed by the czar. But he clung firmly to the necessity for the Bolsheviks to carry out propaganda for an international proleterian revolution and for the seizure of power by a soviet of workers' deputies.

But Lenin's main concern now was to how to leave "this accursed Switzerland" and return to Russia. In wartime all normal means of transport were impossible. But it was Martov's plan that finally succeeded. He suggested approaching the German government and arranging an exchange of Russian exiles for German internees. The plan was adopted: to deliver Lenin and his Bolsheviks to Russia would hasten the collapse of Russia. The "sealed train" with Lenin and his party arrived at the Finland Station in Petrograd on April 16 at 11 P.M., to be greeted by enthusiastic crowds, representatives from the Petrograd Soviet, the Baltic fleet, and a band playing *La Marseillaise*. Addressing the crowds from the turret of an armored car he shouted "Long live the world wide Socialist Revolution!"

The April Theses—The morning after Lenin's arrival it was decided to hold a meeting of the Bolshevik delegates to the All-Russian Congress of Soviets of Workers' and Soldiers' Deputies at the Tauride Palace. The address he gave at the conference, which was recorded as

he delivered it, became known as the April Theses. The singular nature of many of these statements led to his being attacked not only by Mensheviks, which was to be expected, but also by many of his own party. Questions were also asked as to how he had managed to travel through Germany on the "sealed train." Could he have been subsidized by the German High Command? This suspicion continued to haunt Lenin for many years, though it has been proved untrue.

By the time of the next party conference in May, Lenin had overcome most of his critics but the situation was anarchic. Only Kerensky, now minister of war in the Provisional Government, seemed to have any authority. There were Mensheviks in the government, but the Bolsheviks were not asked to join and, in any case, would have refused.

By June the Bolshevik program was rapidly increasing its support. After the Bolshevik failure to take the initiative in the workers' demonstrations in the July Days, and the provisional government's action against the Bolsheviks, Lenin was in imminent danger. Rather than face his accusers he took refuge in a village near Petrograd and then moved to Finland. In August the Petrograd Supreme Court indicted him for treason and the organization of an armed uprising. At the Sixth Party Congress, Lenin was elected to the Central Committee with Zinoviev and Trotsky. They were all either in prison or in hiding.

Lenin then published *State and Revolution*, in which he argued that after the proletarian revolution there would be a period of transition before the ideal Communist state could be established, and this state would be called the dictatorship of the proleteriat. "When the ideal state comes into existence there will be no need for it any more—it will wither away."

On October 9 Lenin returned to Petrograd and on October 10 a meeting was held in the apartment of Nikolai Sukhanov at 32 Karpova. Twelve of the 21 members of the Central Committee were present. Lenin accused them of lacking courage and foresight and demanded an immediate uprising. A vote was taken; ten of the committee were in favor; two, Zinoviev and Kamenev, were against.

The October Revolution—On the morning of October 25 the Bolshevik forces went into action and seized the key points in the city. On October 26 Lenin attended the Second All-Russian Congress of Soviets of Workers' and Soldiers' Deputies. He was elected chairman of Sovnarkom (the Council of People's Commissars) and on October 27 issued the Decrees on Peace and on Land, calling for immediate peace and proclaiming the end of private ownership of land.

While Trotsky organized the defense of Petrograd, Lenin proceeded with the work of government. To a large degree it was government by improvisation. As he later wrote, "Revolutions are the locomotives of history. Drive them at full speed and keep them on the rails." On October 26 he signed a decree ordering elections to be held on November 11. But when the Constituent Assembly met in January 1918 and the Bolshevik motions were defeated, Lenin promptly withdrew them from the assembly and called for the dissolution of the assembly on the grounds that it represented the "old relationship of political forces." This was formally the end of democratic government in Russia.

The peace negotiations with the Germans at Brest-Litovsk were being conducted by Trotsky. Lenin was only able to get the party to agree to accept the quite onerous terms on the grounds that he could not afford to fight a revolutionary war or depend on the revolution's taking place in Germany—which Trotsky and the others were relying on. Nevertheless, he had to threaten resignation in order to get his own way.

In March he moved the center of government to Moscow and lived first in the Hotel National and then in an apartment in the Kremlin with Trotsky as a nearby neighbor. They arranged that the Kremlin bells should play the *Internationale*.

Invasion and Civil War—The Soviet republic was in danger, with White troops menacing Petrograd. Trotsky as commissar for war was responsible for defending the new Soviet republic. But Lenin introduced the most Draconian punishments for anyone involved in resistance to the government. Red Terror became a principal instrument of rule. In July 1918 Left Social Revolutionaries assassinated Count Mirbach, the German envoy to the Kremlin, and the deputies of the Social Revolutionaries were arrested. Lenin sent a telegram to Stalin telling him that "the left SRs who had launched an uprising against us must be mercilessly suppressed." In August there was an attempt to assassinate Lenin by another Left Social Revolutionary, Fanya Kaplan. He was shot in the chest and shoulder, but by October was well enough to speak in public again. His attempted assassination was followed by a mass wave of terror; the Petrograd Cheka alone executed more than 500 immediately.

1919 was the worst year of the civil war. Lenin still had hopes of European revolutions breaking out and they were given temporary substance in Hungary and Bavaria by the setting up of "soviets" there. But they were soon crushed as Rosa Luxemburg and Karl Liebknecht's Spartacists had been in Berlin. In March he established the Third International—the Comintern—and declared optimistically: "The ice is broken. The Soviets have conquered throughout the whole world." By the end of the year the Interventionists had withdrawn and the outcome of the civil war seemed less in doubt.

At about this time Lenin developed a plan for the electrification of the country, declaring that "Communism is the Soviet government plus the electrification of the whole country." In February 1920 he delivered a report to a meeting of the All-Russian Central Executive Committee denying that the Bolsheviks had remained in power by the use of terror and claiming that "we have renounced capital punishment."

In April war broke out between Russia and Poland and, against Trotsky's advice, Lenin ordered the Red Army to advance on Warsaw. The campaign was a failure and the disaster was compounded by Stalin's taking Lvov, ignoring the overall plan. This was not the first time that Stalin had gone against Trotsky; indeed, he had been attempting to poison Lenin's mind against him for some time. Lenin was forced to mediate between them but, on this occasion, he supported Trotsky completely. On October 12 a peace treaty was signed with Poland and, on the same day, Lenin attended the funeral of his friend Inessa Armand, who had died of cholera contracted in the Crimea in August. Lenin was grief stricken.

New Economic Policy (NEP)—In 1921 peace returned to Russia. The enemies of the Soviet Republic, both external and internal, had been mostly defeated, but, as Lenin admitted in a letter written in February, "It is quite useless to work on vast bureaucratic schemes of state economy. We are beggared. That is what we are—starving, destitute beggars." Suddenly there was a new opposition. In March the sailors at Kornstadt called for free elections and the return of small-scale enterprise. This rebellion was ruthlessly suppressed, but Lenin realized that the policies of War Communism could not continue without the entire economy breaking down and with it the government. So at the 10th Party Congress, the "Workers' Opposition" was attacked and the measures known as the New Economic Policy (NEP) were introduced. This was almost immediately followed by the most appalling famine, the result of widespread crop failures on a scale not seen for 30 years.

Conditions in the country improved with a good harvest in 1922 and the new measures to encourage the peasantry to sell their crops. Small-scale industry and commerce had made a wider range of goods available, but Lenin was obsessed with the "swamp of bureaucracy" that was strangling the country. It was perhaps one of the reasons for making the fateful decision to appoint Stalin as general secretary during the course of the 11th Party Congress in April 1922.

Illness—In April Lenin had a small operation to remove one of the bullets that had lodged in his body after Fanya Kaplan's assassination attempt, but on May 26 he suffered from a stroke and was kept at Gorky until September, when he returned to work at the Kremlin. He was supposed to work no more than 5 hours a day but actually worked 10 and held meetings on the days he was not supposed to work. On October 3 he attended a meeting of the All-Russian Central Executive Committee and in November spoke at a session of the Moscow Soviet, where it was noticed that his speech was slurred. In December he had two more attacks and his right side was paralyzed. His doctors ordered him to bed for a complete rest.

Visitors were forbidden but Lenin was allowed to dictate for 5 or 10 minutes daily. He started to write the letters to the congress that became known as his "Testament." A variety of topics were covered but it mainly concentrated on his fears about the future leadership of the party and the possible split he saw developing from a struggle between Trotsky and Stalin. Of Stalin he wrote "Comrade Stalin having become General Secretary has unlimited authority... and I am not sure that he will always be capable of using that authority with sufficient caution.... Comrade Trotsky... is personally perhaps the most capable man in the present Central Committee but he has displayed excessive self assurance.... These two qualities of the two outstanding leaders of the present can inadvertently lead to split." In further installments of his "Testament" he suggested increasing the number of Central Committee members and also went into the question of nationalities. In doing so, he criticized Stalin for his repressive actions in Georgia. He also sent a note to Trotsky asking him to look into the Georgian situation. In January he added a note to his previous comments on Stalin, saying that "Stalin is too rude... which becomes intolerable in a secretary general. This is why I

suggest that the comrades think about a way of removing Stalin from that post."

In March 1923 Lenin learned of Stalin's abusive telephone call to Krupskaya, in which Stalin attacked her for allowing Lenin to discuss political matters. He wrote to Trotsky asking him to raise the matter of the Georgians at the plenum of the Central Committee and to Stalin to decide whether he wished to apologize or break off relations with him.

Death—On March 10 Lenin suffered a third stroke but by October was well enough to be driven to Moscow.

On January 21, 1924, he had a further attack, lost consciousness, and died at 6:50 P.M. On January 23, his body was moved to Moscow and on January 27, against his wishes, it was placed in a mausoleum in Red Square. Thousands of mourners from all regions of Russia flocked to Moscow to pay their last respects to their leader. And at the second All-Union Congress of Soviets the anniversary of Lenin's death was announced as a national day of mourning.

LIGACHEV, YEGOR K. W. 1920–

Politburo member. He is an engineer by profession and a graduate of the Moscow Aviation Engineering Institute, and has been a member of the Communist Party of the Soviet Union since 1944. After World War II he worked as an engineer before joining Komsomol and working for it in Novosibirsk. Several years of party work followed, at the end of which he became secretary of the Novosibirsk Obkom. In 1961 he went to Moscow to work in the Central Committee, dealing with party publications. In 1965, after Brezhnev's reorganization of the party apparatus, he was sent back to Siberia as first secretary of the Tomsk Oblast. He stayed there until 1963 and built a reputation as a hard but fair party leader. Yuri Andropov, who had a high opinion of Ligachev's integrity, brought him back to Moscow as head of the organizational department of the Central Committee. In 1985 he became a full member of the Politburo. Although he supported Mikhail Gorbachev's election to general secretary, Ligachev does not owe his political rise to Gorbachev and is regarded as being firmly on the conservative side of the party. In the summer of 1987, with Viktor Chebrikov then head of the KGB, he published a warning against too radical changes and played a leading role in the dismissal of Boris Yeltsin. He survived the 1989 reshuffle of the Politburo and held his post as chairman of the Central Committee Commission for Agriculture.

LITVINOV, MAXIM (GENOKH KOISSEVICH, MEIER WALLACH). 1876–1951

Soviet diplomat. A Social Democrat from 1898, he joined the Leninists in 1901. After the 1905 Revolution, he moved to London where he worked in an office. He married Ivy Low, a London journalist linked with the Bloomsbury intellectual set. In 1917 he was appointed the Soviet representative in Britain. He was arrested but released in exchange for the head of the British Diplomatic Mission to St. Petersburg, Bruce Lockhart.

Litvinov was deputy commissar for foreign affairs from 1921 to 1930, often representing the Soviet Union abroad at international conferences. He became

commissar in 1931, but Stalin replaced him with Vyacheslav Molotov in 1939 when he wanted to deal with Nazi Germany, either because he was too clearly associated with Western Europe or because as a Jew the Nazis would not talk to him. He was reappointed deputy commissar in 1941 and was ambassador to Washington from 1941 to 1943.

LOCKHART, SIR ROBERT BRUCE. 1887–1970

The first British diplomat to head a special mission to the Bolshevik government in 1918. The Soviets assumed immediately that he was a spy. He spoke fluent Russian and made friends with leaders such as Leon Trotsky. He was imprisoned in the Kremlin, September–October 1918, on suspicion of being behind the assassination of Count Wilhelm von Mirbach (See Mirbach), but released after British protests and threats of retaliation. He was exchanged for Maxim Litvinov.

Lockhart had, in fact, been the paymaster of the British agent in Russia, Sidney Reilly. Together they had arranged help for White agents and planned the assassination of Lenin. The attempt by Fanya Kaplan on Lenin preempted them. For his work in Russia he was decorated and given a knighthood. After 1922 he worked for a bank and as a journalist, writing his memoirs in 1933.

LUKYANOV, ANATOLY I. 1930–

Vice-president of the Supreme Soviet and deputy to Mikhail Gorbachev. A lawyer who has worked for years in Moscow for the Central Committee and the Supreme Soviet, he joined the

BIOGRAPHIES

Politburo in September 1988. Congress ratified his position as vice-president in May 1989 by a huge vote after deputies had quizzed him intently on his role in the suppression of Hungary in 1956 and Czechoslovakia in 1968, of his attitude to the Baltic States, and his views on deported peoples like the Ingush. They seemed assured that he would support *perestroika*.

LUNACHARSKY, ANATOLY V. 1875–1933

The reforming commissar for education and the arts. As a student in Zurich he met Rosa Luxemburg and was associated with the left thereafter. Back in Russia he was arrested and on his release in 1902 he returned to Switzerland, joining Alexander Bogdanov. He met Lenin in Paris in 1904 and took on the editorship of V*pered* and *Proletary*, magazines intended for clandestine circulation in Russia. Late in 1905 he went back to Russia. Because of his philosophical outlook he was now attacked by Lenin, in *Materialism and Empiriocriticism*. He returned to Switzerland in 1914.

In 1917 Lunacharsky went to Petrograd, joining Leon Trotsky and moving toward the Bolsheviks again. His power of oratory impressed many and he became deputy mayor of Petrograd. After the October Revolution he became a member of Sovnarkom and commissar for education and the arts. He successfully campaigned against illiteracy and the 1917 rate of 65 percent illiteracy was reduced by the end of his time to a negligible figure. From 1930 to 1932, before his death, he was with Maxim Litvinov as the Soviet representative at the League of Nations.

LUXEMBURG, ROSA. 1870–1919

Founder of the Communist party in Germany. A Social Democratic agitator in Russian Poland, she moved to Berlin in 1898. She joined with Lenin in the 1906 "Unity" Party Congress in Stockholm, but she was soon at loggerheads with him because of his hostility to the Mensheviks. From 1910 she devoted herself to socialism in Germany. She was killed by soldiers after the failure of the 1919 Communist uprising, and is remembered as one of the great martyrs of communism.

LYSENKO, TROFIM D. 1898–1976

Soviet geneticist. His theories were promoted by Stalin as Marxist, ideologically correct, and, therefore, "true." Of Ukrainian peasant origin, he specialized in low-temperature seeds, especially for Russia's arctic zones. His "neo-Lamarckian" argument stated that heredity was not determined by chromosomes or DNA, but could be modified by environment and, furthermore, that acquired characteristics could be inherited. He was made president of the Academy of Agricultural Sciences in 1938, but dismissed in 1956, after Stalin's death, having been denounced by Nikita Khrushchev for falsifying statistics and issuing diplomas to favorites. Khrushchev, however, also defended him and Lysenko returned to official favor in 1958 and was reinstated as the academy's president in 1961, until his final dismissal in 1963. The geneticist Nikolai Vavilov, who had founded the academy and whose theories were internationally accepted but ran counter to Lysenko's, was arrested and died in detention in 1942.

MAKHNO, NESTOR I. 1889–1935

Ukrainian guerrilla leader. He was born to a peasant family, but he found the opportunity to educate himself when imprisoned in Moscow in 1908 for his anarchist associations. Released by the revolution in February 1917, he returned to his village and became the revolutionary leader of the area. The advance of the German army into the Ukraine made him take up arms, and he led his local group not only against the Austrians and Germans but also against the landowners and the Ukrainian governments of Simon Petlyura and General Pavel Skoropadsky. This extended his fighting area widely and became the rallying point for all insurgents in southern Russia north of the Sea of Azov. He was a pure anarchist dedicated to the destruction of all governments and parties. Although he cooperated with Red forces for a time, he quarreled with his Bolshevik collaborator, Grigorev, and shot him. In 1919, with the French occupation of southern Russia, he built up his peasant army to 40,000 men. As a Ukrainian nationalist he attacked Anton Denikin's Volunteer Army in the rear, leading to its defeat. Makhno was absolute in his anarchism and direct in his dealing: when Baron Peter Wrangel sent him an envoy to discuss cooperation, Makhno had the man shot.

In November 1920 the Red Army, under Mikhail Frunze, broke up ·his army and he escaped from Russia, reaching Rumania in August 1921. Sick and in poverty he went on to Paris, where he stayed for the rest of his life.

MAISKY, IVAN M. 1884–1975

A leading Menshevik and Soviet diplomat since 1917, he held anti-Bolshevik posts until he left the Mensheviks in 1919, joining the anti-Bolshevik government in Samara and was, therefore, expelled from the party. His talents were turned to diplomacy, and he was employed in the Ministry of Foreign Affairs from 1920. He was ambassador to Britain, 1932–43, and deputy commissar for foreign affairs with Maxim Litvinov, 1943–1946, when he retired to private life.

MAKLAKOV, VASILY A. 1870–1957

A Kadet of the right. A lawyer and a member of the Duma from 1905, he was sent to France as ambassador by the Provisional Government in 1917. He gave open support to Lavr Kornilov's calls for military action against the Bolsheviks and welcomed Nikolai Chaikovsky and the terrorist Boris Savinkov to the White "Russian Political Conference" in Paris in 1919. He became the leader of the Russian political émigrés in France.

MALENKOV, GEORGY M. 1902–1979

Soviet leader. A young loyal Communist from 1920, he was on the Central Committee during the purges. During the war he was a member of the committee in charge of military equipment and joined the Politburo in 1941. In 1950, at the 19th Party Congress, he declared that the Soviet grain problem was finally solved (bringing him in direct conflict with Khrushchev's expertise).

After Stalin's death he was head of the collective leadership of the Soviet Union, but it did not take long for Khrushchev to supplant him. He admitted his policy errors and when, in 1957 with Kliment Voroshilov and Vyacheslav Molotov he attempted to challenge Khrushchev, he was expelled from the Central Committee and assigned to the management of a far-off electric power station. His last 12 years of retirement were spent in Moscow.

MALEVICH, CASIMIR. 1878–1935

Painter. He was born in Kiev and studied at the Moscow School of Painting, Sculpture, and Architecture. He took part in the trio of progressive exhibitions before World War I with Mikhail Larionov and Natalia Goncharova. Like them he attempted to combine the principles of cubism and futurism, but later he developed a new geometrical abstract style of his own he called suprematism. He denied the social purposes of painting.

He taught at the People's School of Art in Vitebsk from 1919 to 1922 and in Leningrad from 1923 to 1927. In the early thirties he attempted to get into the mainstream of socialist realism with the painting *The Girl with a Red Staff*, which he produced in 1932. However, he is remembered for the most absolute abstract painting: a white square on a black background.

MALINOVSKY, RODION I. 1898–1967

Soviet military leader. A czarist infantry noncommissioned officer in the Red Army from 1920, he was tough, even brutal, with little formal education. He rose to be a marshal of the Soviet Union. Commanding the Ukrainian Front in World War II, he ended in command of the Transbaikal Front, moving his force rapidly against the Japanese in 1945. He became first commander-in-chief of land forces in 1956, and

then succeeded Georgi Zhukov as minister of defense.

MALTSEV, T. S. 1895–

A well-known figure in Soviet agronomy. Born to a peasant family, he became director of a testing station at the Zavety Lenina Kolkhoz, where he developed a new system of plowing. Used in the Kurgan Oblast, this system produced high yields and in 1935 he was made a Hero of Socialist Labor. His method was less successful in lighter soils, which tended to be subject to erosion.

MANDELSTAM, OSIP. 1892–1938

Poet. When he was arrested in 1934 after reciting a satirical poem about Stalin, his wife appealed to Nikolas Bukharin, who was powerless but spoke to Stalin. Stalin asked Boris Pasternak, who said Mandelstam was harmless but a good poet. Consequently, Mandelstam was simply banned from Moscow. Arrested again in 1938, he died in the NKVD's hands.

His widow, Nadezhda Mandelstam, was also a major poet. Her memoirs, *Hope against Hope* and *All Hope Abandoned*, published abroad in the 1970s, are a revealing account of intellectual life in the Soviet Union. She recounts how they were reduced to begging to avoid starvation in the 1930s because they were officially out of favor. Yet discreet help came from the intellectuals of the official establishment. In 1956 she received a printed notification from the Supreme Court that her husband's death had been due to a regrettable oversight. He was "rehabilitated."

MANNERHEIM, CARL G. E. 1867–1948

A baron and general in the czar's Russian army. He commanded the guards who retook Helsinki after the 1917 Revolution. As regent of Finland, 1918–1919, he fought the Soviet army and ensured Finland's independence. He was made president of the Defense Council, 1931–1939, after threats of a Fascist party takeover and promoted to marshal in 1933. In 1939 when the Soviet Union attacked he assumed supreme command. The Finnish defense line on the Karelian Isthmus became known as the Mannerheim Line. Allied to Germany in the war against Russia, he corresponded personally with Winston Churchill before Britain, with regret, declared war on Finland. (The United States was not at war with Finland and retained a legation there during the war.) In 1942, at the age of 75, he was made marshal of Finland and continued in command of the army. He declined to accept command of the German troops in Finland, since that would have made him one of Hitler's subordinates, preferring to keep Finland's military operations limited and clear of Hitler's grand strategy. He became president in August 1944 and obtained a cease-fire with the Soviet Union on September 4, 1944. He finally declared war on Germany in March 1945 and resigned as president a year later.

MANUILSKI, DMITRI Z. 1883–1959

An old-guard Bolshevik. He was one of those who returned with Lenin from exile in 1917 and who died in retirement. He was a radical activist from 1904, being arrested several times and deported until leaving for France in 1907, where he worked with Vladimir Antonov-Ovseenko and Leon Trotsky as a journalist.

After the October Revolution Manuilski held several posts, including secretary of the Ukrainian party from 1921 to 1923. He worked for the Comintern Secretariat from 1922, imposing its will on the German and French parties. Stalin had confidence in his ruthless methods (hidden under a convivial exterior) and used him to replace Nicholas Bukharin as secretary to the Comintern. He was then appointed deputy to the Bulgarian Georgy Dmitrov, and acted, unofficially, as Stalin's man in the Comintern. In 1945 he was made Ukrainian foreign minister when that republic was given a full seat in the United Nations. He held this post until he retired—already out of favor but allowed to withdraw peacefully—in 1952.

MARTOV, YULI (Y. O. TSEDERBAUM). 1873–1923

Menshevik leader. From a Jewish Odessa family, he suffered from anti-Semitism in Russia, and his rebelliousness caused him to be exiled to Siberia in 1893. He advocated taking Marxism to the workers by being involved in their struggle for better conditions, rather than by intellectualizing and lecturing the elite. Although he and Lenin were confined to Siberia, it was due to his activity that the Russian Social Democrat Labor party was founded. With Lenin, he started the Liberation of Labor group in October 1895, and was also a founder of the *Iskra* group. In 1903 he would not accept Lenin's proposals for a tightly run organization of dedicated revolutionaries, and the party split on the vote—

Martov's faction being the minority, the Mensheviks, with Moscow as his stronghold.

Martov became the official leader of the Mensheviks in 1917 when he returned from exile, racked with tuberculosis. In October he led the assembly as an Internationalist against Alexander Kerensky, but when he attempted to check the Bolsheviks and persuade them to negotiate, Leon Trotsky replied, "Go where you belong: into the trash can of history." He left Russia in 1921 and died an exile in Berlin.

MARX, KARL. 1818–1883

German political philosopher, the founder of modern socialism. He published the *Communist Manifesto* with Friedrich Engels in 1847. Expelled from Prussia, Marx lived in London from 1849, supported by the richer Engels. He completed the first volume of *Das Kapital*, the classic work of Marxian Communist theory, in 1867; it was completed after Marx's death by Engels. He was the founder of the International Workingmen's Association in 1864, known as the First International, but conflicts with the anarchism of Mikhail Bakunin led to its disintegration in 1876.

MASLYUKOV, YURI. 1937–

Politburo member. Having graduated as an engineer from Leningrad, his career led him through management to be head of the technical department of the Ministry of Munitions and then, in 1982, into Gosplan. In 1988 he became chairman of Gosplan, and at the same time he was made an alternate member of the Politburo and a deputy chairman of the Council of Ministers. In 1989

Gorbachev, as he strengthened his party support, made him a full member of the Politburo.

MAYAKOVSKY, VLADIMIR V. 1893–1930

Futurist poet and dramatist. Born in Georgia, he joined the All-Russian Social Democratic Labor party in his youth, although he never became a Communist party member, and was imprisoned in 1909. In 1918 he wrote the first Soviet play, the *Mystery Bouffe*, which was staged by Vsevolod Meyerhold. In 1924 he wrote his famous poem *Vladimir Ilich Lenin*, and also *Hymn to the Attacking Classes*. His poem *Lost in Conference* attacked the hordes of bureaucrats that he saw strangling the revolution. It was approved of by Lenin but did not increase his popularity in the party. Boris Pasternak was his friend and an admirer of his less public poetry. On a visit to the United States in 1925 he wrote a cycle of poems on America praising in his *Brooklyn Bridge* its engineering achievements.

In 1930, out of favor and dogged by personal problems, Mayakovsky committed suicide. Ideologically he was always regarded as sound (and accepted as a practitioner of socialist realism). After his death Stalin treated him as the poet laureate of the revolution. He had the advantage during the Great Purge, the "Yezhovshchina," of being already dead, otherwise he would have been a certain candidate for elimination.

MEDVEDEV, ROY. 1925–

Soviet historian. His work on Stalin and his period, on the October Revolution, and on Nicholas Bukharin and Nikita Khrushchev, using documents hitherto unavailable to historians, has altered our picture of the 20th century. In 1971 his brother Zhores Medvedev published an account, in Britain, of their detention in psychiatric wards. Elected a deputy to the Congress in 1989 and to its Supreme Soviet, he has been outspoken in his calls for democracy.

MENZHINSKY, VYACHESLAV R. 1874–1934

Head of the OGPU (State Political Administration), an aesthete, dilettante, poet and painter, and a Bolshevik from 1903. The son of a rich lawyer, he was accustomed to a luxurious life-style. He was out of Russia from 1907 to 1917, when he returned in time for the October Revolution. He was commissar for finance from October until March 1918, then consul in Berlin up to November 1918. He went to the Ukraine as a Cheka official, and from July 1920 was in charge of the Cheka in the Red Army. From September 1923 he was deputy chairman of the OGPU (as the Cheka had become known), succeeding Felix Dzerzhinsky as chairman in July 1926.

Menzhinsky, known as "the Poet of the Cheka," was responsible for the brutal enforcement of such programs as collectivization, although, never in good health, he delegated much to his deputy Genrikh Yagoda, who succeeded him.

MERKULOV, SPIRIDON AND NIKOLAI.

The entrepreneurial brothers from a peasant family in the Amur Valley who led the National Democratic Union, formed of "conservative socialists," in the Russian Far East in 1920. Spiridon had been a specialist on the region for the czar's Ministry of Agriculture and Nikolai was a Vladivostok industrialist. They owned a newspaper and exercised great influence. Using the Far Eastern Constituent Assembly, elected in 1920, and with Japanese support, they planned an anti-Bolshevik coup. By late 1921 they were under suspicion of corruption and of diverting supplies for their family profit. In May 1922 they declared the assembly dissolved and led their own government with the help of the last of the Imperial navy, but by August they had been ousted and Spiridon was sent to Canada with 30,000 rubles as a payoff. Nikolai retained an official position until October 1922, when he left with others for Japan.

MEYERHOLD, VSEVOLOD. 1874–1940?

Actor and theatrical director. He was born in Penza and was a member of the Communist Party of the Soviet Union from 1918. After studying at the Music and Drama School in Moscow, he joined the Moscow Arts Theatre, where he acted for several years. Dissatisfied with the classical theatre, in 1902 he left to start a theatre of his own, the Society of New Drama. He experimented there with his theories of nonconventional, stylized drama. In 1905 he worked with Konstantin Stanislavsky who was developing his famous and revolutionary methods of training for actors, and then went to St. Petersburg to work with Theodore Komissarjevsky's theatre.

After the revolution he developed the idea of the so-called theatrical October, a style which incorporated political messages into dramatic texts without sacrificing entertainment values. He directed the Meyerhold Theatre from 1920 to 1938. He was an early mentor of Sergei Eisenstein in experimental film work. Meyerhold had always suffered attacks from the authorities for "formal" elements in his work, which was considered a failure to work within the guidelines of socialist realism. He was arrested during 1938, and either vanished into the camps with his wife or was executed. Their exact fate is unknown.

MIKOYAN, ANASTASY I. 1895–1978

Long-serving Soviet politician. An Armenian brought up in Azerbaijan and party member from 1915, he was the sole survivor of the 26 Baku commissars shot in 1919 by anti-Bolsheviks of the Musavat party. He was a leading figure in the events of 1920 when the Red Army occupied Transcaucasia. He was on the Central Committee from 1923 and in 1925 became the youngest member of the Politburo. He replaced Lev Kamenev as commissar for commerce in 1926, and he then took over supplies and then food until 1938. He raised huge sums of hard currency, reputedly over $100 million, through his sales of art treasures to Calouste Gulbenkian, the oil millionaire, and Andrew Mellon, the U.S. financier. Mikoyan studied U.S. food products and introduced a whole range of ice creams to the Soviet Union.

Mikoyan was on the Council of Ministers and the Supreme Soviet, whose chairman (president of the Soviet Union) he was from 1964 to 1965. He was one of the few on Stalin's Politburo both before and after World War II, but

after Stalin's death he moved toward Khrushchev and with Mikhail Suslov went to Hungary in 1956 to determine Soviet policy there. Although a supporter of Khrushchev and seen to have high status, his power was declining during the early 1960s.

Mikoyan was a survivor and died peacefully in retirement. Once, when seen leaving a house in heavy rain without coat or umbrella, he was reported to have said, "Don't worry, I can dodge between the raindrops."

MILYUKOV, PAVEL N. 1859–1943

A Russian historian, a founder of the Constitutional Democrats (Kadets). A member of the Third and Fourth Dumas, he opposed the czar's war policies and was in the Provisional Government as foreign minister from February to April 1917. He fled in October 1917 and, after cooperating with the White Army, settled in Paris where he edited anti-Communist Russian newspapers until the German occupation of Paris in 1940.

MIRBACH, COUNT WILHELM VON. 1871–1918

The German envoy to the Kremlin. He was shot and killed by Cheka men in association with Left Socialist Revolutionaries under Maria Spiridonova in July 1918. He was the representative of the German government, which was still at war in the west, and prepared to pay money to the Bolshevik government to encourage them not to pursue the war.

MOISEYEV, MIKHAIL. 1882–1955

Soviet miliary leader. As the general in

command of the Far East District from January 1987, he succeeded Marshal Sergei Akhromeyev as chief of staff of the armed forces and first deputy minister of defense when the latter resigned in December 1988.

MOLOTOV ("THE HAMMER"), VYACHESLAV M. SCRIABIN. 1890–1986

Leading Soviet politician. A Bolshevik from 1906, he was exiled for his activities. In 1917 he was editor of *Pravda*, and a colleague of Stalin in 1921. Molotov held high office from the beginning. He was a member of the Politburo, 1926–1957, and chairman of the Council of People's Commissars (premier of the Soviet Union), 1930–1941. Then from 1939 to 1941 he was commissar for foreign affairs, replacing the Jewish and less abrasive Maxim Litvinov in order to sign the Soviet-German pact with Joachim von Ribbentrop. After Stalin's death his power waned and an attempt to outmaneuver Khrushchev in 1957 led to his dismissal from the Central Committee and exile to Mongolia as ambassador until 1960. At the age of 94 he was re-admitted to the Communist party.

Molotov looked like the perfect "faceless bureaucrat." Winston Churchill described him as a man who "perfectly represented the modern conception of a robot.... His smile of Siberian winter, his carefully measured and often wise words, his affable demeanor, combined to make him the perfect agent of Soviet policy in the deadly world."

NECHAEV, SERGEI G. 1847–1882

Russian revolutionary conspirator of the 19th century. Claiming to be the leader of a large revolutionary movement and hunted by the police, he went to Switzerland in 1869. There he met other exiles. He fascinated Mikhail Bakunin, producing either with him or in imitation, the *Revolutionary Catechism* that influenced a generation of young Russian revolutionaries, including Lenin. It is reflected in George Bernard Shaw's *Man and Superman* and is still a key to understanding the idea of a "revolutionary."

"The revolutionary is a doomed man," it starts. "The revolutionary can have no friendship or attachment.... He should not hesitate to destroy any position, any place or any man in the world.... The filthy social order can be split up into several categories. The first category comprises those who can be condemned to death without delay."

Extradited for murder from Switzerland in 1872, he spent his last years in close confinement in the Peter and Paul Fortress in St. Petersburg.

NICHOLAS II, ROMANOV. 1868–1918

Czar of Russia from 1894. He succeeded his father, Alexander III, in 1894. The revolution of 1905 forced him to summon a Duma. His reign survived because of the gestures of reform made under the government of Peter Stolypin. His czarina, Alexandra Feodorovna, a granddaughter of England's Queen Victoria, was anxious for the health of their sickly son and brought the family under the charlatan Cregori Rasputin's influence in 1906. This alienated many of the aristocracy, particularly when war against Germany came, and the German-born czarina and Rasputin were suspected of treachery. Nicholas took command of the armies in the face of the defeats of 1915.

When the February Revolution came, he abdicated in favor of his brother Michael in March 1917, although his brother did not take the throne, handing authority to the Provisional Government under Prince Georgy Lvov. Under Bolshevik rule he was sent with his family to Ekaterinburg under guard. On July 16, 1918, when it seemed that White troops were approaching, he, the czarina, and their four children were all shot and their bodies thrown in a marsh.

ORDZHONIKIDZE, GRIGORY (SERGO I.) 1886–1937

A political activist from Georgia and a close associate of Stalin. From early in his career he was a Bolshevik. This was confirmed in 1910, when he made his way to Paris and mixed with Lenin's Bolshevik colleagues. Sent on a mission to Russia he was arrested and exiled to Yakutsk in Siberia.

In the civil war he was the political commissar in Kliment Voroshilov's army and, in February 1921, he joined with Stalin in plotting the invasion of Georgia (which took most other party leaders by surprise) and was the commander of the military force. In 1922 he was the Politburo's representative in Georgia, where he urged the unpopular official line that it should merge into the Transcaucasian Republic. In the course of this he beat up a Georgian Communist leader, provoking an angry reaction from Lenin, who compared him to a czarist bully, "Sergo" was Stalin's instrument and responsible for the Russification of Georgia. His methods dis-

turbed Lenin and led to his viewing Stalin in a different light.

Stalin appointed him to the Politburo in 1930, and in 1932 he was made commissar for heavy industries.

In 1933 he is believed to have resisted, with Sergei Kirov, Stalin's program of Terror and to have opposed the persecution of Nicholas Bukharin. In 1937, Vyacheslav Molotov attacked Ordzhonikidze's powerful commissariat for its protection of "saboteurs." Shortly after this he committed suicide or was murdered— it is not clear which. But he was never denounced or criticized during Stalin's régime. His mistake may have been to have tried to block the rise of a younger and even more ruthless Georgian, Lavrenti Beria.

PASTERNAK, BORIS. 1890–1960

A poet and novelist. His parents were famous Russian artists, his father a painter and his mother a pianist. In 1957 the publication of his novel *Dr. Zhivago* in Italy, and the award of the Nobel Prize for Literature, led to his dismissal from the Soviet Writers' Union. Although in disgrace when he died, his funeral in Moscow was attended by a large crowd. In 1988 his expulsion from the union was, posthumously, cancelled and the novel published in the USSR.

PETERS, JACOB. 1886–?

Early Communist international agent. Born in 1886 in Kurland, he worked in London from 1909 to 1917, where he was a member of the British Labour party. He was arrested with others in December 1910 for the murder of three policemen at Houndsditch in London, tried at the Old Bailey, and acquitted.

There is also some possibility that he was the "anarchist" known as Peter the Painter, hunted by the police and the object of the spectacular "Sidney Street siege" led personally by the Home Secretary, Winston Churchill, who brought in the army in an unsuccessful attempt to capture him. In 1917 he was sent back to Russia by his Communist colleagues in London, where Felix Dzerzhinsky used him to infiltrate the Ministry of Foreign Affairs. In 1919 he was appointed chief of internal defense in Petrograd and stamped out the revolt ruthlessly, sending some 3,000 hostages to Moscow. There is an account of his wearying of endlessly signing death warrants, unread. In October 1920 he left Russia for a period. His wife was an English woman, but in 1923 he was elected a member of the Party Central Committee and was "commandant" of the Kremlin until 1937, when all trace of him ceases. He was presumably shot in the purges, but the latest edition of *The Great Soviet Encyclopedia* gives neither date nor cause for his death.

PETLYURA, SIMON V. 1879–1926

A Ukrainian journalist. He specialized in social matters and became the Ukrainian Rada's secretary for military affairs. Jailed for the four months of the Skoropadsky regime, he reemerged as a Ukrainian military leader. His troops, however, were diminished by the defection of Nestor Makhno's peasant army to the Bolshevik cause. In 1919 he made a deal with the Poles, and the next year cooperated with Josef Pilsudski and retook Kiev on April 25, 1920. The Red Army, however, retook the city in June and Petlyura's campaign ended with his flight from the Ukraine.

PETROV, YEVGENY P. (KATAYEV). 1903–1942

One of the pair of authors known as "Ilf and Petrov" (q.v.). He was the younger brother of the novelist Valentin Katayev.

PILSUDSKI, JOSEF. 1867–1935

A Polish socialist. Exiled by the czarist government to Siberia, 1887–1892, he agitated for Polish independence. In 1914, in World War I, he led an anti-Russian Polish Legion supported by the Austrian Empire. Interned by the Germans in 1917, he was released to command the Polish army after the Brest-Litovsk Treaty. In 1918 the new Poland elected him chief of state and dictator until the constitution of 1922. As marshal of Poland in 1920, he led the campaign against the Bolsheviks, defeating the Red Army and taking Kiev in 1920, with French help, when the Red Army tried to take Warsaw. Although not head of state he retained dictatorial powers until his death.

PLEKHANOV, GEORGY V. 1857–1918

A Narodnik and the leading philosophical Marxist in Russia. He left Russia in 1880, living mostly in Geneva, Switzerland. He founded the Social Democratic party and collaborated with Lenin, but sided with the Mensheviks after 1903. During World War I he took a strongly patriotic and "Defensist" position and opposed the Bolshevik revolution.

PODGORNY, NIKOLAI V. 1903–1983

A Soviet leader. A party member in the Ukraine from 1930, minister of food in 1940, he rose to be the all-union minister and first secretary of the Ukrainian party's Central Committee, 1935–1965. He was then appointed secretary of the USSR Central Committee and chairman of the Supreme Soviet Presidium (president of the USSR) from 1965 to 1977, when Brezhnev pushed him into retirement.

PREOBRAZHENSKY, EVGENY A. 1886–1937

An active Bolshevik from early in his career. Living to the east of the Urals, he saw the revolution there threatened, first, by the arrival of the Czech Legion, shortly followed thereafter by the armies of Alexander Kolchak. He was elected to the Central Committee, taking a hard left-wing position. In 1920, as one of the three party secretaries, he campaigned for democratization, but this brought him into conflict with both Stalin, who opposed his ideas, and Grigory Zinoviev, who felt he had a monopoly in this field. In 1926 he was a leading figure in the New Opposition and was expelled from the party and exiled to Siberia the next year. He capitulated to Stalin and was readmitted to the party in 1929, only to be expelled again. In 1936 he was a witness for the prosecution against Zinoviev and then himself arrested. He vanished from history.

PROKOVIEV, SERGEI. 1891–1953

Composer and pianist. Born in the Ukraine to middle-class parents, he was a child prodigy who wrote his first piano piece at the age of 5 and entered the Leningrad Conservatory at the age of 14. Here he met Nikolai Miaskovsky, who became a life-time friend, and they both became involved with the World of Art group, which was arranging concerts featuring the music of Arnold Schönberg, Richard Strauss, and Igor Stravinsky. In 1914 he won the Anton Rubinstein Prize at the Conservatory with a performance of his own *First Piano Concerto*. He spent the summer of 1917 outside Petrograd writing his *Violin Concerto*.

In 1918 Prokoviev left Russia and went to the United States, where he gave concert performances and tried, unsuccessfully, to write operas including the brilliant *Love for Three Oranges*, which was not actually performed until 1926. He abandoned the United States for Paris, where he worked with Serge Diaghilev and Stravinsky in the theatre and wrote his *Third Piano Concerto*.

In 1933 he returned to Russia, where he spent the rest of his life. His relationship with the authorities was complex and unhappy, though he was not shown the harsh treatment that some artists received. But like every other composer he was subject to the control of the Union of Soviet Composers, and he was certainly not free to indulge in the kind of experimentation that was common in the West. His *Cantata for the 20th Anniversary of the Soviet Revolution* was not performed until 1966. He wrote the music for Eisenstein's *Alexander Nevsky*, and in 1944 his most successful work, the superb *Fifth Symphony*. In 1948 the harsh decree from the Central Committee, which attacked the work of Soviet artists for being riddled with formalist perversions, did not spare him. He attempted to regain favor with an opera based on the life of a well-known war hero but it was badly received. Prokoviev died in Moscow in October 1953, on the same day as Stalin.

PYATAKOV, GRIGORY (YURI). 1890–1937

The leader of the Ukrainian Communist party. He set up a secret government in Kursk in December 1918 and led Red Army troops into an attack on the Ukraine. Stalin accused him of being part of the Trotsky conspiracy, and he was executed after a trial in 1937. His sentence was annulled by the Soviet Supreme Court in June 1988.

RADEK, KARL BERNHARDOVICH (SOBELSOHN). 1885–1939 (1941?)

Journalist and politician. Brought up in Polish-speaking Galicia (then part of the Austrian Empire), he became a socialist in his youth. He traveled to Switzerland and Germany, writing and translating for a living. He entered Russia (without knowing a word of the language) in 1905 and was imprisoned and sent back to Austria in 1907. He joined Lenin and Zinoviev in Switzerland and returned with Lenin in the "sealed train" to Petrograd in 1917.

A brilliant, often outrageous man, looking like a cross between a professor and a bandit, he worked in the Commissariat for Foreign Affairs, specializing in Central Europe. He took part in the Brest-Litovsk negotiations, got himself into Germany in December 1918, and helped found the Communist party there. Imprisoned in Berlin, he turned his cell into the unofficial embassy of the Bolshevik government. On his return he was given the position of secretary of the Comintern. Involved with the attempted Communist takeover in Germany in 1923, accompanied by Larissa Reisner, he was held responsible for its failure and lost his post.

Something of a political turncoat he tried to reconcile the left opposition with Stalin's views, though he remained consistently hostile to Zinoviev. His career was not advanced by his apparently cynical changes of belief, even when events proved him right. In December 1927, with 74 others, he was expelled from the party for opposing its line: he made a prompt about-turn and, with Evgeny Preobrazhensky, joined in a declaration against "right opportunism" and was readmitted. From 1929 to 1936 he was Stalin's adviser on foreign affairs. In 1936 he worked with Nicholas Bukharin on the new Soviet constitution, and that year he joined in condemning Grigory Zinoviev and Lev Kamenev, calling for their death. That year he, too, was arrested and accused of maintaining contact with Trotsky. Sentenced to 10 years' imprisonment, he disappeared and at some point died of a heart attack, or perhaps was murdered by fellow prisoners.

His sentence was annulled by the Soviet Supreme Court in June 1988.

RASKOLNIKOV, (ILIA) FYODOR FEDOROVICH. 1892–1939

Sailor and revolutionary. The illegitimate son of a priest who became a socialist as a student, and worked for *Pravda* in St. Petersburg, with Vyacheslav Molotov and Stalin. He joined the czarist navy during the war as a cadet and sailed with the fleet in the Pacific. When the February Revolution broke out he rejoined *Pravda* and was sent to Kronstadt, becoming vice-chairman of the Kronstadt Soviet on March 17. He was one of the leaders of the Kronstadt sailors who demonstrated in Petrograd in the July Days, and with Trotsky secured the release of Viktor Chernov.

The failure of the demonstration landed him in the Kresty jail until the October Revolution. As an assistant in the new Commissariat for Naval Affairs, he ensured the scuttling of the fleet at Novorossisk in June 1918, and commanded the Volga flotilla that captured Kazan that August. In December 1918 he commanded a destroyer in the Baltic that met a British naval force; his ship was grounded and he was taken a prisoner to Brixton in London until May 1919, when he was exchanged for captured British officers. He then took command of a Caspian-Volga flotilla, which was in action until 1920, when he was appointed "commissar-commander" of the Baltic fleet. "In March 1921," he wrote, "I demobilized myself and was appointed ambassador to Afghanistan."

This revolutionary romantic was married to the beautiful Larissa Reisner, and was in tune with neither the old-guard Bolsheviks nor the newly rising Stalinists, preferring the world of writers and artists. In 1930 he resumed a diplomatic career and was ambassador to Estonia, Denmark, and Bulgaria, where in 1937 he noticed that his own volume of memoirs was on the list of banned books in the Soviet Union. He therefore ignored an order recalling him and went to France. On September 12, 1939, he died in Nice, under unexplained circumstances. His book *Kronstadt and Petrograd in 1917* (Moscow 1925) was reprinted in 1964, but as an émigré he has never been fully rehabilitated.

RASPUTIN, GREGORI. 1871–1916

A mystic living at the czar's court from November 1905. He was believed to have healing power over the czar's son, sick with hemophilia. He was despised for his peasant manners and hated for his influence by the men of the court (but with an effective sexual attraction for many of the ladies). He was suspected generally of working for the Germans and was murdered by courtiers, after many attempts, in December 1916. The name Rasputin means "the profligate."

REED, JOHN. 1887–1920

A U.S. journalist. He was the author of *Ten Days that Shook the World*, published in March 1919, the well-known account of the October Revolution, and was portrayed in the 1982 film *Reds*.

Reed, the son of an Oregon judge, became a journalist after studying at Harvard and went to Russia as a war correspondent in 1917. Impressed by the revolution, he went to work for the Bureau of International Revolutionary Propaganda in December 1917. In 1918 the Bolshevik government proposed him as their consul in New York, but this was unacceptable to the U.S. government. Reed helped to found the U.S. "Communist-Labor party." He returned to Russia, joining the executive committee of the Comintern in October 1919. He died of typhoid while on a mission in Baku.

REILLY (ROSENBLUM), SIDNEY (SIGMUND). 1874–1925

Spy. Born in Odessa, he led a wandering life, marrying in England as Sidney Reilly. In World War I he obtained an arms purchasing agency to sell weapons to Russia. Recruited by the British secret service, he was sent to Russia in 1918 and forced into hiding in the waves of terror that followed the assassination of Count Wilhelm von Mirbach. Reilly escaped through Sweden to London, where he set to work to support Boris Savinkov's Paris-based anti-Bolshevik operation. In the course of this, Reilly passed on the "Zinoviev letter," forged correspondence implicating the British Labour government with the Comintern. Now working independently from the British secret service, Reilly went back into the Soviet Union on the invitation of "the Trust," a supposed group of dissidents. He was captured by the OGPU and vanished.

REISNER, LARISSA M. 1895–1926

Writer. The daughter of a Communist professor, she was brought up in Germany in intellectual circles. She completed her education in Russia and began writing poems and political articles, involving herself with workers' movements and, in particular, the Kronstadt sailors. With the October Revolution she took to arms and fought with the Red Army, being made a commissar. With her husband, Fyodor Raskolnikov, she saw action with the Volga-Caspian flotilla and later joined him in the Soviet embassy in Afghanistan.

Their marriage broke up when they left Afghanistan in 1923. Raskolnikov had ill-treated her, and she went to live with Karl Radek (who later wrote her biography). She then went to Germany on a mission to encourage the Communist rising in Hamburg. Back in Russia she continued writing, but the malaria she had contracted on her travels led to her death at the age of 31.

ROKOSSOVSKY, KONSTANTIN K. 1896–1968

Marshal of the Soviet Union. He joined the Red Guards in 1917; then in 1919 he became a member of the party and joined the Red Army. Among the purged army officers of 1937, he was released early in 1939. He was an outstandingly successful and heroic commander during the war, leading armies outside Moscow in 1941, Stalingrad in 1942, Kursk in 1943, and at the final entry to Berlin in 1945, when he was promoted to marshal of the Soviet Union.

Although of Polish origin, he had been raised in Russia and only spoke Polish with a heavy accent; nevertheless he was given command of the Polish army in 1949, until the Polish leadership removed him in 1956; there were suggestions that he had prepared to take over the government in Moscow's interest. His last military employment was as officer commanding the Transcaucasian Military District.

ROMANOV

The family name of the ruling czars of Russia. The heir-apparent, Alexis, was killed with the rest of the family in 1918.

ROZANOV, SERGEI NIKOLAIVICH. 1856–1919

A White general appointed by Alexander Kolchak in July 1919 to establish military control in the Far East. His cruel administrative methods and his reliance on Japanese support alienated other Russians. When Kolchak fell, he put himself under the protection of the Czechs, who handed him over to his opponents in Irkutsk, where he was executed in February 1920.

RYKOV, ALEXEI. 1881–1938

An early Bolshevik. Espousing moderate leanings, he advocated coalitions with other socialists in 1917. A member of the Politburo, he succeeded Lenin as the chairman of Sovnarkom (Council of People's Commissars) in 1924 until 1930. He was accused of being in the Right Opposition and recanted. He was put in a show trial and executed in the Great Purge.

RYZHKOV, NIKOLAI. 1929–

Politburo member. From the Urals, he started as a mine worker, then qualified as an engineer in 1959. He worked in industry in Sverdlovsk and had close contact with Andrei Kirilenko. In 1974 he came to Moscow via the Planning Commission of the Supreme Soviet, and in 1979 was made first deputy chairman of Gosplan. Under Yuri Andropov he became Central Committee secretary and has been in the Politburo since 1985, becoming premier and chairman of the Council of Ministers under Gorbachev in succession to Nikolai Tikhonov.

SAKHAROV, ANDREI. 1922–1989

Nobel Peace Prize winning physicist and leading dissident. He was a member of the Soviet Academy of Sciences at the age of 22, awarded the Order of Stalin and the Order of Lenin, and made a Hero of Socialist Labor. He is known as the father of the Soviet hydrogen bomb.

In the Khrushchev era he became outspoken, calling for co-existence between the United States and the USSR and for a nuclear test-ban treaty. In 1968 he published as a *samizdat*, *Thoughts on Progress, Peaceful Co-Existence and Intellectual Freedom*, which resulted in internal exile in Gorky. Released in December 1986, he decided to get a nomination to stand for Congress in 1989 from the Academy of Sciences, and would not accept any lesser body, turning down the support of members of "Memorial," a group commemorating the victims of Stalinism, and was in the event elected. In the Presidium of the Congress he became the focus of the new opposition.

SAKHAROV, VLADIMIR. 1944–

Soviet diplomat. He defected to the United States in 1971 and is the source of several personal stories about contemporary Soviet leaders.

SAVINKOV, BORIS. ?–1924

Socialist revolutionary terrorist. He was involved with the assassinations of the Minister Vyacheslav Plehve in 1904 and the Grand Duke Serge in 1905. He was deputy minister of war under Alexander Kerensky, but broke with his party in September 1917, supporting Lavr Kornilov. He was in touch with British intelligence through the diplomat Bruce Lockhart and worked with Sidney Reilly. He set up his own military organization, the "Green Movement," which instigated brief, abortive uprisings in Rybinsk, Murom, Kazan, Kaluga, and Vladimir and, most importantly in July 1918, in Yaroslav. He fled to Paris but kept his groups in action from a Warsaw base as head of a "Russian political committee." In 1924 he was decoyed into the Soviet Union and put on trial. He died in prison, possibly by his own hand.

The English novelist and one-time spy Somerset Maugham described Savinkov as "a genial likeable fellow." Winston Churchill met him in 1919 and thought him "a terrorist for moderate aims." But the British Foreign Office wrote him off as "most unreliable and crooked."

SEMENOV, GRIGORI MIKHAILOVICH. 1890–1946

A Cossack ataman. As czarist military commander, he continued to control Transbaikal until 1920, working with the Japanese interventionist forces. An ambitious and energetic leader, his ruthlessness lost him support among other anti-Soviet soldiers and politicians. His own Cossacks deposed him in June 1921, and in September he left for Japan, leading anti-Soviet intrigues there and in Manchuria, where he led a pan-Mongol movement with Japanese support. At the end of World War II he was captured and brought to Moscow, where he was tried in August 1946 and executed.

SEMICHASTNY, VLADIMIR Y. 1917–

KGB leader. Having risen through party ranks from Komsomol, he was made chairman of the KGB to succeed Alexander Shelepin in 1961, holding the post until 1967, when the powerful Yuri Andropov took over.

SEROV, IVAN A. 1905–

KGB leader. Head of the KGB (chairman of the State Security Committee)

after Stalin's death and Lavrenti Beria's removal. Rumored to have been responsible for the Katyn Forest massacre in 1940, he was in charge of the removal of the Crimean Tatars and others in the period 1943–1944. Georgy Malenkov gave him the KGB post in 1954, but his brutal background caused him to be replaced by Alexander Shelepin in 1958. "Like other high-ranking executives in the security apparatus, Serov had a long record of crime and abuse of power, but he was devoted to Khrushchev and was prepared to act promptly on any order that he received from him," wrote the historian Roy Medvedev.

SHARANSKY, ANATOLY. 1948–

Soviet dissident. The son of a journalist, he became a famous "refusenik" when in 1978 he was tried and sentenced to nine years in the Gulag. He emigrated to Israel after an East-West prisoner exchange in 1986. His memoirs, *Fear No Evil*, were published in 1988. He was proposed as Israeli ambassador to the UN in 1989.

SHCHERBITSKY, VLADIMIR V. 1918–

Senior party official. A party member from 1941, after the war he held a succession of high party posts. Under Leonid Brezhnev he became Ukrainian first secretary and a member of the Presidium of the Supreme Soviet in 1972. He was honored twice as Hero of Socialist Labor, in 1974 and 1977, and awarded the Lenin Prize in 1982. The last member of the old guard, he survived Gorbachev's 1988 rebuilding of the Politburo and stood unopposed for a seat at Dnepropetrovsk, his first party post, in the 1989 Congress election. He was dropped from the Politburo in September 1989.

SHELEPIN, ALEXANDER N. 1918–

KGB leader. From a Komsomol organizer, and its first secretary in 1952, he was made chairman of the State Security Committee (the KGB), 1958–1961. At the 22nd Party Congress he spoke out against Stalin's atrocities. He was one of the younger men of the time and received rapid promotion, moving to be Central Committee secretary, a member of the Politburo, and deputy chairman of the Council of Ministers. In June 1967, after the defection of Svetlana Alliluyeva, he was demoted to a post in charge of trade unions.

SHEVARDNADZE, EDUARD A. 1928–

Soviet foreign minister. A Georgian, he was responsible for an attack on corruption in Georgia. His party career was established in Georgia, becoming first secretary there in 1972, and was strengthened when he ruled that Georgian, not Russian, should remain the official language of the republic. He joined the Central Committee in 1976 and the Politburo in 1978. In July 1985 he succeeded Andrei Gromyko as foreign minister. He visited China in February 1989 to try and rebuild the decayed Sino-Soviet friendship.

SHLIAPNIKOV, ALEXANDER G. 1884–1937

A Bolshevik leader in Petrograd during World War I. He served on the executive committee of the Petrograd Soviet in 1917. He held commissar posts in the Soviet government, but from 1920

he led the Workers' Opposition group in the Bolshevik party, criticizing the centralized bureaucratic control of industry. He was expelled from the party in 1933 and presumably arrested and shot in 1937.

SHMIDT, DMITRI. ?–1937

A Ukrainian Jew who had been a civil war cavalryman and who in 1936 commanded the Red Army's only heavy-tank brigade: he was the first to be shot in the military purges, typifying their extraordinary attack on the loyal, long-serving, and specialist officers.

SHOSTAKOVICH, DMITRY. 1906–1975

Soviet composer. Born in St. Petersburg, he helped support his widowed mother and family by playing the piano in a local cinema. He studied at the Petrograd Conservatory and wrote his first symphony in 1926. In 1936 he was attacked by the authorities for his opera based on a novel, *The Lady Macbeth of Mtsensk District*, and in order to justify himself to the Union of Soviet Composers, he produced his immensely popular *Fifth Symphony*. In 1940 he was awarded the Stalin Prize for his *Piano Quintet*. In 1942, during the war, he produced his *Seventh Symphony*, dedicated to the city of Leningrad then under siege. After the performance in Moscow and Leningrad a score was flown at once to the United States, where it was given a highly publicized performance by Arturo Toscanini with the NBC Orchestra.

After the savage assault on composers by Andrei Zdhanov in 1948, Shostakovich compromised by writing simpler, more accessible music for public performance. One work from this period was entitled *The Sun Shines on our Motherland,* and other more complex and private works such as the *Violin Concerto,* the latter not performed until after Stalin's death. In Khrushchev's time he was inclined to side with the authorities in criticizing experimentation, and his *Twelfth Symphony* was dedicated to the memory of Lenin. He was declared People's Artist of the USSR in 1954 and awarded the Order of Lenin in 1956.

SINYAVSKY, ANDREI. 1925–

A literary critic and dissident. He was arrested in September 1965 and put on trial with Yuli Daniel in 1966. They were "secret" writers of parodies of Soviet life, little known, but read abroad. The trial was in the hands of Yuri Andropov, then head of the KGB, who, unusually for a show trial, allowed them to plead not guilty and had them tried on the charge of libeling the state. That fiction could be judged a libel made the case a notorious travesty of justice and attracted much adverse publicity in the West, but while it reflected the conservative reaction of the time in the party, it also lost the respect of the more able writers. Sinyavsky was given a seven-year sentence, but he was released and emigrated to France in 1966.

SKOROPADSKY, PAVEL P. 1873–1945

A czarist general. From a wealthy Ukrainian family, he was promoted to general in 1912. In February 1917 he renamed his Russian command the First Ukrainian Corps. He was nominated head of the "Free Cossacks" in October, and in March 1918 he became head of the Ukrainian state under German protection. In December 1918, wearing a German uniform, he escaped from a further Ukrainian revolt to Germany. He lived there until his death.

SKVORTSOV-STEPANOV, IVAN. 1870–1928

A Social Democrat in Moscow from 1896. He was first Soviet commissar for finance. He edited *Das Kapital* in Russian, but Lenin described him as "only a theoretical Marxist."

SOKOLNIKOV, GRIGORY. 1888–1939

Deputy commissar for finance in 1921. The paradox of a Bolshevik financier arose from the collapse of the Soviet economy in 1921. There was a massive budgetary deficiency and the currency was becoming valueless. Sokolnikov set guidelines in the 1922 11th Party Congress to attack the problem by backing the paper money with internationally accepted gold and thus forcing state trusts to be measured by their market values. The gold-backed unit of currency—the chervonets, equivalent in value to the czarist 10-ruble gold piece—was successful and the financial crisis was overcome.

Sokolnikov had been a Bolshevik since 1905, although he had disagreed with Lenin over his treatment of the Mensheviks. In 1918, since other leaders would not commit themselves, he was the Russian signatory to the Brest-Litovsk Treaty. At the peak of his career he was on the Politburo, but in 1925 he aligned himself with Grigory Zinoviev, Lev Kamenev, and Nadezhda Krupskaya in the New Opposition. He lost his ministerial post in January 1926 and was ambassador to London, 1929–1932. At the 1934 Party Congress Lazar Kaganovich mocked him as an arrogant enemy of the working class and forced him to recant his former criminal views. He was arrested in July 1936, tried, and sentenced in the following January. He did not survive life in the camps. The rehabilitation of his reputation was made in 1989.

SOLOMENTSEV, MIKHAIL S. 1913–

Politburo member. A factory worker and engineer, he has held many party posts in the USSR, including at Chelyabinsk, Karaganda, Kazakhstan, and Rostov. A member of the Central Committee since 1961, the Politburo in 1983, and chairman of the Party Control Commission until 1987.

SPIRIDONOVA, MARIA. 1884–1941

The most famous Russian woman revolutionary leader. In 1905, as a Socialist Revolutionary activist, she shot the brutal czarist governor of Tambov and was captured, beaten, and raped by his Cossack guard, then sentenced to life imprisonment, which she served in hard-labor camps. At the outbreak of the February 1917 Revolution she was appointed mayor of Chita and celebrated this office by blowing up the town jail. She returned to Petrograd in 1917 and, with Boris Kamkov, founded the breakaway Left Socialist Revolutionary faction. In July 1917, "the little peasants' general," with her pince-nez spectacles, dark hair pulled back, and simple blue dress, led workers, soldiers, and Kronstadt sailors on the march against the provisional government.

Spiridonova was the Bolshevik-supported candidate for the presidency of the Assembly in January 1918 (when the Center-Left Socialist Revolutionary Viktor Chernov was elected). She was arrested after the Left Socialist Revolutionary revolt in July 1918. Thirteen others were executed, and although she admitted ordering the murder of the German ambassador, she was sentenced to only one year's imprisonment by the Moscow Revolutionary Tribunal, then ordered to a sanitorium (possibly the earliest case of the use of mental hospitals for imprisoning dissidents) but eventually exiled to Soviet Central Asia. She never ceased to demonstrate her opposition to the Bolshevik government, was arrested again in the 1930s, and died in a prison camp, possibly in 1941.

STAKHANOV, ALEXEI G. 1906–1977

A coal miner. His output of 12 tons a day so far exceeded the standard that he was praised by Stalin and held up as a model for workers, establishing the 'Stakhanovite movement." His production figures were almost certainly rigged and the objective of a sevenfold increase could not be maintained anywhere without loss of quality.

STALIN (DJUGASHVILI), JOSEPH VISSARIONOVICH 1879–1953

Stalin was born on December 21, 1879, in the small Georgian town of Gori, the fourth child—the previous three had died in infancy—of Ivanovich Djugashvili, a peasant turned cobbler, and his wife Ekaterina. His father's business failed and he got a job in a shoe factory, but he died when his son was 11. Stalin's mother brought him up on her wages as a washerwoman. It is claimed that his father had subjected him to fearful beatings when drunk.

At the age of 9, Stalin was sent to the ecclesiastical school at Gori and, at the age of 14, with the aid of a scholarship, he went to the Theological Seminary at Tbilisi, where he spent the next five years training to be a priest in the Greek Orthodox Church.

Georgia was socially regressive—the freeing of the serfs took place later than the rest of Russia. At the same time, because many of the liberals and later revolutionaries were deported to the province, it was a breeding ground for radical ideas and movements. The seminary itself was frequently accused of harboring such ideas.

Stalin was a good pupil, well read in the Russian classics and an excellent debater, though it is claimed that he disliked being beaten in an argument. He was soon in trouble with the authorities for reading subversive literature. In 1898 he joined Mesami Dasi (the "Third Group"), an illegal Social Democratic group in Tbilisi. He later wrote, "I became a Marxist because of my social position, but also because of the harsh intolerance and Jesuitical discipline that crushed me so mercilessly at the seminary." In May 1899 he was expelled from the seminary for not attending examinations, though Stalin claimed it was for spreading Marxism. He got a job as a clerk in the observatory but was now actively involved in the Social Democratic movement and helped to organize the first May Day parade in the Caucasus. The following year the Okhrana (czar's secret police) came to arrest him and, taking a false identity, he entered the political underground from which he was not to emerge until the 1917 Revolution.

He became a wanted socialist agitator, living under a variety of assumed names and organizing strikes, the distribution of literature, and endless meetings. He impressed the local leadership sufficiently to be elected a member of the Social Democratic Committee of Tbilisi in 1901. At this point he was sent to the oil town of Batumi to carry the socialist message to the workers, and it was here that he took the nickname "Koba," meaning "indomitable" in Turkish. In April 1902 he was arrested by the Okhrana and spent 18 months in jail before being exiled to Novaya Uda in the Irkutsk Oblast of Siberia. In his absence he was appointed a member of the all-Caucasian Federation of the Social Democratic party. By the beginning of 1904 Stalin had escaped from his confinement in Siberia and reappeared in Tbilisi.

The split between the Bolsheviks and Mensheviks had just occurred and Stalin took the side of Lenin and the Bolsheviks. In an article published shortly after his return to Tbilisi he stressed his view of the need for complete uniformity of views inside the party. He took only a local role in the 1905 Revolution, but he had become a leading figure among the Bolsheviks of Georgia and had married Ekaterina Svanidze from an active Marxist family there. Ekaterina died in 1907, leaving a son, Yakov, to be brought up by her family.

At a party conference at Tammerfors in Finland in 1905 he met Lenin for the first time, and he was disappointed by the fact that Lenin did not stage-manage his entrance to the conference, which Stalin wrote, "seemed to me rather a violation of certain essential rules." He attended the Fourth Party Congress in January 1906 in Stockholm, where he disagreed with Lenin about land nationalization—he wanted to divide the land of the large estates among the peasants—and the Fifth Party Congress in London in July 1907. In London he met his great rival, Leon Trotsky, for the first time.

Among his party duties was being coordinator of the "fighting squads," who were raising money for the cause by robbing banks and hijacking treasury vans. Stalin turned his attentions to labor politics in Baku, and organized a series of strikes by the oil workers. During this period he met many of the people with whom he was to become closely involved, including Sergo Ordzhonikidze, later commissar for heavy industry, and Kliment Voroshilov, then secretary of the oil workers' union and later to be a marshal of the Soviet Union. That year both Stalin and Ordzhonikidze were arrested by the Okhrana and exiled to Vologda Oblast, from which he rapidly escaped and returned to Baku. In March 1910 he was again arrested and returned to Vologda. This time he completed his sentence.

In 1912 Lenin, at the Sixth Party Congress in Prague, proclaimed his final break with the Mensheviks. Ordzhonikidze was elected to the Central Committee and Stalin was co-opted on to it by Lenin. In the general round-up of suspects following the assassination of Peter Stolypin, Stalin was once again deported to Vologda, from which, inevitably, he escaped and made contact with the Bolshevik deputies to the Duma. He then prepared the first issue of *Pravda*, which was published on April 22, 1912. At the end of December Stalin left Russia for six weeks, the longest trip abroad he ever was to make. He went to

Cracow for a meeting with Lenin, who sent him to Vienna and suggested he write an essay on *The Problems of Nationalities and Social Democracy*, which appeared under the name K. Stalin. In Vienna he met Nicholas Bukharin who was working on a scholarly thesis on economics, and Leon Trotsky, again who was later to write of the "glint of animosity" in Stalin's yellow eyes directed at himself. There was good reason for the animosity. Trotsky, a brilliant and famous figure in the movement, had criticized the employment of the fighting bands Stalin had organized, and was also attacking Lenin's disruption of the Social Democratic party.

Stalin returned to St. Petersburg at the end of February and was betrayed by Roman Malinovsky, an Okhrana informer on the Central Committee (he was also the leader of the Bolsheviks in the Duma). This time he was exiled to northern Siberia, where he spent four years hunting, fishing, and reading. The war had broken out and the imposition of martial law made it safer to stay in exile. He wrote to his future mother-in-law, Olga Alliluyeva, asking for picture postcards to relieve the dull ugliness of the landscape. It is the only nonpolitical letter of his known to exist.

In 1917 Stalin, Lev Kamenev, and others returned from Siberia and were welcomed in the capital. In the absence of Lenin and other senior members of the movement, Stalin took over the editorship of *Pravda* and was, in essence, for a brief time the leader of the party. At the end of March an All-Russian Bolshevik Conference was held and Stalin presided over it. He took a comparatively moderate stance and was prepared to support a motion suggesting reunification with Mensheviks who would be "anti-Defensist"—against the war. It was this stance that brought Trotsky over to the Bolsheviks.

Lenin's arrival at the conference after his journey across Germany in the "sealed train" had a shattering effect. His April Theses urged the Bolsheviks toward a seizure of power. Stalin, who as editor of *Pravda* had been taking a quite different attitude, rapidly moved into line with his master once more. At another national conference of Bolsheviks in April, Stalin was elected to a new Central Committee with Lenin, Grigory Zinoviev, Lev Kamenev, Yakov Sverdlov, and others. Stalin was assigned the difficult and arduous task of organizing the party groups in the various soviets that were springing up all over the country.

After the July Days, Lenin was forced to go into hiding and Trotsky was arrested. Stalin once again took over temporary leadership but relinquished it in August, when the leaders had been released. In October, against the wishes of Kamenev and Zinoviev, the Central Committee decided on an insurrection for which Trotsky had done the main planning. An immediate excuse for the uprising was provided when the Provisional Government closed the printing presses of *Pravda*. And in the early morning of October 25, 1917, the Bolshevik forces went into action. Throughout the whole of the October uprising Stalin remained very much in the background. Trotsky's view was that Stalin's essential caution kept him on the fence until he could see how it was all going to turn out. Stalin wrote, "The revolution is incapable either of regretting or burying its dead." Prophetic words indeed.

After the October Revolution, Stalin supported Lenin completely and on October 26 became a member of the new

government as commissar for nationalities. With Lenin and Trotsky he resisted the inclusion of other parties in the government.

In March 1918 Stalin left Petrograd for the new seat of government in Moscow. With him came his new wife, the 16-year-old Nadezhda Alliluyeva, daughter of the family he had lodged with in Tbilisi. From a small room in the Smolny Institute, Stalin now had an office in the Kremlin and he set to drafting a constitution for the new Russian Soviet Federal Socialist Republic; it was adopted in July. Stalin foresaw an integrated "Great Russian" state, and he had no sympathy with nationalists, being particularly keen to force the Ukraine away from its aspirations of independence.

The Civil War—In June 1918, Stalin went to Tsaritsyn to supervise the movement of food supplies, but with the Don Cossacks and the Volunteer Army to the south, he required a strong armed escort. By July, seeing that priority lay in defending the revolution, he decided to take charge of the North Caucasian Military District, turning himself into a military man and gathering his support. The old Baku Committee reassembled; Kliment Voroshilov was the commander of the 10th Army, Simeon Budyenny was commanding a cavalry troop, and Stalin's old friend Grigory Ordzhonikidze was a political commissar with the 10th Army. The Tsaritzyn group soon began a fierce conflict with Trotsky, who, as commissar for war, resented Stalin's making decisions about his front without referring them to him. A battle raged around Tsaritsyn for some time before the White Armies were repulsed, for which both Stalin and Trotsky were later to claim the credit. The Tasritsyn affair served to increase the bitterness between the two men but also to magnify the importance of the city for Stalin with momentous consequences during World War II.

Stalin's military adventures went on into 1919; he acted as the political eyes and ears of Lenin and the Central Committee, from Estonia to Kharkov. He also gained permission for Budyenny to lead the highly successful independent 1st Cavalry Army.

Russo-Polish War—In April 1920 war with Poland began and in May Kiev fell to Marshal Josef Pilsudski. When the Red Army repulsed the attack, Stalin sided with Lenin in urging an invasion of Poland, which they hoped would incite a revolution among the working class. The Red Army under Mikhail Tukhachevsky was advancing on Warsaw when Pilsudski counterattacked. Budyenny, in command of the Southern Front, was ordered to attack but, encouraged by Stalin, he changed direction to take Lvov, and the Red Army's attack, its forces divided, was soon in full retreat. On this issue both Trotsky and Tukhachevsky were once again in bitter conflict with Stalin.

Stalin's native Georgia, formally independent and under a Menshevik government, was the subject of his attention in late 1920. Ordzhonikidze, designated party boss for Transcaucasia, received instructions, by-passing Lenin, to "defend" the Soviet Republic against Georgia. In July 1921 Stalin visited the Caucasus and Georgian Menshevism was brutally suppressed.

War Communism and the New Economic Policy—During the period that followed the civil war, Stalin had little to contribute in the theoretical sense. All attention, both in the country and in the world outside, was focused on Lenin and Trotsky. The party was often referred to as the Lenin-Trotsky party but Stalin was, in fact, steadily accumulating power. He had been appointed commissar of nationalities in 1917, then commissar of Rabkrin (the Workers and Peasants Inspectorate), and was named one of the five original members of the Politburo in 1919. As commissar of nationalities he was responsible for dealing with almost 50 percent of the population, from the Ukraine to the farthest fringes of Russia. He used his position to build allies just as he used his command of Rabkrin to build up a unique understanding of the machinery of government. In the Politburo he was the liaison officer with the Orgburo and he became a member in April 1920.

Then on April 3, 1922, following the 11th Party Congress, he was elected to the new post of general secretary of the party's Central Committee, with Vyacheslav Molotov and Valerian Kuibyshev as assistants. The Secretariat prepared the agenda for Politburo meetings and was responsible for the appointments of party functionaries and their careers. It is said that Lenin spoke to his intimate circle about some misgivings concerning the last appointment. "This cook can only serve peppery dishes," he is reported to have remarked. But the sheer drudgery of the work had not tempted any of the other more brilliant figures in the party. There was little concern about the concentration of power in Stalin's hands because he was regarded as Lenin's assistant.

But at the end of May 1922, Lenin suffered the first of the three strokes that were finally to kill him. In October, when Lenin was convalescing, he received a visit from Stalin anxious to put his side of the case concerning Trotsky's criticism of the Inspectorate, and his methods of dealing with the opposition in the Ukraine and Georgia. Lenin gave him his full support then, but in December, having received many more complaints about the general secretary and having had a second stroke, he dictated a memorandum in place of a will in which he spoke of his fears about a split in the party and talked of the opposition between Stalin and Trotsky. Of Stalin he wrote, "Comrade Stalin having become general secretary has concentrated enormous power in his hands; I am not sure that he always knows how to use that power with sufficient caution." Of Trotsky he wrote, "He displays too far-reaching self-confidence and a disposition to be too much attracted by the purely administrative side of affairs."

With Lenin incapacitated, Stalin was pushing the constitutional reform of the Union of the Republics through the 10th All-Russian Congress of Soviets; and on December 30, 1922, USSR became the official name of the country. Lenin, who had learned more about Stalin's methods in Georgia, dictated a postscript to his testament concerning the succession. "Stalin is too rude," he wrote, "and this fault becomes unbearable in the office of general secretary. Therefore I propose to find a way to remove Stalin from that position and appoint to it a man more patient, more loyal, more polite and more attentive to comrades." He then launched a public attack on the Inspectorate and promised to take up the case of the opposition in Georgia. He had also learned of an abusive telephone call to his wife from

Stalin and wrote a letter breaking off personal relations with him. On March 9 Lenin had the third and final stroke. Stalin was at a critical point in his life. If Lenin recovered he would launch an attack on him at the forthcoming 13th Party Congress, at which Stalin had suggested to Trotsky that the latter took Lenin's place. Stalin was careful to make all sorts of concessions to critics of his motions for the congress and got the Politburo to agree not to show Lenin's notes on the Georgian situation to the congress as well.

At the same time, with Zinoviev and Kamenev, he formed a triumvirate in the Politburo with the express purpose of defeating Trotsky in the leadership struggle. The other members, Nicholas Bukharin and Mikhail Tomsky, for example, were unwilling to back Trotsky. Battle was now joined between the triumvirate and Trotsky who appealed to the party and particularly the younger members, talking about degeneration in the old guard of the Bolsheviks; and the new monolithic structure of the bureaucrats—that is, the Secretariat, who no longer wished for debate. Stalin countered this by appealing to Lenin's rules against factionalism in the party. At the conference in January Stalin attacked Trotsky as the mouthpiece of the "petit bourgeois intelligentsia" while his group claimed to represent the proletariat. The conference voted against Trotsky's motions and condemned the opposition on the grounds of "petit bourgeois deviation from Leninism."

Three days later, on January 21, Lenin died. The emergence of the Leninist cult took formal shape at his funeral and the subsequent exhibition of his embalmed body in the mausoleum in Red Square. Stalin and other members of the Politburo arrived at Lenin's home in Gorky within three hours of his death, and on January 27 he helped carry the bier into the crypt of the mausoleum. Trotsky had gone for medical treatment to the Caucasus and did not return for the funeral. He later claimed that Stalin had not informed him of the date.

He also survived the reading of Lenin's personal attacks on him at a plenary session of the Central Committee in May. Zinoviev assured the committee that in this case Lenin's strictures on the nature of the general secretary had proved to be baseless. Both Zinoviev and Kamenev, believing themselves superior in intellect and imagination to Stalin, felt they had nothing to fear from him, whereas Trotsky's charismatic personality and oratorical brilliance frightened them. During the next three years the power struggle among the various factions in the Politburo continued. The most important issues were the controversy over Stalin's "Socialism in one country" versus Trotsky's theory of permanent revolution. Stalin supported the view that although at some unspecified date in the future revolution would undoubtedly take place in all capitalist countries, with determination it was possible to build a socialist society in Russia. Trotsky and his followers believed that a truly socialist society could only be built in cooperation with the revolutionary proletariat of the advanced countries.

The second great debate arose from the policies of the New Economic Policies (NEP), which had caused new alignments to arise within the Politburo. Supporting the Leninist, moderate neocapitalist policies of the right, as they came to be known, were Nicholas Bukharin, Alexei Rykov, and Mikhail

Tomsky. On the left were Zinoviev, and Kamenev, unhappy with the NEP on the grounds that it was the road back to capitalism. Stalin for the moment supported the right.

After the 14th Party Congress in December 1925, Molotov, Voroshilov, and Kalinin were elected to the Politburo—all supporters of Stalin—while Zinoviev and Kamenev with the Leningrad delegates voted against the Central Committee's report and were heavily defeated. Stalin sent Sergei Kirov to Leningrad to deal with the opposition stronghold there. In the spring of 1926, Zinoviev and Kamenev threw in their lot with Trotsky. Voroshilov had now been appointed as commissar of war to replace Trotsky, but his deputy Mikhail Lashevich, an associate of Zinoviev, was now denounced by Stalin for having attempted to form an opposition party in the army. As a result Zinoviev was expelled from the Politburo and then, in October 1926, Stalin expelled Trotsky.

Essentially the opposition had been crushed, though Trotsky and Zinoviev were still members of the Central Committee. The General Secretariat refused to allow publication of their statements intended for the next congress and they printed them in secret. For this they were expelled from the Central Committee. In December 1927 Trotsky was deported to Alma-Ata while Zinoviev, Kamenev, and the remainder of the opposition made a declaration renouncing their views. Having rid himself of the left, Stalin now took on his recent allies, the right. With the help of Molotov, Voroshilov, and Kalinin, and two new members, Valerian Kuibyshev and Jan Rudzutak, Stalin was able to start removing Bukharin's supporters from key points in the party. He described them as the Right Opposition and in April 1929 first mentioned Bukharin as their leader. In January 1929 the Politburo agreed to deport Trotsky from Russia. He then removed the remainder of the Right Opposition from their important positions, and by the end of the year they had all submitted. The cult of Stalin was visibly forming and beginning even to overshadow the cult of Lenin.

1929, The Second Revolution—The 1928 crisis of grain supply threatened not only the food supply to the towns but also the great new plans for the industrialization of the country. Stalin acted decisively and ruthlessly. He decided that the agricultural sector must be industrialized and the kulaks must be dispossessed to provide equipment and capital for the collectives. He also took the optimistic but fairly moderate goals outlined in the industrialization plans and transformed them. He talked about getting an increase in production of 50 percent in a year. In agriculture he succeeded in exploiting the peasant in order to finance his industrial plans but at the most appalling cost in human misery. Millions were deported and uncountable numbers died of disease and starvation. In industry extraordinary results were achieved in the heavy industrial sector, though the interests of the consumer were virtually ignored. In 1931, in a speech to business executives, he revealed the thinking behind his actions. "We are fifty to a hundred years behind the advanced countries. We must make good this lag in ten years. Either we do it or they crush us," he said. One of the ways in which this was achieved was by using forced labor from the vast labor camps peopled by rebellious peasants and other dissidents.

The Purges—On the night of November 8-9, 1932, Stalin's wife Nadezhda killed herself. A change came over Stalin. He had always shown some disinclination to punish those who opposed him. He refused to take drastic action against Trotsky, though urged to by Zinoviev. But there were signs of opposition in the party and in the country and, in June 1934, Stalin signed a decree to the effect that a whole family would be held responsible for the treason of any of its members. Stalin also reorganized the political police, replacing the GPU by the NKVD. Everything changed abruptly when on December 1, 1934, Kirov was assassinated in Leningrad, now generally believed on Stalin's orders. Immediately Zinoviev and Kamenev were arrested and sentenced to penal servitude, and in the spring of 1935 Andrei Zhdanov was sent as governor to Leningrad, where he instituted a reign of terror in which thousands of suspect party members in Leningrad and other Russian cities were deported to camps in Siberia. Stalin's control over the USSR was not only aimed at political opponents; the fields of philosophy, literature, history, and art were brought under the strictest control.

In 1936, after a short pause, the purges began again with a series of show trials. They included not only most of the better-known members of the opposition but, in 1937, a large number of senior army officers. All were charged with an incredible list of crimes including attempting to assassinate Stalin and other members of the Politburo.

Two of the men charged—Genrikh Yagoda and Nicholai Yezhov—were the chiefs of the NKVD who had provided the evidence against the other accused. Most were shot, having confessed to all the crimes with which they were charged. By the end of 1938 Stalin had destroyed much of the Bolshevik old guard, some of whom could have formed an alternative government. He had crippled the army. He had also terrified the country into complete acceptance of his will. To settle accounts with his main opponent, Trotsky, took a little longer. In August 1940, Trotsky, who had settled in Mexico, was killed in his office by an ice pick wielded by an NKVD-trained assassin.

Foreign Policy—Until 1939 Stalin's view of foreign policy can be summed up by his statement to the 16th Party Congress in June 1930: "We do not want a single foot of foreign territory, but we will not surrender a single inch of our territory either." In China he supported Chiang Kai-shek until the Chinese leader, fearful of the power of the Communists, broke off relations with the USSR. Stalin correctly predicted the Wall Street crash and the onset of the Great Depression. But he underestimated the strength of the German Nazi movement when it came to power in 1933. He began to search for anti-Nazi coalitions, but because of the distrust felt for him by Western politicians, got nowhere. He involved the USSR in the Spanish Civil War, but even there did little for his reputation by conducting a witch-hunt for Trotskyites and traitors among the Spanish republicans.

In April 1939 Stalin made diplomatic moves in two directions: a pact with Britain and France and an approach aimed at rapprochement with Germany. In August Hitler, who was about to invade Poland, began to make active advances for a nonaggression pact. This was signed by Molotov and the German Joachim von Ribbentrop on August 23. A secret protocol attached to the pact included the partition of Poland between the two powers and made Finland and the Baltic States part of the Soviet sphere of influence. Both parties to the pact were attempting to win time and freedom of action, but Stalin seems to have overestimated the military strength of France, Poland, and England and to have underestimated the might of the German war machine. In April 1941 Stalin entered into a pact of neutrality with Japan that was to prove of vast importance during the forthcoming struggle with Nazi Germany.

The good will between the new allies did not last long. Though Stalin had been warned specifically by Winston Churchill that the Germans planned to attack the USSR in June, he paid no attention even though there were 150 German divisions massed on the frontier. On June 22 Hitler launched Operation Barbarossa, a full-scale attack on the Soviet Union.

World War II—During the whole of the Second World War, Stalin played a key role in the day-to-day conduct of the war. The Stavka, the Red Army's nerve center, was controlled from his office in the Kremlin, where he stayed even when the Nazi armies reached the suburbs of Moscow in December 1941. He was constantly in touch with all the fronts and armies, but he rarely overrode his generals' plans. But he did take Voroshilov's and Budyenny's commands away from them at the beginning of the war after they had suffered appalling defeats at the hands of the Germans and had revealed themselves as incapable of dealing with modern mechanized warfare. Stalin broadcast messages to the Russian people reminding them of past victories over Napoleon and calling for them to be prepared to make sacrifices against the invading Germans, who were out to restore czarism and the rule of the landlords.

He also made alliances with both the United States and England and obtained vast quantities of supplies from the Allies, most significantly transport. Later in the year the focus of the military campaign shifted south to Stalingrad, which the Germans were determined to take. It became the most significant battle of the war, more for personal than for strategic motives—to Hitler because of its name, to Stalin because of his past associations with the city. The Red Army counterattacked and then surrounded the Germans, who finally surrendered in February 1943. Though there were hard and vicious battles to come, it was Stalingrad that signalled the final defeat of the German invasion. After the battle Stalin took the title of marshal.

During 1943 the Russians recaptured a sizable fraction of the territory occupied by the German armies during the invasion and, in November, Stalin met Winston Churchill and Franklin D. Roosevelt at Teheran. He called, as he had done in 1942, for a second front in France while Churchill, anxious to limit Russia's power in the Balkans, proposed landings in southern Europe. Stalin won the day and the Allies agreed to launch Operation Overlord in May of the next year. By the time the three met again at Yalta in February 1945, the situation had changed dramatically. The Red Army had swept the Nazi armies off Soviet soil and were poised on the Oder for the final assault on Berlin; the Allied armies in the West were dealing with Hitler's last desperate offensive in the Ardennes.

At the Yalta Conference, Churchill and Roosevelt obtained Stalin's agreement to join in the final assault on Japan but did not inform him of the development of the atomic bomb. It is now known that Stalin had already been informed about the bomb by his intelligence staff. When officially informed about it at the Potsdam Conference in August 1945, Stalin was noncommittal, realizing the implications for the balance of power. By Potsdam, Roosevelt had died and, halfway through the conference, Churchill, defeated in the postwar election, had been replaced by Clement Attlee. Signs of conflict between the wartime allies were appearing over the dividing up of Germany and Stalin's policy in the Balkans. But Stalin was still concerned enough about public opinion in the West to agree to send Molotov to the first assembly of the United Nations.

Victory and the Fruits of Victory—Stalin was proclaimed Hero of the Soviet Union and generalissimo after the great Victory Parade in June 1945. His task was then to rebuild a shattered nation that had suffered appallingly from the war. Twenty million had died, most of the cities and towns in European Russia had been destroyed, and much of its population was homeless. His plan for rebuilding the USSR was as ruthless as the first five-year plan. Agriculturally the peasants were to go on suffering—he increased compulsory quotas for the collective farms—to provide cheap food for industry and the industrial emphasis as once again almost entirely on heavy industry at the expense of consumer goods. However he had one resource previously unavailable. As the result of Soviet victories at the end of the war, conquered nations such as East Germany could be plundered for both resources and labor. Even more important, those countries now within the Soviet Union's sphere of influence could be linked economically for the USSR's benefit.

To put this into effect, Stalin inspired and coordinated Communist takeovers in the countries of Eastern and Central Europe and, when this was achieved, virtually sealed off the Eastern bloc from the West. The Iron Curtain of Churchill's famous speech had come to pass, and extended not only to frontiers but even the airwaves. The wartime revival of old themes such as Mother Russia and the restoration of traditional regimental titles such as Guards and Cossack, as well as the celebration of the victorious generals were dropped. Indeed, many of the troops returning from Europe were shipped straight to labor camps. Stalin was fearful that their experience in the West might lead them to demand a better life from the government. What the average worker in Russia received was the harshest and most stringent direction of labor and discipline—the punishment for the most trivial offense was deportation to the Gulag. And the ex-commissar for the nationalities ordered the uprooting of entire nations like the Crimean Tatars, accused of collaboration with the Nazis, and their deportation to Siberia.

Then, in March 1947, U.S. President Harry S. Truman, in a speech to both houses of Congress, declared U.S. support for the Greek government fighting Communist insurgents and offered help to any country fighting communism. The cold war had been declared. The United States launched the Marshall Plan, but Stalin rejected this help for

Eastern Europe. He then founded the Cominform, essentially a revival of the old Comintern, and tightened his grip on Eastern Europe. In Czechoslovakia, a few days after a Communist takeover, Jan Masaryk, the foreign minister who had been resisting Stalin's demands, was found dead on the pavement under his office window.

Stalin announced a blockade of Berlin, hoping to drive the Western powers and their garrisons out of the city. But he had underestimated the strength of the Allies' airpower and Berlin was kept supplied from the air. Another blow to Stalin was the breach with Marshal Tito of Yugoslavia, and this inspired similar stirrings in some other Eastern Bloc countries, which led to a procession of show trials on the Soviet model, followed by executions all over Eastern Europe.

In China, Mao Tse-tung had come to power. He was an old comrade and a formal treaty was signed in February 1950. It was followed shortly by the attack across the 38th Parallel by the Communist North Koreans. China became directly involved in the conflict, but Stalin could see no profit for the USSR in the war.

The Soviet Union had exploded its first atomic bomb in 1949 and in 1953 its first hydrogen bomb. Industry had achieved astonishing feats, reaching a 50 percent increase in prewar production figures by 1952, but agriculture was in a disastrous state. Between 1949 and 1953 the average grain harvest was less than it had been in 1913.

In Stalin's last years in the Kremlin his suspicious and devious nature became more and more pronounced, climaxing in the famous "Doctors' Plot," which has led many to believe that he was about to launch another wave of terror against the remainder of the old guard in his entourage, Nikita Khrushchev relates that at the 19th Party Congress in 1952, Stalin launched a savage attack on Molotov and Mikoyan, and claimed that Voroshilov was a British agent.

On March 6, 1953, Stalin's death was announced. He had suffered a brain hemorrhage and a stroke six days earlier. He was 73. His bier was carried into Red Square and buried in the mausoleum next to Lenin. It did not remain there for long. After the 20th Party Congress in 1956, as a result of the speech by Khrushchev denouncing Stalin as a bloody tyrant, the body was removed and is now buried outside the walls of the Kremlin.

STALIN, EKATRINA SVANIDZE. ?–1907

Stalin's first wife. Their son, Yakov, was born in 1906 and raised in the Caucasus by her parents.

STALIN, NADEZHDA ALLILUYEVA. 1901–1932

Stalin's second wife. He knew her family in Tbilisi. She was in Petrograd with her father in 1917, and she joined the party; They married in 1918. She was expelled from the party in 1921 as nonactive, but Lenin intervened and she was reinstated. She studied at the Industrial Academy, where she met Nikita Khrushchev and introduced him to Stalin. She killed herself in 1932, the night after she spoke out to a small gathering about the miseries being suffered in the country.

STOLYPIN, PETER A. 1862–1911

Czarist politician. Stolypin was a provincial—a simple and direct man. In the 1905 Revolution, while he was governor of Saratov, his personal coolness restored order. Once during a riot, when an agitator seized him by the arm, Stolypin asked him to hold his coat while he carried on, in the face of shooting.

As the czar's prime minister from 1906, he made some moderate reforms, seeking to build a class of peasant farmers as a counter to the Duma liberals and revolutionaries. He promoted the break up of the *mir* and the migration of peasants to Siberia. He introduced a property qualification for membership in the Duma and planned social improvements, but he governed by decree under Article 87, without using the Duma. He ordered court-martials throughout the country to deal with rebels, and had many peasants hanged. In hunting intellectual suspects he encouraged anti-Semitism and the murder gangs of the Black Hundreds.

His home was bombed in 1907, and he survived only to be assassinated four years later in a Kiev theatre.

STRUVE, PETER BERNGARDO-VICH. 1870–1944

A writer on history, politics, and economics. He was at first influenced by Marxist thought, and was responsible for the manifesto at the founding of congress of the All-Russian Social Democratic Labor party in 1898. However he soon came to believe in an evolutionary rather than a revolutionary view of Marxism, broke with the Social Democrats, and helped to found the Liberation of Labor group. In 1906 he joined the Kadet party and was elected to its Central Committee.

But Struve's real commitment was to the idea of liberty. He was awarded an honorary degree from Cambridge University and elected to the Russian Academy of Sciences in 1917. The revolution disturbed him profoundly and the Bolshevik coup in October drove him to support the Whites, whom he believed to be on the side of liberty. When Baron Peter Wrangel was defeated he became professor of political economy at the Russian Juridical Faculty at Prague University. From there he went to Belgrade, and then spent the last two years of his life in Nazi-occupied Paris. He liked to describe himself as a "liberal conservative."

SUKHANOV, NIKOLAI. 1882–1940

A Menshevik supporter of the 1917 October Revolution. He was arrested with other Mensheviks in 1931 and died in prison.

SUSLOV, MIKHAIL A. 1902–1982

A party official from 1921, with a reputation for intellectual rigor. In 1944 he was made chairman of the Politburo in Lithuania and in 1947, editor in chief of *Pravda*. He was appointed to the Politburo in 1952.

He insisted on the total dominance of Russia and the Russians in the Soviet world, not simply by reason of military force, but through cultural domination. With this purpose in 1956 he went to Budapest, just before the uprising was crushed; in 1958 he went to Prague to question Alexander Dubček's ideology; and in 1981, to Poland at the time of the Solidarity strikes. Always strong on correct party lines, in October 1964 he led the attack on Nikita Khrushchev, but in 1970 it was Suslov who stopped Leonid Brezhnev from combining the posts of head of party and head of government. When this survivor of Stalin's regime, the grand old man of the Politburo, died, Yuri Andropov succeeded him in his post.

SVERDLOV, YAKOV M. 1885–1919

An activist in the Bolshevik underground in Russia from its early days. Released from exile in a remote part of Siberia in 1917, he made his way to Petrograd, where he became secretary to the party's Central Committee and head of state as chairman of the All-Russian Central Executive Committee of the Soviets. His organizing ability made him, in effect, the Central Committee's first general secretary before the post existed. In the 1917 July Days, when other Bolshevik leaders were either in hiding or under arrest, he was the party leader. He died of the "Spanish influenza" epidemic at the time, caught while traveling in the Ukraine.

TIKHON, V. I. BELAVIN. 1865–1925

Archbishop of the Russian Orthodox Church in Moscow. He was elected to the post of Patriarch (which had been abolished since Peter the Great) under the Provisional Government in 1917. At once he asserted his authority by refusing to recognize the newly elected head of the Georgian Orthodox Church. He spoke out against the Bolsheviks in January 1918 and protested the seizure of church property in 1919. Seeing the reality of the situation, the failure of the

Whites, and the danger of the Red Terror, he urged his clergy to cooperate with the regime. Resisting seizure of the Church's treasures, he was jailed in May 1922. Priests less hostile to the Bolsheviks then formed the rival "Living Church." He was released in 1923 after he recanted his anti-Bolshevik past. After his death it was two years before his successor, Sergius Stragorodsky, was elected (having also been jailed), but he was not installed until 1943.

TIKHONOV, NIKOLAI. 1905–

An old party member. Loyal to Leonid Brezhnev and Konstantin Chernenko, he retired as premier in 1985 and was succeeded by Nikolai Ryzhkov.

TIMOSHENKO, SIMEON K. 1895–1970

Marshal of the Soviet Union. He began his career as a peasant conscript to the czarist army in World War I. Timoshenko joined the Red Guard in 1918 and was involved in the defense of Tsaritsyn, where he made the acquaintance of Stalin. He became a member of Simeon Budyenny's 1st Cavalry Army and later commanded the 4th Cavalry Division, taking part in the defeat of Baron Peter Wrangel in 1920.

After the civil war he continued to serve in the Red Army as commander of the Northern Military District in 1937 and commander of the Kiev Military District in 1939. In January 1940 he commanded the Northwestern Front in the Russo-Finnish War and in May 1940 he was made people's commissar for defense. On June 22, 1941, at the outbreak of war with Germany, Stalin made him commander-in-chief. In July

he was relieved of this post but appointed to the Stavka, the Army Supreme Headquarters.

During World War II Timoshenko held a series of commands. He was in charge first of the Southern and then of the Southwestern fronts. In the early days of the Stalingrad campaign he was appointed to head this front but was removed a short time later. In 1943 he coordinated the Volkov and Leningrad fronts, and from 1944 to the end of the war was responsible for the Ukraine.

After the war Timoshenko held appointments in military districts. He was a candidate member of the party's Central Committee from 1952 until his death. He was well known for his blunt and outspoken manner, but remained a favorite of Stalin to the end. Under Nikita Khrushchev in 1960 he was quietly put on the shelf as an inspector general of the ministry of defense.

TOMSKY (EFREMOV), MIKHAIL P. 1880–1936

A working-class militant from St. Petersburg. A printer by trade, he tried to organize a union that ended with his arrest and deportation to Tomsk (hence the cover name "Tomsky"). In 1917 he made his way from Siberia to Moscow and, when Lenin returned, to Petrograd. He remained a trade unionist and was president of the Congress of Trade Unions from 1919. His standing in the party (he was one of the eight pallbearers in Lenin's funeral), his popularity with workers, and his administrative ability made him of great use to Stalin. His antipathy to the left-wingers, including Leon Trotsky, put him among the right-wing bloc in 1925. In 1928, with the Left Opposition destroyed, Tomsky found himself, with Nicholas Bukharin and Alexei Rykov, a trio in opposition to Stalin, urging a slowdown in the collectivization process. Despite warnings they refused to give way, and in 1929 were condemned by the Central Committee. Tomsky was expelled from the Politburo and from his union presidency.

Tomsky went through a process of self-criticism at the 16th Party Congress the next year, and he regained some of his status. But when he heard that Andrei Vyshinsky had started inquiries about him, he killed himself in August 1936. Bukharin, later at his own trial, was to name him as the link between the conspirators of the Right Opposition and a group in the Red Army.

TROTSKY (BRONSTEIN), LEV DAVIDOVITCH (LEON). 1879–1940

One of the major figures of the Bolshevik revolution. He was born October 26, 1879, at Yanovka, a small village near Kharkov, the fifth child of a prosperous Jewish farmer. Educated at the St. Paul School in Odessa, he felt "an intense hatred of the existing order, of injustice, of tyranny" from an early age, as he declares in his autobiography, *My Life*.

His father wished him to become a engineer but, stirred by the self-sacrifice of a girl student in Petrograd in 1897, he decided to take up revolutionary politics. He formed a commune of students and workers, but in 1898 they were betrayed to the czarist police and he, with many others, was imprisoned in Moscow and then exiled to Ust-Kut. There he was married, for the first time, to Alexandra Lvovna, a member of the South Russian Worker's Union. During his exile he began his literary career, writing for an Irkutsk paper and

studying Marx, Engels, Plekhanov, and Lenin.

In 1902 Trotsky left his wife and two daughters in their place of exile and escaped, with her blessing, to Europe in order to work for the revolutionary paper *Iskra*. In the autumn of 1902 Trotsky arrived in London by way of Paris and established a relationship with Lenin there and later in Paris. At the Second Congress of the Social Democratic party in London, the party divided into the Menshevik (minority) and Bolsheviks (majority) factions. Trotsky, not approving Lenin's ruthless authoritarianism, sided with the Mensheviks. In the 1905 Revolution, Trotsky played a dominant role in the St. Petersburg Soviet, and was elected chairman while at the same time writing for three papers, *The Russian Gazette*, *Nachalo* (The Beginning), and editorials for *Izvestia*, which was the official organ of the Soviet. During this period he married his second wife, I. N. Sedova, also a political activist.

On December 3 he was arrested with other members of the St. Petersburg Soviet and spent the next 15 months in prison at Berezov. He was able to continue writing pamphlets and books and reading the European classics while in prison. Trotsky escaped from Berezov in January 1907 and left Russia via Finland for a foreign exile that was to last for 10 years.

First Exile—After attending the Fifth Congress of the Social Democratic party in London in 1907, Trotsky settled in Vienna with his wife for the next seven years. His intent was to keep in touch with the political situation, for the German Social Democratic party was regarded by the Russian revolutionaries as a model, with August Bebel and Karl Kautsky as its intellectual gurus.

In 1908 he began publication of *Pravda*, which was smuggled into Russia by members of the underground Seamen's Union. His chief contributor was Adolf A. Ioffe, who later played an active part in the 1917 Revolution. He also traveled in the Balkans and continued to study economics and mingle with both Menshevik and Bolshevik factions of the party.

Immediately after the outbreak of World War I in August 1914, Trotsky and his wife moved to Zurich and entered the life of the Swiss Socialist party. In November 1914 he went to France as a war correspondent and settled down in a borrowed house at Sèvres, attending from there the conference at Zimmerwald.

In 1916 Trotsky was deported from France. He spent a few weeks in Spain with his family, sailed for New York, and arrived there on January 13, 1917. In New York Trotsky met Nicholas Bukharin, but by March 27, with news of the February Revolution, he was on his way to Russia with his family on a Norwegian boat. But at a request from the Provisional Government, they were held at a camp in Halifax, Canada, for a month. Finally in May they arrived in Petrograd, where he was briefly imprisoned but when released made chairman of the Petrograd Soviet, as he had been 12 years earlier. Despite the Bolsheviks imprisoned by Alexander Kerensky, their numbers were growing in the Soviet and increased by the threat of a right-wing coup headed by General Lavr Kornilov.

The October Revolution—At the Second All-Russian Congress of the Soviets on the eve of the October Revolution, Trotsky, replying to Yuli Martov

who was urging the revolutionary party to form a coalition with the Mensheviks and Socialist Revolutionaries, said, "Your part is over. Go to where you belong: into the trash can of history."

At the first meeting of the Central Committee of the party, at Trotsky's suggestion, ministries in the newly formed government were called People's Commissaries, and the government, the Soviet of People's Commissaries. Lenin proposed him as the chairman, which he rejected, just as he also turned down the commissariat of the interior because he feared his Jewish origins might be exploited by their enemies. Finally he accepted the job of commissar of foreign affairs. In doing so he became involved, much to the fury of the Western Allies, in separate armistice talks with the Germans and their allies at Brest-Litovsk.

The negotiations were complex, and on February 7 Trotsky announced to the startled Germans and their allies that the Russian armies had been demobilized. This was an expression of his "neither peace nor war" policy, the merits of which he thought he had convinced Lenin. On March 6, under threat of Lenin's resignation, the treaty was signed. Later in the year Trotsky made a public appreciation of Lenin's part in the Brest-Litovsk decision. He said, "Only Comrade Lenin maintained stubbornly, with amazing foresight, that we had to go through with it to tide us over until the revolution of the world proletariat. And now we must admit that we were wrong."

Civil War—By August 1918 the fate of the revolution hung in the balance, threatened by external and internal counterrevolutionary forces. Trotsky, who had been appointed commissar of war and chairman of the Supreme War Council (VVS), moved to Moscow with Lenin and the rest of the government and started to outfit the armored train that was to become his command post and, indeed, almost his home for the next two and a half years. It contained a secretariat, a printing press, a telegraph station, a radio station, a library, a garage, and even a bath. It also included a squad of handpicked troops armed with machine guns and their own transport. As Trotsky wrote, "We were constructing an army all over again and under fire at that." His first mission with the train was to Sviyazhsk on the Kazan Front where the Czech Legion had just taken Kazan. His inspiring leadership and, where necessary, ruthless discipline restored the situation, and on September 10 Kazan was recaptured. Two days later Simbirsk was recaptured by the First Army commanded by Mikhail Tukhachevsky, one of the many former czarist officer "specialists" whose use by Trotsky met with a great deal of opposition from the ultra-left in the party and led to Trotsky's first direct clash with Stalin. This took place at Tsaritsyn, where Stalin and Kliment Voroshilov ignored the commander of the Southern Front, an ex-czarist officer, and then Trotsky's direct orders. He appealed to Lenin, who directed Stalin to give in which he did with ill grace; but he then attempted to stir up trouble by claiming that Trotsky was recruiting a faction hostile to Lenin.

In March 1919 Stalin was appointed to the Politburo along with Trotsky, Lenin, Lev Kamenev, and Krestinsky, but Stalin was also appointed to the Orgburo, the administrative arm of the Central Committee. His fatal grip on the levers of power was beginning.

Stalin soon caused trouble for Trotsky by persuading Lenin to overrule his decision to remove the commander on the Eastern Front. Trotsky returned to Moscow and admitted that he had been in the wrong, but when the Politburo supported the commander, he resigned from all his posts. Lenin was so appalled by the consequences that he persuaded the other members to change their minds. Fully in charge now and with Lenin's total support, Trotsky reorganized the Southern Front and planned an October offensive on the forces of Anton Denikin. Then he returned to Moscow and persuaded the Politburo to implement his plan for total mobilization in order to save Petrograd, which Lenin had been seriously thinking of abandoning. Arriving in the city in October he threw himself into the battle, actually chasing the retreating troops of an infantry regiment back into action. He stopped Nicholas Yudenich's White Army forces at the Pulkovo Heights outside Petrograd, and, on October 22, drove them back to the Estonian frontier. A month later Andrei Kolchak was defeated in Siberia. Trotsky was awarded the Order of the Red Flag.

The Red Army, now an efficient fighting force, recaptured Kiev from Marshal Josef Pilsudki's Poles in June 1920, but Trotsky was against the attempt to reach Warsaw where Lenin hoped to rouse the workers to revolt. He was proved right and the situation was worsened by Stalin's mistimed attempt to capture Lvov. But, by the end of November, a peace treaty had been signed with Poland and Baron Wrangel had been defeated and driven off Russian soil The revolution was once again safe.

War Communism—In 1920 the economic situation in the country was grave. The peasants were cultivating no more than they needed for their own survival and industrial production was down to a third of what it had been before the war. In certain parts of the country famine was rife. Trotsky had been given the job by Lenin of restoring the railway system. He came back from his tour of inspection in the Urals convinced that the system of expropriation from the peasants would never provide the huge increase in food supplies needed. He suggested to Lenin and the Central Committee that a form of progressive tax on agricultural produce would make it profitable for the peasant to cultivate more land and sell more grain. His suggestions were turned down by the committee. Appointed as economic spokesman at the Ninth Party Congress he therefore suggested the only logical alternative, militarization of the labor force and the trade unions. He personally put the railway workshops under martial law, provoking a storm of protest from the extreme left. Then, in February 1921, following a week of strikes and protests in Petrograd, the tragic Kronstadt rebellion took place. Although it was quickly put down, the committee realized that a crisis had arrived, and at the 10th Party Congress in March 1921 Lenin put forward his proposals for a New Economic Policy (NEP), which mirrored almost exactly those which Trotsky had suggested a year earlier.

New Economic Policy—The new policies had an instant and dramatic effect. The harvest of 1922 was back to about three-quarters of the prewar average and smaller industrial enterprises increased output by more than 50 percent. It was not enough for Trotsky, who insisted that

full-scale economic planning was necessary, though Lenin remained unconvinced.

In April 1922, just after the 11th Party Congress had dispersed, Stalin was designated general secretary at Lenin's suggestion and at the same time, and not coincidentally, Trotsky was asked to become deputy chairman of the Soviet of People's Commissars. He refused, perhaps because there were already two deputy chairmen and he regarded the offer as a slight. Then on May 26 Lenin had a stroke, losing the power of speech and the use of his right arm and leg.

The Struggle for Leadership—Lenin's illness immediately raised the question for the first time of who would succeed him as party leader. This led to the formation of the Stalin, Grigory Zinoviev, and Lev Kamenev triumvirate, whose immediate purpose was to prevent the emergence of Trotsky in this role. He was, after all, a hero of both revolutions, a brilliant orator and thinker with a huge popular following. Zinoviev was envious of Trotsky and Kamenev feared his extremism. Stalin felt about Trotsky much as Zinoviev did, but his jealousy and envy were more extreme, as his ambition was greater.

Lenin was sufficiently recovered by September to ask Stalin to bring up the matter of Trotsky's appointment to the deputy chairmanship again. Stalin, disturbed by the growing closeness between the two men, telephoned Nadezhda Krupskaya, Lenin's wife, and coarsely abused her for allowing Lenin to write to Trotsky "against doctor's orders." Lenin knew nothing of this, but had a second stroke in December.

Later, when he had learned of Stalin's attack on his wife and also of the actions taken by Stalin in Georgia, Lenin asked Trotsky to take charge of the enquiry into the whole affair. Lenin also wrote to Stalin asking him to apologize for his rudeness to Krupskaya on threat of breaking off relations with him. Stalin made his apologies to Lenin before, on March 10, he suffered the third and final stroke from which there seemed little likelihood of recovery.

The 12th Party Congress was due shortly and the triumvirate was anxious to know whether Trotsky would use Lenin's papers on the Georgian affair. Trotsky declared himself against the idea of removing Stalin from the Politburo but declined to deliver the keynote speech at the congress, lest it be thought that he was seeking to replace Lenin as leader. During the congress Stalin secured agreement to increase the size of the Central Committee, many of them being his own candidates.

After the congress, 46 members of the party, some of them close associates of Trotsky, wrote to the Central Committee, complaining of the growth of bureaucracy in the party. For this protest they were condemned for fractionalism. In October Trotsky got soaked through while duck shooting near Moscow, and contracted a fever that lasted on and off for several months. Coming at such a difficult time, it is difficult to resist making a connection between the illness and the extreme stress under which he was now living. He rallied sufficiently to attack his opponents in a letter in which he accused them of attempting to terrorize the party. Zinoviev called for his expulsion from the party, but Stalin, recognizing the depth of feeling which Trotsky could arouse, was more cautious. Then in January 1924 Trotsky's doctors advised him to visit a Black Sea

resort to recuperate. While there he received the news of Lenin's death. He planned to return to Moscow for the funeral but Stalin told him quite falsely, that he would not be in time for it, and he remained in Tiflis.

Just before the 13th Party Congress on May 22, Lenin's "Testament" was presented to a joint meeting of the Central Committee and heads of the delegations. Despite its crushing references to Stalin and its call for him to be replaced as general secretary, the Politburo decided to suppress it. Trotsky could only sit there in impotent rage. Zinoviev, adding insult to injury, called for a recantation of his views. Trotsky refused. In July he lost his place on the executive of the Comintern to Stalin.

Permanent Revolution—In the autumn of 1924 a massive campaign of denigration was launched at Trotsky, aimed at diminishing his role in the revolution and, more specifically, at attacking him on vital ideological matters: First, was his theory of permanent revolution, by which he meant that socialism would be impossible to construct in Russia without the transformation of other Western societies by the same route. Second was his statement that the peasantry was naturally bourgeois in attitude and of necessity would have to be led by the proletariat. Although in the past all these doctrines had been regarded as perfectly respectable, if debatable, statements denying them could always be found in the writing of Lenin, who was now being turned into the icon of the revolution. In December Stalin produced his own theory, largely based on an article of Lenin's, which suggested that because of the unequal development of capitalism, socialism might develop in a limited number of countries at first, perhaps even only one. Stalin called his policy—it became the orthodox view—"Socialism in one country."

In January 1925 the Central Committee met and removed Trotsky as commissar of war, though he was allowed to remain on the Central Committee and the Politburo. He was appointed to the Electro-technical Development Board, where he suggested harnessing the Dnieper River for power generation, an idea at which Stalin sneered, only to adopt it himself 10 years later.

The Leadership Battle Continues—The triumvirate was beginning to break up. Zinoviev, aware now of the menace of the general secretary, launched an attack on his new doctrine in *Leninism*, and with Krupskaya demanded a free debate on the Bukharin policy of indulging the peasantry. It was refused and at the 14th Party Congress he was attacked by a packed meeting. In January Stalin sent Sergei Kirov to Leningrad to purge the party there and to take over from Zinoviev as chairman of the Leningrad Soviet. In April Zinoviev and Kamenev arranged a meeting with Trotsky and suggested an alliance against Stalin. He left for Germany for medical treatment almost immediately. When he returned to Moscow, he and his followers, calling themselves the United Opposition organized small meetings, frequently disrupted by local officials and party members loyal to Stalin. In a letter to the Central Committee, Trotsky put the opposition's point of view, asking for a rapid industrialization program, an end to the "Socialism in one country" idea, and greater democracy in the party. In reply the Politburo ejected Zinoviev,

and he and Kamenev persuaded Trotsky to make a truce with Stalin, which he did, holding fast to his criticism but promising to cease all fractional activities. On October 23, the day before the meeting of the 15th Party Congress, Stalin broke the truce by denouncing the opposition as Social Democrat "Deviationists." Trotsky rose to his feet and, pointing to Stalin, declared, "The First Secretary poses his candidature to the post of Grave Digger of the Revolution." Stalin rushed from the room, slamming the door behind him. Stalin denounced his views at the congress and Trotsky replied in masterly fashion, but the congress stood by Stalin and reaffirmed their strictures on the opposition.

In April 1927 Trotsky had a final opportunity to demonstrate what he considered the "criminal character" of Stalin's support for Chiang Kai-shek, which led directly to the massacre of the Chinese Communists in Shanghai. But it was too late. Almost the last official moves in opposition to the party were made by Trotsky and Zinoviev in Leningrad, at a meeting held to celebrate the introduction by the Politburo of a five-day work week that the United Opposition held to be a fraud. A week later the Central Committee, meeting in an extraordinary session, expelled all the United Opposition leaders and Trotsky and Zinoviev were expelled from the party. At the 15th Party Congress in December, Zinoviev and Kamenev decided to capitulate; and on January 12, 1928, the GPU informed Trotsky that, on account of his counterrevolutionary activities, he would be deported to Alma-Ata in Turkestan.

Exile—Determined that his exile would be seen for what it was, Trotsky locked himself in his house with Natalia and their two sons. He even forced the GPU to carry him onto the train. After complaining to Moscow, he was given a four-room apartment in the town. He immediately set himself up as the headquarters of the United Opposition, writing endless letters and sending telegrams. He was appalled by what he heard of events in Moscow. Bukharin, Stalin's ally on the right of the party, had been disposed of as efficiently as had his previous allies and had submitted to the party will. Almost all of Trotsky's supporters had now been virtually exiled or had submitted.

Trotsky's daughters by his first marriage were ill. Nina died in a sanatorium and Zina was suffering from consumption. Trotsky himself was ill with a recurrence of the fever he had had for the last two years. On December 16 a special representative of the GPU arrived to give him an ultimatum: desist from directing the United Opposition or be exiled from the country. Trotsky refused and on January 20, 1929, he was handed a letter that sentenced him to deportation from the USSR on the grounds of provoking anti-Soviet actions and preparing for an armed struggle against the Soviet power.

Deported—Trotsky refused to sign a confirmation of his deportation order, but by January 22 he and his family were on their way to Constantinople, which had been selected as his place of exile. They arrived on February 12 and the GPU escort handed him the sum of $1,500 "to enable him to settle abroad." He eventually found a house to rent on Prinkipo Island and set about applying for visas to various European countries. He was turned down successively by Germany, Norway, France, and England.

Trotsky settled down to his usual political existence. He found a printer in Paris to produce an Opposition bulletin that circulated widely in Europe, though few copies reached the Soviet Union. He also wrote *My Life. An Attempt at an Autobiography* and started work on the massive *History of the Russian Revolution.*

Although Trotsky continued to denounce Stalin's tactics and his principles, he had little success in building a serious opposition outside the USSR, partly owing to the ruthless suppression of his associates. His daughter Zina, with whom Trotsky had a difficult relationship, arrived with his son Leon. Zina stayed with them for a time but Lyova was sent to Germany. Trotsky, who had correctly forecast the rise of the Nazi party, had hopes that the working class would rise in armed resistance, though he denounced the German Communist party for its tactical liaison with the Nazis. In January 1933 Trotsky was devastated by the suicide of Zina in Berlin. In July some of his French admirers persuaded the government to allow him a residence permit. He found a house in Barbizon, but it was an unhappy situation with severe restrictions on his freedom of action and harassment by the police and the press.

In December 1934 the assassination of Kirov and the massive purge of the Leningrad party signaled the prelude of a campaign of Terror. Within weeks Zinoviev and Kamenev were on trial, though at this time they were given only relatively short prison sentences. But the assault on Trotsky's family began with the arrest of his son Sergei. It was to continue until they had all been eliminated.

Norway—Knowing that he was outstaying his welcome in France, Trotsky managed to get a six-month visa from the new Labor government in Norway. Then, on August 15, 1936, the first of the great show trials was announced. Kamenev, Zinoviev, and 14 others were to stand trial. At the center of the accusations was the charge that Trotsky, with his son Leon Sedov, had been the chief conspirator and that the German Gestapo was involved.

Trotsky promptly denounced this as "the greatest forgery in the world's political history" but the accused, prompted by torture or threats to their families, confessed to a man. Zinoviev, indeed, said that he had been second only to Trotsky in the group that killed Kirov and planned to kill Stalin. Guarantees from Stalin that they would be freed if they made their confessions were followed by the firing squad. Trotsky's attempt to defend himself by giving interviews and statements were cut off by the Norwegian government under pressure from the Soviet Union.

In December 1936, and much to his relief, Trotsky was informed that Mexican admirers of his led by the artist Diego Rivera had persuaded the Mexican president to grant him asylum.

Mexico, the Final Chapter—Trotsky and Natalia had scarcely been made welcome by the Riveras at their house in a suburb of Mexico City when a second show trial opened in Moscow—this time with 14 less well-known defendants but with more specific and absurd accusations involving Trotsky as arch-conspirator. He was accused of conspiring with the German and Japanese governments and of promising them the Ukraine and the eastern Maritime Province in return for being made ruler of Russia when the country was inevitably defeated. Trotsky heard that his son Sergei had been accused of organizing the mass gassing of workers at a factory in Siberia where he was working and executed. In May, Marshal Mikhail Tukachevsky and five other prominent generals were tried and executed, the beginning of the purge of the army that Trotsky had created. Early in February 1938 Trotsky's son Lyova, who had been working for Trotsky in Paris, was admitted to a hospital for an appendix operation. He died on February 16; poisoning by the GPU has been suspected but not proved.

For Trotsky the horrors in Moscow continued. In March, Bukharin, Rykov, and Krestinsky were arraigned. Bukharin was accused of planning, with Trotsky's assistance, the murder of Lenin in 1918. Genrikh Yagoda, who as head of the GPU had been in charge of the whole apparatus of repression and torture, was also charged with being a tool of Trotsky. Bukharin defended himself bravely; the others confessed to all charges. Eighteen of the accused were shot immediately.

Late in 1938 Trotsky fell out with Diego Rivera and moved to a house in Coyoacán paid for by admirers in New York.

In January 1940 Sylvia Angelof, a New York Trotskyite, arrived to work for the family, bringing with her a man known as Frank Jacson. His real name was Ramon Mercader, and he was the son of a Spanish Communist named Caridad, who was the mistress of a senior GPU official. Mercader had been trained by the GPU and he infiltrated the Trotsky household.

In May there was an armed raid on the house using machine guns and explosives, from which Trotsky and his family escaped uninjured. However, one of the guards, a young American, disappeared with the raiders and was later found shot dead. The affair was hailed by pro-Stalinist factions as a put-up job, but no one was ever charged. Then in August, Jacson/ Mercader, who had been on a trip to New York, suddenly started to take an interest in politics and asked Trotsky to look at an article he had written. He returned on August 20, and while Trotsky was reading the article in his study, he drove an ice pick into his head. Trotsky struggled with him but then fell to the ground. He was rushed to the hospital but died on the evening of August 21. Mercader was tried and sentenced to 20 years. In 1960 he was released and was made a Hero of the Soviet Union, and wound up in Czechoslovakia as a radio repair man.

Trotsky's body lay for five days in state and 300,000 people filed past the coffin. A brief note appeared in *Pravda* that said he had been killed by a disillusioned follower.

TSCHAIKOVSKY, see Chaikovsky

TSERETELI, IRAKLY G. 1882–1959

A very active, tall, stylish, and dominating Menshevik from Georgia. He returned from exile in Siberia to become a member of the Petrograd Soviet and minister of posts and telegraphs in the first Provisional Government, up to July 1917. He demanded strong action and called for the disarming of the Bolsheviks. He left the government and moved south to form the Menshevik Georgian government in 1918 and emigrated to France in 1919.

TUKHACHEVSKY, MIKHAIL N. 1893–1937

A czarist Guards officers of noble ancestry. He was made a prisoner of war by the Germans, and escaped through Switzerland in 1917. He joined the Bolsheviks in 1918 and was an early Red Army officer; by May 1918 he was military commissar for the Moscow region. In September he led the successful counterattacks on the Czech Legion at Simbirsk. As an army commander under Mikhail Frunze, he played a leading role in the campaigns of 1919, and his rapid advance beyond the Urals toward Omsk led to the complete rout of Alexander Kolchak's troops. In February 1920 he was in the Caucasus as commander of the Southeast Front, where his organization of the Red Army and his swift advance led to the disintegration of Anton Denikin's army.

With Frunze he began to develop a Marxist "Doctrine of Proletarian War" hostile to the czarist tradition of centralized control, which depended on exploiting partisans and using the maximum offensive mobility possible. In July he had charge of the Western Front against Poland, but the failure to coordinate the armies led to the Red Army's defeat. His study of the campaign laid blame on the lack of command skills in the Southwestern Front, where Stalin preferred to strike independently at Lvov, leaving a gap between the armies that the Poles exploited. Stalin would never forgive him.

Tukhachevsky was the army commander when the Kronstadt revolt was put down in 1921. He held senior army posts and was one of the five officers promoted to marshal in 1935. His modernization and mechanization plans for the Red Army were frustrated by his superior, Kliment Voroshilov, who was Stalin's crony and who still dreamed of cavalry battles. Among his aims was the development of a parachute landing force to drop in advance of the army, though Tukhachevsky saw their role as bringing the oppressed proletariat out in arms against the capitalist oppressors. His outspokenness did not help his reputation among Stalin's friends.

In the purge of the army he was one of the first to be arrested, interrogated, and shot, accused of a conspiracy with Nazi Germany (he had, of course, been involved in the many secret training operations with Germany in the 1920s and 1930s). He was one of the first to have his reputation "rehabilitated" in 1958.

TUPOLEV, ANDREI N. 1888–1972

Aircraft designer. He studied under the pioneer of aircraft design Nikolai Zhukovsky in Moscow, and established an aircraft design bureau in 1916. His rival in design, Nikolai Polikarpov, preferred a small innovative work group, while Tupolev, concentrating on the design and mass production of large multi-engined aircraft, developed a huge, hierarchical organization. Arrested in the purge of 1938 on the ridiculous charge of having sold the plans of the Messerschmitt 109 to the Germans, he continued to work in OGPU detention during the war until he was released and rehabilitated in 1943. His major aircraft designs were the ANT-25, a single-engined monoplane that broke world records for long-range polar flights from the USSR to the United States in 1934, the TU-4 bomber of 1947, copied from U.S. Air Force B-29s that had force-landed in the Soviet Union during the war, and the jet airliners TU-104 and TU-114.

UNGERN-STERNBERG, BARON ROMAN NICOLAUS FEDOROVICH. 1887–1921

A Baltic German baron who, as a former Cossack officer, led White Russian and Mongol forces on the Chinese borders in 1920 with Japanese support. He had a dream of a Greater Mongolia that would liberate Russia from communism (and from Western decadence). He fought his brief war with savagery and sadism. In 1921 he declared himself Emperor of All Russia, but his grandiose, mad schemes collapsed and he was killed by the Red Army.

URITSKI, SEMION PETROVICH. ?–1937

Soviet soldier and intelligence officer. He helped suppress the 1921 Kronstadt rebellion, leading cavalry across the ice. He became head of the 4th bureau, Military Intelligence, in 1935, in succession to General Yan Berzin, and he too was arrested in the Great Purge and shot. But, with Berzin, he was "rehabilitated" in 1964.

USTINOV, DMITRI. 1908–1984

Soviet military leader. He held the rank of marshal as minister of defense, having been a technical specialist in gunnery and military engineering. He reached rank of general, then was minister of the defense industry, 1941–63, and finally Leonid Brezhnev's minister of defense in 1976, after Marshal Andrei Grechko. He also was deputy chairman of Gosplan, 1955–57, chairman of the Dnepropetrovsk ferrous metallurgy industry, 1957–60, and was on the Central Committee from 1966 and a candidate member of the Politburo in 1978.

VALENTINOV (WOTSKY), NIKOLAI. 1879–?

Friend of Lenin, who wrote perceptively about him. His father was a journalist and Nikolai joined the Bolsheviks in 1903. But in 1904 he moved to the Mensheviks and strove to introduce his brand of revisionism. He left Russia for the United States in 1930.

VASILEVSKY, ALEXANDER M. 1895–

Marshal of the Soviet Union. In the czarist army he had risen from a conscript temporary officer to staff captain before joining the Red Army. An early graduate of the General Staff College, in 1941 he was appointed to the Stavka (High Command), heading the operations department, later becoming chief of the General Staff (even though he was for long periods absent with active field commands) and always in close touch with Stalin. Seeing the German advance on Stalingrad he made the overall plan for its defense and took charge of the three Stalingrad fronts in November 1942, which led to the massive German defeat and his promotion to marshal. His final war command was in the north, where he oversaw the armies clearing the Baltic and Prussia. He was then given command of the brief 1945 war against Japan. In 1948 he became chief of the General Staff again and in 1949 minister of defense, replacing Nicholai Bulganin until the death of his

patron, Stalin. He retired from public life.

VLASOV, ANDREI A. 1900–1946

Major-general. Joining the Red Army in 1919, he became a military adviser to Chiang Kai-shek. He served as commander of the 37th Army in the Ukraine and then the 20th Army outside Moscow. A soldier of promise, he was captured with his 2nd Shock Army in June 1942, after it had been overrun during the German advance and was holding out in the forests since March. He was used as a propaganda tool by the Germans. Given the title of chairman of the Committee for the Liberation of the Peoples of Russia in 1944, he raised an army from prison camps to fight on the German side. He surrendered to the Americans in 1945. They handed him back to the Soviets, who hanged him.

VOROSHILOV, KLIMENT E. 1881–1969

Marshal of the Soviet Union. A steel worker and an early member of the Bolsheviks, he was a comrade of Stalin from the civil war, who gave him command of the Soviet troops at Tsaritsyn, although he had no previous military experience. He fought with Stalin on the Southern Front and became a commander in Simeon Budyenny's cavalry. Described by Trotsky as a "hearty and impudent fellow, not overly intellectual but shrewd and unscrupulous," he acquired a reputation among White Army forces for his cruelty and atrocities.

After the civil war Stalin used him as his spokesman on minor military matters, though Voloshilov was known to consult Stalin on even minor military details. During the early thirties the German general Erich von Manstein met him on official liaison visits, and described him as "more of a politician than a soldier." He resisted Mikhail Tukhachevsky's plans to modernize the army. Appointed marshal in 1935, it was he who approved Stalin's liquidation of the rest of the general staff, Tukhachevsky, Vasili Blyukher, and the others. In 1938 he was appointed chairman of the main military council (the RKKA) and in 1941, on the outbreak of war, became a member of the Stavka. In July he was appointed to the State Committee of Defense.

In 1943 with Vyacheslav Molotov he was Stalin's close companion at the Teheran Conference. The British Field Marshal Alan Brooke said of him, "With his squat figure, bluff manner and uncultured speech he seemed a typical Russian peasant." He was also something of a showman, riding out to inspect Cossack troops on a white horse. Ivan Konev said of him, "A man of inexhaustible courage but incapable of understanding modern warfare."

Although a member of the Central Committee from 1921 to 1961 and of the Politburo from 1926 to 1952, by 1948 he had fallen from favor with Stalin, who was toying with the idea, typical of the last years of his rule, that Voroshilov was a British agent and had forbidden him to attend Politburo meetings or to receive any documents. After the death of Stalin in 1953, he was president of the Presidium, nominally president of the USSR, until removed by Nikita Khrushchev in 1958. He was loaded with honors and buried in Red Square.

VOZNESENSKY, NICHOLAS A. 1903–1948

Head of Gosplan during World War II. He recommended allowing the peasants to cultivate their own plots and putting the state retail network at their disposal. He publicly launched the Fifth Five-Year Plan in 1946. He was arrested in 1948 and was shot.

VYSHINSKY, ANDREI. 1883–1954

Stalin's prosecutor in the purge trials. Of Polish extraction he had joined the Social Democrats in 1903 but remained a Menshevik until 1920. Vyshinsky was a lecturer in law at Moscow University and was eventually made rector of the faculty. He became a prosecutor in 1928 and ensured his place in Stalin's favor with the trial of German and Russian engineers accused of sabotage in 1929. As prosecutor general in the Metro-Vickers trial of 1933, on the question of the truth of the charges, he made the classic statement that "We have our own reality," suggesting some special form of Soviet legal truth. He specialized in hurling abuse at the accused: "human garbage," "scum!" or (his favorite) "reptiles!" Among his sneering attacks there was a certain degree of anti-Semitism, when he referred to Jews as "people without a fatherland." He prosecuted Grigory Zinoviev, Lev Kamenev, and 14 others in August 1936 on charges of sedition, and in 1937 Marshal Mikhail Tukhachevsky. In 1938 Nicholas Bukharin, Nikolai Rykov, and Genrikh Yagoda were subjected to his rage and were shot within three days of the trial's end.

Vyshinsky, seen by some contemporary observers as a clear-minded academic, was also the model for Roland Friesler, the hanging judge of the Nazi "People's Courts." In 1940 he was sent to Latvia, recently occupied by the Soviet Union, to introduce Soviet methods of government. In 1947 he succeeded Vyacheslav Molotov as foreign minister and introduced his particular brand of diatribe to the U.N. General Assembly, deliberately alienating the Western democracies. He died in retirement.

WITTE, COUNT SERGEI. 1849–1915

The czarist official who, in October 1905, attempted to establish a constitutional government. He had been in charge of the state's finances and had stabilized them, creating an enormous gold reserve and encouraging foreign enterprise and railroad development, particularly the Trans-Siberian. He negotiated, with the intervention of U. S. president Theodore Roosevelt, the treaty to end the Russo-Japanese war in 1905. He drafted the czar's October Manifesto and became president of the Council of Ministers, the czar's prime minister. He introduced fresh laws to deal with the status of the new Duma, most notoriously Article 87, which allowed the government at any time to declare an emergency and to issue edicts without reference to the Duma.

But however able this masterful, insensitive, and egocentric man was, the left and the right, the liberals and the czar, attacked him and he resigned in May 1906.

WRANGEL, BARON PETER. 1878–1928

White Russian general. This tall, lean czarist general was a baron from an old German Baltic family. As a cavalry officer he had served in the 1905 Russo-Japanese War with distinction and had been commander of the Tsarevich's Own Regiment of Cossacks. In 1914, in World War I, he enhanced his reputation at the early Russian victory of Gumbinnen. In 1918 Wrangel resigned his commission and went to the Crimea, choosing to serve under Anton Denikin. After a series of defeats Wrangel quarreled with Denikin and left Russia, but when Denikin lost the confidence of his fellow generals, they elected Wrangel to succeed as commander-in-chief in April 1920. That month, as the Polish army drove into the Ukraine capturing Kiev, he led his army out of the Crimea and fought until November. Then, driven back to Perekop, he was finally defeated and had to evacuate the remnants of his army—130,000 men in 126 boats—to Turkey. He tried to keep an anti-Bolshevik force in existence, but gave up the attempt in 1925 and left Yugoslavia for Belgium, where he died. He was taken back to Belgrade for burial in the White Russian church there.

YAGODA, GENRIKH. 1891–1938

NKVD head. A Lodz-born son of a chemist, he joined the Red Army and the party. In 1930 he became head of the Labor Camps organization. Vyacheslav Menzhinsky brought him into the NKVD as his prodigy, where he revised the overseas networks and tightened control within the NKVD itself. He took over from Menshinsky in 1934—until he was removed and shot after the first great show trial in 1936. The final irony was that he had gathered the evidence against those shot with him.

YAKOVLEV, ALEXANDER S. 1906–1989

A leading aircraft designer of the Soviet Union. He was born in Moscow and trained at the Zhukavosky Aircraft Engineering Academy. He started by designing gliders, but in 1927 his AIR-1 appeared (at first to a chorus of suspicion from rivals) to take a world record by flying the 1,300 kilometers from Sevastopol to Moscow in 15 hours, 30 minutes. He graduated from the academy in 1931, first joining the Polikarpov Bureau, but then in 1937 setting up his own aircraft design bureau in Moscow.

In 1938 he designed the AIR-22 high-speed reconnaissance aircraft that, after modification, was picked to be put into mass production in 1939; Yakovlev was awarded the Order of Lenin and a premium of 100,000 rubles. He was ordered by Stalin to produce a prototype of a interceptor fighter within six months and did so. This was the YAK-1, manufactured with a wooden wing and steel tubular body, his motto being "simplicity, not primitiveness." The plane carried a 20 mm cannon and two 7.62 mm machine guns, and had an excellent performance comparable to the Spitfire or the Messerschmitt BF-109. It was succeeded by modified versions, the YAK-3, -7, and -9.

In 1940 Yakovlev was made deputy people's commissar of the aircraft industry. His later successful designs included the YAK-15, the first Soviet jet fighter, and in 1958 the YAK-28, the first supersonic tactical bomber. During his life he supervised the design and production of 75 aircraft types, including, from 1944, helicopters, trainers, and a vertical take-off and landing plane. His last plane was the commercial YAK-42, which entered Aeroflot service in 1980.

Yakolev was awarded numerous decorations, including eight Orders of Lenin; in 1972 he received the Lenin Prize. In 1974 he was made a member of the French Légion d'Honneur.

YAZOV, DIMITRI. 1923–

Soviet military leader. An infantry officer during the war, he started with officer cadet training and rose to second in command of a company by 1945. He worked his way up, attending the Frunze Military Academy in 1956 and the General Staff Academy in 1967. He became a divisional, corps, and then army commander in 1974, with command of the Central Asian and Far Eastern Military Districts in 1980. Associated with Mikhail Gorbachev's policies and the withdrawal from Afghanistan, he became a candidate member of the Politburo and minister of defense in 1988.

YELTSIN, BORIS N. 1931–

An "anti-establishment radical." An engineer, graduate of Sverdlovsk, he was first secretary in the Sverdlovsk Oblast from 1976 to 1985. He was transferred to Moscow as Central Committee department head for construction in 1985. In 1986 he went into the Politburo as a follower of Andrei Kirilenko and was taken over by Yuri Andropov. He became Moscow party secretary, but was removed in 1987 after a conflict with more conservative elements. Yegor Ligachev attacked his reforms at the party conference in July, but Mikhail Gorbachev allowed Yeltsin to speak. For the 1989 elections to the new congress, he preferred to stand for the Moscow constituency in opposition to the manager of the Zil limousine factory, rather than his old power-base Sverdlovsk, and was elected with a triumphant majority.

In 1990, Yeltsin was elected president of the Russian Soviet Federated Socialist Republic. At the 28th Party Congress in July, he announced his resignation from the Communist Party.

YEZHOV, NIKOLAI I. 1895–1939?

NKVD head. A St. Petersburg metal worker, he joined the party in 1917 and was with the Red Army until 1921, then filled party posts in various parts of the Soviet Union. In 1927 he became a member of the Central Committee, having responsibilities in 1929–30 for the "liquidation of the kulaks as a class." He was at the 17th Party Congress; in charge of its industrial department, he became secretary of the Central Committee and chairman of the Central Control Commission of the party in 1935, rooting out corruption and red tape. He followed Genrikh Yagoda as head of the NKVD in 1936. On Stalin's orders he launched the terrible purges. Nicknamed "the Iron Commissar" by some and "the Dwarf" by others, he gave the Terror its name Yezhovshchina. In 1938 he was abruptly removed from his post and made commissar for water transport, then arrested. He was, presumably, shot by his former employees. He had moved his way up steadily, showing no sign of viciousness—only loyalty to the party and a Spartan discipline. Yezhov always wore a simple tunic and kept his head shaved in the civil war style.

YUDENICH, NICHOLAS N. 1862–1933

General of the White Army, in command of the Baltic area. With British advisers, he moved from Estonia to Petrograd, whose suburbs he reached in September 1919. The Petrograd Red Guards defeated him, and he retreated as his army disintegrated. He left Russia immediately and went into exile.

ZASULICH, VERA IVANOVNA. 1849–1918

A girl student who, as an ardent admirer of Sergei Nechaev, was used by him to spread the rumor of his great conspiracies. She shot at General Trepov, the military governor of St. Petersburg, was tried, acquitted, and became an exile and an internationally known revolutionary heroine. With Georgy Plekhanov she was the founder of the "Group for the Emancipation of Labor." Lenin met her in Geneva in 1900, where she lived with Yuli Martov, a fellow socialist. She was a co-editor of *Iskra* and worked with the Bolsheviks in their founding days.

ZHDANOV, ANDREI A. 1896–1948

Communist party zealot. He was made secretary of the Leningrad party after the assassination of Sergei Kirov in 1934, and led Stalin's witch-hunt there. As secretary to the Central Committee, he was marked by his adherence to a strict party line and his extreme nationalism, which manifested itself in his antagonism to any Western influence in art or literature. Although he was crudely dictatorial in his methods, he favored a decentralization of authority. After Zhdanov's death in 1948 Stalin became convinced that he had been murdered and a number of Jewish doctors were arrested in 1953 in an episode which later became known as the "Doctors' Plot"; they were released after Stalin died.

ZHUKOV, GEORGI K. 1896–1974

Marshal of the Soviet Union. Mobilized into the cavalry in 1915, he became a much-decorated noncommissioned officer. He joined the Red Army cavalry in August 1918, and was wounded at Tsaritsyn in 1919. After officer training, he fought against Baron Peter Wrangel as a lieutenant in 1920 and from 1920 to 1923 in actions against kulaks. He had senior officer training at the Frunze Military Academy in 1929–30, becoming assistant inspector of cavalry and in 1933 taking command of the 4th Cavalry Division. In 1936 or 1937 he was in Spain, returning in 1937 as commander of the 3rd and 6th Cavalry Corps. In June 1939 he had command of Soviet-Mongolian troops; His August offensive against the Japanese ended in victory.

In Autumn 1939 he was deputy commander of the Ukrainian Military District, then in June 1940 he was commander of the Kiev Special Military District and led troops into Rumanian Bessarabia. From January 1941 he was chief of the General Staff, becoming in March commissar of defense. From July, after the German attack, he took command of the reserve army; in September, of Leningrad; and in October, of Moscow. In February 1942 he had the Western Army Group, then promoted to marshal in January 1943. He led the Red Army in its advance into Germany and received the German surrender in Berlin in 1945.

After the war, Zhukov, although a popular hero, was given a remote posting by Stalin. However, in 1955 Nikita Khrushchev showed his gratitude for his support by making him minister of defense, only to sack him in 1957. Leonid Brezhnev rehabilitated his reputation in 1964, honoring him with the Order of Lenin, but gave him no further employment.

ZHUKOVSKI, NIKOLAI. 1847–1921

The "Father of Russian Aviation." A lecturer in mechanical engineering in the Moscow Higher Technical College, he had studied the theory of flight and had already set up an aerodynamic laboratory before the Wright brothers' first flight. With Andrei Tupolev he worked on designing a bomber for the Red Army. Although this project was a failure, his work team was the foundation for the Soviet's future in aircraft design.

ZINOVIEV (RADOMISLSKY, BORN HIRSCH APFELBAUM), GRIGORY. 1883–1936

Soviet leader. From southern Russia, he was a Social Democrat in 1901. He was a member of the Bolshevik Central Committee, 1907–1927, and was close to Lenin in exile, from 1907. He returned with Lenin in April 1917, but opposed his call for an armed rising. He was head of the party's Petrograd organization, 1918–1926, and head of the Third International, or the Comintern, 1919–1926. In 1924 a letter in his name, addressed to the British Communist party and purporting to be a secret directive from the Comintern, was published. It was a forgery but the effect was to destroy the reputation of the Labor party then in power in Britain. After Lenin's death, with Lev Kamenev and Stalin, he formed a triumvirate but was soon allied with Leon Trotsky and Lev Kamenev against Stalin, as a leader of the United Opposition, 1926–1927. He was expelled from the party for this, but after admitting his errors he was readmitted in 1928 but finally expelled again in 1932. He was arrested in 1934 and accused of complicity in the murder of Sergei Kirov, tried in 1935, and given a jail sentence. He was tried again in August 1936 and executed. His sentence was annulled by the Soviet Supreme Court in June 1988.

PART THREE

CHRONOLOGY

Note: *Dates are given in old style (13 days' difference) up to February 14, 1918. Imperial Russia adopted the Julian calendar in 1700, just as the rest of Europe was abandoning it in favor of the Gregorian calendar. The Bolsheviks joined the rest of the Western World in 1918.*

1905

The Russian Empire is at war with Japan. In 1896 the Russians had arranged a treaty with the Chinese Empire to run the Trans-Siberian railway through Manchuria to Vladivostok, in return for guaranteeing China's territorial integrity and paying off its debt to Japan. Russia now comes into conflict with Japan over its interests in Korea and Port Arthur. The Imperial Russian army and navy are incompetent in the face of the Japanese forces.

January 1—The surrender of Port Arthur by the Russians to the Japanese is announced, and popular discontent with the war breaks out.

January 22—"Bloody Sunday": Russian Orthodox priest Father Georgy Gapon, organizer of a workers' union but also associated with the police, leads a march to the czar's Winter Palace in St. Petersburg to present a petition. Troops, called in anticipation of trouble, open fire on the marchers, killing about 150. The reaction to the massacre is a general strike.

February 17—Grand Duke Sergei, governor of Moscow and uncle of the czar, is killed in the Kremlin by a bomb planted by the "combat section" of the Socialist Revolutionary party.

March 1–9—The Japanese army routs the Russians at the Battle of Mukden.

March 29–30—The police discover the "combat section's" dynamite store in St. Petersburg and arrest most of the group's members.

April–May—The Third Congress of the Social Democratic party is held in London, including only Bolsheviks; the Mensheviks hold their congress in Vienna.

May 2—Striking workers at a large textile mill in St. Petersburg elect a group of workers to carry their demands to the owners. It is the first of the worker's soviets, a pattern which will spread.

May 27—The Battle of Tsushima: the Imperial Russian fleet, having sailed from the Baltic around South Africa and across the Indian Ocean, meets the Japanese fleet and is mostly destroyed in forty-five minutes' action in the Sea of Japan.

June—There are general strikes in Odessa and other major cities.

Soviets (councils) are organized in cities and, after the harvest, with the help of Socialist Revolutionaries, peasant "republics" are declared in the countryside. The landlords are moved off their estates and their houses often burned.

June 14—The crew of the battleship *Potemkin*, of the Black Sea fleet, mutinies, kills many of the officers, and sails from port, shelling Odessa before taking refuge in Rumania.

August 29—The Treaty of Portsmouth (New Hampshire), after mediation involving U.S. President Theodore Roosevelt and negotiations between the czar's prime minister, Count Sergei Witte, ends the war with Japan, with Russia giving up Port Arthur, all claims on Korea, half the island of Sakhalin, and the southern half of Manchuria. These losses are a scar on Russia's memory for 50 years.

October—A railway strike throughout the empire is called by the large and effective workers' union. To end the chaos, trains are sent from east and west of the Trans-Siberian Railway, with officers and soldiers ordered to disarm and execute mutinous troops who join the strikers.

October 7—A soviet is set up in Petrograd to coordinate the workers' strikes. The Socialist Revolutionaries and Social Democrats dominate, and Trotsky, a Menshevik, is a leading figure. The movement lasts 50 days before it is suppressed.

October 17—The czar issues a manifesto, declaring an amnesty and agreeing to a popularly elected Duma (parliament). Freedom of the press, free speech, and religious toleration are also promised. Under the amnesty many political prisoners are released, including those arrested in March. The October Manifesto is drafted by Prime Minister Witte.

The Duma will not be able to control the army or navy, or get foreign loans; under the new Article 87 of the fundamental laws, the czar's government can make any laws it likes if it deems the situation an emergency. The State Soviet, a council of ministers made up of nominated members, officials, and others from zemstvos (county councils), universities, the church, and so on, is changed into an upper house, to balance the elected Duma and to join in passing or rejecting its proposals.

October—The Constitutional Democratic (Kadet) party is formed from zemstvo unions and illegal liberal organizations. It had been founded in Stuttgart in 1902 as the Liberation party, now a middle-class liberal faction that believes the revolution has been achieved. The Kadets see a democratic parliamentary future ahead, with liberal capitalist economic policies; they will oppose the 1917 October Revolution. In 1905, led by Pavel Milyukov, they demand free elections for a national assembly.

November—The St. Petersburg Soviet calls for a general strike, but does not meet with total success.

The moderate Octobrist party is formed by Alexander Guchkov to ensure success of the Duma and continuation of the czarist regime. The party represents large commercial interests and supports the czar's October Manifesto, and will become a majority constituent of the Third and Fourth Dumas.

November 1—The religious mystic Gregori Rasputin comes to stay in the czar's household, holding the tsarina, fearful for her hemophiliac son, under his influence.

November 8—Lenin arrives in St. Petersburg, and calls for a general strike but there is little response.

December 3—The government feels strong enough to break up the St. Petersburg Soviet and arrest the leaders. Leon Trotsky is sentenced to exile but he escapes.

December 9–19—The Moscow Soviet, where Trotsky is a leader, encourages workers in a strike, leading to rioting and brutal army suppression.

December—First Conference of Social Democratic party is held at Tammerfors.

1906

January—The army makes punitive expeditions against uprisings, particularly in the Baltic provinces, where the Letts and Estonians have attacked their German landlords. Hundreds, probably thousands, of executions are carried out.

April—The First Duma is elected. The

Socialist Revolutionaries (SRs) have large numbers elected under the name of a Peasants' Union (since many of the SRs themselves are hunted by the police). The Bolshevik Social Democrats boycott the elections while the Mensheviks have success among the factory workers, but the Kadets are the dominant party.

The Duma presents its proposals to the czar, but there is doubt that it has any constitutional right, including for land reform. One of the czar's ministers lectures the members on their inadmissible demands and the Duma passes a vote of censure. There being no constitutional precedent, the ministers do not resign.

Fourth Congress of the Social Democratic party (known as the "Unity Congress") is held in Stockholm. There is a Menshevik majority.

July 20—When the Duma, frustrated by the government's refusal to consider its land reforms, decides to appeal to the people, it is dissolved and Peter Stolypin is appointed prime minister. Stolypin uses Article 87 to rule, setting up court-martials that deal out death sentences. He also uses his powers to give all (male) peasants voting rights.

August 25—A bomb attempt by the Socialist Revolutionaries' "combat section" on Stolypin's house fails, but severely injures his daughters. From then on he lives as a guest of the czar in the Winter Palace.

November 9—Stolypin, aiming to build peasant support, gives them the right to claim parts of common village land. Later the Bolsheviks will claim that the number of kulaks is being deliberately increased and encouraged.

November—Second conference of Social Democratic party (the first All-Russian) is held at Tammerfors.

1907

January—Lenin moves to Finland.

March 5—The Second Duma is elected and meets with many of the same members. The Kadets continue to dominate but there are nine party groupings. The Socialist Revolutionaries enter under their own party name and the Social Democrats have both Menshevik and Bolshevik deputies.

A new small group is the Union of the Russian People, established in 1905. It is avowedly nationalistic, monarchist, and anti-Semitic, and the open front for the Black Hundreds, led by Vladimir Purishkevich.

April–May—The Fifth Congress of the Social Democratic party is held in London with over 300 attending, 105 of whom are Bolsheviks, 97 are Mensheviks, and the remainder are from other organizations, including the Jewish Bund.

June 3—The Second Duma is dissolved after an Imperial manifesto accuses it of having plotted against the czar. There had been two attempts by the Okhrana (czarist secret police) to implicate Socialist Revolutionaries and Social Democrats in acts of treason. The 65 Social Democratic deputies are arrested and exiled to Siberia.

June 16—A new electorate law restricts suffrage to landowners and the professional classes.

The Third Duma is predominantly right of center with Alexander Guchkov of the Octobrists leading the largest party, 153 deputies, and a stronger right-wing representation of 50 representatives from the Union of the Russian People and 89 nationalists. Of 442 deputies, only 54 were Kadets, 20 were Social Democrats, and 13 were Socialist Revolutionaries, with 18 Polish deputies and others of minority interests.

July–August—Third Conference of Social Democratic party is held at Korka in Finland.

November—Fourth conference of Social Democratic party is held in Helsingfors, in Finland.

1908

The Social Democrats are driven from Russia, some to Western Europe and some to Siberia.

December—Fifth conference of Social Democratic party is held in Paris. The Bolsheviks, led by Lenin, accuse the Mensheviks of failing to follow the policies of the party and of collaborating with the Duma.

1911

August 31—Peter Stolypin, chairman of the Council of Ministers, is shot at a Kiev theatre by Dmitri Bogrov, a revolutionary who also acts as a police agent, and dies a few days later.

1912

January—Sixth Congress of the Social Democratic party is held in Prague. The Bolsheviks constitute a separate party, having split from the Mensheviks and elected a Central Committee. Lenin, Sergo Ordzhonikidze, Yakov Sverdlov, Grigory Zinoviev, and (in his absence) Joseph Stalin are the leading members; they are now the Russian Social Democratic Labor party (Bolshevik).

The Fourth Duma is elected by a narrow franchise, consisting exclusively of substantial property-owning men who in general favor a Western-style parliamentary democracy. The extreme right

despises the plan and the left is represented only by moderates who have avoided exile. Apart from parties representing minorities (Lithuanians, Ukrainians, and 30 Muslims who are aligned with the Kadets), the balance of parties is:

Social Democrats (12 Mensheviks and 6 Bolsheviks)	3%
Trudoviks	2%
Moderate left (Kadets and Progressives)	25%
Octobrists and other centrists	31%
Moderate right and nationalists	21%
Extreme right	15%

April—At the Lena gold fields 2,000 striking workers are fired on by troops and at least 200 are killed. The massacre sparks strikes throughout the empire. Alexander Kerensky is sent by the Duma to the gold fields to investigate.

The newspaper *Pravda* is founded in St. Petersburg as the organ of the Bolsheviks.

1914

May 1—On May Day an estimated half-million workers march in cities across the empire, where 1.25 million people are on strike.

June 15—The heir to the throne of the Austrian Empire, Archduke Francis Ferdinand, and his wife are shot at Sarajevo in Austrian Bosnia. Many are convinced that this is an assassination inspired by Serbia, and Austria demands war against Serbia. There is a chain reaction as nations throughout Europe look to their defenses and allies.

Baku oil workers' strike.

July 13—Warfare breaks out between Austria and Serbia.

In the St. Petersburg general strike,

workers put up barricades against the police.

July 17—The czar decides, after hesitation, to mobilize in view of the Austro-Serbian crisis and in fear of pre-emptive strikes. This continues the chain of military reactions in Europe, compelling Germany toward war.

July 19—Russia and Germany declare war after Russia declines to halt its mobilization.

July 25—Austria declares war on Russia and invades Russian Poland.

August 2—Russian troops invade eastern Prussia and Galicia. The aim is not simply defensive but also to annex "Russian" lands in the Austrian Empire. Troops are also honoring the Russian agreement with France to attack Germany "in the rear."

August 16—Germans defeat and rout the Russian army at Tannenberg and inflict heavy defeats at the Masurian Lakes. But the Austrian reverses in Galicia, where the Russians have captured Lvow, mean that German forces have to be moved to their support.

August 18—The capital of Russia is renamed Petrograd, since "St. Petersburg" sounds German.

October 16—The Black Sea ports of Odessa and Sebastopol are bombarded by the Turkish navy and war with Turkey starts. This closes the Black Sea to Russia, which can now receive munitions only through Murmansk and Archangel or Vladivostok.

November 6—The five Bolshevik members of the Duma are arrested and exiled to Turkestan for urging Russians to fight their government rather than the Germans. The arrests spark protests they had been intended to suppress.

November 10—Although the Russians force the Austrians back in Galicia, the Germans take Lodz. Already the Russian army is running short of guns and munitions.

December—A Turkish army under Enver Pasha invades the Caucasus, intending to raise a revolt there. It is heavily defeated by the Russians at Sarikamis.

1915

January—Enver Pasha, left with one-seventh of his army, falls back to re-form.

Two hundred Finns, with an independent Finland in mind, go for military training in Germany. In May 1916 they became the 27 Königliche Preussische Jäger battalion, which grows to about 2,000 men, and are sent to the German Eastern Front near Riga.

February—The Russian 10th Army is encircled by the Germans at Masuria, while the Austrian attacks in the Carpathians collapse.

March—In counterattacks against the Austrians, the Russians take Przemysl in Galicia, with 120,000 Austrian prisoners.

April 24—Thousands of Armenians living near the Russian border are killed by the Turks in preventive measures. Officials and teachers are particular targets.

May—Austro-German offensive defeats Russians in Galicia, forcing a retreat.

July—A further offensive toward Russian Poland leads to over a million Russian casualties.

July 20—The All-Russian Union of Zemstvos for the Relief of Sick and Wounded Soldiers is formed; it coordinates the supply of necessary resources and helps with hospitals and supplies. Its chairman is Prince Georgy Lvov. This network of voluntary organizations and local committees becomes a focus of criticism regarding the government's conduct of the war.

July 22—The Germans take Warsaw.

August 1—The Duma, with strong feelings on the conduct of the war, meets and proposes the creation of a defense council.

August 22—The leaders of the Duma's central and liberal groups meet and form a Progressive Bloc. They call for a "government of confidence."

August 23—The czar assumes command of the armies, moving to the Stavka (Army Supreme Headquarters), leaving palace politics in the hands of the empress and the notorious, unpopular Rasputin. His move is against the advice of the Progressive Bloc and the Council of Ministers.

The czar appoints the commander of the Northwest Front, General Mikhail Alekseev, his chief of staff. The Russian army has retreated 125 miles east of Warsaw.

September 8—The Progressive Bloc puts forward a reform program calling for an end to religious and racial discrimination, the lifting of restrictions on trade unions, and amnesty for political offenders.

September 15—In the face of Russian defeats, the All-Russian Union of Zemstvos and industrialists call for a reorganization of the war effort. The Progressive Bloc in the Duma presents its case but the czar responds by dismissing the ministers who show sympathy with the bloc.

September 16—Czar discontinues the meetings of the Duma. The socialist conference in Zimmerwald, Switzerland, calls for the end of the imperialist war. Lenin and the Bolsheviks form an international committee (the nucleus of the Third International) and, in contrast to the Mensheviks of Martov, want the war to be turned into a civil war in which the workers will seize power.

1916

February—An attack on the German Front fails with a costly retreat, but it succeeds in taking pressure off the French on the Western Front.

April—Russian troops push through Turkish Armenia to Trebizond.

A socialist conference is held at Kienthal, Switzerland.

June 4–October—The Brusilov offensive (the only offensive of World War I to be named after its commander, Alexei Brusilov) gains some territory south of the Pripet Marshes, crossing the Dniester River and taking half a million Austrian prisoners, but it results in a further million Russian casualties. Pressure on the French at Verdun is relieved, and Rumania comes into the war on the side of the Allies.

June 25—Decrees for a military callup of non-Russian peoples, previously exempt, causes resentment, anger, and revolt in Russian Asia. In Turkestan and Kazakhstan many thousands of people are killed in riots.

September–October—The food shortages and heavy war casualties lead to strikes in Russian cities and mutinies by soldiers at the front. Proposals to conscript soldiers in Russian Central Asia cause a revolt among the Kazakhs and Kirghiz that is suppressed, but some of the rebels take to the hills and, in rebellion against Russian rule, form a basis for the future anti-Bolshevik Basmachis. It is those people that the revolutionaries of 1917 mistakenly expect to join their cause.

November—Admiral Alexander Kolchak's mining of the Bosphorus Sea blocks Turkish trade and regains control of the Black Sea for Russia.

December 31—Rasputin is murdered

by aristocrats in the Winter Palace. His influence over the empress was suspected of being evil and pro-German.

By now, 14.6 million Russians have been put in uniform; 6.9 million of them in the field, 2 million in the rear, and the remaining 5.5 million wounded, prisoners, or dead. There are also 60,000 Russian troops assisting French armies in France and Salonika who will hear of the 1917 Revolution only through French newspapers.

1917

January 9—Some 300,000 workers stage a strike in Petrograd commemorating "Bloody Sunday" of 1905.

February 14—The Duma meets and the Progressive Bloc calls, unsuccessfully, for a government that will have national confidence.

February 22—With severe food shortages and an atmosphere of revolt, there are riots in Petrograd. Police fire on the crowds.

February 23—On International Women's Day, women from textile factories go to the streets calling for bread, bringing others to join them, some 50,000 in all. The Cossacks show a reluctance to charge the crowds. The next day nearly 200,000 take to the streets. Although they are dispersed, the hesitancy of the Cossacks is noticed.

February 25—Soldiers start to join the strikers and demonstrators; the czar orders suppression of the trouble.

February 26—More soldiers mutiny and join the people, providing weapons for the demonstrators. The czar suspends the sitting of the Duma.

February 27—Prince Golitsyn, chairman of the Council of Ministers, and all members of the cabinet resign. The Progressive Bloc forms a Provisional Committee of the Duma and proclaims that, as a committee of state, it has replaced the czarist government and has taken responsibility for national and public order.

The Petrograd Soviet of Workers' and Soldiers' Deputies is formed with Nikolai Chkheidze, the leader of the Mensheviks in the Duma, as chairman. It is an informal body of between 2,000 and 3,000 members, modeled on the 1905 Soviet and occupying part of the same building, the Tauride Palace, as the Duma. The most dominant person is Irakly Tsereteli, a Menshevik.

February 28—*Isvestia* calls on people to take power. Czar Nicholas leaves the Stavka (Army Supreme Headquarters) to join his wife and family at Tsarskoye Selo.

March 1—The Petrograd Soviet declares the army under its control, and in Order No. 1 calls for soldiers' soviets, thus removing the authority of officers over men. The order is circulated throughout the army although it is intended for Petrograd only.

March 2—A Provisional Government is agreed upon between the Provisional Committee and the Petrograd Soviet. It puts Prince Georgy Lvov at its head as prime minister and commissars are to replace the ministers, most of whom are arrested. The Ministry of Foreign Affairs is under Pavel Milyukov, War under Alexander Guchkov, and Justice under Alexander Kerensky. Czar Nicholas II abdicates in favor of his brother, Grand Duke Michael, and confirms the new government. He and his family are in Tsarskoye Selo, effectively as prisoners.

March 3—Grand Duke Michael refuses to become czar.

March 4—The Ukrainian Rada (council) is established in Kiev, mainly by socialists.

March 11—Grand Duke Michael is removed from his post as commander-in-chief and replaced by General Mikhail Alekseev.

March 12—The Provisional Government abolishes the death penalty in the army.

April 3—Lenin returns from exile to Petrograd via the "sealed train." He is met at the Finland Station by Nikolai Chkheidze, the Menshevik president of the Petrograd Soviet, as a matter of courtesy.

April 7—Alexei Kuropatkin, the governor-general of Turkestan, is arrested and a Turkestan Committee of the Provisional Government is organized.

An All-Russian Congress of Soviets votes to continue the war; the Bolsheviks, led by Joseph Stalin and Lev Kamenev of the Petrograd Soviet, press for the Provisional Government to open peace negotiations, but Lenin opposes this. Lenin argues in favor of no support for the government in any way, and that there can be no peace without the overthrow of capitalism. This, his April Theses, becomes Bolshevik policy.

First Kazakh conference, nationalist and anti-Russian, is held at Orenburg.

April 16–23—A congress of Muslims of Turkestan makes nationalist resolutions, but no action is proposed.

April 24—Seventh conference of (Bolshevik) Social Democratic party meets, for the first time openly, in Petrograd. Lenin elaborates on his April Theses.

May—Meeting of the First All-Russian Congress of Peasant Deputies, with 1,350 elected deputies.

May 3–5—Petrograd troops mutiny against prowar ministers Guchkov and Milyukov, who resign from the govern-

ment. Lavr Kornilov resigns his command in Petrograd.

May 5—A revised government under Prince Georgy Lvov includes socialists and Kerensky becomes minister of war.

May 22—General Alexei Brusilov is appointed commander-in-chief replacing Mikhail Alekseev, who reverts to his post as chief of staff in order to launch an offensive against the Germans.

June—First All-Russian Congress of Soviets is held. In Tiflis, where there are Socialist Revolutionary and Menshevik factions formally united but rivaling each other, Bolsheviks are elected to the Soviet.

The Ukrainian Rada sets up a General Secretariat, which assumes some of the functions of government.

June 10—The Bolshevik Central Committee calls for street demonstrations, but these are forestalled by Nikolai Chkheidze's warnings and abandoned. Irakly Tsereteli calls for disarmament of the Red Guards but he is overruled.

June 18–26—An offensive on the Southern Front with 44 divisions is opened by General Alexei Brusilov, with initial success. However, it results in losses of 60,000 men and further mutinies. Lavr Kornilov insists on an end to the offensive and is made commander-in-chief replacing Brusilov.

June 18—Menshevik and Socialist Revolutionary leaders at the first All-Russian Congress of Soviets call for demonstrations in support of the offensive, but the demonstrators, with Bolshevik organization, show hostility to the war.

June 19—A general congress (the Krug) of the Don Cossacks, held in Petrograd, elects General Alexei Kaledin as ataman.

July—The czar and his family are moved to Tobolsk.

July 2—Kadet (Constitutional Democrats) ministers resign when the Provisional Government proposes to deal with the Ukrainian Rada. They see it as a movement to separate the Ukraine from Russia.

July 3—The July Days. Over 30,000 soldiers, sailors from Kronstadt, and workers demonstrate in Petrograd against the war to protest low wages and to show their hatred of the government. They are called out by the Bolsheviks with the slogan "All power to the Soviets." But the march is led by Left Socialist Revolutionary Maria Spiridonova, and the Bolsheviks are not in control. Although there are rank and file Bolsheviks marching, Lenin and the Bolshevik leadership think it premature. Trotsky tries in vain to stop them, but the workers are dispersed by troops loyal to the Provisional Government.

July 4—After the further disorder, the Provisional Government issues warrants for the arrest of leading Bolsheviks, partly on the grounds of their supposed support from Germany. Lenin flees to Finland, where he has friends.

July 9—Prince Georgy Lvov resigns, and Alexander Kerensky becomes prime minister and forms a new government.

July 12—The Provisional Government, at the demand of Lavr Kornilov, reintroduces capital punishment and court-martials for the army.

July 18—Kornilov is appointed commander-in-chief to replace Alexei Brusilov.

July 21–26—A second Kazakh conference is held in Orenburg, but its anti-Russian nationalism still attracts only narrow support.

July 26–August 3—The Sixth (Bolshevik) Party Congress, with Lenin still in Finland, decides that any possibility of transfer of power to the soviets is now

impossible and that a "revolutionary proletariat" must seize power when possible.

August 3—Alexander Kerensky resigns, but forms a new government.

August 5—In Belorussia a rada (council) is formed with a largely Socialist Revolutionary policy; it hopes to become something like an autonomous republic under the Petrograd Provisional Government.

August 12–15—Kerensky holds a state conference in Moscow to settle differences among the moderate left, the center, and the right; Nikolai Chkheidze and Irakly Tsereteli support him. Kornilov comes and is greeted as a hero, demanding greater powers to control anarchy.

August 21—The Russian army of the Baltic is broken and Riga falls to the Germans. The Petrograd Military District is put under Kornilov's command.

August 27–29—The "Kornilov affair": Kerensky suspects that troops moving toward Petrograd have been sent to instigate a coup d'état. The reason for the move remains obscure, but Kerensky orders the arrest of Kornilov and other generals. Kornilov claims he is acting in the defense of the Russian people, with no political ambition. As Kornilov's cavalry approaches Petrograd, the workers in the city see the Red Guards as their defense against the military counterrevolution. Kerensky assumes the position of commander-in-chief of the Russian army.

August 31—A majority of the Petrograd Soviet votes with the Bolsheviks.

September 1—Kornilov submits to arrest. With other generals he is moved to detention in Bykhov.

September 5—Moscow Soviet now has a majority voting with the Bolsheviks, and elsewhere Bolshevik groups are taking control of towns such as Tsaritsyn.

September 9—General Mikhail Alekseev resigns as chief of staff to protest treatment of Kornilov.

September 12—In Tashkent, Bolsheviks and Socialist Revolutionaries attempt to take over the Provisional Government.

September 20—A Southeastern Union of Cossacks is declared, pledging the independence of the various Cossack groups and hostility to the Bolsheviks.

September 21—The Bolshevik Central Committee decides to take part in Kerensky's Pre-Parliament.

September 25—Trotsky becomes chairman of the Petrograd Soviet Presidium, which now has a Bolshevik majority among the soldiers' delegates.

October 6—The Duma and State Council are formally dissolved. The Kuban Rada declares its independent existence.

October 7—Kerensky organizes a Pre-Parliament in anticipation of the elected Constituent Assembly due in November. The Pre-Parliament meets but owing to a lack of purpose, produces no effective action. In Petrograd the Bolsheviks collaborate with it; however, Lenin, from Finland, urges them not to do so but to aim to seize power.

October 10—Lenin, clandestinely in Petrograd at a meeting of the party's Central Committee, wins over the majority to his policy of taking power since now, unlike in July, the Bolsheviks have a majority. Lev Kamenev and Grigory Zinoviev still hope for a parliamentary victory, but the Central Committee approves of an insurrection in principle.

October 20—Although he is aware of the Bolsheviks' preparations, Kerensky does not order defensive preparations; he probably believes his troops are adequate.

The Bolsheviks set up a Military Revolutionary Committee organized by Trotsky, with commissars appointed to military units. They will issue orders and control stores of ammunition. There are 20,000 Red Guards, 60,000 Baltic sailors, and 150,000 soldiers of the Petrograd garrison under its control.

October 23–25—An armed uprising is called by the Military Revolutionary Committee. Red Guard detachments occupy, without bloodshed, key points in Petrograd: the telephone exchange, the post office, the railway stations. At the call of the committee, some 5,000 sailors and soldiers from Kronstadt land in the city and a further 3,000 arrive in the next four days.

The Winter Palace, where the government is in session, is threatened by the guns of the cruiser *Aurora* and the Peter and Paul fortress, which is used as military headquarters of the Military Revolutionary Committee. Red Guards, soldiers, and sailors surround the palace, which, after a little resistence, surrenders. The ministers are taken into custody but Kerensky has already left, looking in vain for military support.

Petrograd remains outwardly calm, with restaurants and theatres open: Feodor Chaliapin sings *Boris Gudunov* at the opera.

October 25—The second All-Russian Congress of Soviets opens with a Social Democrat (but not Bolshevik) majority.

A Don Cossack state is proclaimed by Ataman Alexei Kaledin. It boycotts the congress on the ground that the Provisional Government is the only valid authority.

October 26—The All-Russian Committee for the Salvation of the Country and the Revolution is set up by the Presidium of the Pre-Parliament. On it are Mensheviks, Socialist Revolutionaries, and others, including representatives from the trade unions.

The Congress of Soviets elects a Sovnarkom (Council of People's Commissars), with Lenin as its head and including Stalin as commissar for nationalities. All the members are Bolsheviks, although they are later joined by Left Socialist Revolutionaries. It becomes the effective, decision-making body ruling the nation.

October 27—The third All-Russian Congress of Soviets issues two decrees: (1) Decree of Peace calls for an immediate just peace without indemnities; neither the Western Allies nor the Central Powers take notice of this; (2) Decree of Land declares all land the property of the people, to be redistributed by village soviets. This is Socialist Revolutionary rather than Bolshevik policy and, although it has popular appeal, it tends to increase the proprietorial instincts of the peasants. Promulgated on the 57th anniversary of Czar Alexander's decree emancipating the serfs, one of its clauses defines the object of a socialist agricultural program to develop the collective system of agriculture, because it is more economical with respect to both labor and products at the expense of individual holdings.

October 29—Officer cadets, under orders from the Committee of Salvation, attempt a counter-uprising, but it fails with heavy casualties.

Kerensky is in Pskov to raise an anti-Bolshevik force.

October 30—Cossack troops are defeated in an attempt to move into Petrograd by a force of sailors, workers, and Red Guards.

November 1—In the city of Tashkent, Bolsheviks and Socialist Revolutionar-

ies regain control; there are no Muslims among them.

November 2—Ataman Alexei Kaledin assembles an anti-Bolshevik army of Don Cossacks under the command of General Mikhail Alekseev. This is the first White Army of the Don.

Decree on the rights of nationalities is issued by the Petrograd Soviet.

Transcaucasian Commissariat is declared by the separatist Musavat party in Azerbaijan.

November 3—Bolsheviks, with 30,000 Red Guards, take power in Moscow after several days of fighting and after reinforcements arrive from Petrograd. The majority of the troops stay neutral.

November 6—The Ukrainian Rada declares an independent republic and groups all soldiers of Ukrainian origin as an army. The rada takes repressive measures against the Bolsheviks.

November 10—The second All-Russian Congress of Peasant Deputies meets in Petrograd. The delegates are equally socialist Revolutionaries (led by Viktor Chernov) and Bolshevik, combined with the Left Socialist Revolutionaries (led by Maria Spiridonova). Spiridonova is elected chair rather than the popular Chernov by the soldiers' deputies because they hate the war and Chernov's "Defensist" position. The congress breaks up and many of the Socialist Revolutionaries leave Petrograd; Chernov goes to Samara and later to Ufa.

November 12—Elections to the Constituent Assembly are held; the Bolsheviks had promised to ensure this; 41 million votes were recorded:*

Socialist Revolutionaries	370 seats
Bolsheviks	175
Left Socialist Revolutionaries	40

Mensheviks	16
Kadets (Constitutional Democrats)	17
Other minority national groups	89
	707

*(These figures are from Soviet sources: Socialist Revolutionary historians differ slightly.)

November 13—A Tatar Constituent Assembly assumes authority in the Crimea, led by the Tatar National party and the Kadets.

November 15—Estonia proclaims its sovereignty.

In Belorussia, an armored train and troops from Petrograd arrive and a Bolshevik coup d'état succeeds. The rada acquiesces, and Bolshevik rule is established.

November 20—Ensign Nikolai Krylenko, a young Bolshevik soldier and lawyer nominated to take command of the army, arrives at the Stavka (High Command) in Mogilev and arrests the general staff of the army and shoots General N. N. Dukhonin, the acting commander-in-chief, when he refuses to start armistice negotiations with the Germans. Negotiations with Germany start toward an armistice.

November 21—Felix Dzerzhinsky sets up the Special Commission for the Struggle Against Counter-Revolution and Sabotage (Cheka) in the offices of a former insurance company in Lubyanka Street, Moscow. It is directly under the authority of the Sovnarkom (Council of People's Commissars).

November 22—The All-Turkestan Muslim Congress at Kokand declares autonomy for South Central Asia.

November 23—Led by nationalists re-

sisting Russification, Finland proclaims independence.

November 26—Eight Socialist Revolutionaries join the Sovnarkom with the Bolsheviks.

November 28—The old Provisional Government, now in hiding, calls the Constituent Assembly to meet.

December 2—Agreement on an armistice with Germany is reached.

December 3—Bolsheviks occupy the Stavka at Mogilev. An appeal to Muslim workers of Russia and the East is issued by Lenin, but without noticeable effect.

December 2–3 and December 5–13—The third and fourth Kazakh conferences are held at Orenburg, under the protection of the Cossack general Alexander Dutov. He uses the conferences to take Orenburg for the anti-Bolshevik cause. The conferences again fail to attract support for Kazahk rights.

December 6—Kornilov and the generals escape from detention in Bykhov and, singly, reach the Don headquarters of the Volunteer Army, commanded by General Alekseev.

December 9—Russo-German negotiations for a peace treaty start at Brest-Litovsk.

December 18—The Volunteer Army agrees to the military command of Kornilov, but politically relations with both civil authorities and foreign powers are to be under Alekseev.

1918

January 5–6—The Constituent Assembly opens. But the Bolsheviks and the Left Social Revolutionaries withdraw when their resolution that the assembly have only limited power is defeated. Red Guards stop delegates from entering the assembly and it disperses.

January 9—The Ukrainian Rada declares independence.

January 15—The Workers' and Peasants' Red Army is established by decree.

Independence is declared by the "Baltic Knighthoods" under German influence.

The Bolshevik Revolutionary Committee for the Don demands that power be handed over to them, and Alexei Kaledin finds that the Volunteer Army is not prepared to support him.

January 26—The Siberian Regional Duma in Tomsk is dissolved by the local soviet, and they create an anti-Bolshevik provisional government, claiming to rule Siberia.

February—The Russian Muslim Assembly in Kazan proposes an autonomous Volga-Ural Muslim state, but non-Muslim Russian socialists block it.

A new Red fleet is decreed; many sailors are removed from Kronstadt as the Black Sea fleet is reorganized.

Ottoman Turkish troops move into the Caucasus to protect Muslims against Armenian revenge.

February 1–14—Gregorian calendar is introduced.

Note: *All dates are now given in "new style," in common with the rest of the Western world.*

February 6—Red troops from Tashkent, with Armenian Dashnak troops in support, attack the Turkestan Muslim autonomous government in Kokand. There is a massacre in the city and the resulting dispersal of Central Asians is partial cause of the formation of Basmachi groups.

The attack by Red troops on Bokhara is beaten back.

February 8—Soviet troops occupy Kiev.

February 9—The Ukraine concludes a peace treaty with the Central Powers—Germany and Austria—who recognize its independence.

February 10—Russians break off negotiations with the Central Powers because the Bolshevik Central Committee has voted for Trotsky's proposal of "neither peace nor war," which means they will declare the war at an end but will not accept the Austro-German annexations.

February 11—Alexei Kaledin commits suicide.

February 16—Lithuania declares independence.

February 18—Germans resume fighting in the Ukraine. They control the Donets Basin coal area.

Attempts to install a Soviet government on the Don are frustrated by the anti-Bolshevik Cossack Krug (assembly), which prefers a Don-Caucasian union with German support.

February 23—Following the vote of the All-Russian Congress of Soviets in January to create its own military organization (the Workers' and Peasants' Red Army), mass meetings are held and in Petrograd alone 60,000 volunteer. (Today, this is celebrated as Red Army Day.) Facing the threat to their revolution of the German advance, Lenin issues the proclamation: "The Socialist Fatherland is in danger."

February 24—The Central Committee and the All-Russian Congress of Soviets accept the German terms for peace. Trotsky resigns as commissar for foreign affairs and becomes commissar for war.

Estonia declares independence, while Latvia waits for changes in its circumstances.

The Volunteer Army, with about 4,000 men, is led by Lavr Kornilov on the "Ice March" across the Steppes, south toward the Kuban.

February 25—The Red Army occupies the Don capital and most of the Cossack forces submit.

The main body of the Finnish Jäger battalion (formed in 1915)—about 2,000 well-equipped, German-trained men— arrives in Finland, providing the nationalist General Carl Mannerheim with an anti-Bolshevik, anti-Russian force.

March 1—A treaty of friendship with the Finnish Socialist Republic is signed, but is with a short-lived revolutionary government and the Finnish nationalists continue to fight.

March 2—Germans reoccupy Kiev and restore rada rule.

March 3—Brest-Litovsk Treaty between Russia and the Central Powers (the German and Austrian empires) is signed by Grigory Sokolnikov, because major Bolshevik figures will not risk putting their name to it. Russia cedes Poland and territory on the Baltic, and allows independence for Finland and the Ukraine. There are supplements to the treaty signed with Bulgaria, Rumania, and Turkey. Russia surrenders Kars, Ardahan, and Batum to Turkey. The Left Socialist Revolutionaries vote against the treaty and resign from the Sovnarkom. The treaty is later invalidated after the 1918 Allied victory.

In Baku there are race riots, continuing through the month, between Armenians and Azeri Muslims; 3,000 are killed.

March 6–8—Seventh Party Congress (now the RCP(B) or Russian Communist party [Bolsheviks]) is held in Petrograd.

March 10—An offensive against the Whites in Finland starts. Germany supports the Finns with troops.

March 12—The Soviet government moves from Petrograd to Moscow. The Kremlin becomes the seat of national government.

March 15—The Brest-Litovsk Treaty is ratified by the Seventh Party Congress.

March 25—The nationalists in the Belorussian Rada see the opportunity for independence, and meet to declare a national republic.

March 27—The first group of the Czech Legion, the military unit formed in 1916 of Czech prisoners of war and émigrés, starts to leave by rail across Siberia to Vladivostok. It had been agreed that the legion would be returned to its home by the only possible route.

April—A Bolshevik and left-Menshevik soviet is established in Baku.

April 5—Allied troops land at Murmansk (their declared purpose being to protect the dumps of Allied arms and ammunition there). A Japanese contingent lands at Vladivostok shortly afterwards.

April 13—Lavr Kornilov, leading the anti-Bolshevik Volunteer Army, is killed by a shell and Anton Denikin takes his place as military commander.

Germans take Odessa.

Trotsky, who has taken command of the Red Army, becomes commissar of war.

April 14—The Finns, led by Mannerheim with German support, take Helsinki.

April 22—As an outcome of the Brest-Litovsk Treaty, the Democratic Federal Republic of Transcaucasia declares independence, with Turkish and German troops present.

Turkish troops move into the territory around Kars ceded to Turkey under the treaty. They continue deep into the Caucasus, to Tiflis and Erivan.

April 23—Germany makes a trade agreement with the Ukraine.

April 29—The Germans throw out the Ukrainian Rada and set up their own government there under Pavel Skoropadsky, a wealthy landowner and a relative of the German army commander.

April 30—German troops take the Black Sea naval base of Sevastopol and demand the removal of the Russian fleet, which the Bolsheviks order back to port, but the sailors scuttle the ships. The Germans install a puppet government in the Crimea.

The Turkestan Autonomous Soviet Socialist Republic is declared.

May 4—The Bolsheviks sign an armistice with the German-controlled Ukraine.

May 8—The Germans enter Rostov.

May 11—The North Caucasian Federal Republic is founded by Georgian Mensheviks in Tiflis.

May 14—A fight between some Hungarians and Czechs at Chelyabinsk causes the Czech Legion to take up arms in its defense, which brings the Czechs into conflict with the local ruling soviet.

May 15—The Finnish nationalists take the last Bolshevik-held fort on the Karelian Isthmus.

May 25—Trotsky orders any armed Czech found on the Penza-Omsk Line to be immediately shot. This gives the Czechs even greater determination to defend themselves, since they see Trotsky and the Bolshevik government as allies of their enemies, the Germans.

May 26—Transcaucasian independence: the Georgian Soviet Democratic Republic is proclaimed by Irakly Tsereteli and recognized by the Moscow Soviet in August. This starts the breakup of the Caucasian Republic into three: Georgia, Armenia, and Azerbaijan.

May 28—Azerbaijan establishes its own government. It starts negotiations with the new Turkish leader, Kemal Ataturk.

May 29—Although the Red Army is now 300,000 strong through volunteers, conscription is introduced. Anton Denikin's Russian Volunteer Army is in control of much of the south, having

pulled back into the Steppes from the Kuban, but taking Novorossisk after the Red fleet has sailed. He plans to move to control Azerbaijan, but the British presence blocks him.

May 30—Armenia announces its independence.

June—Turkey makes an agreement with the Azerbaijani Musavat party and moves toward its objective, Baku.

June 1—At Omsk a Socialist Revolutionary-dominated West Siberian Commissariat, with its own white and green flag (snow and forest), profiting from the activity of the Czech Legion, proclaims the autonomy of Siberia in continuity with the January Siberian Regional Duma and in support of the Constituent Assembly. By the end of the month this government is taken over by the right-wing government of western Siberia.

June 8—Czechs move to Samara; their presence allows the Socialist Revolutionaries to form a government accepting the authority of the Constituent Assembly. The SRs hope to establish an all-Russian pro-Allied, anti-Bolshevik government.

June 12—An armistice is signed with Pavel Skoropadsky's Ukrainian regime.

June 13—Revolutionary Military Council is established east of the Ural Mountains to deal with the Czech Legion.

June 14–20—The Menshevik, and Right Social Revolutionaries are expelled from the Kronstadt Soviet, as they have been throughout Russia.

June 18—Committees of Poor Peasants are set up, with the purpose of extracting grain from the kulaks and the rich.

June 26—Kerensky appears unexpectedly at a British Labour party conference in London. He says that the Russian people are fighting and will continue to fight against tyranny (meaning Germany).

July—A Transcaspian government is set up at Orenburg, mainly by anti-Bolshevik railwaymen. When the British leave Baku in September, this government is without protection.

July 4—At the fourth All-Russian Congress of Soviets, Maria Spiridonova leads an attack on the Brest-Litovsk Treaty.

July 10—The constitution of the RSFSR (Russian Soviet Federal Socialist Republic), adopted by the fourth All-Russian Congress of Soviets, is published.

July 16—The German ambassador, Count Wilhelm von Mirbach, is shot and killed in Moscow by two Left Socialist Revolutionaries under the orders of Spiridonova. They are also Cheka officials.

July 16–17—At Ekaterinburg, on threat of an anti-Bolshevik attack (in fact, the approach of the Czech Legion), Czar Nicholas, Empress Alexandra, and their four daughters and son are shot by their Cheka guards.

Abortive anti-Bolshevik risings in Yaroslav (as in others centers, Rybinsk, Murom, Kazan, Kaluga, and Vladimir) are organized by the former Socialist Revolutionary Boris Savinkov.

July 25—The Czech Legion enters Ekaterinburg.

August 2—A government is set up in Archangel under Nikolai Chaikovsky, with about 13,000 Allied troops landing.

August 6–7—The Czech Legion (now considered by the Bolsheviks to be White forces) moves from Samara and captures Kazan, where it finds the czarist government's gold reserves. The legion would have advanced south to Saratov, but it was halted by the brilliant partisan leader Vasily Chapeyev.

Denikin advances toward the Volga River and besieges Tsaritsyn, where Stalin is sent as the party's representative. With him are Simeon Budyenny, Grigory Ordzhonikidze, and Kliment Voroshilov. They successfully stand the siege.

August 14—British forces land at Baku, ostensibly to defend the area against the Turks, but also to protect the oil fields.

Japanese troops, with British and Americans, land at Vladivostok; some 20,000 troops are involved.

August 16—The capital of the Kuban is taken by Denikin's troops.

August 26—Denikin occupies the Black Sea port of Novorossisk, where the Imperial fleet has already been scuttled by the sailors.

August 30—Lenin is shot and injured by Fanya Kaplan, a Right Socialist Revolutionary.

September 2—The Revolutionary Military Council of the Republic is set up under Trotsky to control all military operations, but, given the communication problems, local councils continue to act on their own.

September 5—The Sovnarkom issues sweeping powers to the Cheka. This is the beginning of the Red Terror.

September 8—Conference at Ufa of non-Bolshevik governments.

September 10—Trotsky's Red Army recaptures Kazan.

September 14—The British depart Baku, leaving a local anti-Bolshevik administration in charge.

September 15—The Musavat party in Baku makes an alliance with the Turks, who are seen as enemies by the Armenians and Georgians.

September 20—Twenty-six Bolshevik commissars, the leaders of the earlier attempt to take control of the area, are taken from Baku and shot. British complicity in this is assumed. The only survivor of the Bolshevik leadership there is Anastasy Mikoyan.

September 23—White forces at Ufa set

up the Directorate, an all-Russian provisional government of five members.

September 25—The leaders of the Volunteer Army and the Georgian Republic meet to debate their responsibilities, the Georgians arguing that the army is there solely to fight the Bolsheviks, not to determine states' right or borders.

October 8—The Red Army takes Samara and the Whites are forced back to east of the Urals.

October 9—The Directorate, forced from Ufa, sites its capital at Omsk.

October 11—The Socialist Revolutionary Central Committee at Ekaterinburg calls on the party to resist the rightist tendencies of the Directorate at Omsk.

October—Mikhail Alekseev, who has been ailing a long time, dies and Anton Denikin assumes both military and political command of the Volunteer Army.

November 11—Armistice is concluded between the Allies and Germany.

November 13—Soviet government, following the armistice, denounces the Brest-Litovsk Treaty.

November 17—Another British contingent arrives at Baku and is met by an Azerbaijan Musavat government it cannot recognize unless the government admits to being part of Russia.

Latvia, with a strong working-class movement and strong sympathies to the Bolsheviks on the one hand and Baltic-German nationalists supported by *Freikorps* (German ex-soldiers organized into efficient fighting units) on the other, finally declares independence.

November 18—The Omsk Directorate is overthrown by officers, with the tacit approval of Allied officers there. Alexander Kolchak assumes full powers as Supreme Rule of All Russia.

November 25—An Allied naval squadron receives the surrender of the German fleet at Sevastopol (it consists of seized czarist ships).

December 14—The Skoropadsky puppet regime collapses in the Ukraine. The Ukrainian Social Democrat Simon Petlyura re-emerges as commander-in-chief. With his forces growing rapidly to 100,000 and allied with the anarchist Nestor Makhno's peasant guerrillas, he takes the capital, Kiev.

December 17—French land troops in Odessa as part of a plan to maintain order and ensure the evacuation of the Germans.

The Ukrainian Directorate proclaims the restoration of independence. Petlyura's forces advance rapidly toward Odessa, where he stops outside the city not wishing to be in conflict with the French. But elements of the Volunteer Army there try to persuade the French troops into action against the Ukrainians, declaring them to be enemies of Russia.

December 23—The Central Committee decides to establish a Belorussian Soviet Socialist Republic.

December 29—A coalition government for Azerbaijan in Baku is accepted by the British, who also have outposts at Batum and Tiflis. The Georgians are assured by the British that they, too, will receive a form of recognition.

1919

January—The Russian Political Conference is held in Paris, consisting of senior Imperial Russians abroad at the time, including ambassadors. Prince Georgy Lvov is designated chairman. It is hoped that this body will coordinate the governments in Russia: south (Denikin), Siberian (Kolchak), and northern (Chaikovsky). Unity is never achieved nor is recognition of the conference by the Western allies, since the conference is seen as one of a stream of representatives from minority nationalities with good claims to be heard. Russia thus does not have a seat at the Versailles Peace Conference.

Red Army takes Orenburg, defeating Kolchak and thus opening the way to Central Asia. However, Kolchak's offensive in March rules out any chance of the Red Army's linking forces with Tashkent.

January 1—Belorussian Soviet Socialist Republic is formally declared.

January 3—The Red Army takes Riga in Latvia, where Baltic Germans have been in power, and Kharkov in the Ukraine.

January 5—An agreement is alleged to have been signed, between the Bolsheviks and the German Communist Karl Liebknecht, that the Bolsheviks will assist, with "Russian gold," the establishment of a German Soviet Republic. Karl Radek is in Berlin with the hope of stirring the German revolutionaries and is arrested. During that month German soldiers murder Liebknecht and Rosa Luxemburg, following an attempted uprising in Berlin.

January 6—The Osipov coup d'état in Tashkent: a young ex-czarist officer working with the Bolsheviks, but hostile to Muslims and disillusioned with Moscow's policies, declares Bolshevik rule in Central Asia at an end, but in two days the Red Guards in the town—mostly railway workers—have reversed the position. Osipov gets away with the money from the Central Bank and is never heard of again.

January 16—The Ukrainian Rada declares war on the Soviets.

February 6—Red Army takes Kiev. Petlyura's force has lost Makhno's partisans, who now are siding with the Communists.

Vladimir Antonov-Ovseenko, the Red Army commander, moves rapidly through the southern Ukraine.

February 15—Denikin assumes supreme command of the White forces in southeastern Russia.

March—Polish armies under Marshal Josef Pilsudski advance into Lithuania, the Ukraine, and Belorussia. Belorussia is proclaimed part of Poland. At the same time the Belorussian Soviet Socialist Republic declares that Lithuania is merged with it.

March 2–7—The Communist International holds its first congress in Moscow. The Comintern is formed, in the expectation of the revolution's spreading throughout the world.

March 13—Kolchak starts an offensive from the Urals, hoping to advance to the northwest, linking up with the White forces around Archangel.

March 18–23—Eighth Party [RCP(B)] Congress is held in Moscow. A Secretariat and Politburo are set up; both are already functioning in effect, although the Politburo, with the Orgburo, is not formally in the party's statutes until December 1919. Stalin is a member of both bodies.

March 21—The withdrawal of Allied troops from Russia is decided. Plans for a Franco-Ukrainian offensive are abandoned in the face of Antonov-Ovseenko's advance, and the French troops at Odessa withdraw.

March 27—Marshal Ferdinand Foch's plan for an anti-Bolshevik crusade is rejected by the Allied Supreme Council.

April—General Eugene Miller, a czarist staff officer who has just returned from Italy to become leader of the Whites in Archangel, acknowledges Kolchak's authority.

April 5—British troops decide to leave Transcaucasia, having helped Armenia occupy territory, such as the province of Kars. They have been caught between the demands of the Georgians for self-determination and the insistence by Denikin on Russian imperial rights in Georgia.

April 8—French troops leave Odessa, having been under pressure since mid-March from pro-Bolshevik partisans. The French are also anxious to leave since they do not accept Denikin's right to rule there. The city is crowded with refugees, but the French manage to evacuate 30,000 as well as 10,000 in the Volunteer Army.

The Ukrainian Soviet Republic is formed.

April 10—The Red Army enters the Crimea.

April 15—The People's Commissariat for Internal Affairs (NKVD) officially institutes labor camps run by the Cheka.

April 24—Beginning of Russo-Polish War. The Poles destroy Bolshevik rule in Lithuania.

April 30—Sevastopol is evacuated by the French, who take with them the Crimean government after having agreed to a truce with the Red Army.

May 4—Kolchak is defeated on both his Center and Southern fronts.

May 19—The Denikin offensive starts. The Volunteer Army is now named the Armed Forces of South Russia. The army at this date has 64,000 men in the line but will soon grow to its largest number—150,000 men.

May 22—Riga, in Latvia, is liberated from Bolshevik forces.

May 26—The Armenians declare their territory, combined with former Turkish lands, the Armenian Republic.

A Georgian Soviet Democratic Re-

public is proclaimed and recognized by the Moscow Soviet in August.

May 30—Denikin retakes Kharkov in the Ukraine.

June—The advance of General Nicholas Yudenich's northwestern White Army forces the evacuation of over 16,000 women and children from Kronstadt. The city's mainland fortress of Krasnaia Gorka mutinies and defects to the Whites.

June 4—The Social Democrat Simon Petlyura's Ukrainian nationalist forces take the key Galician town of Kamenetz-Podolski. The Galicians, however, seeing the advance of Polish troops eastward into the Ukraine, prefer to put themselves under the protection of the White general, Anton Denikin.

June 9—Red Army under Mikhail Frunze takes Ufa.

June 14—Mensheviks and Socialist Revolutionaries are expelled from the Central Executive Committee of the Soviets. The Mensheviks have maintained their ideals and gained popular strength but have no political power, newspapers, or armed forces. They continue to gain seats on soviets throughout the country and to hold, individually, senior posts, especially in trade unions, until 1921.

June 16—Krasnaia Gorka is recaptured and a purge begins on Kronstadt; hundreds are shot after brief court-martials.

July 1—Baron Peter Wrangel captures Tsaritsyn, having accepted command of the Army of the Caucasus, largely Cossack, on Denikin's right flank.

July 10—A Kirghiz Revolutionary Committee is appointed.

July 12—The United States recalls all its military missions in southern Russia, since they are becoming involved in what is seen as local problems of recognizing statehood.

July 15—Red Army takes Chelyabinsk, putting Kolchak's Siberian army on the retreat.

August—British troops leave Azerbaijan via Iran; British troops in Georgia move to Batum for evacuation.

August 23—Denikin takes Odessa.

August 31—Denikin takes Kiev.

September 19—Allied troops evacuate Archangel.

September 20—Denikin's Whites, the Armed Forces of Southern Russia center group, take Kursk after the failure of a Red Army offensive.

September 28—White Army General Nicholas Yudenich's offensive reaches the suburbs of Petrograd.

October 14–20—Denikin takes Orel, and his army moves toward Tula, the last major city before Moscow. But he is forced back, starting a general White Army retreat as Budyenny's Red Army cavalry breaks through the Volunteer and Don forces.

November 14—Yudenich is defeated by the energetic defense of Petrograd. He receives no help from the Finns nor from the Estonians.

November 15—Petlyura is given full authority as head of the Ukrainian Rada. Omsk is taken by the Red Army; Kolchak abdicates in favor of Denikin.

November 17—The White Army loses Kursk, and the center group commander of Kursk is replaced by Baron Peter Wrangel, who also takes command of the Volunteer Army.

December—The eighth (seventh All-Russian) conference of the party is held in Moscow.

December 6—Petlyura goes to Warsaw for talks with the Polish government.

December 12—Kharkov is taken by the Red Army.

December 16—Kiev is taken by the Red Army, and the reorganized Bolshevik regime takes power in the Ukraine.

December 31—An armistice with the Soviet government is signed in Estonia.

1920

January–February—The Soviets now gain control of most of eastern Siberia.

January—The Sovnarkom issues a plan for the general mobilization of labor, including work books that will state if the owner is carrying out socially useful work. The mobilization of labor is extended to returning troops, and Trotsky and Bukharin suggest the militarization of labor to solve the problems of industry.

January 4—Kolchak resigns as Supreme Ruler of All Russia, abdicating in favor of Denikin, and appoints Grigory Semenov commander of the White forces in the Far East.

January 8—Rostov is taken by the Red Army. This is Denikin's last stand and his troops retreat into the Crimea.

January 15—The Czech Legion hands over Kolchak to a Revolutionary People's Army in Irkutsk, which is in sympathy with the Bolsheviks.

January 31—General Sergei Rozanov is overthrown in bloodless coup in Vladivostok.

February—Frunze takes command of the Red Army in Central Asia and captures Khiva; the khanate of Khiva is declared a People's Republic.

February 1—An armistice with the Soviet government is signed in Latvia.

February 2—Soviet government signs a peace treaty with Estonia at Tartu (known in German as Dorpat). This follows negotiations after the defeat of Yudenich in October 1919. It is seen by Georgy Chicherin as a first experiment in peaceful coexistence with bourgeois, capitalist states.

February 7—Kolchak is executed in Irkutsk.

February 19—The northern White government of General Eugene Miller in Archangel falls.

March—Ninth Party Congress is held. The Orgburo of the Central Committee, which includes Stalin and the three secretaries, now controls the naming to posts of party officials.

March 9—The Kirghiz Revolutionary Committee liquidates all nationalist opponents.

April 4—Wrangel takes over from Denikin and starts reorganizing the civil administration in the Crimea.

April 6—The Far Eastern Republic is founded, made up of the territories east of Lake Baikal, north of Mongolia and Manchuria to the sea, including Vladivostok. Its capital is Chita. Although nominally independent, it is Bolshevik-controlled and acts as a buffer against possible Japanese or Chinese ambitions. Although recognized as a separate state by the Soviets, it will return to the Russian Soviet Federal Socialist Republic next year.

April 21—Polish-Ukrainian treaty of friendship is signed.

April 24—Russo-Polish War; Poles under Pilsudski invade the Ukraine.

April 27—Ordzhonikidze enters Baku and the independent government of Azerbaijan is ended. A provisional revolutionary committee is formed.

April 29—A "declaration of friendly relations" is signed with Japan.

May 6—Poles take Kiev.

May 7—Peace is agreed to with the Georgian Republic.

May 11—A treaty is signed with Turkey and the Republic of Armenia under its Dashnak government.

June 6—Wrangel launches an offensive northward out of the Crimea. He tries to make the Ukrainian partisans allies, but Nestor Makhno simply hangs his envoy.

June 12—Kiev is retaken by the Red Army.

July—Batum (ceded to Turkey under the Brest-Litovsk Treaty) is occupied by Georgia after British troops leave.

The peasants of Tambov, 260 miles southeast of Moscow, take up arms in protest against Bolshevik rule; within the year they are 10,000 strong. Their leader is A. S. Antonov and their opposition is not halted until Lenin receives a delegation in February 1921.

July 11—The Red Army retakes Minsk from the Poles.

July 12—The Treaty of Moscow is signed with Lithuania, recognizing its independence. Vilnius (Wilno, in Polish), occupied by the Red Army, is ceded to Lithuania.

July 19—After the treaty with Lithuania, parts of Belorussia are handed over to Lithuania.

August 10—Western Allies sign the Treaty of Sèvres with the Turkish Ottoman Empire, ending its rule outside Asia Minor; the Armenian Republic is given parts of Turkey. The new ruler of Turkey, Kemal Atatürk, refuses to accept the treaty.

The Soviet Union makes a military agreement with the Armenian Republic.

August 11—The Treaty of Riga is signed with Latvia, confirming Soviet relations with the third Baltic Republic.

August 17—Red Army units get near Warsaw but are beaten back by a Polish counteroffensive. This ends the last real hope of the Communist revolution spreading to the rest of industrialized Europe.

Second Congress of the Comintern is called. Lenin advocates Communist support for the overthrow of the colonialist feudal-landlord order. This supposes that even if national movements may not be Communist, they should be supported to take power and then be taken over themselves at a second stage. The Indian Communist M. N. Roy argues that the bourgeoisie and nationalist movements in colonies are essentially reactionary and that a workers' and peasants' revolutionary movement is needed. Lenin's argument prevails and the nationalist movements are deemed revolutionary. The revised Marxist slogan is adopted: "Workers of the World, and of Oppressed Nations, Unite!"

August 26—The Kirghiz Autonomous Soviet Socialist Republic is set up in Orenburg. The name Kirghiz is later dropped and Kazakh used for this territory (the Kirghiz people are to the south).

September—The ninth conference of the party is held.

Frunze's Red Army troops enter Bokhara after four days of fighting and the emir flees to Afghanistan; a Soviet Republic of Bokhara is declared (later included in Uzbekistan with Khiva).

September 13—The Khorezmian People's Socialist Republic, the former khanate of Khiva, is recognized by the Soviet Union.

September 21—Russo-Polish peace talks start.

September 28—Turkey attacks the Armenian Republic after it had intervened in Turkish Anatolia over persecuted Armenian minorities. In a two-month campaign 200,000 Armenians are killed.

A Comintern Congress of Peoples of the East is held at Baku. It includes delegates from Turkey, China, and Russian Central Asia. The argument

that the eastern, Muslim world has a different class structure and that the nationalist petite bourgeoisie are the key to revolution is rejected and ignored in Moscow. The congress also promises that independent Asian countries will have its cooperation while colonial countries will be urged to revolt.

October 9—Polish troops occupy the Lithuanian capital, Vilnius, and hold it until 1939 as part of Poland, by League of Nations agreement.

October 12—Russo-Polish peace treaty is signed.

October 14—Finland and Russia sign a peace treaty at Tartu (Dorpat). While the Arctic port Pechenga (Petsamo) is given to Finland and a good boundary on the Karelian Isthmus, parts of Karelia are included as an autonomous republic in the Russian Soviet Federal Socialist Republic. Finnish fortifications are also to be demolished.

October 28—Frunze, sent to deal with Wrangel, attacks the Taurida Front.

November 2—Wrangel is defeated and forced back into the Crimea.

November 11–14—Wrangel's forces are evacuated from the Crimea; 150,000 refugees are taken to Turkey. 60,000 of them are soldiers but they are soon dispersed as an army. The remnants of the Imperial Russian navy sail to French Tunisia and are maintained there for several years, still recruiting and training.

November 23—Lenin introduces a policy of concessions to the hostile capitalist world on the country's borders. Trade relations are to be established and breathing space gained in which to rebuild the economy.

November 29—The Soviet Union mediates between Turkey and Armenia and, in the process, sets up a new Soviet Armenian government and accepts an earlier agreement on partition of Armenia and Azerbaijan, which produces the anomalous status of Nagorno-Karabakh.

December—Seventh Congress of Soviets of Workers', Soldiers', and Peasants' Deputies' is held. Socialist Revolutionaries and Mensheviks attend.

The Sovnarkom decrees that payment for rations is to be abolished, thus confirming the statement made earlier by the All-Russian Central Committee of the Soviets welcoming moneyless transactions "with a view to total abolition of the monetary system"

December 2—Turkey signs treaties with both the Dashnak Armenian Republic and the Soviet Armenian Republic, recognizing their national status and frontiers.

December 20—The Ukrainian Soviet Socialist Republic signs a treaty of alliance with the Soviet Union.

1921

January 16—The Belorussian Republic is recognized and an alliance with Soviet Russia is signed.

February—Baron Ungern-Sternberg captures the Mongolian capital of Urga, thinking to use this as an anti-Bolshevik base against Siberia.

February 13—The last public appearance of the Anarchists in Russia, as their survivors are released from prison for the day of Peter Kropotkin's funeral.

February 14—A peace treaty with Lithuania is signed.

Lenin meets a delegation from Tambov, where the peasants have been in revolt since the summer of 1920.

February 16—The Soviet Union moves troops into Georgia, with Stalin supervising the occupation.

February 20—A treaty of friendship is signed with Persia.

February 21—The Red Army moves into Dushanbe, the capital of the future Tajikistan.

February 22—Gosplan, the State Planning Commission, is established. At its foundation are economists and statisticians rather than political planners.

Demonstrations take place in Petrograd, where food and fuel have become scarce.

February 24—Petrograd factory workers go on strike.

February 25—The Menshevik Georgian Soviet Democratic Republic is overthrown in Tiflis, with help from the Red Army, ending its independence. It becomes the Georgian Soviet Socialist Republic. With Armenia and Azerbaijan, it will be joined into the Transcaucasian Federation in 1922.

Zinoviev is put in charge of a defense committee to deal with the Petrograd demonstrations.

February 27—Martial law is proclaimed in Petrograd. A delegation of Kronstadt sailors visits Petrograd and returns to report the failure of Bolshevik rule and to demand a nonparty conference.

February 28—A treaty of friendship is signed with Afghanistan.

The sailors of the battleship *Petropavlovsk* at Kronstadt call for free elections of new soviets, freedom of speech, liberation of all socialist political prisoners, equal rations for all, and full rights for land-holding peasants and small industrialists who are not employers.

March 1—Mikhail Kalinin, the nominal head of state, goes to Kronstadt to appeal to the sailors and to warn them. The outcome is a mass meeting that elects a non-Bolshevik revolutionary committee. There are 16,000 sailors, soldiers, and workers in revolt under the slogan "Soviets without Communists." They send delegates to Petrograd.

March 8—An attempt by Soviet troops to take Kronstadt fails. In Petrograd the Defense Committee takes emergency powers and troops are gathered to storm the naval base.

March 8–16—The 10th Party Congress is held. There are now nearly three-quarters of a million party members, but a "cleansing operation" is launched at the congress, removing a quarter of a million members in the first party purge. Lenin announces the New Economic Policy (NEP). A resolution against party factions is passed.

March 11—Turkish troops occupy Batum.

March 16—A trade agreement is signed with Great Britain, culminating negotiations begun in May 1920. This marks a major change in Soviet world status, for it means *de facto* recognition of a major international power. Other nations follow to take advantage of the new trade opportunity.

A treaty is signed with Turkey, giving Batum to the Soviet Union and Kars and Ardahan to Turkey.

Stalin is elected to the Politburo and Orgburo of the party's Central Committee.

March 17–18—Under Trotsky's Defense Committee, Mikhail Tukhachevsky and Lev Kamenev mobilize a force of 50,000 that, under cover of heavy machine gun and artillery fire, goes over the ice to enter Kronstadt. 8,000 sailors escape to Finland; thousands others are drafted to other naval units or labor camps and hundreds are rounded up and shot.

March 18—The Treaty of Riga involving the Soviet Union, the Ukraine, and Poland ends the war and defines the border. Poland gains a frontier farther to

the east than the earlier proposed Curzon Line.

March 25—The U. S. Secretary of State, Charles Evans Hughes, in response to an approach by Maxim Litvinov, states that no trade relations are possible as long as the Soviets do not recognize "the sanctity of private property, the sanctity of contract, and the rights of free labor."

April—Famine in the Volga region.

April 10—The Soviet Union fails to gain the cooperation of China over the regime of the former czarist general, Baron Roman Ungern-Sternberg, and sets up a nominal Communist Chinese government.

May—The 10th conference of the party is held.

May 6—A Soviet-German agreement is signed, opening up the possibility of trade. A secret agreement is also made to start the manufacture of German Junkers aircraft in Russia, financed by the German government. Three factories are built.

May 21—An alliance with the Georgian Soviet Socialist Republic is signed.

May 27—Ungern-Sternberg, in the Mongolian capital Urga, declares himself Emperor of All Russia and moves his Cossack and Chinese troops into the Soviet Union, where a government of the Mongolian People's Republic is in exile, waiting. After brutal fighting, in which all prisoners are killed, Ungern-Sternberg is captured. Independent Mongolian republics are set up as the autonomous protectorates of Inner and Outer Mongolia (with Urga, renamed Ulan-Bator, as its capital).

June 26—*Pravda* reports that 25 million people in Russia are starving.

July 12—Third Comintern Congress is held. The emphasis is on the search for new tactics, seeing the lack of progress toward a world revolution. Lenin gives the main task of winning over the majority of the working class, but he also expresses his hopes for nationalist revolutionary movements in Asia.

A rebellion by the people of Soviet East Karelia is supported by the Finns who, with Estonia, appeal to the League of Nations for a settlement.

July 13—Maxim Gorky issues an appeal to the world for aid for the Russian famine.

July 23—Herbert Hoover, chairman of the American Relief Administration (ARA), offers assistance to the starving; the Soviet government accepts.

August—Tannu Tuva, a minor czarist Russian protectorate on the border of Mongolia, is established as an independent people's republic. The territory had been abandoned by Russian officials in 1918, taken over by Chinese rulers, and used by White Russian troops. It will become an autonomous region within the Russian Soviet Federal Socialist Republic in 1944.

August–September—The Turks under Kemal Ataturk decisively defeat the Greek occupation forces in Anatolia. This transforms the weakened Turkish Ottoman Empire into the strong modern republic of Turkey, situated on the border of the Soviet Transcaucasian Federation.

August 20—Famine relief agreements are signed with the American Relief Administration and the Red Cross. In the next two years the ARA feeds 11 million people and clothes millions more. Fridtjof Nansen, for the Red Cross, raises huge sums of money and ships over 90,000 tons of food, but his plea to the League of Nations to take a lead in the relief of Russia fails.

September 15—Ungern-Sternberg is put on trial in Novosibirsk and shot.

October 13—The Soviet-Turkish Treaty of Kars sets the borders with Turkey for Armenia, Azerbaijan, and Georgia.

November 5—A treaty with the Soviet-Mongolian People's Republic is signed; the Soviet Union no longer recognizing Chinese authority there.

November 8—Enver Pasha, who had escaped from Turkey and now lives in Russia, arrives at Bokhara, sent by Lenin to persuade the Muslim population to drop support for the rebel Basmachis, but instead he joins them, planning to lead a holy war.

December—The 11th conference of the party is held.

December 7—An agreement is signed with Austria, along the lines of the German agreement of May.

1922

January–March—Soviet troops crush the revolt in East Karelia, which started in July 1921.

January 2—Turkey signs a treaty of friendship with the Ukraine.

February—The Cheka is reorganized as the GPU, or State Political Administration.

February 14—Enver captures Dushanbe, then raids Bokhara and gains control of most of the former kingdom.

March–April—The 11th Party Congress is held. It defines the limits of the New Economic Policy, with the state retaining control of large-scale industry, national transport, and foreign trade; Lenin shows great optimism on foreign trade.

April 3—Stalin is elected general secretary of the party. Lenin is in convalescence after an operation to remove two bullets from the shooting in August 1918.

Patriarch V. I. Tikhon is arrested and the Orthodox Church Holy Synod is dissolved.

April 10–The Conference of Genoa includes 34 nations but not the United States, and deals with the matter of economic reconstruction. Georgy Chicherin counters claims against Russia with accounts of damages caused by intervention during the civil war. The right of the Russian Soviet Federal Socialist Republic to represent the other Soviet republics is accepted, a step toward the formation of the Union of Soviet Socialist Republics.

April 18–The Treaty of Rapallo is signed by the Soviet Union and Germany, mutually renouncing reparations for war damage and establishing diplomatic and economic relations. One outcome is the establishment of the clandestine German-staffed flying school at Lipetsk in central Russia.

April 29–The Soviet Union gives Turkey arms, ammunition, and a credit of 100 million gold rubles to reestablish its army, thus enabling Turkey to end its war with Greece victoriously.

May–Enver Pasha, leading 7,000 Basmachi, demands the withdrawal of Soviet troops from Turkestan. He is in touch with King Amanullah of Afghanistan.

May 26–Lenin suffers a stroke, losing his power of speech. Stalin becomes the principal link between Lenin and the Politburo.

June 1–A new agreement with Finland is made to settle their frontier disputes.

June 14–Enver Pasha is defeated by the Red Army and his forces are dispersed.

July 17–The Afghan ambassador leaves Bokhara, accused of actively assisting the Basmachis. The Emir of Bokhara and his entourage remain in Afghanistan,

but Amanullah abandons any hope of detaching Bokhara from the Soviet Union.

August–The 12th conference of the party.

August 4–Enver Pasha is killed in fighting in Turkestan, ending his insurrection.

September 26–At Gorky, Stalin disputes with a convalescing Lenin the status of national minorities in the future Soviet Union. Stalin, organizing the federation of the Russian, Ukrainian, Belorussian, and Transcaucasian republics, proposes that they all come into a "Russian federation" and that minorities would be adequately represented, but with "Great Russian" dominance.

October 2–Lenin returns to Moscow.

November 5–December 5–Fourth Comintern Congress. The slogan of the Third Comintern Congress is repeated ("To the Masses") with tactics for implementing united fronts; that is, persuading workers' movements to voice support for revolution. Delegates are given the task of winning over the majority of the working classes of Europe and the United States.

November 20–The Far Eastern Republic (former eastern parts of the czarist empire) is dissolved and joins the Russian Soviet Federal Socialist Republic under the same name.

December 13–23–Lenin suffers further strokes, but he continues working and dictates his letters to the congress, also known as his "Testament"; they contain the often-quoted adverse comment on Stalin, the praise of Trotsky, and the ambiguous remarks on Zinoviev and Kamenev.

December 30–The USSR, or Union of Soviet Socialist Republics, is formed by the federation of the republics of Russia, Ukraine, Belorussia, Transcaucasia, Khorezm, Bokhara, and the Far Eastern Republic.

December 31–Azerbaijan enters the USSR as the Azerbaijan Soviet Socialist Republic and part of the Transcaucasian Federation with Georgia and Armenia.

1923

January 4–Lenin dictates a codicil to his "Testament," warning of Stalin's ambitions and proposing his removal from the post of general secretary.

March 9–Lenin suffers a third stroke. It renders him permanently without speech.

March 11–Frunze becomes chief of staff of the Red Army.

April–The 12th Party Congress is held. The "scissors crisis," as described by Trotsky, the economic situation in which the cost of manufactured goods rose and the peasants' incomes fell sharply, faces the party, Stalin, ignoring Lenin's arguments, reports on party organization and national minorities.

The "Living Church," accepted by the party, declares the Patriarch of the Orthodox Church unfrocked and abolished. This "official" church dies away in two years. Patriarch Tikhon, after imprisonment, calls on his followers to observe civic loyalty.

June–The American Relief Administration ends its operation in the Soviet Union.

July 24–Treaty of Lausanne is signed between Turkey and the Western Allies, determining its frontiers, including that with Armenia.

October–Mikhail Borodin arrives in China as a special representative of the Soviet Union. His aim is to reform the ruling party of Sun Yat-sen; Vasili Bluykher accompanies him to found a military academy and to strengthen the Soviet Union's position in China.

October 21–A Communist uprising in Germany, in which Karl Radek is involved, fails to materialize and the army takes control in many centers. Radek escapes from Hamburg. The failed uprisings are in impetus to Hitler's first attempt at an anti-Communist coup d'état in Munich in November.

December 5–Trotsky publishes a letter warning that the revolutionaries might degenerate into bureaucrats, since officials were now appointed from above rather than elected. This makes the conflict between himself and Stalin (who is responsible for the appointments) public.

1924

January–The 13th conference of the party; Stalin openly attacks Trotsky for being against the party organization and inciting party members against it.

January 21–Death of Lenin. The three who had been leading the party during his illness (Stalin, Zinoviev, and Kamenev) block Trotsky's gaining a majority in the Politburo.

The Mongolian People's Republic is established as a Soviet protectorate.

February 1–The USSR is recognized by Great Britain as the *de jure* ruler of the territories of the old Russian empire.

February–New bank notes are issued as part of a struggle against inflation, ending the successful gold-backed unit of currency, the chervonets, introduced in 1921 to deal with the collapse of the Imperial ruble.

February 3–Rykov is elected prime minister of the Russian Soviet Federal Socialist Republic. The USSR is recognized by Italy and Sweden.

April–Stalin's *Foundations of Leninism* is published.

May–A treaty is signed between the Soviet Union and China, giving the Soviet Union rights over the railway through Manchuria, as czarist Russia had held.

The Turkestan Republic is replaced by the Turkmen and Uzbek Soviet Socialist republics.

May 23–31–The 13th Party Congress is held. Zinoviev demands Trotsky's recantation of his theory of permanent revolution. Many of the delegates are new to the party and are strongly influenced by the economic distress; they support the status quo rather than revolutionary proposals. The Trotskyite Left Opposition is isolated.

The Central Committee decides to support Stalin and to suppress Lenin's "Testament" recommendation to remove him from the post of general secretary. Petrograd is renamed Leningrad.

July 8–The Fifth Comintern Congress decides that all Communist parties should be "Bolshevized"—that is, remodeled along Russian lines. The failure of the German uprising of 1923 is examined and blame is put on Radek for working with Social Democrats.

October 24–The "Zinoviev letter" is published in Britain. It is purported to be a secret directive from the Comintern to the British Communist party, and is confirmed as such by British intelligence. There are anxious reactions arising from fear and misunderstanding of "international" Bolshevism. The letter leads to the crushing of Britain's Socialist Labour party at the next election and years of mistrust of the USSR.

October 28–France recognizes the USSR.

November–Publication of Stalin's *Trotskyism or Leninism?*

December–Abortive Communist coup in Estonia.

1925

January 21–Japan recognizes the Soviet regime, and its forces finally leave eastern Russia.

January 26–Trotsky is dismissed as commissar for war and replaced by Mikhail Frunze, who had been high in Lenin's favor. Frunze, with Mikhail Tukhachevsky, starts a program to reorganize the Red Army.

March 15–The Tajik Autonomous Soviet Republic is formed as part of the Uzbek Soviet Socialist Republic.

April–The 14th conference of the party. Stalin presents his thesis, "Socialism in one country." Bukharin says, "We must tell the peasants, 'enrich yourselves.'"

August–The Central Committee issues a resolution on the control of literature. Some writers see this as the party's protection against extremists and zealots.

October–Frunze dies after an operation and is succeeded as commissar for war by Kliment Voroshilov, Stalin's wartime comrade.

October 12–A further trade agreement is made with Germany.

December–The 14th Party Congress is held; the party is now called the AUCP(B) —All-Union Communist Party (Bolshevik), which becomes known as the CPSU(B), the Communist Party of the Soviet Union (Bolshevik), keeping that name until 1952. Kamenev and Zinoviev are defeated when they oppose Stalin's industralization plan and fail in the vote of no confidence in Stalin that they try to bring. Delegates from Zinoviev's political base in Leningrad are cowed by Stalin's supporters and do not vote for

Zinoviev. Zinoviev is demoted in his Politburo rank.

1926

January–Sergei Kirov is made party secretary in Leningrad, ousting Zinoviev after the Central Committee orders new elections.

Stalin publishes his *Questions of Leninism*, an anthology of his writings, which will become a standard party textbook.

April 24–Treaty of Berlin is signed with Germany, a nonaggression pact.

June 12–The British government protests the Soviet Union's gifts of money to strikers in Britain.

July 14–Zinoviev is expelled from the Politburo on grounds of opposing the party's program of industrialization.

July 20–Dzerzhinsky, the head of the GPU (State Political Administration), dies and is replaced by Vyacheslav Menzhinsky.

August 31–A treaty with Afghanistan, agreeing that neither will join in any pact or trade agreement directed against the other, ends the hostility between the regimes.

September 28–Treaty of neutrality and nonaggression is signed by the Soviet Union and Lithuania.

October 19–At the 15th conference of the party, Stalin attacks the United Opposition; Zinoviev is removed as chairman of the Comintern and Kamenev is replaced as commissar for foreign trade by Anastasy Mikoyan.

1927

January 17–Trotsky and Kamenev are expelled from the Politburo, admitting their disloyalty to the party, following

the 15th conference of the party. The Politburo now consists of Stalin, Bukharin, Rykov, and Tomsky (the so-called moderates), being neither of the left (Trotsky and Zinoviev) nor of the right (Bukharin and Trotsky), with the newly added members Kalinin, Molotov, and Voroshilov.

April–Fourth Congress of the Soviets of the USSR.

April 12–Chiang Kai-shek, the Chinese nationalist successor to Sun Yat-sen, captures Shanghai but then turns on his Communist supporters and massacres them. The Comintern agent Borodin is forced to flee. The Soviet left accuses Stalin and Bukharin for this failure of Soviet diplomacy.

May–Great Britain breaks off diplomatic relations with the USSR (until 1929), after a raid on the Soviet trade office turns up documents confirming Soviet support for British strikers. Britain also cancels the 1921 trade agreement.

July 29–**August 9**–The Central Committee discusses the United Opposition's letter criticizing Stalin.

October–Trotsky and Zinoviev are expelled from the Central Committee and then from the party. Stalin arranges this with the Central Committee and the Rabkrin (Commission of Workers' and Peasants' Inspection).

November–Trotsky and Zinoviev try unsuccessfully to raise public demonstrations against the New Economic Policy.

December–15th Party Congress is held. Trotsky and his supporters are refused a hearing; complete recantation is demanded. Stalin delivers the main report of the work of the Central Committee. The policy of collectivization is established. Diplomatic relations with China are broken off.

1928

January–Stalin visits Siberia and issues orders to obtain grain by force from the peasants.

January 16–Trotsky is banished from Moscow; he is put on a train at night by the GPU and sent to Alma-Ata in Central Asia.

January 27–Kamenev and Zinoviev publish in *Pravda*, as a capitualtion to Stalin, a denunciation of the Trotskyites. Collectivization starts.

May–The public trial of mining engineers accused of sabotage at the Shakhty mines in the Donbas is held. Among them are Germans, and it is suggested that they are included to show that the Soviet Union is not dependent on German aid.

Gorky returns to the USSR, having lived in Italy since 1921.

July–August–Sixth Comintern Congress. Social Democrats are labeled "Social Fascists" and declared the main enemy of Soviet communism.

1929

January–Bukharin's article in *Pravda* advocates nonviolent cooperation between peasant and industrial worker.

Trotsky is expelled from the USSR and is exiled to Turkey.

February 9–Litvinov, on behalf of the USSR, joins the Kellogg-Briand Pact outlawing war.

April–Stalin attacks the "new bourgeoisie" and the moderates (Bukharin and others) at the Central Committee, accusing them of counterrevolution and consorting with the Left Opposition.

The 16th conference of the party. The First Five-Year Plan (1928–1933) is presented, with optimistic output targets for the industrialization of the Soviet Union.

October–Wall Street stock market crash. This confirms to the Soviet Union the imminent collapse of the democratic capitalist world.

November–Bukharin is removed from the Politburo by the Central Committee.

Stalin announces a program of mass collectivization and the liquidation of the kulaks as a class.

December–Vasili Blyukher's Far Eastern Army defeats the Chinese, who withdraw form Manchuria, allowing the railway to operate.

Bukharin and his colleagues, now called the "Right Deviationists," make a public confession of their errors.

December 5–Tadjikistan becomes a union republic of the USSR, having been separated from Uzbekistan.

December 11–16–The Kazakh party's Central Committee decides on collectivization and the resettlement of nomads; 544,000 of 566,000 households are to be settled by 1933.

1930

February–Decree on collectivization, describing the categories of kulak to be dealt with in the process of deportation or confiscation of goods. By this time, half of all the peasants are officially said to have joined collectives. In fact, many left the collectives after a few weeks, but the process continues until, by 1936, 90 percent of peasant households are collectivized.

March–Stalin's article, "Dizzy with Success," calls for moderation in the program of collectivization.

March 10–Kazakhstan declares that it has achieved 56.6 percent collectivization, but only 20 percent resettlement of nomads. There is armed resistance to the program; fighters are either called Basmachi ("bandits") or blame is put on the Alash Orda of 10 years earlier.

June–July–The 16th Party Congress adopts the slogan, "Fulfill the Five-Year Plan in Four Years." Molotov becomes chairman of the Council of People's Commissars, and Litvinov, succeeding Chicherin, is commissar for foreign affairs.

Opening of the Turkish Railway. Construction had started in 1913; this links Turkestan with the Siberian railway system.

October–Unemployment is stated not to exist anymore in the USSR.

November–The trial of the "industrial party," a number of engineers and scientists accused of working for France and trying to wreck the Soviet economy and overthrow the government, is held. Principal among them is Professor Leonid Ramzin, who with four others, is sentenced to death. The sentences are commuted and Professor Ramzin, a leading expert on thermodynamics, returns to lead a distinguished academic career in Moscow and is later much praised by Stalin.

1931

June–Stalin, in his "Six Points" speech to industrial managers, declares that the period of "wrecking" is past, and calls for a new attitude toward the intelligentsia and toward managers and technicians.

Ex-Mensheviks and ex-Socialist Revolutionaries working in Gosplan on the five-year plan are accused of working with émigré Mensheviks in a plot to retard industrial development. They are tried and sentenced to imprisonment.

September 18–Japan invades Manchuria. Japan assures the Soviet Union that its action will be limited and will not touch the Chinese Eastern Railway.

December 8–Japan demands that Chinese soldiers who had fled into the Soviet Union and were interned should not be repatriated. These soldiers are later rearmed by the Soviet Union and sent against Chiang Kai-shek in northern China.

1932

January–February–The 17th conference of the party.

January 21–Nonaggression pact with Finland is signed.

February 5–Japanese troops occupy the former Russian city of Harbin.

Nonaggression pact with the Latvia is signed.

February 18–Japanese invasion of Manchuria ends with a new state, Manchukuo, being proclaimed as a Japanese puppet.

April–Famine in Kazakhstan and Kirghiz, partly as a result of farmers having slaughtered their herds. As the Kazakh, Kirghiz, Bashkir, or Chuvash people die, they are replaced by immigrating Russians.

April 23–A Central Committee decree on literary-artistic organizations abolishes all existing artists and writers groups.

May–The organizing committee of the new Writers' Union starts, with the new creed of socialist realism.

May 4–Nonaggression pact with Estonia is signed.

June 29–Nonaggression pact with China is signed.

Zinoviev and Kamenev are exiled to Siberia.

The Dnieprostroi Dam in the Ukraine

is completed. This is hailed by the Soviets as a world record in speed of concrete laying and the largest electric plant in Europe.

Famine. It is particularly severe in the Ukraine, but Stalin refuses to admit its existence.

July 25–Nonaggression pact with Poland is signed.

November 8–9–Nadezhda Alliluyeva, wife of Stalin, commits suicide.

November 29–Nonaggression pact with France is signed.

December–A system of internal passports is set up; they are forbidden to collectivized farmers, preventing movement from the farms.

1933

Zinoviev and Kamenev are allowed to return, while Tomsky, Rykov, and Bukharin recant their errors; Bukharin admits his responsibility for the Right Opposition of 1928–29.

January–The Communist party orders a purge of its members, mainly to weed out undesirables who have joined since 1929. A new central Purge Commission is formed. By the end of 1933, one-third of the party will have been examined, some 1,149,000, of whom one in six will be expelled. This purge is similar in its methods to earlier party purges.

Recruitment to the party is suspended.

April–Japan stops all rail traffic between Manchuria and Siberia. The region is infested with armed bands of ex-soldiers, and the Soviet Union offers to sell its share of the railway to Japan.

Metro-Vickers trials are held.: Russian technical experts and British engineers are charged with being agents of foreign capitalism.

May 25—An order from Stalin and Molotov is issued to release half of those in labor camps as a result of collectivization. This is seen as a sign of liberalization.

August 2–The White Sea Canal, dug largely with labor from camps, is opened.

September 5–Petr Baranov, the commander of the Red Air Force, is killed in a plane crash.

There are famine conditions. The Ukraine suffers particularly.

Second Five-Year Plan, 1933–1937, goes into effect, although it is not formally adopted until the 17th Party Congress in 1934. Its aim is to "eliminate completely the capitalist elements." It includes much development in the east, a second track on the Trans-Siberian Railway, the Baikal-Amur Railway, metallurgical works on the Amur, and electric power stations in the area.

November–The United States and the USSR establish diplomatic relations.

1934

January–Japanese troops attacking northern China move through the Mongolian People's Republic, causing a serious military incident. The Japanese claim they are on Manchurian territory; the Soviet Union says it is an invasion of their ally.

January–February–The 17th Party Congress, the "Congress of the Victors," is held. Soviet economic success is hailed. Andrei Zhdanov, an expert in ideology, is elected secretary of the Central Committee. Nikolai Yezhov, a director of the 1933 party purge, becomes chairman of the Party Control Commission.

The Second Chinese Congress of Soviets (held at the same time) is praised as the best section of the Communist International, although the Chinese party is losing ground to the nationalist Kuomintang.

February 22–Bukharin becomes editor of *Isvestia.*

June 8–The law of the "Betrayal of the Motherland" is issued, making the death penalty obligatory for those found guilty and making members of a family collectively responsible for violations of the law.

July–The GPU (State Political Administration) is reorganized as the NKVD (People's Commissariat for Internal Affairs). The NKVD is forbidden to pass death sentences without the authority of the Soviet Union Procurator.

August 17–First Congress of Soviet Writers. Leading speakers are Gorky, Radek, Bukharin, and Zhdanov.

September 18–The USSR is admitted to the League of Nations.

October–The Chinese Communist army is forced to abandon its territories and starts on its Long March of 5,000 miles to the east and north of China.

November–The Central Committee abolishes food rationing and approves private plots and personal livestock on collective farms.

December 1–Sergei Kirov is murdered in Leningrad by Leonid Nikolayev. Andrei Zhdanov is sent to replace him as party secretary. Stalin visits Leningrad. Arrests are made of suspects and supposed accomplices, who are accused of being Zinoviev supporters. This begins Stalin's period of Terror.

1935

January 22–Zinoviev, Kamenev, and 17 others are arrested for complicity in the murder of Kirov.

March–The British Foreign Minister, Sir Anthony Eden, visits Moscow.

March 23–The Chinese Eastern Railway, between Manchuria and Siberia, is, after long negotiations, sold by the Soviet Union to Japan.

April 9–A trade agreement with Germany is signed. This agreement with Nazi Germany contradicts official Soviet hostility to facism.

April 13–A campaign to verify the documents of all Communist party members is announced, with process due to be completed in October.

May–The Moscow Metro, the underground railroad, is opened. Nikita Khrushchev, first secretary of the Moscow Obkom, is awarded the Order of Lenin for his part in the construction.

May 2–Pierre Laval, the French minister of foreign affairs, visits Moscow and signs a mutual assistance pact.

May 4–Stalin, in a speech, declares "cadres decide everything," stressing the importance of training and developing party workers, the need to stimulate the rank and file, and the goal of breaking through party bureaucracy.

May 16–An assistance pact is signed with Czechoslovakia.

June–Czechoslovak President Edward Benes visits Moscow.

July–August–Seventh Comintern Congress is held in Moscow. Under pressure from the rise of Hitler's Nazi Germany, the general secretary Grigory Dimitrov calls for a change of tactics, promoting Popular Fronts and cooperation with democracies against facism. The Chinese leader Mao Tse-tung is elected to the executive committee.

July–A constitutional commission is formed to revise the 1924 constitution under Stalin's chairmanship, with Zhdanov, Molotov, and others regarded as loyal to Stalin, but also including Bukharin and Radek, who, in fact, do most of the drafting, and publish discussion articles on the commission's program.

August 31–The coal miner Alexei Stakhanov is claimed to have hewed 12 tons of coal in a day, overfulfilling the quota by 1,400 percent. The "Stakhanovite movement" is announced, urging workers to achieve such overproduction and be rewarded with honor and money.

September 22–Conventional ranks are reintroduced for officers in the Red Army.

October–The Chinese Communist Long March ends at Yenan, south of Soviet Mongolia.

November–The verification of Communist party membership is completed; of 1.8 million checked, 9 percent (170,000) are expelled.

December–A series of incidents on the Mongolian border are described as invasions of Manchukuo by the Japanese.

1936

March 12–A mutual assistance pact is signed with the Mongolian People's Republic, giving warning to Japan to keep out of Mongolia.

June–The new constitution is published. It provides for wider suffrage in elections to soviet bodies, including the new Supreme Soviet.

June 18–Maxim Gorky dies. Stalin believes he has been murdered.

August–The Soviet Union accepts the Anglo-French proposal for a nonintervention agreement in the Spanish Civil War. At the same time Stalin decides on involvement in that war.

August 19–24–A public show trial convicts Zinoviev, Kamenev, and 14

others of the Kirov assassination plot. All are shot.

September 26–Yagoda is replaced by Nikolai Yezhov in NKVD. The Great Purge, the "Yezhovshchina," starts.

November–Eighth All-Russian Congress of Soviets gives formal approval to the new Soviet constitution.

The Soviet Union is now declared to have reached the stage of socialism on the road to communism.

Zhdanov in Leningrad as party secretary warns the Baltic States that their planning to ally themselves for defense is an anti-Soviet activity.

Enrollment in the Communist party, frozen since 1933, is restarted.

November 25–Germany and Japan sign the Anti-Comintern Pact. This binds each nation to not enter into political treaty with the Soviet Union and if either is threatened by the Soviet Union, to support the other.

Mikhail Tomsky commits suicide.

December 5–The new constitution is adopted.

The Kazakh ASSR becomes a Soviet Socialist Republic.

1937

January–Radek and 16 others are publicly tried for treason; 13, including Radek, are executed.

February 1–Ordzhonikidze commits suicide at the intimation of his arrest.

The Central Committee receives reports from Stalin, Molotov, and Yezhov on the need for a purge of class enemies from the party and the state.

May 11–Marshal Tukhachevsky is dismissed. The purge of the Red Army starts.

May–Political commissars are reintroduced into the Red Army.

June–The Soviet Union occupies two islands in the Amur River in Manchuria and Japan, occupying the opposite bank of the river, demands their evacuation. There are clashes between patrols and gunboats in the area. When the Soviets withdraw, the Japanese, in spite of protests, occupy the islands.

June 11–Marshal Tukhachevsky and eight other senior army officers are executed after a trial for breach of military duty and oath of allegiance, treason to their country, treason against the peoples of the USSR, and treason against the workers and peasants Red Army.

July 7–Japan begins its invasion of China. This is a relief to the Soviet Union, removing the threat of a direct war with Japan.

August 21–A Soviet-Chinese non-aggression pact is signed with the Kuomintang government. It does not promise assistance, but two countries pledge not to attack or become an ally of an attacker. After the treaty, the Soviet Union sends 400 aircraft and flying instructors to China. A supply road into central China is built. The Chinese government and the Chinese Communists now have a form of truce and alliance.

1938

January–The Central Committee tries to curb "errors" in the purge of party and state.

Khrushchev is appointed acting party secretary in the Ukraine, to clear out nationalists and suspected dissenters. He is made a candidate member of the Politburo.

March–Bukharin, Yagoda, Rykov, and others are put on public trial for treason. They are found guilty and shot.

March 13–The Russian language becomes a required subject in all schools throughout the USSR.

All heads of oblasts, or provincial, governments have now been removed and replaced at this stage of the purge.

July 18–August 10–The "Lake Khasan incident": there is fighting on the Manchuria-Korea-Siberia border, at Chankufeng south of Vladivostok, against the Japanese. The Soviet Union had started to build a submarine base when the Japanese occupied the hill, dominating it. The battle comes near to full war, and it is ended by a truce with both sides claiming victory. Japan is disappointed that Germany does not offer to come to its aid.

September 2–The Soviets ask the French to have a joint-staff military conference on assistance to Czechoslovakia.

September 27–Stalin assures the Czech president, through the leader of the Czech Communists, Klement Gottwald, that the Soviet Union will assist him against Germany even if the French do not cooperate. Soviet troops are massed in the Ukraine, and the Rumanians permit Soviet planes to fly over their territory. Poland refuses to cooperate with the Soviet Union in allowing the transit of troops. The Soviet Union protests against Polish troops massing on the Czech border, warning them that any action against Czechoslovakia will be an act against the Soviet Union. When Germany gains concessions, Poland occupies part of Czechoslovakia— Teschen. Poland also threatens Lithuania over its claims to Vilnius.

September 30–The Munich Agreement among Germany, Italy, France, and Britain gives Czech territory to Germany. Stalin is angered at the Soviet Union's being left out and assumes that France and Britain will take Germany's side against the Soviet Union

The *Short History of the CPSU* is published. Although edited and authorized by the Central Committee of the Communist party, it is written by Stalin's own secretariat and parts, especially the digest of Marxist dialectics, are by himself. It is a history emphasizing or exaggerating Stalin's role. Cheap editions are obligatory reading for all Communists throughout the world for the next 15 years.

November–Marshal Blyukher, the successful commander in the east, is arrested and shot.

December–Yezhov is disgraced and Beria takes over the NKVD. Yezhov may have overstepped the mark in his zeal to purge by naming men close to Stalin, including Beria, in a list of suspects.

1939

January 3–A new military oath is administered to all members of the Red Army.

March 10–15–The annexation and division of Czechoslovakia by Germany takes place, with Hungary taking Ruthenia.

March 10–21–The 18th Party Congress is held. Stalin speaks of the Great Purge as a thing of the past.

Stalin declares that the Soviet Union will fight to help nations defend their independence; he blames France and Britain for appeasing Hitler and the Japanese for concessions and for turning down offers of collective security.

Mao Tse-tung sends the party greetings from a China at war with Japan.

March 18–Stalin proposes a conference with Britain, France, Poland, and the Balkan countries to discuss ways to stop Hitler. The British turn down the idea and propose that Britain, France, Poland, and the Soviet Union declare their support for any threatened European nation. Maxim Litvinov agrees if the other nations do, but Poland refuses for fear of provoking Hitler.

March 23–Lithuania gives the Baltic port of Klaipeda (Memel) to Germany. Memel had been in the German Empire, but Lithuania seized it in 1923. At Hitler's demand—and on his arrival there on a battleship—no resistance was offered. There was little or no international protest.

April 17–Stalin proposes a Soviet-Anglo-French agreement, but Britain, fearing this might provoke Hitler, turns it down.

May 2–Litvinov, the advocate of an alliance with the West, is replaced by Molotov as commissar for foreign affairs. Stalin is abandoning hope of an alliance with the West, and it is possible that he thinks that Litvinov might not be able to negotiate with the anti-Semitic Nazi Germany.

May 20–September 16–In a major battle at Khalkin-Gol in Manchuria, the Red Army blocks the advance of the Japanese.

May 20–Molotov tells the German ambassador that the Soviet Union wishes better relations with Germany.

June 2–Molotov gives the British and French ambassadors a draft treaty guaranteeing the independence of small European states. When Britain hesitates on the details, this is taken as rejection.

July 18–The Soviet Union offers to discuss a trade agreement with Germany.

August 11–A Franco-British military mission arrives in Moscow to discuss cooperation.

August 19–A Soviet-German trade

agreement is signed. Hitler, conscious of the sensational effect on the world of his diplomatic moves, would have liked to deepen the effect by allowing at least a week to pass before the next treaty, but his program for war on Poland is already rolling. He encourages his foreign minister, Joachim Ribbentrop, to continue dealing with Molotov.

August 20–The Red Army under General Zhukov goes on the offensive against the Japanese on the Manchurian-Mongolian border, completing the victory at Khalkin-Gol.

August 23–Stalin agrees to a treaty with Germany and, in Moscow, Molotov signs a nonaggression pact with Ribbentrop, who flies in from Germany. Protocols on spheres of influence are secretly included, acknowledging the Soviet Union's interest in the Baltic and southeastern Europe, with Poland divided on the Vistula River, giving back to the Soviet Union those parts of the Ukraine and Belorussia lost in 1920.

August 25–The Anglo-French military team leaves Moscow for home, their negotiations having become useless.

Communist parties throughout the world are in shock, and now have to change their line and explain the Soviet's abandonment of the "popular front" tactic and the treaty with the hated fascists.

August 31–All Japanese are driven out of Mongolia, defeated by an army with superior mechanization, tanks, and artillery.

September 1–The German army attacks Poland, aiming immediately for Danzig, while bombers attack cities, including Warsaw, and airfields. By the end of the day the Polish air force is almost destroyed.

September 3–France and Britain issue ultimatums to Germany to withdraw from Poland, which expire and bring these nations to war with Germany.

September 15–A cease-fire and a neutrality agreement are signed with Japan.

September 17–The Red Army moves west into Poland, after only four hours' notice to the Germans, taking the agreed parts of the Ukraine and Belorussia, 78,000 square miles of land and over 12,000,000 people.

Soviet casualties are small. Between 180,000 and 250,000 Polish soldiers surrender to the Red Army. Most are sent east for detention; of 15,000 army officers arrested, 4,000 will probably be shot in 1940.

September 28–A boundary and friendship treaty with Germany, including secret protocols on the resettlement of Ukrainians and Belorussians, is signed by Stalin and Ribbentrop. On the same day an assistance pact with Estonia is signed by Molotov, providing for 25,000 Soviet troops to be placed there.

October 5 and 10–Assistance pacts are made with Latvia and Lithuania. The Baltic republics are forced to accept Soviet bases with troops stationed in them.

October 12–Discussions with Finland start in Moscow, with Stalin and Molotov demanding that Finnish territory in the Leningrad area be ceded for the Soviet Union's defense.

November 3–Communist activists in the newly acquired territories in the Ukraine and Belorussia form committees and arrange for a popular vote for them to be taken into the Soviet Union. NKVD men remove local administrators, officials, businessmen, and others they think may be opposed to the Soviet Union and send them to Kazakhstan or Siberia. Soldiers found in civilian dress are arrested and sentenced to eight years' hard labor; later a new Polish army will be recruited from these soldiers. Estimates of the numbers removed vary from half a million to 1.5 million.

November 9–Soviet-Finnish talks break down, because the Finnish parliament does not trust Soviet dealings.

November 12–Talks between Ribbentrop and Molotov start in Berlin to discuss their worldwide interests.

November 30–After declaring that Finland is threatening them, the Soviet Union bombs Helsinki and invades Finland. The Soviet 7th Army proves to be ill trained and ill equipped for the sturdiness of the Finnish defense lines and the severe winter.

December 14–The USSR is expelled from the League of Nations without any nation voting in its support.

December 31–The Japanese ambassador returns to Moscow and an agreement is reached with Japan on the final payment by Manchukuo for the Chinese Eastern Railway, on fisheries, and on the start of a new trade agreement.

1940

January 7–General Kirill Meretskov is removed from overall command of the Finnish war and Simeon Timoshenko made commander-in-chief of all Soviet forces in Finland.

January 15–The Red Army launches an attack on the Finnish Mannerheim Line, preceded by a heavy artillery barrage.

January 31–Relations with Japan, though improved, are still imperfect, and the Japanese demand that the Soviet Union cease its support of their enemies in China. The Soviet press is again attacking Japan, particularly on border matters.

February 11–An agreement with Germany guarantees it food and raw materials from the Soviet Union, with reduced freight charges on the Trans-Siberian Railway for imports from Manchukuo. In return, Germany is asked for examples of its most modern aircraft, warships, guns, machinery, and equipment.

February 17–Soviet tank forces sweep around the Mannerheim Line and drive back the Finnish troops.

February 27–Norway and Sweden refuse an Anglo-French force passage to Finland.

March–May–Over 4,000 Polish officers are shot by the NKVD in the Katyn Forest, near Smolensk. The discovery is made in 1943 and is blamed on the Germans. Later examination proves the contrary.

March 12–Finland stops fighting against the Soviet Union and signs the original treaty to which extra demands are now added. The Finnish army has lost 25,000 men, but the Red Army casualties are much greater, possibly 200,000, reflecting appalling military blunders. German military opinion rates the Red Army very low.

April 9–Germany invades Denmark and Norway. Anglo-French forces try unsuccessfully to hold back the invasion.

May 7–Timoshenko is promoted to marshal of the Soviet Union and people's commissar for defense. Kliment Voroshilov is demoted to deputy chairman of the Defense Committee.

May 10–Germany invades the Netherlands and Belgium, overrunning them and sweeping on into France.

May 16–Timoshenko issues Directive No. 160 to the Red Army, with a new strict disciplinary code, restoring officers' ranks and insignia, saluting, and the wearing of medals. The role of the political commissar in the army is limited. Some 4,000 purged officers are released and reinstated.

June 3–The British army completes its evacuation from France at Dunkirk.

June 8–The last British troops leave Norway.

June 9–The Soviet Union and Japan agree to cease fighting on the Manchurian-Mongolian border.

June 15–Soviet forces move into Lithuania, following a series of border incidents. With NKVD teams, Vyshinsky goes to Latvia, Zhdanov to Estonia, and Dekanazov to Lithuania, where they arrange for new governments to be formed and elections to be held. Leading officials, businessmen, soldiers, and policemen are deported to Siberia.

June 22–France signs an armistice with Germany.

June 28–Germany indicates to Rumania that its provinces of Bessarabia and Bukhovina are likely to be claimed by the Soviet Union, and the Red Army moves into them.

July 21–Newly elected governments in Estonia, Latvia, and Lithuania, supposedly with over 99 percent support, are formed and all ask to be incorporated into the USSR.

August 20–Trotsky is assassinated in Mexico.

September 27–Without informing the Soviet Union, Germany, Italy, and Japan sign the Tripartite Alliance of mutual military assistance, which they say does not affect their previous agreements with the Soviet Union.

October–German troops enter Rumania, ostensibly to train its army, but do not move into the provinces of Bessarabia and Bukhovina, which have been annexed by the Soviet Union.

October 2–By decree, nearly 1 million youths between the ages of 14 and 17 are directed to industrial training schools. The decree ends free education in secondary schools, with heavy fees for those who wish to remain.

October 26–Soviet troops occupy islands at the mouth of the Danube, putting pressure on both Rumania and Bulgaria.

November 12–14–Molotov visits Berlin and is offered an agreement dividing Europe and Asia, with parts of China and India to be in the Soviet sphere; Molotov suggests also Bulgaria, Turkey, Afghanistan, Iran, and Iraq. He also demands that German soldiers leave Finland, which was to be in the Soviet sphere. Germany offers to add the Soviet Union to the Tripartite Alliance. At the end of the meetings, in an air-raid shelter, when Ribbentrop declares that Britain is finished, Molotov asks, "Then why are we in this shelter, and whose are those bombs that are dropping?"

November 26–Stalin replies to Hitler's treaty offer by listing his sphere-of-influence demands in Europe and Asia.

December 18–Hitler issues the orders for Operation Barbarossa, the invasion of Russia.

December 23–29–The Red Army commanders hold a conference in Moscow, which is followed by a war game simulating a German attack. The result leads to a decision to increase the number of tanks for the army.

1941

February 15–20–The 18th conference of the party.

March 1–Bulgaria allies itself to

Germany, joining the Tripartite Alliance. German troops immediately enter the country.

March 20–The head of the GRU (Soviet Military Intelligence) tells his department to regard all claims that war is imminent as either British or German deceptions.

March 25–The Tripartite Alliance is signed secretly with Yugoslavia, but the next day the news causes a coup d'état in Belgrade and the government is turned out.

March–April–Yosuke Matsuoka, the Japanese foreign minister, visits Moscow then Germany and Italy, returning to Moscow. He reassures Stalin that Hitler does not plan to attack him and signs an agreement on peaceful relations and acceptance of present frontiers.

April 6–The new Yugoslav government signs a pact with the Soviet Union. That day German troops cross the frontier into Yugoslavia and dash through to Greece.

April 13–A neutrality pact with Japan is signed by Stalin and Matsuoka.

May 2–Richard Sorge, the GRU spy in Japan, signals Germany's intention to invade. His later information suggests June 22 as the invasion date. The Soviet spy network in Western Europe, known as the *Rote Kapelle*, also warns of German invasion plans, at first giving May 15 as the date, then telling of its postponement to June 22. Through another Soviet spy group, the "Lucy Ring" in Switzerland, the British try to send information they have on the June invasion plan. These warnings are ignored by Stalin.

May 6–Stalin becomes chairman of the Sovnarkom (Council of People's Commissars).

June 4–The commander of the Red Army Military District in Belorussia reports German troop concentrations on the border.

June 11–17–Trade agreements are signed with Japan to ensure the flow of goods for Germany on the Trans-Siberian Railway.

June 13–The Soviet news agency, Tass, issues a statement decrying rumors of war between Germany and the Soviet Union.

Simeon Timoshenko asks Stalin's permission to alert and redeploy forces on the border. Stalin refuses permission.

June 21–Bearing news from German deserters, Timoshenko and Georgi Zhukov go to Stalin, demanding action against the troops on the border. Stalin allows only a limited and unspecific warning to go out, but it is transmitted too late.

June 22–Operation Barbarossa, the German invasion plan, is put into operation. At 3 A.M. the Black Sea fleet reports attacks on the Sevastopol harbor, and the Baltic fleet reports attacks in the Gulf of Riga. Admiral Nikolai Kuznetzov, the commissar for the navy, cannot get news to Stalin.

At 3:30 A.M. the Minsk Military District tells Zhukov that Ukrainian towns are being bombed, and the Baltic Military District reports raids on Lithuania. Zhukov reaches Stalin's office and is ordered to assemble the Politburo. The Germans have sent specially trained units ahead to destroy communications and secure bridges.

At 4:30 A.M. Stalin orders the German embassy to be telephoned for information. The German ambassador meets Molotov and transmits a message which is, in effect, a declaration of war.

At 7:15 A.M. Timoshenko issues Defense Commissar Directive No. 2, ordering forces to fight back, but restricting air activity and forbidding pursuit across the border.

Before noon the German air force claims to have destroyed more than 800 Soviet aircraft on the ground. In all probability, 1,800 are destroyed during the day. At 12:15 P.M. Moscow Radio broadcasts a brief message by Molotov, stating that German troops have attacked and calling on citizens to rally to the party and to Comrade Stalin.

June 23–Baltic: German troops, having marched 40 miles through Lithuania, now enter Latvia.

Ukraine: In the Ukraine, the advancing German armored forces meet resistance instead of the expected collapse of the Red Army. The Soviets fall back to the Pripet Marshes, an easily defended area.

June 24–Northwest: The Red Army attempts a counterattack near Grodno in Belorussia, but without air or artillery cover the Soviets losses are very heavy.

June 25–Finland: Finland declares war on the Soviet Union. Finnish forces advance to the old 1939 frontier on the Karelian Isthmus and to the Svir River between Lakes Ladoga and Onega, where the line stays until 1944; in spite of a strong German presence, the Finns only make such military operations as are in their interest and play no part in Hitler's grand strategy. Marshal Mannerheim declines an offer to take command of the German troops there, since that will demote him, in effect, to being one of Hitler's generals.

Northwest: The Red Army makes a stand on the Dvina River, but the Germans cross the next day.

June 26–U.S. Secretary of State Sumner Welles announces that the Neutrality Act will not be invoked against the USSR, meaning that the United States may supply munitions.

June 27–Hungary declares war on the Soviet Union. Its troops are to form a link with the German armies in Poland and Rumania.

June 28–Baltic: Riga falls, although the Red Army escapes, leaving large quantities of equipment and tanks.

Northwest: Minsk is taken by the Germans.

June 29–Ribbentrop suggests to Matsuoka that Japan take the opportunity of seizing Vladivostok, but Japan maintains neutrality. American ships carrying supplies are sent to the port of Vladivostok. When Japan and the United States are at war, the ships will fly Soviet flags and continue to sail; Japan thus tries to demonstrate neutrality toward the USSR.

Northwest: Bialystok, attacked and cut off on the first day, falls to the Germans. Two Soviet armies are encircled in the same area.

June 30–A State Committee of Defense is appointed with Stalin as its chairman and Molotov, Malenkov, Voroshilov, and Beria as members. It will control the wider aspects of the war—political and economic as well as military.

July 3–Stalin gives his first wartime broadcast to the people. While defending the Soviet-German pact as securing a year of peace, he calls on the people to defend the country and not allow anything, whether a machine, an animal, or a sack of grain, to fall into German hands. He calls on the Soviet Union to fight a patriotic war.

July 7–British Prime Minister Winston Churchill sends a personal message to Stalin offering assistance.

July 8–Ukraine: The Soviet defense

line on the pre-1939 frontier with Poland is pierced, and the Germans are within 90 miles of Kiev.

July 9–Northwest: Vitebsk is surrounded and taken.

July 10–Stalin becomes chairman of the Stavka (High Command), which has been under Timoshenko's control since June 23. Three army areas are organized:

    Northwest—Voroshilov, with
        Zhdanov as the political adviser
    West—Timoshenko and Bulganin
    Southwest—Budyenny and
        Khrushchev

Baltic: The German Army Group North starts an offensive from Estonia toward Leningrad, where the Soviet Northwest armies have lost much material but have survived as a large fighting force.

Ukraine: The Germans marching toward Kiev are attacked in the flank by Red Army units from the Pripet Marshes and their supply lines are cut.

July 11–Ukraine: German and Rumanian armies advance toward the Dniester River, where the Red Army is waiting and heavy rain and thick mud allow only slow progress.

July 12–A military pact is signed in Moscow between Britain and the Soviet Union.

July 16–Moscow: Smolensk is captured and another encirclement of Soviet armies is delayed because the Germans are spread out too widely.

July 18–Agreement with the Czechoslovak government in exile in London to work together for the conduct of the war and to agree to the formation of national troop contigents in the Soviet Union.

July 19—Stalin takes over from Timoshenko as commissar of defense, while he takes command in Leningrad.

Moscow: Hitler orders his Army Group Center to advance on Moscow, but without their armor, one part being sent toward Leningrad and the other south to the Ukraine.

July 29–Ukraine: Zhukov advises withdrawing and surrendering Kiev. Stalin relegates him to the reserve armies.

U.S. President Franklin D. Roosevelt sends his personal representative, Harry Hopkins, to Moscow to discuss military supplies with Stalin. Hopkins is impressed by Stalin's determination and realistic appraisal of the Soviet Union's chances, and convinces Roosevelt that U.S. help would be effectively used.

July 30–Agreement with the Polish government in exile in London, similar to the agreement with the Czechs earlier in the month (see July 18).

August 2–Ukraine: Twenty Soviet divisions are cut off near Uman in the southern Ukraine.

August 5–Moscow: 300,000 men and 3,000 tanks are surrounded and captured near Smolensk. In Belorussia the Germans have advanced over 500 miles and have taken about 600,000 prisoners.

Ukraine: Some 100,000 Soviet soldiers are captured at Uman.

August 23–Voroshilov's Northwest area is broken up into a Leningrad Front, under Markian Popov and Andrei Zhdanov, a Karelian front and a Northwest Front.

August 25–The Soviet Union and Britain enter Iran, to deny it to Germany.

Leningrad: In a move to cut Leningrad off and to link with the Finns, the Germans take Novgorod and cross the Volkhov River.

August 26–Taking stock, the German army records 440,000 casualties (including 94,000 dead), but only 217,000 reinforcements. Units are beginning to beg for refitting and restaffing.

August 31–Some 300,000 Germans of the Autonomous Volga Republic are ordered to move east.

September 4–Baltic: All Estonia and nearly all the southern coast of the Gulf of Finland are cleared of Soviet troops by the German army.

September 5–Hitler decides that Leningrad is a secondary theatre and orders an attack on Moscow before the onset of winter. Armored forces are, therefore, brought back from the Ukraine. Directive No. 35 on the attack is issued the next day.

September 11–Zhukov takes command of the Leningrad Front. The Western Front is given to Ivan Konev and Bryansk to Andrei Eremenko.

September 13–Ukraine: Budyenny is removed from his command when he asks to be allowed to retreat beyond Kiev.

September 16–26–Ukraine: Around Kiev, about 130 kilometers in width and depth, the Red Army is encircled. Kiev falls and 450,000 soldiers are taken prisoner.

September 24–Crimea: The Germans fail to get into the Crimea at the Perekop Isthmus.

September 26–Total German casualties are now 534,000. Frontline generals report anxiety that the Red air force is beginning to be active again, and that antitank guns are proving ineffective against Soviet tanks, particularly the T34.

September 28–A high-level Anglo-American supply mission to Moscow— the British newspaper magnate and minister in the Cabinet Lord Beaverbrook and Roosevelt's envoy, Averell Harriman—agrees to send munitions,

accepting the proviso that the requests will not be justified or explained by the Soviets.

September 30–Moscow: The German offensive on Moscow begins, moving around Bryansk to reach Orel in four days.

October–November–About 75,000 Karachai people are deported from their Caucasian home to the east.

October 6–South: On the Black Sea coast, another 106,000 Soviet troops are captured. The route to the Caucasus is now only thinly guarded.

Moscow: The first snow falls on the German Army Group Center.

October 7–Zhukov returns to Moscow on Stalin's orders, taking command of first the Reserve Front and then the Western Front. Budyenny is briefly missing in the chaos.

October 8–The Japanese mount a campaign to end Germany's war with the Soviet Union, so that Germany can direct its energies against the British Empire. Japan's new cabinet feels that the Soviet Union's difficulties may induce it to reduce support for China, but that war against the Soviet Union would not be in Japan's interest; neutrality is observed until 1945. The Soviet Union is able to withdraw its troops from Asia to the west.

October 9–The German army reports supply shortages of 30,000 tons a month and an inability to deal with captured weapons or munitions; some of these will fall into the hands of partisans. Heavy snow and rain are now falling and transport of Army Group Center is becoming bogged down.

October 11–South: The German Army Group South is also stopped by bad weather north of Taganrog.

October 16–Moscow: Moscow is evacuated of nonessential civilians (many in panic); Stalin, the Stavka, and his government remain.

Crimea: Odessa is evacuated. Its 80,000 troops and many of its 350,000 civilians move to the Crimea.

October 17–South: Taganrog is taken and the Germans are in the Donets Basin—the main coal area of the Soviet Union—at Kharkov, and approaching Rostov.

October 18–Moscow: German tanks are at Moscow's second defense line, 60 miles from the city, but snow is now slowing movement.

October 18–28–Crimea: The Germans, short of tanks on this front, attack the Perekop Isthmus, which is heavily fortified and where the Red air force has local control. Although they break through, taking over 100,000 more prisoners, they meet more resistance on the Crimea, where the Soviets have both air and sea command.

October 19–A state of siege is declared in Moscow.

October 31–Moscow: The German Army Group Center, exhausted, cold, and unable to advance further, is given a fortnight's pause for reinforcement.

November 5–South: A German army attacks toward Rostov.

Crimea: In the Crimea, a Sebastopol Defense Command is set up, with a garrison of about 50,000 and strong defenses around the city.

November 7–Stalin speaks publicly in Moscow on October Revolution Day.

November 8–Leningrad: Tikhvin near Leningrad is taken, but counterattacks regain part of the town and the German advance is held.

November 15–Moscow: With clear frosty weather and harder ground, the

Germans resume their move toward Moscow.

November 18–Leningrad: Leningrad is beseiged, but Lake Ladoga now freezes over and truck convoys bring supplies across it.

November 20–South: Rostov is captured, but Timoshenko's' reorganized Southwest area counterattacks successfully.

November 28–Moscow: The Germans cross the Moskva-Volga Canal and are 25 miles northwest of Moscow.

November 30–South: Hitler issues an order to his troops around Rostov to stand firm and sacks his general, but the Germans retreat from Rostov back to Taganrog.

December–380,000 Kalmyks are deported from their autonomous republic, northwest of the Caspain sea, to Soviet Central Asia.

The Russian Orthodox Church pledges its support for the war.

Stalin and the Polish General Wladislaw Sikorski sign a Polish-Soviet Declaration of Friendship and Mutual Aid.

December 5–Moscow: Zhukov counterattacks outside Moscow. He now has the support of half the strength of the Far Eastern Command, which has been transferred west of the Urals—nearly a million experienced, trained, and well-equipped soldiers.

December 6–Britain declares itself at war with Finland after long diplomatic attempts to persuade that country to keep off Germany's side. Finland, in fact, does little more in the war than regain its 1939 frontier.

Moscow: The Russian counterattacks north of Moscow succeed (to Zhukov's surprise, since he does not appreciate the exhaustion and lack of equipment of the Germans) and drive 20 miles to the

German rear. To the west of Moscow the Germans also retreat 15 miles.

December 7–The Japanese attack the United States at Pearl Harbor, bringing that country into the war.

December 11–Hitler declares war against the United States. This act of solidarity with Japan ensures that the United States becomes an enemy and the war ally of the Soviet Union. However, the Soviet Union declines to give the U.S. air bases in Siberia, since it would invite war with Japan.

December 13–South: Soviet armies attack on the right to Timoshenko's Southwest Front and capture, for the first time in the war, quantities of German soldiers and weapons.

December 15–Parts of the government evacuated from Moscow are ordered to return.

December 16–19–The British foreign secretary, Anthony Eden, visits Stalin but avoids discussion of postwar European frontiers and fails to get any promise of war against Japan.

December 20–A "stand and fight" order is issued by Hitler, though withdrawals continue.

December 25–Crimea: At Sebastopol the German attack, in bad weather, meets low morale among the Soviet troops.

December 26–Moscow: Finding a gap between the German armies, the Red Army around Tula advances quickly to Smolensk, but, after five days frost and lack of supplies stop it. However, the Stavka orders another move from the Northwest Front to envelop the Germans.

Crimea: Red Army detachments from the Transcaucasus are landed on the eastern end of the Crimea, holding the Kerch Peninsula. The effect is to break

off the siege of Sebastopol, where the defenses are crumbling.

1942

January 1–A revised German army handbook on the Red Army is issued for the staff, recognizing that the Soviets have greater abilities to recover and re-equip from stocks than had been anticipated.

January 7–Leningrad: An offensive is launched from the Volkhov River to the east of Leningrad to relieve the city. The Soviets advance slowly for a month to within 40 miles east of Leningrad.

January 9–Moscow: Launching a winter offensive on the Northwest Front on Stalin's orders, the Red Army begins its advance of 200 miles toward Velikiye Luki and Vitebsk, and German armies have to retreat to avoid encirclement. The arms of the Soviet pincer are a hundred miles apart.

January 13–Moscow: Under General Vlasov a specially strengthened army moves through the center of the German pocket.

January 21–Moscow: To reinforce the flanks of the Soviet attack, units are moved from the center, relieving the pressure on Vlasov's offensive. The Germans are able to stand and fight back.

January 28–Crimea: Stalin designates the Crimea as a front, giving the siege of Sebastopol priority.

February 1–Moscow: Zhukov is given command of the Western Front. The advance and completion of encircling movements cannot now be accomplished by the overstretched Red Army.

February 8–Moscow: The Red Army succeeds in cutting off about 90,000 Germans at Demyansk, south of Lake Ilmen. The Germans mount a large air supply operation that ensures the survival of their troops. At first 230 aircraft are used and eventually 600 are deployed, flying in over 270 tons a day and taking 22,000 wounded out and bringing 15,000 reinforcements in.

February 27–Crimea: The Soviet attempts to drive the Germans from Sebastopol and the Kerch Peninsula die out. German attacks are equally unsuccessful.

March 20–Moscow: A further Soviet attack beyond Moscow is ordered but within 10 days it is stopped. The Red Army is exhausted, stuck in the spring mud.

April 18–Five U.S. airmen of the Doolittle bomber raid on Tokyo make a forced landing in the Russian Far East and are interned. They are joined by other U.S. airmen who land in the Soviet Union and are interned in a special camp near Tashkent, as part of the Soviet Union's neutrality in the U.S. war against Japan. In 1943 their escape through Iran is arranged, probably by NKVD border guards.

April 21–Moscow: A specially created corps forces a narrow corridor through to the encircled Germans at Demyansk, who are then reinforced and act as a springboard for the later offensive.

May–A central partisan staff is established in the Stavka. In 1941 there had been stragglers or units cut off from the main force, which made uncoordinated attacks on convoys or camps. Now partisan actions are to be part of the Red Army's plans, although their effect is not fully felt until 1943.

May 12–Center: Timoshenko starts a spring offensive with an attack aiming at Kharkov. His left wing, to the south, does not drive home armored attacks as he planned.

May 15–Crimea: In the Crimean spring offensive, the Germans take the Kerch Peninsula. Rumanian soldiers are now conducting the Sebastopol siege. Hitler's objective is no longer Moscow and Leningrad, but to destroy the Red Army to the west of the Don and take the oilfields of the Caucasus.

May 26–A 20-year Treaty of Alliance is made between the Soviet Union and Britain.

May 29–Center: Timoshenko's failed offensive ends with the loss of Kharkov, as two Soviet armies are surrounded and cut to pieces and 214,000 are taken prisoner.

June–Moscow: General Vlasov and his army, cut off in the forests north of Lake Ilmen, is driven out; he is captured with 33,000 men.

June 7–Crimea: The Germans return to the siege of Sebastopol. There is desperate fighting.

June 28–Center: The Germans, with heavy air support, attack in the direction of Voronezh.

June 10–26–Center: In two operations, the Germans force the Soviet armies of the Southwest back toward the Don River.

July–Hitler moves to his advanced headquarters at Vinnitsa to watch his troops advance into the Crimea, the Caucasus, and over the Volga at Stalingrad.

July 4–Crimea: Sebastopol finally falls. Hitler is so pleased that he proposes to move the victorious troops to the siege of Leningrad.

The loss of the Crimea leads to creation of a new Soviet command: the North Caucasus front, commanded by Budyenny. Timoshenko's Southwest command is reduced, with parts directly controlled by the Stavka.

July 6–Center: Voronezh is taken and the Germans cross the Don. Soviet troops avoid being trapped and regroup on their side of the river.

July 8–Stalingrad: German armor crosses the Donets River, but again the Red Army avoids being trapped and retreats intact, although Hitler is convinced that they must have been destroyed.

July 12–Stalingrad: The Stavka creates the Stalingrad Front under Timoshenko, with Khrushchev as the political adviser. Timoshenko is replaced shortly afterwards.

July 23–South: Germans take Rostov, but again the Red Army falls back in good order, though weakened.

July 25–Stalingrad and South: The Germans attack from three bridgeheads over the Don River. One army swings north toward Stalingrad. To the south, on a hundred-mile front, they break through Soviet defenses and a rapid advance starts.

Budyenny's Caucasus command is now mixed with the South Front, with him in nominal command.

July 28–Stalin issues an order of the day, "Not a step backwards," that the Red Army should yield no more ground west of the Don. Although it leads to a large number of casualties, a small bridgehead over the Don is held.

August–Voroshilov is made commander-in-chief of the partisan movement.

August 12–16–Churchill meets Stalin in Moscow and discusses the war, particularly the possibility of an Anglo-American second front being opened in Europe.

August 12–Stalingrad: The Stalingrad Front is put under General Eremenko of the Southeast Front.

August 18–Caucasus: The Germans reach the mountain passes entering the Caucasus.

August 23–Stalingrad: A force heavily supported by the German air force crosses the Don and reaches the Volga River north of Stalingrad. The evacuation of the civilian population and the fortification of the city now begins.

September 1–Caucasus: The German advance in the Caucasus halts at the Terek River to wait for reinforcements.

September 12–Stalingrad: General Vasily J. Chuikov is selected by Khrushchev to command the 62nd Army on the Stalingrad Front. This army will hold the city.

September 14–Stalingrad: The Germans under Friedrich von Paulus nearly succeed in taking all of Stalingrad, the old town city center and railway station. With street fighting the Red Army begins to make small gains, supported by cover fire from the far side of the Volga River.

September 28–Stalingrad: The Stavka gives Konstantin Rokossovsky the Don Front north of Stalingrad, and Eremenko, with Khrushchev, the Stalingrad Front.

November 2–Caucasus: The German offensive in the Caucasus gets within five miles of Ordzhonikidze, the farthest east reached by the invading army.

November 8–Hitler receives the news of the Anglo-American landings in North Africa. This and the news of the defeat of his army in Libya at El Alamein by the British distracts him from Russia; when the Soviet offensive comes, his generals will have to wait indecisively for his instructions.

November 17–Center: Zhukov is sent

to coordinate the offensive against the German Army Group Center.

November 19–Stalingrad: General Alexander Vasilevsky, who has been assigned the leadership of the Stalingrad counteroffensive, attacks and in four days encircles the 6th German Army there. The Germans expect the attack but are surprised by the strength of it. Von Paulus is ordered to defend his position in Stalingrad; he has six days' of supplies and he is promised an airlift based on the experience of Demyansk in February. There are about 250,000 Germans and Rumanians encircled there.

November 25–Stalingrad: The German air force attempts to airlift 700 tons a day to their 6th Army, but ice and fog, and losses of 488 aircraft, bring the total lifted by mid-December to only 3,300 tons.

December 12–Stalingrad: A German army under Fritz von Manstein tries to reach Stalingrad but is halted 40 miles outside. Without artillery or infantry support, his armor is outgunned and runs out of fuel.

December 16–Stalingrad: On the Southwest Front, north of Stalingrad, an Italian army on the Don is broken and abandons its positions; the Red Army under General Nikolai Vatutin makes an advance of 150 miles.

December 18–Stalingrad: In Stalingrad the Germans decide against attempting a break-out, hoping to hold out longer.

December 19–Stalingrad: Although now threatened in the rear, a German force gets within 30 miles of Stalingrad.

December 24–Stalingrad: The Russian breakthrough north of Stalingrad reaches the main airfield supplying the beleaguered Germans.

December 27–Stalingrad: The German Army Group Don is itself nearly encircled by Eremenko's advances, through the Rumanians, in the south and Vatutin to the north. These advances also threaten Rostov and all the German forces north of the Caucasus.

The Germans create a Russian National Army under the captured General Vlasov.

1943

January 7–Caucasus: Forward units of Eremenko's army reach the headquarters of the German troops in the Caucasus, 30 miles from Rostov, and the Germans start to leave the area. The Soviets are not powerful enough to stop them.

January 12–Leningrad: The siege of Leningrad is lifted by a narrow passage south of Lake Ladoga, but the front outside remains unchanged.

Roosevelt and Churchill hold a conference at Casablanca in North Africa, to which Stalin is invited but does not come, given the pressure of the war and his belief that all his allies should do is to attack in the west. The plans outlined at Casablanca mean that the USSR will continue to bear the brunt of the fighting until the next year.

January 13–Center: On the Voronezh Front the Hungarian army is attacked, smashed, and its line broken. Zhukov and Vasilevsky are briefly attached to this front for the offensive and Zhukov draws up plans to move on to Kharkov.

January 17–Stalingrad: The Stalingrad siege is now fought at minus 30 degrees centigrade; German rations are reduced to 200 grams of horsemeat and 75 of bread. The pocket is half its original size and only one supply airfield remains. Aircraft have 300 miles to fly and only bring 60 tons a day.

January 23–German munitions of the Russian Front are reported dangerously low. From 3,300 tanks used at the invasion of June 1941 there are now only 495 battle-ready tanks on the Eastern front and the Soviet KV and T34 tanks are proving superior. The Red air force is increasing in number and improving in fighting quality. However, the Germans have the new Tiger and Panther tanks and new fighter planes on the way.

January 31–Stalingrad: The German von Paulus is promoted to field marshal, but, despite this encouragement, he surrenders at Stalingrad with 91,000 soldiers and 24 generals (16,700 had already surrendered and 70,000 had died.)

February 16–Center: Kharkov, evacuated by the Germans, is taken. However, counterattacks throw back the Red Army on the Voronezh Front.

March 6–Stalin styles himself marshal of the Soviet Union.

March 12–Center: Kharkov is retaken and the Soviets recoil, losing the initiative they have held since last November.

April–The NKGB (People's Commissariat for State Security) is made independent, relieving Beria's NKVD of state security and concentrating it on public order and the smooth functioning of the war economy. The special NKVD sections are removed from the army and converted to an independent organization (this develops into SMERSH, or the General Section for Terror and Diversion).

April 26–Stalin breaks off diplomatic relations with the Polish government in exile in London, in protest at its accusations after the discovery of the Katyn Forest massacres.

May 15–The Comintern is dissolved, encouraging the United States to believe in the end of the Soviet Union's international ambitions.

July 1–Hitler assembles his commanders and prepares for a new offensive in the Soviet Union. The Stavka recognizes that there will be a German offensive and decides to wait for this and then counter firmly, using a reserve force placed opposite the Kursk salient. The front commanders are Rokossovsky of the Central Front, Vatutin of the Voronezh Front, and Konev with the Steppe Front in reserve.

July 5–August 23–Center: The biggest tank battle in the history of warfare takes place in and around Kursk, where, on July 10, the German offensive is halted by Rokossovsky's artillery and effective antitank weapons with the demoralizing use of antitank rockets from aircraft.

July 10–Anglo-American forces land on Sicily. This is the first landing on Europe by the Western Allies.

July 12–Center: The Western and Bryansk fronts attack toward Orel and Kharkov.

July 25–Mussolini, the Italian leader, is arrested and a new Italian government is formed. Italy no longer wants to fight, forcing the Germans into a war on two European fronts. Needing troops for Italy, Hitler orders his Army Group Center to evacuate its salient at Orel.

August 3–Center: On the Voronezh and Donets fronts the Red Army surprises the Germans and moves toward Kharkov, which they reach on August 13.

Stalin makes his only wartime visit to a fighting front, southwest of Moscow.

August 5–Center: Orel is retaken.

August 6–Soviet papers start a campaign to show that the only effective anti-Japanese force in China is the Communist army and not Chiang Kai-shek's nationalists.

August 23–Center: Kharkov falls, but the Red Army's advance comes to a halt.

August 26–Ukraine: Rokossovsky attacks from beyond Kursk as part of a general broad-front Soviet attack, and the Germans fall back in the Ukraine and in the south.

September 8–Orthodox ecclesiastical administration and seminaries are allowed to be reestablished. Metropolitan Sergius is elected patriarch and is officially received by Stalin.

September 21–Ukraine: Moving rapidly, at 15 miles a day, the Red Army reaches the Dnieper River, soon holding 400 miles of is eastern bank and making a number of crossings.

October 9–Crimea: The German forces on the Crimea are isolated; Hitler has decided to hold it as a protection for Rumanian oil and lest its loss change the attitude of neutral Turkey.

October 15–30–Conference of Allied Foreign Ministers (Britain, China, United States, and USSR) in Moscow. The United States demands that China be one of the four major countries to sign the Declaration of the Four Nations on General Security. This gives the first agreement to demand unconditional surrender from Germany but the possibility of negotiating with other enemies, and provides for the administration of both liberated lands and former enemy countries.

November–Tito, the Communist leader of Yugoslavia, achieves Allied recognition.

The Karachai Autonomous Region is dissolved because of the belief that they had collaborated with the Germans and the surviving people deported eastward.

November 6–Ukraine: After breaking through from a Dnieper bridgehead, Soviets retake Kiev.

November 26–Ukraine: Exhaustion and mud stop further movement and a German counterattack halts the Soviets.

November 28–December 1–Allied conference at Teheran; China is not present, at Stalin's insistence. Stalin demands a second front by the Anglo-Americans in 1944 and tells Roosevelt and Churchill that the Soviet Union will join the war against Japan, but only after the defeat of Germany. Postwar Europe is discussed. The Soviet Union demands and gets the promise that its borders will be at least those of June 1941, and that part of East Prussia will be included. Poland will not have any part of the Ukraine or Belorussia. The Soviet Union claims those parts of Poland east of the Curzon Line and it is allowed to move its borders westward to the Oder River. It is agreed that Finland will maintain its national identity. On the Far East, Stalin requires an ice-free port and Dairen is suggested with Soviet use of the Manchurian Railway.

Roosevelt proposes to Stalin a postwar international organization of about 40 nations, with a small group of the big-four nations and a few others as an executive committee. This is the seed of the United Nations.

December 24–Ukraine: The winter campaign starts from the Ukraine.

December 27–The Kalmyk Autonomous Republic is dissolved after claims that they had collaborated with the German occupiers and its people are deported to the east.

1944

January 5–Ukraine: Under Konev the Red Army's Ukraine offensive starts against fierce German opposition, but surrounds large numbers of them south of Kiev.

January 12–Following a broadcast by the Polish government in London, affirming its rights to its former territory, Molotov asserts that the people of all Belorussia and the Ukraine have chosen to join the USSR and that the Poles should enter into an agreement with the Soviet Union about future frontiers. He also points out the anti-Soviet tone of statements by Polish generals and leaders of the underground.

January 14–Leningrad and Baltic: The Soviet offensive starts from the bridgehead west of Leningrad and is followed by attacks to the south, which cut off the Germans in Novgorod.

January 27–Leningrad: Leningrad is relieved after 870 days of siege.

January 29–Ukraine: Vatutin's troops on the Ukrainian Front cross the 1939 Polish frontier.

February–About 400,000 Chechen and 75,000 Ingush Sunni Muslims are deported from their Caucasus home to Kazakhstan and western Siberia as a result of their anti-Soviet uprising, following the German occupation of their area in 1942. They are rehabilitated in 1957.

February 4–Ukraine: The Germans encircled in the Ukraine are supported by air drops. A relief force gets near them and there is a breakout. Half escape but return to the German army with an infectiously low morale.

February 15–Baltic: Hitler agrees to a retreat on the Baltic coast out of Russia into Estonia. Both sides now get into defensive positions, with their main forces in Belorussia and the Ukraine.

February 23–Finland secretly discusses terms with the Soviet Union through Alexandra Kollontay, its ambassador in Sweden.

February 24–Ukraine: Soviet forces regroup to complete the clearing of the Ukraine. The partisans are no longer all pro-Soviet, some being nationalist Ukrainians and some anti-German and anti-Russian Poles. Khrushchev (with Brezhnev as his deputy) sets the NKVD to weed out the Ukrainian nationalist UPA (Insurgent Army).

February 29–Vatutin is shot and killed by Ukrainian partisans. Zhukov replaces him.

March 6–South: An encircling movement in the southern Ukraine aims at Odessa. Although Zhukov moves his army 200 miles in six weeks, the Germans escape.

March 8–The Kabardino-Balkarian Autonomous Republic temporarily loses the "Balkaria" part of its name, as the 40,000 Turkic-speaking Balkars from the Caucasus Mountains are deported to the east because of collaboration with the Germans. They are permitted to return to their lands after 1957.

March 9–South: The Red Army reaches the Rumanian border.

March 30–Japan closes her concessions on northern Sakhalin Island and a five-year fishery agreement is signed. With the war in both west and east turning against the Axis, Japan is anxious not to quarrel with the Soviet Union.

April 8–Crimea: The Soviet attack on the Crimea starts. Hitler has ordered the Crimea to be defended.

April 10–South: The Red Army retakes Odessa.

May 5–Crimea: In the Crimea, all but Sebastopol is cleared of German and Rumanian troops.

May 10–Crimea: Sebastopol's defenses collapse after heavy artillery and air bombardment, and Germans take the city.

June–The Crimean Tatar Autonomous Republic is dissolved and 200,000 Crimean Tatars are deported, accused of having helped the Germans in the occupation of their country.

June 6–D-Day. The United States and Britain make landings on Normandy beaches of France. At this time the German army is deployed with 54 divisions in the west, 27 in Italy, 25 in the Balkans, 15 in Scandinavia, and 164 on the Russian fronts.

June 9–Finland: An attack on Finland drives the Finns back to their 1940 lines on the Karelian Isthmus.

June 10–The U.S. ambassador to the Soviet Union, Averell Harriman, asks for air bases in the Far East; Stalin agrees but progress is very slow since Stalin does not wish Americans on Soviet territory.

June 23–Center: Two weeks after the Anglo-American landings in France, the Soviet summer Belorussian offensive begins. Two marshals of the Soviet Union command: Vasilievsky to the north of the sector and Zhukov to the south. The Germans are prepared to defend the Ukraine, but the Red Army, now heavily outnumbering the Germans in men, tanks, guns, and aircraft, strikes through Belorussia toward the Baltic. Vitebsk is surrounded and Hitler, in Bavaria and not realizing the hopelessness of the situation, orders its defense.

July 4–Center and Baltic: Red Army takes Minsk, the capital of Belorussia, and a huge breach is opened leaving the way clear to the Baltic states and East Prussia.

July 13–Baltic: The Red Army takes Vilnius.

July 14–Ukraine: The Soviet offensive in the Ukraine, after two days of artillery barrage and probing reconnaissance raids, starts with overwhelming air superiority. One group surrounded includes an SS division recruited from Galician Ukrainians.

July 25–Poland: The Vistula River is reached with elements of the Soviet-created Polish army following.

A rada (Committee of National Liberation) is set up as a Soviet-controlled Polish government and Lublin is declared the capital.

July 27–Poland: The Red Army enters Lvov after several days' fighting.

July 28–Poland: Brest-Litovsk falls after attempts to defend it by the Germans, and the northern offensive reaches the Baltic coast near Riga, cutting off a large German army.

July 30–Stanislaus Mikolajcek, the head of the Polish government in London, arrives in Moscow, hoping to make some agreement with the Soviet Union in the belief that it needs his cooperation with the Polish underground.

August 1–Finland: The Finnish president resigns and is replaced by Marshal Mannerheim. He gets Sweden's promise of food supplies and is able to act independently of Germany.

Poland: As the Red Army reaches the outskirts of Warsaw, the 35,000-strong Polish Home Army rises against the German occupiers. Not under the control of the Soviet Union, it wishes to take Warsaw itself and not be liberated by, nor in debt to, the Russians. The Soviet Union publicly declares that there is no uprising, but if there is one it is of a group friendly to the Germans, or if neither of these, then they are criminally wasting Polish lives.

August 7–8–Mikolajcek speaks to the Polish Committee of National Liberation and to Molotov. He is offered a place in the government and advised not to return to London but to go to Warsaw. He refuses.

August 10–Poland: A Soviet bridgehead on the east bank of the Vistula goes on the defensive as the Red Army advance loses its momentum.

August 16–The Soviet Union tells Britain that it will not go to the help of the Polish Home Army and refuses British-U.S. aircraft permission to land a supply-dropping mission.

August 20–Balkans: The Red Army moves into Rumania, whose army offers little resistance and leaves German units to fend for themselves.

August 21–At Dumbarton Oaks in the United States, there are British-Soviet-U.S. talks on plans for the future United Nations.

August 23–Balkans: The Rumanian dictator Ion Antonescu is overthrown and there is an immediate armistice with the Soviet Union. More than 150,000 German troops are lost in the surrender.

September 4–Finland: Finland sues for peace and an armistice is signed. German troops are expelled after fighting.

September 7–Balkans: Soviet troops, having crossed the southern Carpathian Mountains, are in Hungarian Transylvania. Hungarian troops begin to run away from the German lines.

September 8–Balkans: The Soviet army enters Bulgaria with which it is not at war (although Bulgaria is at war with Britain). Under these pressing circumstances Bulgaria declares war against Germany.

September 14–Baltic: On the Baltic Front German offensive starts, but after 10 days it is halted after the German Army Group North has withdrawn from Estonia and is cut off in Kurland. The Stavka now reorients the northern attack toward the west.

September 21–Tito, the Yugoslavia guerrilla leader who has been in close cooperation with the British, flies to Moscow and meets Stalin, who promises him military help.

October 2–Poland: The last of the Polish Home Army in Warsaw surrenders. The special SS police who have been given the task of putting down the uprising, do so with terrible brutality.

October 6–Balkans: Under Timoshenko, Soviet troops, with Rumanian allies, thrust into Hungary.

October 9–Churchill and Eden are in Moscow. With Harriman, the U.S. ambassador, they ask Stalin how long it will be before the Soviet Union declares war on Japan. Stalin agrees to U.S. air bases in Siberia, and this matter is raised again in 1945 at Yalta. A further Lend-Lease program of assistance to the Soviet Union is agreed upon. They review the present military situation and describe how the Germans will finally be conquered. An agreement is reached on the control of the Balkans, with the Soviet Union dominating Bulgaria and Rumania; Britain, Greece, but Hungary and Yugoslavia to be shared equally.

October 15–Balkans: Admiral Miklos Horthy, the Hungarian dictator, attempts to make peace but he is arrested and taken to Germany. By the end of the month Soviet troops are just outside Budapest, which they gradually surround.

October 22–Germany: Soviet troops

enter their first German territory, East Prussia.

November 14–The Committee for the Liberation of Russia is set up in Prague, with its armed forces under the nominal command of Andrei Vlasov.

December–A Hungarian provisional government is set up at Debrecen and declares war on Germany.

Zhdanov is moved from Leningrad to Moscow to run party affairs for Stalin.

December 2–General de Gaulle of France, newly liberated, comes to Moscow. The meeting culminates in a Franco-Soviet accord.

1945

January 12–Poland: Konev on the Ukrainian Front begins an offensive from the Vsitula to the Oder rivers. The attack is made at the earliest possible moment, to relieve some of the pressure on the American and British under attack in the Ardennes. Hitler, in the west, switches reserves from East Prussia to support the defenses. Konev's men are soon racing to the Oder River.

January 14–Germany: Rokossovsky's offensive starts north into East Prussia, where Hitler has weakened his forces.

January 19–Baltic: Rokossovsky's men reach the Baltic east of Danzig. The Germans here, now called Army Group Kurland, are cut off and stay there until the end of the war.

January 23–Germany: Konev's Ukrainian Front reaches and crosses the Oder River.

February–The Japanese approach the Soviet ambassador with proposals for peace with the United States. This approach is not reported to the United States.

February 3–Poland: German forces withdraw from Warsaw.

February 4–11–The heads of the allied governments, the Great Powers, meet at Yalta in the Crimea; Stalin, Roosevelt, and Churchill attend.

Stalin agrees to end the Russo-Japanese neutrality pact of 1941 and to declare war on Japan two or three months after Germany's surrender, providing:

(1) the Mongolian People's Republic is maintained:

(2) the 1904 gains by Japan against czarist Russia including Sakhalin, are returned, Dairen is made an international port, the Soviet Union will have a naval base at Port Arthur, and the railways are brought back under Sino-Russian control;

(3) The Kurile Islands are given to the Soviet Union.

February 8–Germany: Konev moves into Lower Silesia. His men draw level with the Belorussian Front troops of Zhukov in Pomerania. Breslau is surrounded and the Germans in it fight on.

February 10–Germany: Rokossovsky's offensive in northeast Germany halts, worn out and short of ammunition.

February 11–Balkans: The last surviving German troops on Balkan Front try to leave Budapest and most of them are killed.

March 5–Balkans: A German offensive is mounted in southern Hungary and Yugoslavia, and for 10 days it advances until troops and ammunition are exhausted.

March 16–Balkans: The Soviets counterattack in southern Hungary, nearly cutting off part of the German army, which escapes and is followed into Austria.

March 25–Germany: Soviet and U.S. forces meet on the Elbe River.

March 28–Poland: Gdynia and, two days later, Danzig (Gdansk) are taken with large numbers of prisoners and 45 German submarines captured. The surviving garrisons with a mass of refugees move into the estuary of the Vistula River, where they hold out until after the war.

April 5–Molotov renounces the neutrality pact with Japan. Japan assumes this to be the beginning of the agreed upon 12-month notice of the ending of the pact.

April 6–Germany: An assault on the city of Königsberg in East Prussia starts. Resistance is fanatical and fighting goes on for six days, followed by terrible atrocities and revenge by the Red Army.

April 13–Austria: The Soviets occupy Vienna after seven days of street fighting.

April 15–Germany: Zhukov starts his final assault toward Berlin. When the Soviet armies reach the city from north, east, and south, they have to fight every inch of the way.

April 29–Italy: The German army in Italy surrenders to the British.

April 30–Germany: As Soviet troops reach the center of Berlin, Hitler kills himself in his bunker headquarters.

May 1–The first negotiations for a cease-fire start in Berlin.

May 2–All fighting in Berlin stops.

May 7–Unconditional surrender is signed by the Germans with Britain and the United States.

The National Liberation Army, the Russian army under Vlasov created by the Germans, takes Prague from German SS troops.

May 9–A second surrender document, ratifying the first, is signed in Berlin.

June–In Poland a Government of National Unity is set up. Stalin assumes the rank of generalissimo, confirming his status as victor of the Great Patriotic War.

July 1–13–A Sino-Soviet conference in Moscow confirms the terms of the Yalta agreement. China receives a pledge from Stalin that any Soviet troops will be withdrawn from Chinese territory three months after Japan's surrender and that the Soviet Union will give the Chinese nationalist government military support. This seems to repudiate support for the Chinese Communists.

July 17–August 2–The Potsdam Conference is attended by Stalin, Truman, and Churchill (whose place is taken by Clement Attlee after the British elections).

The Oder-Neisse Line is agreed upon as the western frontier of Poland.

Truman asks Stalin formally to cooperate in joint action against Japan.

August 6–The United States drops the first atomic bomb on Japan at Hiroshima. The Soviet Union is not consulted.

August 8–The Soviet Union declares war against Japan.

August 9–The Red Army under Marshal Vasilevsky attacks in Manchuria and meets only weak resistance.

August 10–The Chinese Communist army commander Chu Teh orders his men to accept the Japanese surrender and to move into Manchuria to meet and work with the Soviet army. Chiang Kai-shek's order to the Communist army to remain in place is ignored.

August 12–Soviet forces land in Korea.

August 14–Japan offers to surrender. The USSR's official line is that Japan's surrender is caused by the Soviet Union's decisive contribution to victory, not the atomic bombs.

August 20–The Japanese Kwantung army is defeated.

September 2–The Japanese surrender ceremony is held on the U.S. battleship *Missouri*, the Soviet General K. N. Derevyanko present.

Soviet losses in this campaign are put officially at 8,219 dead against 80,000 Japanese dead.

Stalin proposes to U.S. General Douglas MacArthur that General Vasilevsky be an equal commander in Tokyo. This is not accepted—there is to be no four-power control of Japan. However, Vasilevsky had command of Manchuria and North Korea, and Japanese forces north of the 38th parallel are ordered to surrender to him. In Manchuria the Soviet Union begins to remove industrial units and to control the railways. Chinese Communists of Manchurian origin (some who had been in the Soviet Union since the 1930s) occupy the land. A conference of foreign ministers in London ends in a deadlock over the Balkan issues.

November 9–Chinese Communists block the entry of Chinese nationalist troops to Manchuria, while Soviet troops control the ports of entry.

December 15–At the foreign ministers' conference in Moscow, including George Marshall from the United States and Ernest Bevin from Britain, Molotov obtains agreement that both Soviet and U.S. forces will withdraw from China. Korea is not to be immediately reunified, but there will be a trusteeship of the USSR in the north and the United States in the south, with a future government based on democratic parties. However there is to be no part for the Soviet Union to play in Japan.

Khrushchev is appointed first secretary of the Ukrainian Communist party.

1946

January–About 250,000 Soviet occupation troops move into North Korea. Kim Il-sung, a former Communist party secretary in Manchuria, is sent there.

January 16–February 5–A Soviet-U.S. conference on Korea in Seoul ends without decisions.

January 21–All Japanese industrial developments in Manchuria, described as the property of the Japanese army, are deemed booty of war by the Soviet Union.

February–Stalin announces the Fourth Five-Year Plan. He says that in 15 years the Soviet Union will produce 500 million tons of coal, 60 million tons of steel, and 60 million tons of oil, perhaps outstripping the United States. In fact all these long-term targets are achieved (with the initial help of 2 million German prisoners of war and the industrial plant shipped as reparations from Germany and Manchuria).

February 13–Nationalist China accepts the independent status of Outer Mongolia (the Mongolian People's Republic) and establishes diplomatic relations with it.

March 5–Churchill gives the Iron Curtain speech at Fulton, Missouri. Stalin tells the U.S. ambassador that he demands a base in the Turkish Dardanelles.

March 20–A second Soviet-U.S. conference on Korea ends in failure, with accusations that the Americans have blocked Korean unity.

May–The foreign ministers' conference on Germany, having assumed the 1932 level of production as the norm (unattainable under the conditions of 1946), and basing German reparations on this, the United States finds this unjust and declines to make further shipments of good or machinery to the Soviets.

May 31–After demonstrations in universities and cities of China, Soviet troops finally leave Manchuria. At this time, many of the Russians living there in exile after the civil war, especially in Harbin, are made Soviet citizens and many return to the Soviet Union.

July–The British and U.S. occupation zones of Germany are merged into one economic unit, while the French zone remains separate, pending that country's claims on the Saar. This makes a powerful economic unit, dividing the country effectively into East and West Germany.

USSR, with postwar occupation forces in Iran, takes steps to annex Iranian Azerbaijan and to integrate it into the Soviet Azerbaijan Republic. Iran appeals to the United Nations and the Soviet troops are withdrawn.

August–The "Zhdanovshchina" in Leningrad, purging the party that survived the siege, begins.

August 2–Vlasov and his associates are hanged in Moscow.

December–Construction of the first Soviet nuclear reactor begins.

1947

January 5–The U.S. State Department demands that Dairen become a free port, according to the 1945 agreement. The Soviet Union replies that since the war with Japan (in the sense of a peace treaty) has not ended, Dairen is still in its hands.

February–The USSR signs peace treaties with Bulgaria, Finland, Hungary, Italy, and Rumania.

March–April–A foreign ministers' conference is held in Moscow (Molotov,

Bevin for Britain, and Marshall for the United States) to prepare a peace treaty with Germany.

March 12–U.S. President Truman responds to Soviet moves in Iran and Turkey with a message formulating the Truman Doctrine: the U.S. policy is to support "free peoples to work out their own destinies their own ways." U.S. military assistance to Turkey and Greece follows. The Truman Doctrine is accepted by the U.S. Congress in April.

June–Aid is offered to all of Europe under the Marshall Plan, formulated by the U.S. secretary of state. Stalin refuses aid. Czechoslovak coalition government (with its Communist premier Klement Gottwald) decides to accept it.

September–Zhdanov denounces both the Truman Doctrine and the Marshall Plan as the "twin forks" of U.S. imperialist policy. He claims the support of the people's democracies and also other freedom-loving people, including what will come to known as the Third World.

October–Cominform is established at Warsaw Conference, but Yugoslav leader Tito rejects control by Moscow and claims each nation's right to its own "road to socialism."

December 16–Currency reform is announced in the USSR, rendering all existing bank notes useless but exchangeable, 1 old for 1 new ruble in cash, with varying exchanges for amounts held legally in banks. The aim is to wipe out profits of wartime speculators.

1948

January–A United Nations Special Commission visits Korea, but the USSR does not take part, although the delegate for the Ukraine (a full member of the United Nations) has been nominated to the commission.

January 13–Solomon Mikhoels, the Jewish actor and leader, is killed in Minsk, in a traffic accident arranged by the MGB (Ministry of State Security).

February–A full Communist government takes over in Czechoslovakia after claims that Edward Benes was going to form a government without Communists. Although there are riots, the Communist leader Klement Gottwald forms a new coalition government, including the liberal Jan Masaryk. There is a purge of officials and academics. Masaryk dies in a fall from a window in his office. This is either suicide or murder, but the facts are concealed.

The joint Allied Control Commission in Berlin ceases to function.

March–In Berlin, the Soviet commander walks out of the four-power Military Control Council.

April–Travel restrictions are imposed by Soviets on movement between their zone and the Allied zones of western Germany.

June–The Soviets refuse further collaboration with the Berlin four-power Military Control Council.

June 28–The Cominform, at its first meeting, expels Yugoslavia, after Stalin has failed to obtain its submission.

Berlin blockade: Berlin, lying within the Soviet occupation zone of Germany and divided into four sectors, each controlled by one of the Allies, is seen as an obstruction to Soviet control of its zone. Soviets try to isolate the city by land, closing the roads and railways from the Western zones, which means that food and fuel supplies are cut off. The Western Allies respond with a massive airlift of fuel, food, and other supplies. The blockade and airlift last nearly a year.

July 31–August 7–Stalin gives public support to Trofim Lysenko's biological theories through a session of the Academy of Agricultural Sciences.

August 31–Zhdanov, the powerful secretary to the Central Committee and leader of the Leningrad party, dies at the age of 52. His death is followed by the arrest and execution of many of his associates, with thousands sent to camps. This is the Leningrad Purge.

October 10–The first Soviet long-range guided missile is launched. During 1948 there are revolts in forced labor camps, of which there are not yet full details. Notably in Vorkuta, prisoners who had held field officer rank rise up and are only subdued by the use of bomber aircraft.

1949

January 5–10–The Soviet Academy of Sciences condemns "Western idolatry," forcing scientists to turn away from research conducted outside the USSR. Anti-cosmopolitan campaigns are launched; these are also effectively anti-Semitic.

January 25–COMECON, an organization to stimulate trade and economic cooperation, is set up in Moscow. The founding members are the USSR, Bulgaria, Czechoslovakia, Hungary, Poland, and Rumania.

March–Andrei Vyshinsky becomes foreign minister.

Treaty with Korea.

April 4–NATO, the North Atlantic Treaty Organization, is formed.

May–A Communist government takes over in Hungary.

May 12–The Berlin blockade is lifted.

September 25–Tass announces the testing of the first Soviet atomic bomb.

October 1–The Communist People's Republic of China is formed.

November–Soviet Control Commission in Berlin is constituted. Marshal Rokossovsky is appointed supreme commander in Poland. He holds this post until 1956.

December–On Stalin's 70th birthday there are major public celebrations. Foreign Communist leaders visit Moscow, including Mao Tse-tung.

1950

January 10–The Soviet delegation to the United Nations objects to Nationalist China's being seated rather than the People's Republic. In protest the Soviet Union boycotts the United Nations for the next six months.

February 14–A treaty of friendship with China is signed. Stalin attends Mao Tse-tung's reception in its honor.

Stalin's letter on linguistics, attacking Nikolai Marr, a philologist who claimed language to have class basis and that rulers and the oppressed speak, in effect, in different languages; Stalin rules that language is a matter of nationality not class. This signals attacks on large areas of academic research, in sociology, archeology, and ethnology.

June 25–Outbreak of Korean War. This conflict between the Koreans, with Chinese participation against the United States and its allies, lasts until July 1954, with the Soviet Union keeping itself out of direct involvement.

July 7–The United Nations Security Council, which the USSR is boycotting over the issue of China and so cannot veto, votes to establish a United Nations military command in Korea.

During 1950 there is a wave of executions in forced labor camps.

1951

Fifth Five-Year Plan.

The forced labor camps on Sakhalin break into revolt.

1952

March 10–The Soviet Union sends a diplomatic note to the United States, proposing a peace treaty with Germany, with all Germany becoming a neutral area. The United States does not accept this.

October 5–15–The 19th Party Congress. Stalin's paper on "Economic Problems of Socialism in the USSR" is put forward. The term "Bolshevik" is dropped from the party's title and the Politburo is to be renamed the Central Committee Presidium. The possibility of peaceful co-existence with capitalist countries is expressed.

1953

January 13–The "Doctors' Plot": nine Kremlin doctors, seven of whom are Jewish, are arrested, accused of espionage for a U.S. Jewish organization and of murdering party leaders including Zhdanov. Confessions are obtained (although two of the doctors die during the investigation).

March 5–After a heart attack, Stalin dies. A specialist, with the "Doctors' Plot" in mind, hesitates to examine him.

A conference of Politburo members and the Council of Ministers is held. Malenkov takes over Stalin's posts as chairman, or premier; and party secretary. Beria retains control of the security services and Bulganin takes over the armed forces. A week later Khrushchev is moved from party secretaryship for

Moscow and appointed to the party's Secretariat.

March 14–Malenkov is relieved of his functions in the party's Secretariat.

April–The arrest of the doctors is condemned in the press as having been irregular and unlawful. *Pravda* attacks MGB (State Security) men for having caused dissension among "people of different nationalities." This is the end of the anti-Semitic campaign of Stalin's last years.

June 17–Riots in Berlin are put down, using Soviet tanks.

July–Beria, suspected by the other leaders of trying to take power from them, is arrested in the Kremlin on orders signed by Voroshilov. At a signal from Malenkov, soldiers led by Zhukov seize Beria and take him to the headquarters of the Moscow Military District, while Khrushchev, Bulganin, and Molotov reveal the extent of Beria's ambitions to other party leaders.

Under Ivan Serov,the MVD (Ministry of Internal Affairs) is neutralized; new troops are put on guard at the Kremlin and all senior MVD men in Moscow and throughout the Soviet Union are detained.

July 27–After Korean truce talks are initiated in the United Nations by the Soviet Union, an armistice is signed by the U.S. commander of the United Nations force and the commander of the North Koreans.

August 9–Malenkov makes the first of several speeches calling for consumerism: an increase in the production and consumption of goods and food, a decrease in military expenditures, and an increase in money in the hands of the people. He turns against the Stalinist doctrine that heavy industry has priority. To the Supreme Soviet he states that people have the right to demand consumer goods of high quality.

August 20–The first Soviet hydrogen bomb test is announced.

September–Khrushchev is elected first secretary of the party's Central Committee.

December–Execution of Beria and other leading MVD officers is announced.

The second Soviet hydrogen bomb test is carried out at a great altitude, showing that the Soviet Union now has the most powerful missile in the world.

1954

January 25–February 18–At a four-power conference in Berlin, of Britain, France, the United States, and the USSR, Molotov proposes a peace treaty with Germany, with both states, East and West, signing as equals (this ensuring the recognition of two Germanys). The conference ends without a decision.

January 22–In contrast to Malenkov's consumerism, Khrushchev proposes to the Presidium that the country improve its economy through the Virgin Lands campaign, using fallow land for increased grain production.

In Kazakhstan there are protests about this policy because it will also lead to use of traditional and necessary grazing land, and the extra work involved will mean the importation of more Russians.

Khrushchev also argues that the need to use fallow land should take priority over the improvement of existing agricultural resources. He appeals directly to the Komsomols to carry out this policy.

March–The Central Committee resolves that 13 million hectares be plowed for the Virgin Lands campaign and that corn alone should be planted there.

USSR helps to negotiate the treaty at Panmunjom to end the Korean war.

April 26–A conference is called on East Asia, with Britain and the Soviet Union co-chairing, and representatives from France, China, the United States, and the Indochina states. It agrees to elections in both North and South Korea and after the French evacuation of Indochina, to the setting up of North and South Vietnam.

June 5–The Virgin Lands target is raised to 30 million hectares.

June 27–The first nuclear power station is put in operation at Obninsk, near Moscow.

October 12–Khrushchev and Bulganin visit Peking. A friendship agreement is signed.

November 22–Andrei Vyshinsky dies in New York.

December–Abakumov trial is held. Vikor Abakumov, who had been minister of internal security from 1947 to 1951 and had succeeded Zhdanov in the Leningrad Purge, is put on trial with other security men on charges of corrupt behavior. The case reveals scandals of the Stalinist period. All the accused are found guilty and executed.

1955

February 8–Malenkov is dismissed as premier, on charges of mismanagement of industry and agriculture. Bulganin takes his post.

April 18–27–Asian-African Conference in Bandung. Twenty-nine countries of Asia and Africa (including Communist China, but excluding the USSR) meet in Indonesia. Dissatisfied with the quarrels of the USSR and United States, the conference attempts to make the Third World a force in international politics.

May 14–The Warsaw Pact, a military alliance among the USSR, Bulgaria, Czechoslovakia, East Germany, Hungary, Poland, and Rumania, is signed. It is a response to the inclusion of West Germany in the North Atlantic Treaty Organization.

May 27–June 2–Bulganin and Khrushchev visit Yugoslavia, seeking reconciliation with Tito.

July 18–23–Geneva Summit Conference. Bulganin, U.S. Pres. Dwight D. Eisenhower, British Foreign Secretary Sir Anthony Eden, and Edgar Faure meet.

July 27–USSR agrees to peace with Austria and ends its military occupation.

August–There is a better Soviet harvest, but this is on traditional lands; the fallow lands suffer from a drought.

September–Konrad Adenauer, chancellor of West Germany, visits Moscow: there is agreement on recognition of West Germany through diplomatic relations.

November–December–Khrushchev and Bulganin visit Southeast Asia.

1956

January–Porkkala, a port on the Gulf of Finland granted to the USSR in the peace treaty, is returned to Finland as a gesture of good will.

February 14–25–The 20th Party Congress. The most important session excludes the press and features Khrushchev's "secret speech" attacking Stalin and the "cult of personality," and revealing for the first time details of the purges.

March–Riots in Tbilisi, Georgia.

April–Bulganin and Khrushchev visit Britain.

June–Food riots in Poznan, Poland.

Peoples including Kurds, Turks, and Islamic Kemshin Armenians are exonerated of treason during the war.

June 2–Shepilov succeeds Molotov as foreign minister.

July–Karelo-Finnish Soviet Socialist Republic reduced to the status of an autonomous republic, bringing the total of republics in the Soviet Union down from 16 to 15.

In the Virgin Lands campaign, 30 million hectares are cultivated. While the program is successful in neglected arable land, on the virgin lands there are severe problems of erosion.

September 11–The Crimean Tatars are exonerated of war crimes by the Supreme Soviet Presidium.

October 21–Wladislaw Gomulka is appointed Polish party secretary in spite of Soviet protests and a visit by Khrushchev.

October 23–Riots in Budapest, the capital of Hungary, against the Communist regime.

October 24–Imre Nagy becomes premier in Hungary and promises reforms, including elections and a break of the military treaty with the USSR. This causes Khrushchev to take firm action to protect Soviet interests.

November 4–Khrushchev sends Soviet tank forces to crush the Hungarian revolt. Imre Nagy is later shot, in 1958, without an open trial. He is "rehabilitated" in 1989.

Russian student groups organize meetings and distribute leaflets condemning Soviet intervention in Hungary. Many of the protesting students are arrested, expelled from the university, or sent to detention camps.

1957

January–Chinese Foreign Minister Chou En-lai visits Moscow, Warsaw, and Budapest.

February 16–Gromyko replaces Shepilov as foreign minister.

March–Khrushchev makes new economic proposals, reducing the functions of Gosplan, decentralizing economic planning, and introducing new local economic councils (sovnarkoz).

April–Directives to decentralize the economy are issued.

May–Sixty central industrial ministries are abolished in Moscow replaced by sovnarkhoz, in the hope that local interests will produce more effective planning.

June–There is a plot to depose Khrushchev by leading Stalinists in the Politburo including Molotov, Kaganovich, Bulganin, and Voroshilov. They claim that he has undermined the reputation of the party internationally and put Malenkov forward as leader. However, the army and the KGB do not support them and Khrushchev counters with a meeting of the party's Central Committee, which backs him. No members of the factional group are expelled from the party, in contrast to the practices of Stalinist times.

June 29–Kaganovich, Malenkov, Molotov, and Shepilov are removed from the Presidium and Central Committee.

The Cominform (which had replaced the Comintern) is abolished.

October 4–*Sputnik I*, the world's first artificial satellite, is launched. This causes considerable consternation in the West; the first U.S. satellite will not be launched until 1958.

Boris Pasternak's novel *Dr. Zhivago* is published abroad, first in Italy, having been rejected by Soviet publishing houses.

Khrushchev visits China, signing agreements on aid and nuclear cooperation.

October 26–Zhukov is removed from the Central Committee and his post of minister of defense while on a visit to Yugoslavia. He is accused of withdrawing the army from party control and of a "cult of personality." He is also perhaps felt to have political ambitions and to object to Khrushchev's amassing power. He is replaced by R. I. Malinovsky, a senior officer with no political weight.

November 7–Fortieth anniversary of the October Revolution. Conference of Communist party leaders of the world, including Mao Tse-tung but not Tito, is held in Moscow.

1958

January–The decision to reduce the Soviet armed forces by 300,000 men as an economy move meets with resistance from senior officers.

February 26–Motor Tractor Stations (MTS) are reorganized: the tractor stations are dissolved and their machinery is sold to the kolkhoz.

March 26–Khrushchev is appointed chairman of the Council of Ministers, while Bulganin is relegated to chairman of the State Bank, having been accused of taking part in the previous year's attempt to oust Khrushchev.

The Sixth Five-Year Plan (1956–60) is dropped, since its targets are seen to be overly optimistic and a new Seven-Year Plan (1959–65) is instituted with the aim of improving the standard of living.

May–Soviet credit to Yugoslavia is cancelled in retaliation for Tito's align-

ment with the Third World and with the West.

Soviet Union makes loans to support the economy of the West African state of Guinea, from which France has cut off all its aid. One totally inappropriate item is said to have consisted of an entire airport and all necessary equipment, including the standard snow plow for use in the (Russian) winter.

August 24–27–Race riots in Grozny, the capital of Chechen-Inguish Autonomous Soviet Socialist Republic to the west of the Caspian Sea in the Russian Soviet Federal Socialist Republic, whose former inhabitants wish to return to their home after banishment.

September–Bulganin and Voroshilov expelled from the Presidium. There's a record grain harvest, although meat production is not as high as planned. Oblasts are ordered to double their meat production.

October 23–The Pasternak affair: Boris Pasternak is awarded the Nobel Prize for Literature for *Dr. Zhivago*, while in the Soviet Union he is attacked by the Writers' Union and the Komsomol. Condemned via mass meetings, he is obliged to write a letter recanting the novel.

November–Educational reforms are introduced, adding practical training to the secondary school curriculum. The earlier intention to increase the compulsory 7-year schooling to 10 years is dropped, and an 8-year system is introduced. Post-school training is increased, and the number of correspondence or evening students is increased to exceed the full-timers.

Ivan Serov, head of the KGB, is demoted to run the GRU (Military Intelligence) on the pretext of the Belgian queen's crown (stolen during the war) having been found in his possession. This is followed by the retirement of many long-serving KGB officials.

December–By the end of the year most communal farm machinery and Motor Tractor Stations (MTS) have been closed since larger farms now have their own. This leaves the large number of average or smaller farms ill equipped, with ill-maintained machinery, and unable to achieve their targets.

1959

January–Khrushchev and Gromyko visit China. After this, Sino-Soviet relations deteriorate since the Chinese Communists regard Khrushchev as a "revisionist" of Leninism and so a dangerous influence.

21st Party Congress adopts the Seven-Year Plan, as the Sixth Five-Year Plan is an admitted failure.

New party leaders are promoted: Frol Koslov, Alexei Kosygin, Polyansky, and Mikhail Suslov.

A new *History of the Communist Party of the Soviet Union* is published. Stalin's *Short Course* of 1939 had been removed from the party's reading list after the 20th Congress in 1966. This is intended as an uncontroversial version, but it is never widely circulated.

February–British prime Minister Harold Macmillan visits Moscow.

May–Khrushchev visits Albania, attempting to save off a threatened rift.

June–Sino-Soviet atom agreement is rescinded by the USSR.

July–U.S. Vice Pres. Richard Nixon visits U.S. exhibition in Moscow. In a demonstration house, Nixon and Khrushchev hold the "kitchen debate" in which Khrushchev promises that Soviet Un-

ion will "teach America a lesson" and that it "will bury you all."

September–Russian rocket *Lunik II* lands on the moon.

The Chinese express anger at the Soviet's failure to support them in their claim for Indian territory. Khrushchev visits the United States, staying with President Eisenhower. He holds a press conference, then visits farms in Iowa and steel mills in Pittsburgh.

1960

January–The Supreme Soviet cuts the authorized numbers of the army and navy from 3.6 million to 2.4 million. This is half the 1953 strength, and consequently there are numbers of disgruntled prematurely retired officers who add to the growing lack of support for Khrushchev in the forces. It is expected that this demobilization will include 250,000 officers, some of them generals and admirals.

February–Khrushchev visits India, has meetings with Nehru, visits the Bhilhai steel works, which are being funded by the Soviet Union, and signs agreements on economic and cultural cooperation.

Mikoyan visits Cuba.

March–Khrushchev visits de Gaulle in Paris.

April–A shake-up in the military high command removes opponents of Khrushchev's policies, puts Ivan Konev in command of Warsaw Pact forces, and retires old friends of Stalin, such as Timoshenko.

May–Kozlov is elected to the Central Committee Secretariat.

Voroshilov is replaced by Brezhnev as chairman of the Presidium of the Supreme Soviet.

Marshal Sacharev is appointed chief of the General Staff.

May 1–The U.S. U2 reconnaissance aircraft piloted by Gary Powers is shot down near Sverdlovsk. This results in formal protests and cancellation of a summit meeting with Eisenhower in Paris. At first Khrushchev reports to the Supreme Soviet only that the plane had been shot down, without saying that Powers had been captured. He thus traps the U.S. state department into making easily disprovable statements denying the purpose of the flight.

May 30–Novelist and poet Boris Pasternak dies.

July–Economic and technical aid to China is stopped. Soviet experts are recalled.

September–Khrushchev loses his temper at a U.N. General Assembly meeting, interrupting a Western delegate by banging with his shoe on the desk and walking out of the meeting.

October–A missile at the Tura Tam test range blows up on the launch pad and kills the chief marshal of artillery, M. I. Nedelin, and perhaps 300 other officers and scientists.

December–Cuban delegation visits Moscow.

December 9–Volga Power Works is opened.

1961

January–M. A. Olshansky, a follower of Trofim Lysenko, is appointed minister of agriculture.

January 25–The crew of the U.S. plane shot down in 1960 is released.

April 12–Yuri Gagarin orbits the world in the spaceship *Vostok I*.

May–A Ukrainian Workers' and Peasants' Union is uncovered; its leaders are tried and condemned for anti-Soviet activity in planning to set up a separate Ukrainian socialist state.

June–Khrushchev and President John F. Kennedy meet in Vienna.

July 29–The Supreme Soviet revises the penal code and introduces the death penalty by shooting for those convicted of currency speculation.

August–Soviet Union demands, from the United States, Britain, and France, peace treaties with the two Germanys.

August 6–7–Gherman Titov makes the second fully orbital space flight, circling the earth 17 times in over 25 hours.

August 13–The Berlin Wall is erected, cutting off West Berlin. It is built as a result of the Western Allies' refusal to sign peace treaties with the two Germanys.

Khrushchev, in response to America's increased military budget and the Berlin crisis, cancels further cuts in the armed forces.

The Soviet Union resumes nuclear testing.

Albania breaks off relations with the Soviet Union.

September–The Belgrade Conference: 35 Mediterranean and Afro-Asian countries meet and agree on the principles of the Bandung Conference in 1955 and declare a policy of nonalignment. This conference is an embarrassment to the Soviets, since the dissident Communist leader of Yugoslavia, Marshal Tito, is the host.

Kwame Nkrumah, the president of Ghana, tours the Soviet Bloc after the Belgrade Conference.

October 17–31–22nd Party Congress.

The Seven-Year Plan is replaced with the Seventh Five-Year Plan (1961–65).

Khrushchev speaks both of increasing consumer satisfaction and of holding traditional budgetary policies.

October 30–Stalin's body is removed from the Lenin Mausoleum in Red Square.

1962

March–Khrushchev criticizes Soviet agriculture.

June–COMECON meeting is held in Berlin.

Food prices are increased. In Novocherkassk, in the industrial Donbas, there are riots in protest.

September–The Cuban missile crisis. Soviet guided anti-aircraft missiles are sent to Cuba, but President Kennedy warns that he will not tolerate such weapons in Cuba.

October–Kennedy orders a blockade of Cuba and puts U.S. forces on alert. Soviet troops are also placed on alert. Soviet ships are halted outside the blockaded area. After messages between the two leaders, the weapons are returned to the USSR.

November–The reorganization of the Soviet Union's administrative apparatus starts.

Alexander Solzhenitsyn's *One Day in the Life of Ivan Denisov* is published in *Novy Mir*, possibly on the instructions of Khrushchev.

1963

Brezhnev becomes secretary of the Central Committee

June 14–Khrushchev is attacked in the Chinese press, and in a letter to the Communist Party of the Soviet Union as "the Great Revisionist."

June 16–Valentina Tereshkova becomes the first woman to travel in outer space.

July 5–19–Sino-Soviet talks in Mos-

cow show further deterioration in relations. Cooperation between the two countries is almost at an end.

At an international conference in Tangyanika, President Julius Nyerere warns of a second scramble for Africa in the form of Sino-Soviet rivalry.

August 5–Détente: an agreement to ban the testing of nuclear weapons in the atmosphere is signed by Soviet Union, United States, and Britain.

August 31–The Moscow-Washington telephone hotline is installed.

The very poor harvest following bad weather leads to food shortages, and Soviet Union is obliged to import grain from Canada and the United States, bringing disrepute to Khrushchev's agriculture policies.

November–There are provocative Sino-Soviet border incidents between herdsmen and frontier guards.

The USSR offers to establish for Somalia an army of 10,000 men with an air force.

Chinese Premier Chou En-lai visits Africa and, in 1964 at the end of his tour, will say "Africa is ripe for revolution."

1964

A revolution in Zanzibar puts Sheikh Karume's Afro-Shirazi party in power: the USSR supports this group, even though its Marxist elements are soon discarded.

May–June–Khrushchev visits Egypt and Scandinavia.

July–Mikoyan replaces Brezhnev as chairman of the Presidium of the Supreme Soviet.

September–Khrushchev decides to increase consumer production.

October 13–14–While Khrushchev

is on holiday at the Black Sea, meetings of the Politburo, Presidium, and Central Committee lead to agreement to dismiss him. He accepts reluctantly and is retired quietly with a pension.

Khrushchev is replaced by Leonid Brezhnev as first secretary, and Alexei Kosygin as chairman of the Council of Ministers (Premier).

November–Party reorganization takes place.

1965

February–Kosygin visits Paris.

March–Alexei Leonov becomes the first person to walk in space. A new agricultural plan to expand production by increasing investment, lowering delivery quotas, cancelling kolkhoz debts, and awarding higher prices and higher wages is announced.

International Communist Conference is held in Moscow.

July 4–Brezhnev demands rearmament, citing increased defense expenditure in the United States.

August 28–The Volga Germans are exonerated of treachery during the war.

September–Yuli Daniel and Andrei Sinyavsky, underground writers of parodies of Soviet life—little known in the USSR, but read abroad—are arrested.

December–Podgorny succeeds Mikoyan as chairman of the Presidium of the Supreme Soviet.

Nyerere, sensitive to international feelings, maintains his Third World nonalignment, but says, "I gather that even the suits I wear have been adduced as evidence of pernicious Chinese influence."

1966

January 3–11–USSR mediates at Tashkent between India and Pakistan. A USSR–Mongolian treaty of friendship is signed.

February 10–14–Daniel and Sinyavsky trial results in sentences of five and seven years, but they give a bad impression of Soviet justice and of censorship throughout the world.

March–A U.S.–Soviet agreement on cultural and technical exchanges is made.

March–April–The 23rd Party Congress. The Seven-Year Plan is scrapped and a new Five-Year Plan introduced. The Politburo is reintroduced to replace the Central Committee Presidium and bring in younger men.

June 20–July 1–De Gaulle visits Moscow and a Soviet-French communiqué is issued that reduces East-West tension, heightened during the Vietnam war, by promising cooperation in several areas, notably in the Soviet Union's offering France assistance in launching space satellites.

1967

April–Svetlana Alliluyeva, Stalin's daughter who had left the Soviet Union in December 1966, refuses to return from abroad.

June–The Presidium of the Supreme Soviet renounces the accusations of treason against the Soviet Kurds, Turks, and Muslim Armenians made during the war.

September–The Crimean Tatars are exonerated of wartime treason.

1968

Prague Spring. The reforming government of Alexander Dubcek in Czechoslovakia encourages steps to give "socialism a human face." Many of those imprisoned or executed since 1948 are rehabilitated and the previous Communist governments blamed for injustice. Controls on industry are relaxed and a program of freedom is announced, removing censorship and giving people the right to travel freely.

April 21–Crimean Tatars celebrating in Uzbekistan are dispersed by police action.

August 21–The Soviet Union and Warsaw Pact allies invade Czechoslovakia. Dubcek and the central Committee are replaced with hard-liners led by Gustaf Husak.

October 26–Space ship *Soyuz* 3 is launched.

December–The TU-144 supersonic airliner makes its maiden flight.

1969

January 15–The first Soviet space station is put into orbit.

March–A border clash occurs between Soviet and Chinese troops, over an island on the Ussuri River.

A military coup takes place in Somalia, led by General Mohammed Siad Barre, who proclaims a Marxist state.

May 16–United States' *Venus* 5 space craft makes a landing on the planet Venus.

September–Kosygin meets with Chou En-lai to open border negotiations.

November – December – Preliminary SALT talks are held in Helsinki.

December–The Soviet budget allows for a 5.9 percent increase in defense spending for the coming year.

1970

March–USSR–Czechoslovak treaty of friendship is signed.

The Russo-Finnish treaty is extended.

July–A treaty of friendship, cooperation, and mutual assistance is signed with Rumania.

August 11–A treaty between the USSR and West Germany is signed by Chancellor Willy Brandt and Leonid Brezhnev.

October–Alexander Solzhenitsyn is awarded the Nobel Prize for Literature.

1971

February–Details of the Ninth Five-Year Plan call for greatly increased production of consumer rather than producer goods.

April–The 24th Party Congress emphasizes the need for a new European security settlement.

U.S. President Nixon gives figures for US–USSR relative missile strengths at the end of 1970:

	U.S.	USSR
ICBMs	1,054	1,440
Submarines launched	656	350

July–Ninety Soviet diplomats and other officials are ordered to leave Britain on grounds involving espionage.

Zhores Medvedev papers are published in Britain, revealing the experiences of himself and his brother Roy in Soviet psychiatric hospitals.

September 11–Nikita Khrushchev dies.

October–Kosygin announces that the emigration of Jews in the past eight months has exceeded the emigration of the past 20 years.

December–Brezhnev visits France, meets President Georges Pompidou, and signs a joint declaration of cooperation between France and the USSR.

1972

January–*Samzidat* journals in Moscow and Ukraine are suppressed after large-scale police searches.

May–Riots take place in Kaunas, Lithuania, in support of greater religious and political freedom. A 20-year-old worker, Romas Kalenta, burns himself alive to protest persecution of the church.

May 22–President Nixon visits Moscow, signing the first SALT antiballistic missile treaty, an interim agreement on offensive missiles, and establishing a U.S.–USSR Commercial Commission. This is the first-ever visit of a U.S. president to the USSR.

Berbera in Somlaia is made a Soviet military base and more military aid is given to the country.

1973

February–A report from the London School of Economics claims that there are 1 million prisoners in 1,000 Soviet labor camps, and that 10,000 of them are political prisoners.

May–Brezhnev visits the Federal Republic of Germany, signing cultural and economic agreements.

June–Brezhnev visits the United States, signing agreements on the prevention of nuclear war and to promote trade. He makes a TV broadcast to the U.S. nation.

The TU-144 airliner crashes at the Paris Air Show.

July–The International Lenin Peace Prize is presented to Brezhnev.

1974

Brezhnev agrees to a golf course near Moscow (in 1989 this proposal was renewed).

February–Demonstrations take place in Moscow and Tallinn by Volga Germans wanting to leave Russia and Estonia.

Solzhenitsyn is expelled from the USSR after publication of *Gulag Archipelago*.

July–On Nixon's second visit to the USSR, agreements on nuclear arms control are signed.

November–U.S. President Gerald R. Ford meets Brezhnev in Vladivostok.

The Somali army reaches 22,000, with equipment and jet fighters from USSR.

Ethiopian Emperor Hiale Selaisse is overthrown by a coup and U.S. military support is withdrawn.

1975

January–Soviets decide not to ratify USSR–U.S. trade agreement of 1972.

February–COMECON and European Economic Community secretariats meet in Moscow.

July 15–21–A joint Soviet-U.S. space flight, involving *Soyuz 19* and *Apollo* is made.

August 1–Thirty-two European heads of state, with Canada and the United States, hold a meeting with Brezhnev in Helsinki. The final act of the conference is signed, confirming the post-1945 frontiers, giving permanence to newly shaped countries such as Poland and East Germany. In exchange, the Soviet Union agrees to recognition of basic human rights. A result of this in the Soviet Union is the setting up of dissident "Helsinki groups" to monitor the behavior of Soviet authorities.

December–The Nobel Peace Prize is awarded to the Soviet scientist Andrei Sakharov.

1976

Menigistu Haile Miriam, having emerged as the leader of the Derg, the Ethiopian ruling group, makes declarations of Marxism and concludes an arms deal with the USSR.

February–The 25th Party Congress. Brezhnev reports shortcomings in achievements of agriculture and light industry.

An open letter protesting conditions is sent to the congress by Soviet dissidents.

The 10th Five-Year Plan is announced. The production goals of consumer goods promised by the Ninth Five-year Plan is announced. The production goals of consumer goods promised by the Ninth Five-Year Plan are not fulfilled. This plan again calls for emphasis on producer goods.

The 1975 grain harvest is announced as the worst for 10 years; total grain imports from the United States, July 1975–January 1976, have been 13 million tons.

May 28–Treaty on Underground Nuclear Explosions is signed by the United States and USSR.

1977

June 16–Brezhnev is made chairman of the Presidium of the Supreme Soviet, nominal head of state.

September–Hunger strike is conducted by the inmates of Perm prison camps.

October 7–Fourth (since 1917) Soviet constitution is adopted.

Somalia and Ethiopia come to war over Eritrea, whose ownership they dispute—two Soviet-armed states in conflict. Forced to take sides, the USSR chooses Ethiopia as its ally.

1978

January–Gromyko protests the possible introduction of the neutron bomb.

February–Soviet nationals are expelled from Canada for involvement in espionage.

June–August–The trial and sentencing of dissidents Orlov, Anatoly Sharansky, and Alexander Ginsburg. This arouses strong reactions in the United States.

August–China and Japan sign a treaty of peace and friendship, which the Soviet Union protests.

1979

January–In the United States there is anger when it is disclosed that 20 MIG-23 fighters have been delivered to Cuba in the previous year.

Viktor Korchnoi, the chess grandmaster living in Switzerland, is deprived of Soviet citizenship, under a law endorsed in December 1978.

July 18–SALT II (the Soviet–U.S. Strategic Arms Limitation Treaty) is signed by Brezhnev and U.S. President Jimmy Carter, in Vienna.

In Cambodia the Khmer Rouge is ousted and replaced by a Soviet-backed Vietnamese government.

December 24–The Soviet Union invades Afghanistan. By 1988 Soviet casualties will be 13,000 dead and 35,000 wounded.

1980

January–Sakharov is exiled to Gorky, after openly protesting the invasion of Afghanistan.

February–The U.S. CIA estimates that Soviet defense spending, given the present military activity, must increase from 11 percent to 15 percent of the GNP by 1985.

August–After strikes in Polish industrial centers, the independent trade union Solidarity is formed.

October–Negotiations on normalization of relations with China are suspended, owing to Soviet invasion of Afghanistan.

October–December–Kosygin resigns, and dies shortly afterwards.

1981

February 24–March 3–The 26th Party Congress. Guidelines for the next five-year plan are affirmed.

April–The United States lifts the embargo on grain sales to the USSR.

July–China protests the Soviet occupation of the Wakhan salient in Afghanistan on their mutual border.

December–Leningrad Writers' Union's monthly journal *Aurora* devotes an issue to Brezhnev's 75th birthday, with a satire on a man resembling Brezhnev.

1982

January 25–Mikhail Suslov dies.

February 22–*Pravda* makes indirect comments on Galina Brezhnev's daughter Galina and "Boris the Gypsy," her blackmarketeer circus performer lover.

November 9–Manager of the major store Gastronom No. 1 is arrested and charged with fraud; he is a friend of Galina Brezhnev; he is sentenced on November 25, 1983, and shot in July 1984.

November 10–Leonid Brezhnev dies.

November 12–Yuri Andropov is elected general secretary of the party's Central Committee.

1983

January–Andropov is elected chairman of the Supreme Soviet Presidium.

September 1–A South Korean airliner, having strayed off course, is shot down by Soviet fighters, killing 269 people on board.

1984

February 9–Yuri Andropov dies.

February 13–Konstantin Chernenko is elected general secretary and president of the Presidium.

Sharaf Rashidov is removed from post of party secretary of Uzbekistan after 24 years. This is part of the uncovering of the Uzbekistan corruption scandal.

October 1–The Lena-to-the-Pacific-Coast section of the Transbaikal-Amur Railway is opened.

1985

March 10–Konstantin Chernenko dies.

April–Mikhal Gorbachev is elected general secretary of the party's Central Committee.

July 2–Gromyko is elected chairman of the Presidium of the Supreme Soviet, or head of state.

August 6–The Soviet Union announces a unilateral moratorium on nuclear explosions.

September–Nikolai Ryzhkov succeeds Nikolai Tikhonov as premier.

1986

February 24–March 6–27th Party Congress. Mikhail Gorbachev stresses the need for radical change after the stagnation of the Brezhnev years. He calls for a restructuring (*perestroika*) of Soviet society. The party adopts his line and follows his call for a greater openness (*glasnost*) in public dealings. *Perestroika* and *glasnost* become words frequently used in reporting and debating current Soviet problems.

April 26–Chernobyl: the atomic power station explodes. Thirty-two people are killed at once; a fall-out cloud drifts westward over Europe and four years later there is still a 30-mile exclusion zone around the site.

August 18–The 1985 ban on nuclear explosions is extended to 1987.

September 22–Thirteen kilograms of gold from the British cruiser *Edinburgh*, sunk in 1942 during World War II, is recovered by a British diving team. The gold, payment for wartime munitions, is divided between Britain and the USSR.

October 2–The remaining Chernobyl atomic reactor is buried under a security mound of metal and concrete.

December–In Kazakhstan there are seven deaths in a students' nationalist protest demonstration.

1987

February 12–Some 140 dissidents, accused of anti-Soviet statements or actions, are pardoned.

February 26–An underground nuclear test is carried out, ending the unilateral moratorium.

March–Muslims riot in Tajikistan.

March 10–11–A Soviet–U.S. meeting is held in Moscow on the future of Angola and the Cuban presence there.

March 18–A U.S. nuclear test in Nevada is observed by a Soviet team as part of an experiment in the international monitoring of such tests.

March 28–April 1–Margaret Thatcher, the British prime minister, visits the Soviet Union.

June 29–30–The Supreme Soviet approves the restructuring of the national economy, with laws on state enterprises and on procedures for suing officials who infringe citizens' rights.

July–Crimean Tatars protest in Red Square against their continued exile.

November 2–Mikhail Gorbachev, reporting as general secretary of the party at the 70th anniversary of the 1917 Revolution, points out the existence of conservative resistance to change.

1988

February 27–28–Twenty-six Armenians killed by Azeris at Sumgait, in an outbreak of racial violence. This signals the resurgence of old antagonisms the Soviet system had thought buried.

Nikolai Bukharin (shot after trial in March 1938) is "rehabilitated" by a commission set up to study the trials.

April 15–The withdrawal of Soviet troops from Afghanistan begins.

May 21–The first announcement is made by Tass of the Nagorno-Karabakh (autonomous region cut from Armenia by Stalin in 1923) dispute.

May 26–Law on cooperatives gives impulse to private enterprise. The published "theses," or platform for the party's Central Committee for June 28, give blueprint for greatest social changes since 1917.

May 28–Hints appear in the Soviet press admitting the Soviet Union, not the Nazis, was responsible for Katyn Forest massacre of 4,000 Poles.

May 29–June 2–U.S. President Ronald Reagan and Mikhail Gorbachev hold a summit meeting in Moscow.

May 30–Boris Yeltsin, former party chief in Moscow, calls for removal of Yegor Ligachev, from party leadership, accusing him of opposition to *perestroika*.

June 3–Andrei Sakharov endorses *perestroika*.

June 4–Moscow demonstrators chant (among other things) down with the KGB.

June 5–17–1,000th anniversary of Russian Christianity is celebrated.

June 9–Igor Muradian, Armenian activist, says that party leaders of Armenia and Azerbaijan have decreed that the Armenian enclave, Nagorno-Karabakh, in Azerbaijan cannot be handed over by Azerbaijan to Armenia, but might be raised to "autonomous republic."

June 10–Pravda admits Communist party's loss of control in Nagorno-Karabakh. Two-day general strike begins as the recently appointed Armenian party chief, Suren Arutyunyan, speaks to crowd of 300,000 in Erevan, assuring them that the Armenian Soviet would back demands for a return of Nagorno-Karabakh to Armenia.

June 11–In Moscow reports are confirmed that an Azeri policeman was killed in an anti-Armenian riot in Baku, the Azerbaijan capital.

June 13–Mikhail Gorbachev opens dialogue with the Vatican, breaking years of hostility.

Lev Kamenev and Grigory Zinoviev, executed in August 1936, have their sentences annulled by the Soviet Supreme court, as are those of Yuri Pyatakov (executed after a trial in 1937) and Karl Radek (who died in a labor camp during a 10-year sentence).

A Moscow "Beauty Queen" crowned: a 16-year-old Komsomol, another break with previous practices.

June 28–July 1–19th Party Conference (the first Conference, held between Party Congresses, since 1941). Discussion of *perestroika* occupies the main part of the conference.

November–The names "Brezhnev" and "Chernenko" are removed from towns and institutions, being linked with the period of stagnation.

November 30–Yuri Churbanov, son-in-law of Brezhnev, is found guilty of taking bribes and the abuse of power while deputy interior minister and sentenced (December 30) to 12 years hard labor in a camp. Two former deputy interior ministers, Tashtemir Kakhramanov and Khaidar Yakhyayev (in office 1964–79), are released. The investigator of the case had stated in February 1989 that the trial had shown the accused as petty criminals and had covered up the real extent of the bribe-taking and blunted the struggle against organized crime.

December 7–Mikhail Gorbachev's speech to the United Nations General Assembly includes a promise to cut Soviet forces in Europe by 500,000 as part of the MBFR (Mutual Balanced Force Reduction talks). Marshal Sergei Akhromeyev, the head of the forces resigns but later publicly justifies the reduction both politically and militarily.

An earthquake destroys part of northern Armenia at 11:41 A.M. Of a population of three million, half a million are homeless. Spitak, the center of the earthquake, loses 11,000 of its 22,000 inhabitants.

1989

January 10–Mikhail Gorbachev addresses the Central Committee of the party, meeting to draw up its list of candidates for the Congress elections in March. He tells them that they have "no God-given right to rule," but must earn their position in "the political vanguard of society."

January 18–Mikhail Gorbachev announces that the Soviet Union's military budget will be cut by 14.2 percent, the personnel by 12 percent, 240,000 men from Europe starting in April and 200,000 from Asia, particularly 75,000 from Mongolia and 60,000 from the frontiers of Afghanistan, Iran, and Turkey. He states that 10,000 tanks will leave Europe and all aircraft will leave Mongolia. The conservative, official daily paper *Pravda* accuses the pro-*glasnost* weekly magazine of the intelligentisia, *Ogonyok*, of distorting history and setting itself up as the judge of the country's cultural, political, and moral life. Estonia's parliament votes (204 for, 50 against, and 6 abstaining) to enforce the use of the national language and giving it primary official status.

Tajikistan is reported to have had anti-Russian and anti-Uzbek riots.

February–Eduard Shevardnadze, the foreign minister, visits China; this is the first visit by a minister since 1959.

February 6–The Polish government starts talks with the rebel trade union movement, Solidarity.

February 15–The last Soviet troops leave Afghanistan.

February 22–The Czech government sentences the dissident playwright Vaclav Havel to nine months in prison.

March–Elections for the new Congress of People's Deputies result in many defeats for the old guard party members.

April 9–In Tbilisi, Georgia, troops of the interior ministry and the army use gas and clubs to attack a protest meeting of thousands, killing 20, mainly women and children. Over 4,000 are injured, many by anti-riot gas.

April 14–The party leadership in Georgia resigns, accepting blame for the shootings in Tbilisi.

April 17–The Polish court lifts the ban on the Solidarity movement.

April 25–Andrei Gromyko and 109 others are purged from the Central Committee of the party.

April 27–Demonstrations against the Chinese party's rule are held in Tiananmen Square in Peking by 150,000.

May 22–China's government is paralyzed by the demonstrators in Peking.

May 25–The new Congress of People's Deputies meets.

June 4–Troops move against the Chinese protestors, and hundreds, perhaps thousands, are killed in Tiananmen Square.

Solidarity wins free elections in Poland.

June 17–The remains of Imre Nagy, executed in 1958, are disinterred and given a hero's burial in Budapest.

July 10–Coal miners go on strike in Mezhdurechensk, western Siberia. This is followed by strikes in the Donbas. In all 300,000 miners are on strike.

July–Russian workers in Estonia strike, protesting against discriminatory laws. The strikers are linked with the "United Front of Workers", a recently formed body backed by Yegov Ligachev.

July 24–In Tbilisi, Georgia, a demonstration of 20,000 people shout "Down with the Russian Empire!"

July 30–An unofficial opposition in the People's Congress, the "inter-regional group," is formed by over 200 Soviet deputies, with Boris Yeltsin as leader and including Andrei Sakharov.

August 8–The West German mission in East Berlin is closed after 130 East Germans take refuge there.

August 16–A draft law is published giving workers the right to strike.

August 23–Two million people form a chain across Estonia, Latvia, and Lithuania to mark the 50th anniversary of the Soviet occupation of the Baltic states.

September 10–Hungary opens its border with Austria, allowing 6,000 East Germans to leave for the West. Thousands more follow in the following weeks.

September 21–At Semipalatinsk in Kazakhstan interracial riots leave three dead.

September 22–The RSFSR congress votes for further elections to be by straightforward consituencies, without special seats for party organization appointees, and with no exclusive or leading role for the party.

October 2–The Supreme Soviet imposes a ban on all strikes in key industries.

October 18–Erich Honecker, the East German chairman of the council of state and the Politburo, resigns. The Central Committee replaces him with a more liberal Politburo member, Egon Krenz.

October 26–Miners in the Arctic city of Vorkuta walk out on strike, claiming that the promised improvements had not reached them.

Mikhail Gorbachev abandons the "Brezhnev doctrine," letting the countries of the Eastern Bloc find their own solutions to political and economic problems.

November 4–Czechoslovakia opens its border to East Germans and thousands travel through to West Germany.

November 7–In Moldavia crowds disrupt the parade celebrating the anniversary of the October Revolution. The party secretary is forced to resign.

The East German government resigns.

November 9–The Berlin Wall is broken open by the East German government.

November 10–Todor Zhivkov, the Bulgarian head of state, resigns.

November 17–A large demonstration in Prague is attacked by the police and many are severly beaten.

November 24–The Czechoslovak party leadership resigns.

November 29–Direct rule in Nagorno-Karabakh, the Armenian enclave, is ended and it returns to Azerbaijani administration.

December 1–President Mikhail Gorbachev meets Pope John Paul II in the Vatican, the first ever encounter between the leader of the world's 800 million Catholics and the head of an officially atheist super power.

December 3–Mikhail Gorbachev meets with the U.S. president, George Bush, in Malta. They declare the Cold War over.

December 10–A non-Communist government is formed in Czechoslovakia.

December 12–The Congress of Deputies voted by only a small majority against a revision of the constitution to remove the party's statutory position.

December 15–Andrei Sakharov, the winner of the 1975 Nobel Peace prize and defender of human rights who had emerged from exile to become the leader of the radicals in the Congress of People's Deputies, dies.

December 17–Demonstrations in Timisoara, Rumania, are crushed; first reports overestimate the deaths as many thousands.

December 22–The rule of Nicolae Ceaucescu in Rumania ends.

December 25–Ceaucescu and his wife Elena are captured, tried, and shot.

December 28–Alexander Dubcek, who had been deposed in 1968, is elected chairman of the Czechoslovak parliament.

December 29–Vaclav Havel, jailed

in February, is sworn in as president of Czechoslovakia.

1990

January 5–Azerbaijani Muslims demonstrate at the Iranian frontier, calling for the opening of the border dividing them from their fellow Azeris in Iran.

January 6–In the Azerbaijan capital of Baku there are demonstrations calling for the return of their control of Nagorno-Karabakh. Twenty-five Armenians are killed in later riots.

January 7–Renewed rioting and fighting in Georgia between Ossetians and Georgian nationalists takes place.

January 15–Algirdas Brazauskas is elected president of Lithuania by a majority (228 to 4) of the republic's Supreme Soviet.

February 8–In Odessa at a large demonstration Ukrainian members of the nationalist Rukh party call for political change.

February 9–Mikhail Gorbachev, at a meeting with U.S. Secretary of State James Baker, agrees to destroy "a significant part" of Soviet chemical weapons.

In the Tajik capital of Dushanbe rioters attempt to storm the local police headquarters. At least 22 are killed.

February 13–The Soviet Communist Party Central Committee issues its revised policies, including guarantees of human rights, with a high court to protect them, emphasis on the production of consumer goods, and the development of a market economy. The nation's government should be based on an electoral system allowing political parties, abandoning the monopoly of the Communist party, and instituting a presidential head of state, responsible to the Congress of People's Deputies but

with powers to ensure the functioning of the state. On the federation of nations within the Soviet Union there should be "unity in diversity" and attempts at secession should be opposed.

February 25–Elections are held in Lithuania, Moldavia, Tajikistan, and Kirghizia.

In the Belorussian capital of Minsk a Popular Front rally of 150,000 people demands extra funds from Moscow to help overcome the results of the 1986 Chernobyl disaster. 100,000 people are still to be relocated.

February 28–The Congress of Deputies passes a new law to redefine rights to own property and land. Peasants will choose to be in kolkhozes or to receive their own allotment of land.

March–In Donetz, in the Ukraine, coal miners go out on strike. They claim that their action is not affected by the ban of October 1989 because it is for political, not economic, purposes. They call for full democracy in the Communist party. Although in the Ukraine, the miners are believed to have strong links with Russia but are beginning to support the Rukh party.

March 3–There are further anti-Mashketian riots in Uzebekistan. Uzbeks attack the camps where refugee Mashketians are housed.

March 4–Elections in the RSFSR, Ukraine and Belorussia. In the RSFSR alone there are 6,700 candidates contesting 1,068 seats.

March 6–The Congress of Deputies passes a further law on property, allowing ownership of assets and shares in enterprises and the right to pass these on to heirs. This is intended to provide the ground for a new market economy.

March 11–Lithuania declares itself independent after 124 delegates to its new parliment vote in favor with none against. They also vote to change the republic's name by dropping the words "Soviet Socialist".

March 13–1,800 out of 2,000 delegates to the Congress of Deputies vote to alter the constitution by removing the Communist party's supremacy and instituting an executive presidency.

March 14–The congress votes to appoint Mikhail Gorbachev as president of the Soviet Union. He is the only candidate but only 60 percent vote for him, the remainder being 495 hard line conservatives and 426 who abstain. Anatoly Lukyanov, one of eight candidates, with only 54 percent of the votes, is elected to succeed Gorbachev as head of the congress.

The congress also passes a resolution with a large majority that the Lithuanian declaration of independence has no legal force.

March 21–The Alliance for Germany backed by West Germany's Christian Democratic party wins the biggest share of the votes in the first free East German elections. The Social Democratic party comes in second, despite having led in the opinion polls throughout the election.

March 22–Mikhail Gorbachev, using his new powers as president, increases pressure on Lithuania by forbidding the ownership of guns, and tightening immigration and customs controls on the republic. There is also a show of strength in the capital, Vilnius, as the Red Army patrols the streets in armored cars.

April 8–Results of the first democratic elections in Hungary are announced: the Democratic Forum, led by Jozsef Antall, wins a landslide victory of 156 seats, and agrees to form a coalition with the Independent Smallholders

with 43 seats, and the Christian Democratic Peoples' party with 21 seats. The Communists win a total of 33 seats.

April 21–The Soviet Union imposes an economic blockade on Lithuania, including the reduction of oil and gas supplies. The Lithuanian government under its president Vytautas Landsbergis asks for economic assistance from the West.

May 5–At the annual May Day parade in Moscow, Mikhail Gorbachev and the rest of the Soviet politburo are booed off the rostrum by a mixed crowd of demonstrators including nationalists from the republics and anti-communist party elements.

May 9–The Estonian Soviet Socialist Republic changes its name to the Republic of Estonia and reinstates its prewar constitution. This is followed by Russian workers laying siege to the parliament building in the capital, Tallinn.

May 26–In the Rumanian elections two-thirds of the vote goes to the National Salvation Front, the party which assumed power immediately after the revolution in December. There are protests on the grounds that the party still contains too may unreconstructed Communists.

May 30–Boris Yeltsin is elected president of the RSFSR and declares that Russian laws should have priority over Soviet laws.

May 31–Mikhail Gorbachev goes to Washington for a summit with Pres. George Bush. The main topic of the meeting is the question of whether a unified Germany should be a member of NATO. No formal conclusions are reached.

June 2–Ethnic unrest breaks out in the Kirghiz Republic among the minority Uzbeks. Forty-eight die and there are many casualties. A state of emergency is declared and the border with Uzbekistan is closed.

June 8—The Hungarian defense minister says that Hungary wishes to leave the Warsaw Pact and will not take part in its manuevers this year.

At a one-day summit meeting the Warsaw Treaty organization declares its intention to become mainly a political body; the details are to be worked out at a meeting to be held in November.

June 10—Civic Forum wins a landslide victory in the Czechoslovak elections. The Christian Democrats come in second, but the Communists get 13 percent of the vote, better than expected.

In Bulgaria, the reformed Communist Party, now known as the Socialist Party, wins 48 percent of the votes, followed by the Union of Democratic Forces with 35%, and the Agrarian Party with 8 percent.

June 11—The Soviet and West German foreign ministers meet at Brest in Belorussia to discuss the problems arising from a united Germany. It was at Brest (then Brest-Litovsk) in March 1918 that the Bolsheviks signed a peace treaty with Imperial Germany.

June 12—The RSFSR's new parliament under Boris Yeltsin proclaims its right to determine its own economic and political future.

June 13—The Central Committee announces that there have been over 130,000 resignations from the party in the previous six months, as many as in the whole of 1989. This is announced as a preliminary to the 28th Party Congress.

GAZETEER

Changed or alternative place names

Akmolinsk now Tselinograd, in Kazakhstan, since 1961

Alma-Ata formerly Vernyi

Aleksandropol now Leninakan

Andropov formerly and now Rybinsk

Arkhangelsk Archangel

Ashkhabad formerly Poltoratsk 1919–27

Berdyansk known as Osipenko 1939–58

Bobriki now Novomoskovsk

Chapayevsk in the Kuibyshev Oblast, formerly Ivashchenkovo, then Trotsk from 1919–27

Chistyakovo now Torez

Chkalov now Orenburg

Detskoye Selo now Pushkin

Dnepropetrovsk formerly Ekaterinoslav

Donetsk formerly Yuzovka (after the 19th-century Welshman John Hughes, who founded a coal mining and iron foundry there), then Stalin from 1924 and Stalino, 1935, and Donetsk from 1961

Dorpat Tartu

Dushanbe sometimes Dushambe; known as Stalinabad, 1929–61

Dzaudzhikau now Ordzhonikidze

Ekaterinodar now Krasnodar

Ekaterinoslav now Dnepropetrovsk

Ereven Yerevan

Frunze formerly Pishpek (capital of the Kirghiz SSR) until 1926

Gorky formerly Nizhny Novgorod (Gorky's birthplace)

Hayastan Armenia, in the Armenian language.

Ivano-Frankovsk formerly Stanislav, in the Ukraine, 1945–62, spelled Stanislau to 1919 and, in Polish, Stanisławow, 1919–45

Izhevsk now Ustinov

Kalinin formerly Tver

Kaliningrad formerly Königsberg

Kkelmitsky formerly Proskurov, until 1954

Khodzhent now Leninabad

Kirov since 1936, formerly Vyatka

Kirovograd in the Ukraine, was Elizavetgrad to 1924, then Zinovievsk until 1936; it was called Kirovo between 1936 and 1939

Klaipeda Memel (German)

Königsberg now Kaliningrad

Krasnodar formerly Ekaterinodar

Kuibyshev formerly Samara

Kuznetsk Now Novokuznetsk

Lemberg the German name for Lvov

Leninabad in the Tajik SSR, formerly Khodzhent or Khojend, to 1936

Leninakan in the Armenian SSR, Aleksandropol to 1924

Leningrad changed from the German-sounding St. Petersburg in WW I to Petrograd and changed to Leningrad in 1924 after Lenin's death

Leninskoye a village in the Jewish Autonomous Oblast, Khabarovsk, RSFSR; was Mikhailovo-Semyonovskoye, then Blyukherovo until 1939

Lugansk now Voroshilovgrad

Lvov See also Lwow and Lemberg

Lwow the Polish spelling (see also Lemberg) of Lvov

Mariupol known as Zhdanov 1948–89

Mary formerly Merv

Memel German name for Klaipeda

Merv now Mary, since 1937

Molotov now, as formerly, Perm

Molotovsk now, as formerly, Severodvinsk

Nikolskoye now Ussuriysk

Nizhny Novgorod now Gorky

Novoazovsk Novonikolyevka to 1935 and Budyonnovka 1935–66

Novokashirsk a suburb of Kashira, Moscow Oblast; until 1935 was Ternovsk, from 1935–57, Kaganovich

Novokuznetsk Kuznetsk to 1931, Stalinsk 1931–61

Novomoskovsk Bobriki to 1934; Stalinogorsk 1934–61, near Tula

Novosibirsk Gusevka to 1903 and Novonikolayevsk until 1925

Ordzhonikidze formerly Vladikavkaz until 1932, then Dzaudzhika 1944–54

Orenburg known as Chkalov, 1938–57

Osipenko now Berdyansk

Perm known as Molotov 1940–57, in the Urals

Petrograd now Leningrad

Pishpek now Runze

Poltoratsk now, as formely, Ashkhabad

Proskurov now Khmelmitsky

Pushkin formerly Tsarskoye Selo, then Detskoye Selo 1917–37

Reval the German form of the Russian Revel; the Estonian name Tallinn is now used

Rybinsk known as Shcherbakov, 1946–57, later Andropov

St. Petersburg now Leningrad

Shcherbakov formerly and now Rybinsk

Samara now Kuibyshev

Severodvinsk known as Sudostroy 1918–38 and Molotovsk 1938–57, in the northwest of the RSFSR

Sovetsk formely Tilsit

Stalin now Donetsk

Stalinabad Dushanbe; known as Stalinabad 1929–61

Stalingrad formerly Tsaritsyn, now Volgograd

Stalinogorsk now Novomoskovsk

Staliniri now Tskhinval

Stalino now Donetsk

Stalinogorsk now Novomoskovsk

Stalinsk now Novokuznetsk

Stanislav now Ivano-Frankovsk

Stavropol now Tolyatti

Sudostroy now Severodvinsk

Sverdlovsk formerly Ekaterinburg (or Yekaterinburg), 1924

Tallinn formerly Reval

Tartu Dorpat

Tbilisi formerly Tiflis

Tolyatti (Togliatti, the Italian Communist) formerly Stavropol

Torez (Thorez, the French Communist) since 1964, formerly Chistyakovo, in the Ukraine

Tsaritsyn now Volgograd

Tsarskoye Selo now Pushkin

Tselinograd since 1961, formerly Akmolinsk; Tselino means "virgin soil"

Tskhinval capital of South Ossetian Autonomous Oblast in Georgia, formerly Staliniri 1934–61

Tver now Kalinin

Ussuriysk Nikolskoye to 1926, Nikolskoye-Ussuriysk 1926–35 and Voroshilov 1935–57

Ustinov formerly Izhevsk in the Udmurt ASSR

Vernyi now Alma-Ata

Vilna Wilno (Polish), Vilnius (Lithuanian)

Vladikavkaz now Ordzhonikidze

Volgograd formerly Tsaritsyn and Stalingrad

Voroshilov now Ussuriysk

Voroshilovgrad formerly Lugansk, to 1935; renamed Lugansk 1970 but later reverted to Voroshilovgrad

Vyatka now Kirov

Yerevan Erivan

Yuzovka now Donetsk

Zhdanov Mariupol, known as Zhdanov 1953– 1989

Note: in 1988 a number of places named after either Brezhnev or Chernenko reverted to their original name. See also Adrian Room, *Place-Name Changes Since 1900* (Metuchen, N.J.: Scarecrow Press, 1979).

BIBLIOGRAPHY

Aganbegyan, Abel. *The Challenge—Economics of Perestroika*. London: Hutchinson, 1988.

Akiner, Shirin. *Islamic Peoples of the Soviet Union*. London; Boston: Kegan Paul International, 1983. Routledge Chapman Hall.

Amnesty International. *Prisoners of Conscience in the USSR*. London: Quatermaine House Ltd, 1975.

Armstrong, John A. *Ukrainian Nationalism*. 2nd ed. Englewood, Colo.: Libraries Unlimited, 1980.

Auty, Robert, and Dimitri Obolensky. *An Introduction to Russian Art*. Cambridge: Cambridge University Press, 1980.

Ball, Alan M. *Russia's Last Capitalists: The Nepmen, 1921–29*. Berkeley, Calif.: University of California Press, 1987.

Boyd, Alexander. *The Soviet Air Force Since 1918*. New York: Stein and Day, 1977.

Breslauer, George W. *Khrushchev and Brezhnev as Leaders*. Boston:Allen and Unwin, 1982.

Brown, Archie, and Michael Kaser (ed). *Soviet Policy for the 1980s*. Bloomington, Ind.: Indiana University Press, 1982.

Brun, Capt A. H. *Troublous Times*. 1931 [Tashkent 1917–19]

Carr, E. H. *The Bolshevik Revolution*. 3 vols. New York: W. W. Norton, 1985.

Central Committee of the CPSU(B) (ed). *History of the Communist Party of the Soviet Union (Bolsheviks)*. Moscow, 1941.

Chorley, Katherine. *Armies and the Art of Revolution*. London: Faber and Faber, 1943.

Clark, Ronald W. *Lenin: the Man Behind the Mask*. New York: Harper & Row, 1988.

Cohen, Stephen F. *Bukharin and the Bolshevik Revolution*. New York: Oxford University Press, 1980.

Cole, J. P. *Geography of the Soviet Union*. London: Butterworth, 1984.

Conolly, Violet. *Beyond the Urals*. New York: Oxford University Press, 1967.

Conquest, Robert. *The Great Terror*. New York: Macmillan, 1968.

——. *Stalin and the Kirov Murder*. New York: Oxford University Press, 1989.

Crankshaw, Edward. *Khrushchev*. New York: Viking, 1966.

Dallin, David J. *Soviet Russia and the Far East*. New Haven: Yale University Press, 1949.

Daniels, Robert V. (ed). *The Stalin Revolution*. Lexington, Mass.: DC Heath, 1972.

Deacon, Richard. *A History of the Russian Secret Service*. New York: Taplinger, 1972.

Dyker, David A. (ed). *The Soviet Union under Gorbachev*. Armonk: M. E. Sharpe, 1987.

Dziewanowoki, M. K. *A History of Soviet Russia*. Englewood Cliffs, N.J.: Prentice Hall, 1985. (2nd edition)

Erickson, John. *Stalin's War with Germany*. 2 vols. Boulder, Colo.: Westview Press, 1975.

Eudin, X. J., and H. H. Fisher. *Soviet Russia and the West 1920–1927*. Palo Alto, Calif.: Stanford University Press, 1957.

Fairhall, David. *Russia Looks to the Sea: The Expansion of Soviet Marine Power*. London: Deutsch, 1971.

Feis, Herbert. *Churchill-Roosevelt-Stalin*. Princeton, N.J.: Princeton University Press, 1967.

Ferro, Marc. *The Bolshevik Revolution: A Social History*. Routledge, Kegan Paul, 1980.

Fleischhauer, Ingeborg, and Benjamin Pinkus. *The Soviet Germans*. London: C Hurst & Co, 1986.

Footman, David. *Civil War in Russia.* London: Faber & Faber, 1981.

Frankland, Mark. *The Sixth Continent.* New York: Harper & Row, 1987.

Getty, J. Arch. *Origins of the Great Purges.* Cambridge: Cambridge University Press, 1985.

Getzler, Israel. *Kronstadt 1917–1921.* New York: Cambridge University Press, 1983.

Gorbachev, Mikhail. *Perestroika.* New York: Harper & Row, 1987.

Hart, B. H. Liddell. *History of the Second World War.* New York: Putnam, 1970.

Haupt, Georges, and Jean-Jacques Marie (trans. C. I. P. Ferdinand and D. M. Bellos). *Makers of the Russian Revolution.* Ithaca: Cornell Univ. Press, 1974.

Heller, Mikhail, and Aleksandr Nekrich (trans. Phyllis B. Carlos). *Utopia in Power: The History of the Soviet Union from 1917 to the Present.* New York: Summit, 1986.

Hill, Ronald J. *Soviet Union.* London: Francis Pinter, 1985.

Hingley, Ronald. *Russian Writers and Soviet Society: 1917–1978.* New York: Random House, 1979.

Hosking, Geoffrey. *The First Socialist Society.* Cambridge, Mass.: Harvard Univ. Press, 1985.

Jacobs, Dan N. *Borodin, Stalin's Man in China.* Cambridge, Mass.: Harvard University Press, 1981.

Jukes, Geoffrey. *The Soviet Union in Asia.* Berkeley: Univ. of California Press, 1973.

Kapur, Harish. *Soviet Russia and Asia 1917–1927.* Geneva: University of Geneva, 1965.

Katz, Zev, with Rosemarie Rogers and Frederic Harned (ed). *Handbook of Soviet Nationalities.* New York: The Free Press, 1975.

Kilmarx, Robert A. *A History of Soviet Air Power.* London: Faber, 1962.

Kolarz, Walter. *Russia and Her Colonies.* Hamden, Ct.: Archon Books, 1952.

Kolkowicz, Roman. *The Soviet Military and the Communist Party.* Boulder, Co. & London: Westview Press, 1985.

Laquer, Walter. *Europe since Hitler.* Revised edition. New York: Penguin, 1982.

Levytsky, Boris. *The Uses of Terror: The Soviet Secret Service 1917–1970.* New York: Coward, McCann & Geoghegan, 1972.

———. *The Stalinist Terror in the Thirties.* Palo Alto, Calif.: Stanford University Press, 1974.

Lincoln, W. Bruce. *Passage through Armageddon.* New York: Simon & Schuster, 1986.

Longworth, Philip. *The Cossacks.* New York: Holt, Rinehart & Winston, 1969.

Lubachko, Ivan S. *Belorussia under Soviet Rule 1917–1957.* Lexington, Ky.: University Press, 1972.

Luckett, Richard. *The White Generals.* New York: Viking, 1971.

McAuley, Mary. *Politics and the Soviet Union.* New York: Penguin, 1977.

McCauley, Martin. *The Soviet Union since 1917.* Longman History of Russia series. New York: Longman, 1981.

McNeal, Robert H. *Stalin: Man and Ruler.* London: Macmillan, 1988.

Marshall, Richard H., Jr (ed). *Aspects of Religion in the Soviet Union, 1917–1967.* Chicago: University of Chicago Press, 1971.

Mawdlsey, Evan. *The Russian Civil War.* Boston: Allen & Unwin, 1987.

Medvedev, Roy. *Khrushchev.* Garden City, N.Y.: Anchor Press/Doubleday, 1982.

———. *On Stalin and Stalinism.* New York: Oxford University Press, 1979.

——. *The October Revolution.* New York: Columbia University Press, 1979.

——. *Nikolai Bukharin.* New York: W. W. Norton, 1980.

Medvedev, Zhores. *Andropov.* New York: W. W. Norton, 1983.

——. *Gorbachev.* New York: W. W. Norton, 1986.

——. *Soviet Agriculture.* New York: W. W. Norton, 1987.

Mett, Ida. *The Kronstadt Uprising.* London: Solidarity, nd (1987?).

Mezhenkov, V. (ed). *Soviet Scene 1987.* London: Collets, 1987.

Michel, Henri. (trans. D. Parmée). *The Second World War.* New York: Praeger, 1975.

Miller, R. F., and J. H. and T. H. Rigby. *Gorbachev at the Helm.* London: Croom Helm, 1987.

Misiunas, Romuald J., and Rein Taagepera. *The Baltic States.* Berkeley: University of California Press, 1983.

Morris, L. P. *Eastern Europe since 1945.* London: Heinemann Educational Books, 1984.

Mosley, Nicholas. *The Assassination of Trotsky.* London: Michael Joseph, 1972.

Munting, Roger. *The Economic Development of the USSR.* New York: St. Martin's Press, 1982.

Murphy, Paul J. *Brezhnev.* Jefferson, N.C.: McFarland & Co., 1981.

Nekrich, Aleksandr M. (trans. George Saunders). *The Punished Peoples.* New York: W. W. Norton, 1978.

Nove, Alex. *An Economic History of the USSR.* Revised edition. New York: Penguin, 1982.

Novosti Press Agency. *USSR Yearbook '88.* Moscow: Novosti Publishing House, 1988.

——. *USSR Yearbook '89.* Moscow: Novosti Publishing House, 1989.

Pares, Sir Bernard. *The Fall of the Russian Monarchy.* New York: Vintage, 1939.

Paxton, John. *Companion to Russian History.* New York: Facts on File, 1983.

Payne, Robert. *The Life and Death of Lenin.* New York: Simon & Schuster, 1964.

Pearson, Michael. *The Sealed Train.* New York: Putnam, 1975.

Radkey, Oliver H. *The Sickle under the Hammer.* New York: Columbia University Press, 1963.

Raleigh, Donald J. *Revolution on the Volga: Saratov in 1917.* Ithaca: Cornell University Press, 1986.

Read, Anthony, and David Fisher. *The Deadly Embrace.* London: Michael Joseph, 1988.

Ripka, Hubert. *Eastern Europe in the Post War World.* New York: Praeger, 1961.

Robottom, John. *Modern Russia.* 2nd edition. New York: McGraw Hill, 1971.

Ro'i, Yaacov (ed). *The USSR and the Muslim World.* Winchester, Mass.: Unwin Hyman, 1984.

Saikal, Amin, and William Maley. *The Soviet Withdrawal from Afghanistan.* Cambridge: Cambridge University Press, 1989.

Salazar, General L. A. S. *Murder in Mexico.* London: Secker & Warburg, 1950.

Schmidt-Häuer, Christian. *Gorbachev— The Path to Power.* Topsfield, Mass.: Salem House, 1986.

Schwarz, Boris. *Music and Musical Life in Soviet Russia, 1917–1970.* Bloomington: University of Indiana Press, 1972.

Seaton, A. *The Russo-German War 1941–1945.* New York: Praeger, 1971.

Seaton, Albert, and Joan Seaton. *The Soviet Army: 1918 to the Present.* New York: New American Library, 1987.

Segal, Ronald. *The Tragedy of Leon Trotsky.* London: Hutchinson, 1979.

Serge, Victor, and Natalie Trotsky. *The Life and Death of Leon Trotsky.* New York: Basic Books, 1975.

Seton-Watson, Hugh. *Nationalism and Communism.* London: Methuen, 1964.

Shapiro, Leonard. *The Origin of the Communist Autocracy.* New York: Macmillan, 1977.

———. *Soviet Treaty Series.* 2 vols. Washington, D.C.: Georgetown University Press, 1950–55.

———. *The Communist Party of the Soviet Union.* London, 1970.

———. *1917 The Russian Revolutions and the Origins of Present Day Communism.* Maurice Temple Smith, 1984.

Shukman, Harold (ed). *The Blackwell Encyclopedia of the Russian Revolution.* Oxford: Blackwell, 1988.

Silverlight, John. *The Victors' Dilemma: Allied Intervention in the Russian Civil War.* New York: Weybright and Talley, 1971.

Smith, Canfield F. *Vladivostok under Red and White Rule.* Seattle: University of Washington Press, 1975.

Staar, Richard F. *Communist Régimes in Eastern Europe.* Stanford: Hoover Institution Press, 1982.

Steele, Jonathan, and Eric Abraham. *Andropov in Power.* Garden City: Anchor Press/Doubleday, 1983.

Talbott, Strobe T. R. *Khrushchev Remembers.* London: André Deutsch, 1971.

Tatu, Michel. (trans. Helen Katel). *Power in the Kremlin.* New York: Viking, 1969.

van Goudever, Albert P. *The Limits of Destalinisation in the Soviet Union.* London: Croom Helm, 1986.

von Rauch, George. *A History of Soviet Russia.* 5th edition. New York: Praeger, 1967.

Veen, Hans-Joachim (ed.). *From Brezhnev to Gorbachev.* Leamington Spa: Berg, 1987.

Voline (Vselvolod Mikhailovich Eichenbaum). *The Unknown Revolution, 1917–1921.* New York: Free Life Editions, 1974.

Wade, Rex A. *Red Guards and Workers' Militias in the Russian Revolution.* Palo Alto, Calif.: Stanford University Press, 1984.

Walker, Martin. *The Waking Giant.* New York: Pantheon, 1986.

Warner, Oliver. *Marshal Mannerheim and the Finns.* London: Weidenfield & Nicholson, 1967.

Werth, Alexander. *Russia at War: 1941–1945.* New York: Dutton, 1964.

Westwood, J. N. *Endurance and Endeavour: Russian History, 1812–1986.* 3rd edition. New York: Oxford University Press, 1987.

Wildman, Allan K. *The End of the Russian Imperial Army.* Princeton, N.J.: Princeton University Press, 1980.

Wistrich, Robert. *Trotsky: Fate of a Revolutionary.* New York: Stein and Day, 1979.

Zaleski, Eugène. (trans. MacAndrew and Nutter). *Planning for Economic Growth in the Soviet Union, 1918–1932.* Chapel Hill: University of North Carolina Press, 1971.

MAPS

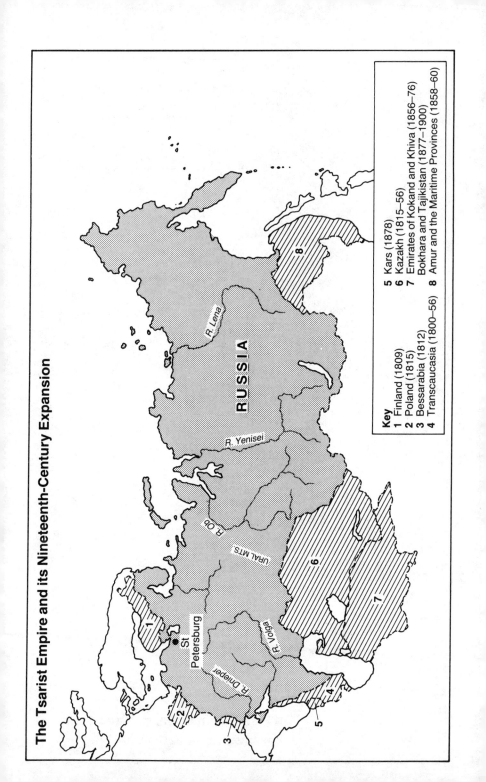

The Tsarist Empire and its Nineteenth-Century Expansion

Key
1 Finland (1809)
2 Poland (1815)
3 Bessarabia (1812)
4 Transcaucasia (1800–56)
5 Kars (1878)
6 Kazakh (1815–56)
7 Emirates of Kokand and Khiva (1856–76)
  Bokhara and Tajikistan (1877–1900)
8 Amur and the Maritime Provinces (1858–60)

RUSSIA

St Petersburg

R. Lena
R. Yenisei
R. Ob
URAL MTS
R. Volga
R. Dnieper

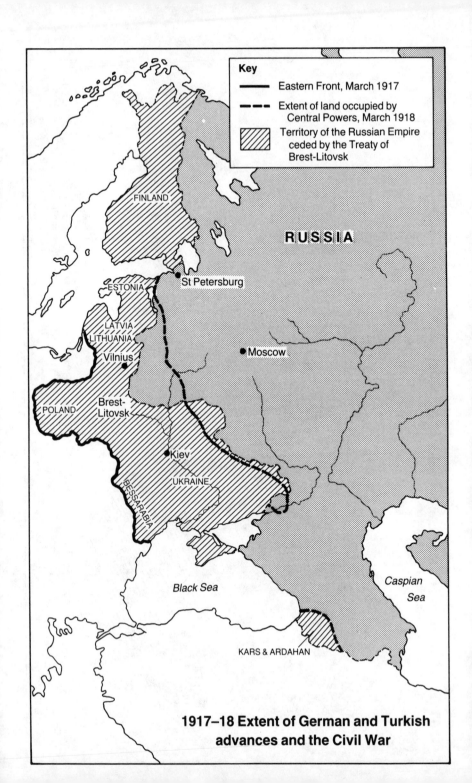

Key

— Eastern Front, March 1917

--- Extent of land occupied by Central Powers, March 1918

▨ Territory of the Russian Empire ceded by the Treaty of Brest-Litovsk

FINLAND

RUSSIA

ESTONIA

● St Petersburg

LATVIA
LITHUANIA

● Vilnius

● Moscow

POLAND

Brest-Litovsk

BESSARABIA

● Kiev

UKRAINE

Black Sea

Caspian Sea

KARS & ARDAHAN

1917–18 Extent of German and Turkish advances and the Civil War

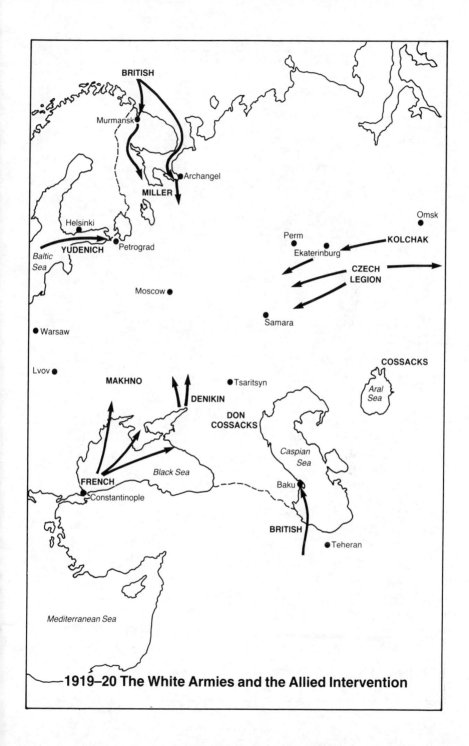

1919–20 The White Armies and the Allied Intervention

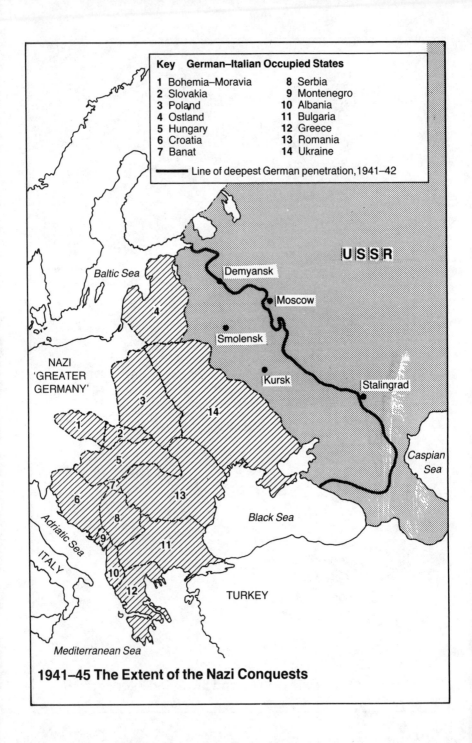

1941–45 The Extent of the Nazi Conquests

Key   German–Italian Occupied States

1 Bohemia–Moravia
2 Slovakia
3 Poland
4 Ostland
5 Hungary
6 Croatia
7 Banat
8 Serbia
9 Montenegro
10 Albania
11 Bulgaria
12 Greece
13 Romania
14 Ukraine

— Line of deepest German penetration, 1941–42

USSR

Baltic Sea

NAZI 'GREATER GERMANY'

Demyansk

Moscow

Smolensk

Kursk

Stalingrad

Caspian Sea

Black Sea

Adriatic Sea

ITALY

TURKEY

Mediterranean Sea

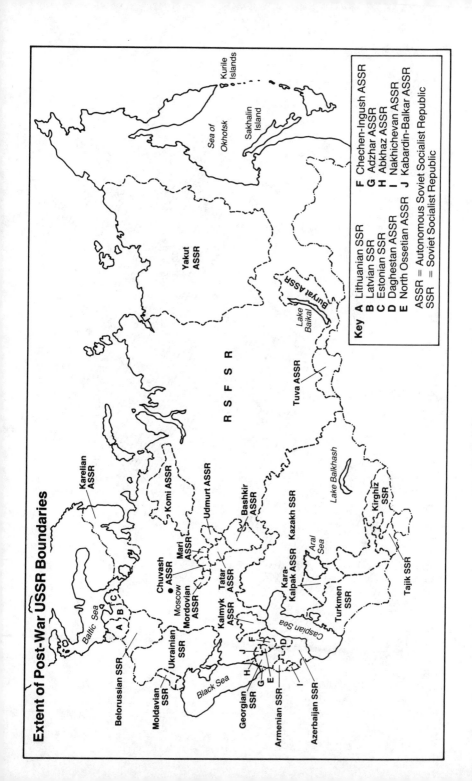

Extent of Post-War USSR Boundaries

Key
A Lithuanian SSR
B Latvian SSR
C Estonian SSR
D Daghestan ASSR
E North Ossetian ASSR
F Chechen-Ingush ASSR
G Adzhar ASSR
H Abkhaz ASSR
I Nakhichevan ASSR
J Kabardin-Balkar ASSR

ASSR = Autonomous Soviet Socialist Republic
SSR = Soviet Socialist Republic

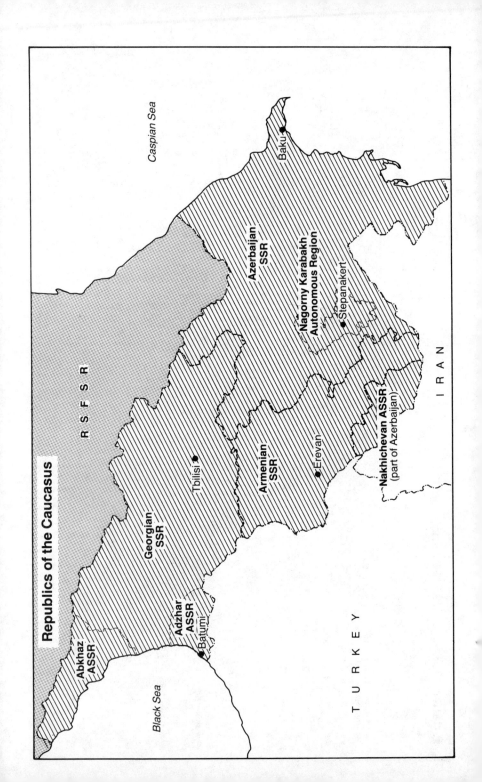

Major Industrial and Agricultural Areas

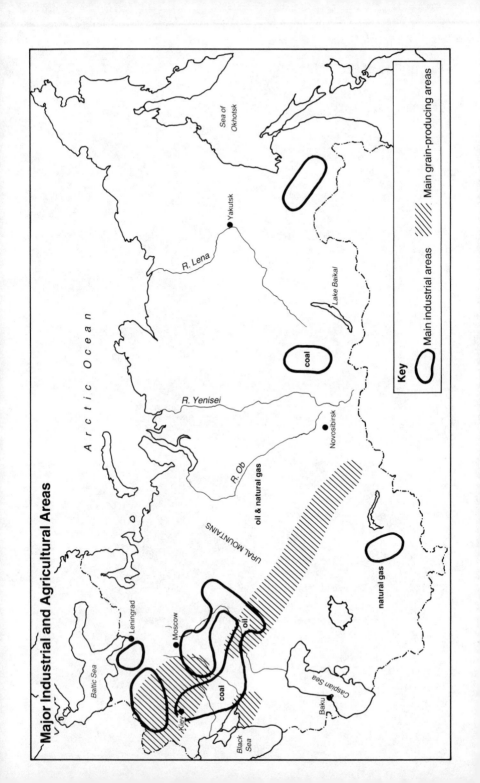

Key

◯ Main industrial areas

⬭ Main grain-producing areas

Arctic Ocean

Baltic Sea

Leningrad

Moscow

Kiev

Black Sea

Caspian Sea

Baku

natural gas

URAL MOUNTAINS

oil

coal

oil & natural gas

R. Ob

R. Yenisei

Novosibirsk

coal

Lake Baikal

R. Lena

Yakutsk

Sea of Okhotsk

Index

Index

Index

Index

Index

Index